Rivals for Power

Rivals for Power

Presidential-Congressional Relations

Third Edition

Edited by
James A. Thurber

ROWMAN & LITTLEFIELD PUBLISHERS, INC.
Lanham • Boulder • New York • Toronto • Oxford

ROWMAN & LITTLEFIELD PUBLISHERS, INC.

Published in the United States of America
by Rowman & Littlefield Publishers, Inc.
A wholly owned subsidiary of The Rowman & Littlefield Publishing Group, Inc.
4501 Forbes Boulevard, Suite 200, Lanham, Maryland 20706
www.rowmanlittlefield.com

P.O. Box 317, Oxford OX2 9RU, UK

British Library Cataloguing in Publication Information Available

Library of Congress Cataloging-in-Publication Data

Rivals for power : presidential-congressional relations / edited by James A. Thurber.—3rd
ed.
    p.   cm.
  Includes bibliographical references and index.
    ISBN 0-7425-3682-3 (cloth : alk. paper)—ISBN 0-7425-3683-1 (pbk. : alk. paper)
    1. Presidents—United States.   2. United States. Congress.   3. United
States—Politics and government—20th century.   I. Thurber, James A., 1943–
JK585.R59   2005
320.973—dc22   2005007832

Printed in the United States of America

∞ ™ The paper used in this publication meets the minimum requirements of American
National Standard for Information Sciences—Permanence of Paper for Printed Library
Materials, ANSI/NISO Z39.48-1992.

*To Claudia, Mark, Leonor, Kathryn, Greg,
and my grandchildren, Tristan, Bryan, and Kelsey*

Contents

Preface   ix

1   An Introduction to Presidential-Congressional Rivalry   1
James A. Thurber

2   Partisan Polarization, Politics, and the Presidency: Structural
Sources of Conflict   33
James P. Pfiffner

3   Presidential Leadership of Congress: Structures and Strategies   59
Stephen J. Wayne

4   The Impact of Campaigns on Presidential-Congressional
Relations   85
Richard E. Cohen

5   Successful Influence: Managing Legislative Affairs in the
Twenty-First Century   101
Gary J. Andres and Patrick Griffin

6   The Presidency and Congressional Time   125
Roger H. Davidson

7   The Legislative Presidency in Political Time: Party Control
and Presidential-Congressional Relations   151
Richard S. Conley

8   The Institutional Context of Veto Bargaining   183
C. Lawrence Evans and Stephen Ng

9   Politics of the Federal Budget Process   209
Leon E. Panetta

10 Ending a Transatlantic Trade War: The Art of Coalition
Building on Capitol Hill   233
   Mark J. Oleszek and Walter J. Oleszek

11 The Making of U.S. Foreign Policy: The Roles of the
President and Congress over Four Decades   267
   Lee H. Hamilton

12 Justifying War against Iraq   289
   Louis Fisher

Index   315

About the Contributors   331

Preface

This book builds on the knowledge of a variety of scholars and practitioners from the White House and the Hill and is designed to explain the political dynamic between the president and the U.S. Congress. The examination of the rivalry between the president and Congress uses a variety of approaches and perspectives. The title *Rivals for Power: Presidential-Congressional Relations* highlights the continued competition between the two branches, whether the White House and Congress are controlled by the same party or by different parties. The book focuses on the divisions in our democracy that create the rivalries between the president and Congress. It explores the structural, political, and behavioral factors that establish incentives for cooperation and conflict between the two branches.

As director of the Center for Congressional and Presidential Studies at American University and as a former congressional staff member, I have spent over thirty years studying and teaching about the relationship between the White House and Congress. Much of my understanding of this complex rivalry comes from a combination of my independent research and the knowledge from scholars, White House staff, members of Congress and staff, and the press. All of these are essential sources for this book. I have many professionals from the White House and the Hill to thank for sharing their knowledge and expertise; not the least are U.S. Senator Hubert H. Humphrey and U.S. Representative David Obey, for whom I worked. Many interviews with persons in Congress and the White House were helpful to me in preparing this book.

Rivals for Power is intended for students, scholars, public officials, the media, and the general public. Each chapter reports on original research on Congress and the relationship between the president and Congress from unique viewpoints, often as players from inside the policy making process. Scholars, journalists, and political practitioners have contributed to this volume. Most of the scholars are experienced hands who have worked in Congress and the White House.

This book relies on the support of people from Rowman & Littlefield and American University who contributed their expertise and dedication to assure its publication. I thank Rowman & Littlefield for their support of this work. Jennifer Knerr, executive editor, has been a friend for many years and has provided invaluable encouragement and support to me and to this project . I particularly thank Alden Perkins, production editor, and Cheryl Hoffman, for her masterful copyediting. I also thank Renee Legatt from Rowman & Littlefield for her assistance in the production of this book. At American University, I first want to thank the staff of the Center for Congressional and Presidential Studies, especially Melissa Castle, Sam Garrett, and Emily Charnock, for their dedication and help. Their careful research and editing are appreciated.

I have special thanks for the support of the Center and this project from William LeoGrande, dean of the School of Public Affairs. As chair of the Department of Government, Saul Newman has been a friend and strong supporter of the work of the Center. My close friend and colleague Neil Kerwin, Provost of American University, has been unfailing in his enthusiastic support of my efforts to build the Center for Congressional and Presidential Studies and to continue our scholarship about the president and Congress.

This book is clearly a collective effort. I thank all the contributors who have contributed original and important scholarship to each chapter. As editor and author, I take full responsibility for any omissions or errors of fact and interpretation.

1

An Introduction to Presidential-Congressional Rivalry

James A. Thurber

After one of the longest and most intense, expensive, and closely contested campaigns with Democrat John Kerry, Republican George W. Bush was reelected to the presidency in 2004 with 51 percent of the vote. Bush won both the popular vote, by a margin of over 3.5 million people, and the Electoral College vote, unlike the 2000 election when Bush received five hundred thousand fewer votes than Al Gore. The 2004 election showed once again that presidents are chosen by Electoral College votes; thus the candidates focused their resources of time, people, and money on a handful of battleground states where the contest was close and made a difference in the outcome of the election. The 2004 campaign (just like the 2000 campaign) was waged primarily in Florida, Pennsylvania, Ohio, Michigan, Minnesota, Wisconsin, Iowa, and New Mexico. The Republicans increased their majority in the U.S. Senate and the U.S. House of Representatives with fifty-five GOP senators and 231 representatives.

Unlike the 2004 election, in just about every respect the 2000 election made history. In 2000 George W. Bush was elected to the presidency in one of the closest national elections of all time, on the promise that he would reach across the aisle to be a reformer working in the middle of the political spectrum. The reality of the president's first year in office saw the development of a conservative political agenda that alienated the very lawmakers the president had pledged to work with during his campaign.

The 2000 election was essentially tied (with its outcome uncertain for five weeks) for the U.S. Senate and, effectively, for the U.S. House of Representatives. It marked only the fourth time in U.S. history—and the first time since 1888—that the winner of the electoral vote did not win the popular vote. George W. Bush's Electoral College win with 271 electors, to 267 who voted for Gore, was the second smallest ever in the Electoral College. The popular vote totals for former vice president Al Gore (50,996,000) and President George W. Bush (50,456,000) were the second- and third-highest totals ever. Gore's edge of nearly 540,000 votes constituted the third-smallest margin in the popular vote since 1900. Al Gore's margin in the popular vote was also the largest margin of any candidate not to ascend to the presidency. The result of the 2000 election was power sharing in the Senate with fifty Democrats and fifty Republicans and a House with an exceedingly narrow margin for the Republicans, 212 to 211 with 2 independents. George W. Bush won the presidency without a majority of the popular vote, with no clear mandate or overwhelming majority in the Senate or House. Any hint of a mandate was further undermined by Bush's controversial win with the U.S. Supreme Court. Here a court normally devoted to federalism overruled twice, in 5–4 votes, a state's highest court on the interpretation of state electoral law.

Over 40 percent of all presidential elections since the early nineteenth century have produced "minority" winners, including Abraham Lincoln, Grover Cleveland (twice), Woodrow Wilson (twice), Harry S. Truman, John F. Kennedy, Richard M. Nixon, Bill Clinton (twice), and George W. Bush (in 2000). These sub–50 percent winners often have at least one of the following three factors to help them govern: a clear-cut edge in the popular vote, a decisive advantage in the Electoral College, or party allies firmly in command on Capitol Hill.

President George W. Bush in 2000 had none of these advantages at the beginning of his administration and faced a unique problem involving legitimacy considering the outcome of the five-week Florida recount and the ultimate forum, the courts. That changed dramatically with the 9/11 terrorist attack on the United States with a rallying of U.S. citizens, Congress, and the world community behind President Bush; his invasion of Iraq and later his win in the 2004 election further changed his agenda and the Republican majorities in the House and Senate. Events and election results shape the context for presidential-congressional relations by setting the agenda (9/11) and through the partisan majorities in Congress (2002 and 2004).

Congressional Democrats lost ground politically during the Clinton presidency, both in the Senate and in the House, but it did not guarantee a new Congress that would work easily with President George W. Bush. The 2000 elections left the Democrats with forty-six fewer House seats and seven fewer Senate seats than when Clinton was first elected in 1992. Every two-term president in the twentieth century has lost seats in the House and the Senate (save for FDR's first eight years, when the Democrats picked up seven Senate seats), and Clinton was no exception to this trend. President Bush was an exception to this trend with Republican gains in the House and Senate mid-term elections in 2002 (and with Republican gains in 2004).

The historic 1994 midterm congressional election reversed a generation of Democratic dominance in the House, brought divided party control of government again, and dramatically reshaped the rivalry between the president and Congress. Every election since 1996 has reinforced the dominance of the Republicans on Capitol Hill, except in 1994 when Senator Jeffords switched parties and gave the Democrats a majority of one in the Senate from mid-2001 to 2002. The 1994 election not only brought an overwhelming victory for the Republican Party and major changes in the policy agenda and the structure of Congress, but it also dramatically changed the balance of power between the president and Congress.[1] Having received an electoral mandate to implement their legislative program of cutbacks, devolution, and deregulation, Republicans in Congress boldly set about dictating the policy agenda. In contrast, President Clinton found that his negotiating power had been significantly diminished after the 1994 election. The Republicans centralized the decision-making system in the House of Representatives and, in the process, limited the president's ability to influence Congress. These changes did not last long.

After the historic 1994 midterm election, President Clinton was compelled to reach out to the new Republican leadership in the House and the Senate. Speaker Newt Gingrich (R-GA) received a boost in power from a highly unified House Republican Conference and the structural reforms that it imposed upon the House. President Clinton's activist agenda during the 103rd Congress was overshadowed by the Contract with America and the GOP-led drive to balance the budget and cut back the federal government.[2] However, ultimately, neither President Clinton nor the new Republican leadership could govern effectively without the cooperation of the other. Elections can have an impact on presidential and congressional relations, as shown so clearly in the dramatic shift in political mood and policy agenda from 1992 to 1994.

The 1992 presidential election brought Democrat Clinton to the White House and unified party control of government for the first time in twelve years. At the heart of the 1992 presidential campaign was President Clinton's promise to fix the economy and to use the presidency to do so. He believed in an activist role for the federal government. The election produced the largest turnover of membership in the House of Representatives in more than forty years; 110 new members took office in January 1993. President Clinton had a majority of Democrats in the House and Senate, unified party control of government, and many new members of Congress who wanted change. However, he discovered quickly that 43 percent support in the election (all but four House members ran ahead of him in absolute votes) did not translate into a mandate or easy coalition to push his activist agenda.[3] Although he was a "New" Democrat from the Democratic Leadership Council (DLC), Clinton sent strong signals to the Hill that he wanted to cooperate with a policy agenda along centrist lines. However, it was difficult for the president to find common ground for his centrist agenda with the Republicans and liberal or "Old" Democrats who were aligned with organized labor (opposing the DLC).

Unified party control of government did not bring an end to the rivalry between the president and Congress for President Clinton (in 1993–1994), nor did it for President George W. Bush. Within a few months, bitter struggles had broken out, pitting both of these presidents with their own parties and against opposition party leaders. Although Presidents George W. Bush and Bill Clinton presented themselves as moderate, pragmatic, and bipartisan, they had serious problems building centrist coalitions to support their programs. Both had to work with the majority of their party members, whose centers of gravity had moved to the left on the political spectrum for the Democrats and to the right for the Republicans and who, as a result, frequently opposed the presidents' policies. For example, in 2001, President Bush had major opposition within his party from key committee chairs to his first legislative initiatives: a $1.6 trillion tax-cut proposal and major changes in education policy (No Child Left Behind Act). In 2005 Bush was also confronted with opposition to his Social Security privatization reforms and to certain budget cuts and permanent tax cuts. Although Clinton also had unified party government for his first two years in office (1993–1994), eleven Democratic House subcommittee chairs voted against President Clinton's economic package in May 1993, and the president's program barely survived. In a clear indication of the lack of discipline in the Democratic Party, in response to a subsequent demand by some House members, especially freshmen, the House leadership rejected the proposal that the eleven be stripped of their chairmanships.[4] Clinton also had to build cross-party coalitions with more conservative Republican leaders to pass several major bills on his agenda, such as the North American Free Trade Agreement (NAFTA), the General Agreement on Tariffs and Trade (GATT), and normal trade relations for the People's Republic of China. Many of President Clinton's initiatives were stopped or amended so thoroughly that they bore little resemblance to his original proposals. Unified government did not guarantee presidential dominance in Clinton's relationship with Congress.

In 1989 President George Bush (senior) had similar conflicts with Congress. Immediately after his inauguration, President Bush, also in a gesture of goodwill like his son George W. Bush, praised Congress: "To the Members of the Congress, to the institution of the House of Representatives and the Senate of the United States, may they flourish and may they prosper."[5] In response to President Bush's efforts to build better relations with Congress, Thomas S. Foley (D-Wash.), then House majority leader, said, "That's another example of President Bush reaching out. We're going to respond very positively to that."[6] Despite all this, President Bush went on to have one of the lowest records of support for his policy initiatives in Congress in the last fifty years (43 percent in his fourth year in office) (see table 1.1). President Clinton and the two Bush presidents had every good intention to work with

Table 1.1.   Presidential Success in Congress

Presidential Success Scores: History			
Year/President	Success Scores	Year/President	Success Scores
1953 Eisenhower	89.16	1979	76.80
1954	78.26	1980	75.11
1955	75.27	1981 Reagan	82.35
1956	69.70	1982	72.45
1957	68.38	1983	67.07
1958	75.68	1984	65.79
1959	52.00	1985	59.89
1960	65.12	1986	56.07
1961 Kennedy	81.38	1987	43.50
1962	85.41	1988	47.40
1963	87.10	1989 G. Bush	62.57
1964 Johnson	87.92	1990	46.77
1965	93.07	1991	54.17
1966	78.95	1992	43.03
1967	78.77	1993 Clinton	86.39
1968	74.53	1994	86.43
1969 Nixon	73.95	1995	36.17
1970	76.92	1996	55.07
1971	74.82	1997	53.62
1972	66.27	1998	50.65
1973	50.65	1999	37.80
1974 Nixon	59.56	2000	55.05
1974 Ford	58.20	2001 G. W. Bush	86.67
1975	60.99	2002	87.76
1976	53.85	2003	78.74
1977 Carter	75.45	2004	72.62
1978	78.33		

Source: CQ Data, 2005

broad bipartisan centrist coalitions in Congress, but whether with unified or divided party control of government, it did not work out that way.[7]

Goodwill does not generally characterize the institutional relationship between Congress and the president. In his first four years in office, President George W. Bush earned the highest presidential support scores, 81 percent (the percentage of presidential proposals that are approved by Congress calculated annually by *Congressional Quarterly Weekly Report*), since President Jimmy Carter (see table 1.1). President Clinton also earned high presidential support in his first two years of office (in the mid-1980s), but the percentage dropped for the last six years during divided party and government to the mid-50s to below 40 percent in 1999 (see table 1.1).[8] He was impeached stemming from an affair with a White House intern and his health-care reform failed. Personal scandal followed him from his political career in Arkansas through his eight years in office into retirement, which affected his ability to build support in Congress. However, while in office he did continue to reduce the federal budget deficit, to build bipartisan support for successful passage of NAFTA and GATT, the family and medical leave law, normal trade relations with the People's Republic of China, and a variety of other programs.

In his first two years in office, President George W. Bush fared better than most presidents elected in the postwar era, winning over 80 percent of the roll-call votes on which he took an unambiguous position (see table 1.1). Bush's success rate during his fourth year of presidency was 72.6 percent, which was higher than any president in the fourth year of his term since Eisenhower in 1956 except for Johnson (at 74.5 percent) and Carter (at 75.1 percent).[9] On the other hand, despite President George H. W. Bush's popularity with the American people during Desert Storm (the highest in the polls of any postwar president at the end of his first year) and his sincere efforts to build bridges between the White House and Capitol Hill, executive-legislative relations during his presidency remained deeply rooted in political and institutional divisions, divided party government. His presidential success score for 1992 (his fourth year in office) was the lowest in the past fifty-one years at 43 percent. The partisan divisions that George H. W. Bush experienced did not evaporate for President Clinton with unified government in 1993–1994, and they were clearly revealed in Clinton's relationship with Congress until he left office January 20, 2001. Clinton's fourth-year presidential success scores were 55.1 percent.

President George W. Bush also called for bipartisanship, comity, and a more civil relationship with Congress in his 2000 campaign and during the early days of his first four years in office. However, he also inherited a long-seated rivalry and difficulty in building coalitions around his policy initiatives (especially in the Senate). Where does this conflict come from? What are the roots of the rivalry between the president and Congress? Why does the president's success with Congress vary over time?

"The relationship between the Congress and the presidency has been one of the abiding mysteries of the American system of government," according to Arthur M. Schlesinger Jr.[10] The answer to this mystery lies in a variety of factors. In this introduction, I will examine several root causes of the rivalry and balance of power between the president and Congress: the constitutional design with its formal presidential and congressional powers; different electoral constituencies for the president, the House, and the Senate; varying terms of office; increased partisanship and polarization of Congress; the ongoing competition for power between Congress and the president; the permanent election campaign; narrow majorities in both houses; congressional individualism; the impact of the media in the twenty-four-hour, seven-days-a-week news cycle; and the nature of interest groups and American pluralism.

CONSTITUTIONAL DESIGN

The framers of the Constitution bequeathed to Americans one of the most enduring rivalries in government, that between the president and Congress.[11] The Constitution separates the three branches of government (legislative, executive, and judicial) but combines their functions, creating conflict and shared powers.[12] As Richard Neustadt observed, the constitution created a government "of separated institutions sharing powers," which makes it difficult for presidents to bridge the constitutional gap even in the best of political circumstances. The Constitution gives the president and the Congress different powers, and each is jealous of the other's constitutional prerogatives regardless of context.

The Constitution invests Congress with "all legislative Powers," (lawmaking), but it also authorizes the president to recommend and to veto legislation. Article I, Section 7 of the Constitution requires the president to approve or disapprove all bills passed by Congress. If the president vetoes a bill, "it shall be reposed by two-thirds of the Senate and the House of Representatives" (Article I, Section 7). Because it is so difficult for Congress to gain a two-thirds vote, presidential vetoes are usually sustained. Since the beginning of the federal government in 1789, thirty-five of forty-three presidents have exercised their veto authority on a total of 2,550 occasions (see table 1.2). Of that number, 1,484, or 58 percent, have been returned vetoes, that is, the rejected legislation was returned to the congressional house of origin while it was in session with a presidential message of explanation. One thousand sixty-six (or 42 percent) were "pocket vetoes" not subject to congressional override or while Congress was adjourned. Congress overrode presidential vetoes slightly more than 7 percent of the time (106 times) when it had the opportunity to vote on them (see table 1.2).[13] Because vetoes are so difficult to override, the veto power makes the president very powerful if he wants to stop legislation. President George W. Bush did not use a veto in his first four years in office. The threat of a veto in the legislative process gives the president an important bargaining tool; however, George W. Bush did not use this tool in his first term, and President Clinton did not use this tool until 1995, when he vetoed a $16 billion rescission bill. Clinton used the veto in his confrontation with the Republican-led Congress over the cuts in Medicaid, Medicare, welfare, education, and federal environmental programs in the fiscal year 1996 federal budget. This showdown ultimately helped to shut down government and stop the drive of the Contract with America supporters in the House and Senate. The greatest power of the president in divided government is often the power to say no, as President Clinton did in his last six years of office. It is easier to stop legislation than it is to pass it. President Clinton embraced that notion in his historic budget battle in 1995 when he said, "This is one of those moments in history when I'm grateful for the wisdom of our Founding Fathers. The Congress gets to propose, but the president has to sign or veto, and the Constitution gave me that authority and one of the reasons for the veto is to prevent excess. They knew what they were doing and we're going to use the Constitution they gave us to stand up for what's right."[14]

Congress is given broad powers in Article I, Section 8 of the Constitution, but the greatest power of Congress is its authority to pass laws directly binding upon all citizens (lawmaking). Also of great importance is the power of the purse, the power to authorize and appropriate funds for the president and executive branch agencies. Presidents may propose budgets for the federal government, but Congress has the final say on spending. This creates an automatic rivalry between the two and conflict over spending priorities. Congress also has the power to levy and collect taxes, to borrow and coin money, and to regulate foreign and interstate commerce. A central element of the rivalry between the president and Congress has been battles over tax and trade policy. The powers to declare war, to provide for a militia, and to adopt laws concerning bankruptcy, naturalization, patents, and copyrights are also bestowed on Congress. The interpretation of presidential and congressional war power has changed over time and is another contemporary source of conflict. Congress has the authority to establish or eliminate executive branch agencies (e.g., intelligence reform of 2004) and create new departments (e.g., Department of Homeland Security in 2003) and to oversee their opera-

Table 1.2.   Presidential Vetoes, 1789 to Present

President	Congresses coincident with terms	Regular vetoes	Pocket vetoes	Total vetoes	Vetoes overridden
Washington	1, 2, 3, 4	2	—	2	—
Adams	5, 6,	—	—	—	—
Jefferson	7, 8, 9, 10	—	—	—	—
Madison	11, 12, 13, 14	5	2	7	—
Monroe	15, 16, 17, 18	1	—	1	—
J.Q. Adams	19, 20	—	—	—	—
Jackson	21, 22, 23, 24	5	7	12	—
Van Buren	25, 26	—	1	1	—
W. H. Harrison	27	—	—	—	—
Tyler	27, 28	6	4	10	1
Polk	29, 30	2	1	3	—
Taylor	31	—	—	—	—
Fillmore	31, 32	—	—	—	—
Pierce	33, 34	9	—	9	5
Buchanan	35, 36	4	3	7	—
Lincoln	37, 38, 39	2	5	7	—
A. Johnson	39, 40	21	8	29	15
Grant	41, 42, 43, 44	45	48	93	4
Hayes	45, 46	12	1	13	1
Garfield	47	—	—	—	—
Arthur	47, 48	4	8	12	1
Cleveland	49, 50	304	110	414	2
B. Harrison	51, 52	19	25	44	1
Cleveland	53, 54	42	128	170	5
McKinley	55, 56, 57	6	36	42	—
T. Roosevelt	57, 58, 59, 60	42	40	82	1
Taft	61, 62	30	9	39	1
Wilson	63, 64, 65, 66	33	11	44	6
Harding	67	5	1	6	—
Coolidge	68, 69, 70	20	30	50	4
Hoover	71, 72	21	16	37	3
F. D. Roosevelt	73, 74, 75, 76, 77, 78, 79	372	263	635	9
Truman	79, 80, 81, 82	180	70	250	12
Eisenhower	83, 84, 85, 86	73	108	181	2
Kennedy	87, 88	12	9	21	—
L.B. Johnson	88, 89, 90	16	14	30	—
Nixon	91, 92, 93	26	17	43	7
Ford	93, 94	48	18	66	12
Carter	95, 96	13	18	31	2
Reagan	97, 98, 99, 100	39	39	78	99
G. H. W. Bush	101, 102	29	15	44	1
Clinton	103, 104, 105, 106	36	—	36	2
G. W. Bush	107, 108	—	—	—	—
	Total	1,484	1,066	2,550	106

Source: U.S. Congress, Secretary of the Senate, *Presidential Vetoes, 1989–1996*, S.Pub. 105-22 (Washington, D.C.: GPO, 1992), p. 12; U.S. Congress, Secretary of the Senate, *Presidential Vetoes, 1789–1988*, S.Pub. 102-12 (Washington, D.C.: 1992), p. 595.

tions. The Senate must approve cabinet nominees, ambassadors, and Supreme Court and federal judicial appointees before they can take office. A president cannot enter into a binding treaty with a foreign government without a two-thirds vote of the Senate, nor can the president "declare war," a power the Constitution purposely gives to Congress. All of these constitutional congressional and presidential powers force both institutions to confront each other in governance, which more often than not creates rivalry and conflict.

A dramatic but rarely employed check on the president is impeachment. President Clinton's impeachment was historic yet rare. The president and executive branch officials can be impeached (formally accused) by a majority vote in the House and tried in the Senate. If two-thirds of the senators vote to convict, the official is removed from office. Only President Andrew Johnson and Bill Clinton have been tried on impeachment charges. The vote fell one short of the number required to convict Johnson, and the Senate did not convict Clinton by a significant majority. The House Judiciary Committee recommended that Richard M. Nixon be impeached for transgressions in connection with the Watergate burglary involving the Democratic National Committee offices and the ensuing cover-up. Nixon, however, resigned the presidency before a full session of the House could vote on the impeachment issue. The threat of impeachment establishes an important check on the president and executive branch officials, limiting the power of the president.

The Framers of the Constitution deliberately fragmented power between the national government and the states (federalism) and among the executive, legislative, and judicial branches (separation of powers).[15] They also divided legislative powers by creating two coequal houses, a bicameral Congress with different constituencies, which further magnifies rivalry and conflict. Although divided, Congress was designed to be independent and powerful, able to check the power of the executive and to be directly linked with the people through popular, periodic elections. The Framers wanted an effective and powerful federal government, but they also wanted to limit its power in order to protect personal and property rights. Having experienced the abuses of English monarchs and their colonial governors, the Framers were wary of excessive executive authority. They also feared "elective despotism," or excessive legislative power, something the Articles of Confederation had given their own state legislatures.

Congress has the functions of lawmaking, oversight, deliberation, and education. Therefore, the Framers created three branches of government, with none having a monopoly. This separation of powers restricted the power of any one branch, and it required cooperation among the three in order for them to govern effectively. Today, as then, political action requires cooperation between the president and Congress. Yet the Constitution, in the way it divided power between the two branches, created an open invitation for conflict.[16] In sum, in creating a separated presidency and two equal legislative chambers, the framers guaranteed checks and executive legislative power over ongoing rivalry.

DIFFERENT CONSTITUENCIES

The U.S. system of government, unlike parliamentary systems throughout the world, elects the executive and members of the legislature independently. The president is elected from vastly broader national electoral coalitions (271 electoral votes, generally from "battleground" or competitive states) than are representatives' homogeneous districts and senators' heterogeneous states. Members of Congress, even those who belong to the president's party or hail from his home state, represent specific interests that can conflict with the interests of the president, who represents the nation as a whole. James Madison well understood this dichotomy of interest as an important source of conflict between the president and Congress: "The members of the federal legislature will be likely to attach themselves too much to local objects. . . . Measures will too often be decided according to their probable effect, not on the national prosperity and happiness, but on the prejudices, interests, and pursuits of the governments and the people of the individual States."[17] Presidential elections have been extremely competitive, but narrowed in the last weeks of the election campaigns to very few battleground states (e.g., in 2004, Pennsylvania, Ohio, and Florida). House seats have become less and less competitive than Senate elections. Senate elections have produced an upper chamber that is effectively tied on major issues. The different campaign strategies, messages, and policy promises in the three types of elections often create conflict between the president, House, and Senate. Members of Congress give voice to diverse local and state needs, demands, and viewpoints. Presidents (and their vice presidents) are elected nationally. They must create a broad coalition of voters that is not necessary for lawmakers. Only presidents can claim to speak for the nation at large, thus they view policies and problems from different perspectives and time periods. Presidents are limited to four years, at most eight, to win adoption of what they have promised to a national constituency. Members of Congress do not have term limits and wait for a president to leave office in order to get what they want.

VARYING TERMS OF OFFICE

The interaction of Congress and the president is shaped not only by their different constituencies and electoral competitiveness but by their different

terms in office. The constitutional structure of U.S. government, which separates the Congress and the president, sets different terms of office for representatives (two-year terms), senators (six-year terms), and the president
(four-year terms) and ensures they will be chosen from different constituency
bases. Presidents have only four years, possibly eight, in which to establish
their programs. They are expected to set the national policy agenda and usually move rapidly in the first year, before their decline in popularity.[18] Presidents are not concerned about reelection after the first four years of office.
They focus on legacy, establishing lasting, good public policy and an honored
place in history as their first priority. Other interests are certainly operative,
but the drive for reelection for members of Congress is most important.[19]
Legislators, then, are often reluctant to allow their workload and policy
agenda to be dictated by a president who has no electoral mandate to do so.
They are often driven by short-term motivations to be reelected rather than
by long-term policy goals.

Congress moves more slowly than the president; it is deliberative and inef-
ficient primarily because it represents a vast array of local interests. Congress
passes new laws slowly and reviews old ones carefully. The House of Representatives of the 104th through the 108th Congresses centralized power and
was more efficient than the House of any other modern Congress, but this,
too, caused conflict with President Clinton's and President Bush's agendas.
The decision-making pace of Congress and of the president is not the same
because of their different terms of office, electoral base, and perceived constituency mandates. The result of these varying terms of office is rivalry, conflict, extreme partisanship since 1995, and often deadlock over major policies.

POLITICAL PARTIES

The federal system of state-based political parties contributes to the independence of members of Congress from the president. The president must work
with decentralized political party organizations that often exercise little control over recruitment of candidates who run under their party label, weak
discipline, and even less leverage over members. Senators and representatives
usually run their own races with their own financing. The way they respond
to local conditions has little to do with national party platforms or presidential politics. Members freely pursue their own interests without fear of discipline from the president.

Independence from political parties and the president allows legislators to seek benefits for their own constituents and to serve specialized interests. Thomas Mann argues further that

> the changes that swept through the political system during the 1960s and 1970s—the increase in split-ticket voting, the growing cost of campaigns and reliance on contributions from special interests, the rise of television, the expansion and growing political sophistication of interest groups in Washington, and the democratization and decentralization of Congress—may well have weakened the classic iron triangles, but they also heightened the sensitivity of politicians to all forms of outside pressure.[20]

However, for Republican members of the House, the 1994 election deviated from the normal individualistic election. The Contract with America, signed by three hundred Republican candidates for the House, "nationalized" the campaign for most of those candidates. No incumbent Republican House member lost in the 1994 election. Republicans earned a net gain of seventeen in the fifty-two open-seat House contests and lost only four Republican-controlled House open seats to the Democrats. Thirty-five House incumbent Democrats lost. With the Democrats losing fifty-two seats in the House and eight Senate seats, the mandate of the new Republicans was to be loyal to the contract, to the House Republican leadership, and to the reduction of individualism in the House. Party discipline came from the congressional party leaders, not from the grassroots party organizations throughout the United States. This was unique in modern congressional elections and created the basis of more discipline and centralized power in the House of Representatives, and conflict with President Clinton and party leadership helped President George W. Bush's agenda into the 109th Congress.

There is a continuing trend in both chambers away from bipartisan cooperation and toward ideological and political loyalty. An analysis of party unity votes, defined by *Congressional Quarterly* as votes where a majority of one party votes against a majority of the other, shows that Republicans and Democrats have record levels of polarization. Party unity has steadily increased since 1970, from the low average party unity score of the low sixties to the high eighties in 2004 (see table 1.3). For example, on votes in which party leaders took clear opposing positions, Senate Republicans voted to support the party position 90 percent of the time and House Republicans 88 percent of the time. Senate Democrats supported the party position 83 percent of the time and House Democrats 86 percent of the time. These party voting patterns have revealed the parties to be much more ideological and polarized.

Table 1.3. Party Unity: Average Unity Score by Party, 1960–2004

Year/President	Republicans	Democrats	Year/President	Republicans	Democrats
1960 Eisenhower	68	64	1983	74	76
1961 Kennedy	72	71	1984	72	74
1962	68	69	1985	75	79
1963	72	71	1986	71	78
1964 Johnson	69	67	1987	74	81
1965	70	69	1988	73	79
1966	67	61	1989 G. Bush	73	81
1967	71	66	1990	74	81
1968	63	57	1991	78	81
1969 Nixon	62	62	1992	79	79
1970	59	57	1993 Clinton	84	85
1971	66	62	1994	83	83
1972	64	57	1995	91	80
1973	68	68	1996	87	80
1974 Nixon/Ford	62	63	1997	88	82
1975	70	69	1998	86	83
1976	66	65	1999	86	84
1977 Carter	70	67	2000	87	83
1978	67	64	2001 G. W. Bush	90	85
1979	72	69	2002	89	86
1980	70	68	2003	92	87
1981 Reagan	76	69	2004	89	86
1982	71	72			

Source: CQ Data, 2005

PARTY CONTROL OF GOVERNMENT

Another electoral base impediment to legislative-executive cooperation is divided government, as shown by the dramatic election of 1994, which left a Democrat in the White House working with Republican majorities in the House and Senate.[21] There are two varieties of divided government (the condition that exists when the majority party in either or both houses of Congress differs from the party of the president): divided party control of Congress, and split control of Congress and the White House. From 1901 through 2005, we have had unified party control of government for sixty-five years, almost 62 percent of the time, and divided party control of government for forty years, or 38 percent of the time (see table 1.4). Opposing parties have controlled the presidency and one or both houses of Congress in twenty-two of the past twenty-eight years (79 percent of the time from 1969 through 1996), with the Republicans mainly controlling the White House and the Democrats controlling Congress. From 1887 to 1954, divided party control of government occurred in only eight years (14 percent of the time), but from President Dwight D. Eisenhower's first year (1953) through President Clinton's fourth year in office (1996), it occurred twenty-eight years (56 percent of the time). Although President George W. Bush has had unified party government most of the time, divided party control of government at the federal level has been the norm in modern U.S. politics (see table 1.4).

Presidents are more likely to be successful in their relationship with Congress with unified party government than with divided government. This has been especially true since the post-1980 resurgence of party-line voting and party cohesion in Congress. Overall, Reagan and Bush had low presidential support scores in Congress because of divided party government. Clinton's victories on votes in Congress during his first two years (1993–1994) in office averaged over 86 percent in the House and Senate and dropped to 36 percent in 1995 when the Republicans captured the Congress (see table 1.1). Although President George W. Bush had unified Republican government for the first time since 1954, the closeness of the election and the tie in the Senate created the foundation for conflict and in effect divided government.

The trend toward ticket splitting between presidential and congressional candidates further exacerbates already strained relations. Election returns for Congress have increasingly diverged from national presidential returns; "the range in the . . . variance, which measures the extent to which changes in local returns differ from the change in national returns, has more than dou-

Table 1.4.   Unified and Divided Party Control of Government, 1901–2005

Year	Party Control	Number of years	Percentage

Unified party control of government (64 years) 61.3%
Divided party control of government (41 years) 39.0%

Year	Party Control	Number of years	Percentage
1901–1920	Unified	16	80
	Divided	4	20
1921–1940	Unified	18	90
	Divided	2	10
1941–1960	Unified	12	60
	Divided	8	40
1961–1980	Unified	12	60
	Divided	8	40
1981–2000	Unified	2	10
	Divided	18	90
2001–2006	Unified	4	80
	Divided	1	20

bled."[22] During the past thirty years, as the power of political parties has declined significantly, there has been a corresponding rise in individualistic candidacies for the presidency, the Senate, and the House. Fewer and fewer members of Congress ride into office on the electoral "coattails" of the president. This has led to the election of presidents who find it difficult to translate electoral support into governing support. The scarcity of presidential coattails by George H.W. Bush in 1988, Clinton in 1992, and George W. Bush in 2000 brings the conclusion that "the emperor has no coat."[23] The elder Bush was the first candidate since John F. Kennedy to win the White House while his party lost seats in the House. Clinton ran behind all but four members of the House. With the decline of presidential coattails, strong-willed members of Congress are largely beyond the president's control. They are often more responsive to district and specialized interests than to the national agenda of the president.

Unified party control of government does not mean the two branches will work closely together. Divided government does not always mean that the two branches will fight. David Mayhew found that when it comes to passing major legislation or conducting investigations, it "does not seem to make all that much difference whether party control of the American government happens to be unified or divided."[24] However, we do know that it was generally easier for presidents to govern during periods of unified control.

The balance of power between and within the institutions of Congress and the presidency is dynamic and conflict is inevitable, another root cause of the rivalry between the president and Congress. The congressional institutions of a stable committee system, party leadership organizations, the seniority system, and behavioral norms such as reciprocity all have an impact on congressional-presidential relationships. The 1994 election brought the most centralized power structure in the House since Republican Speaker Joseph G. "Czar" Cannon, who served from 1903 to 1911.[25] Just one year before, the 103rd Congress, under Speaker Thomas Foley, was decentralized and fragmented. What the public expects from each institution varies over time, as dramatically shown by the differences between the 103rd and 104th Congresses.[26] For two hundred years Congress has continued to represent local interest and to respond (some think too much) to political preferences and public pressures.[27] Nevertheless, the institution has changed dramatically. The reforms of the past two decades have made Congress even more representative and accountable and, in the 104th Congress, more centralized. The reforms of the last twenty years have changed the way it makes laws, passes budgets, oversees the executive branch, and confronts the presidents. The degree of centralization or fragmentation of power among committees and members has major consequences for Congress's power vis-à-vis the president. It is difficult for the president to build predictable coalitions around a highly fragmented legislature, but it can also play into his favor if divided party government exists.

As the congressional leadership is centralized and made more effective by one party, the power of a president of the opposition party is often diminished, as we saw in the 104th Congress. This creates more tension between the two branches, with a clash between the president's national policy agenda and the agenda of Congress. President Clinton's legislative successes during the 103rd Congress (1993–1994) were impressive, with a remarkable 86 percent win record on the votes on which he took a position. The 1994 election changed his success and the competitive environment with Congress; he was overshadowed by the Contract with America, the leadership of Speaker Newt Gingrich, and the Republican drive to balance the budget. Unified government and a decentralized Congress helped his legislative successes in 1993 and 1994; a massive loss in the midterm elections to the Republicans created conflict and a deadlock between the two branches. If the president is popular with the American public, he has electoral coattails bringing many new members into Congress who are beholden to him, and if he has a well-organized and well-run White House and administration, he is more able to control the national policy agenda. An example of a president meeting these criteria is President Lyndon Johnson during his first two years of office, before the war in Vietnam undermined his influence in Congress and popularity with the American voters. His central core of authority in dealing with Congress reduced conflict between the two branches. Structural reforms within the presidency (for example, the establishment of the Bureau of the Budget and, later, the creation of the Office of Management and Budget and the expansion of the post–World War II White House staff) and change in Congress (for example, the centralization of power by the Republican Party's congressional leadership and increased party unity in the 104th Congress) have direct impacts on the ability of the president to dominate the legislative agenda and for the Congress to act independently from the president. Thus, cooperation and conflict between the two branches are the norm.

Pressure to check the power of the president through the War Powers Resolution of 1973 and the Budget and Impoundment Control Act of 1974 brought changes that helped Congress reclaim some of the power it had lost to the president during the previous decades. Many institutional reforms of the 1970s, however, resulted in decentralization, which made Congress more democratic but also less efficient. With the new openness came greater accountability and responsiveness but at the price of efficiency and effectiveness as a lawmaking body. Modern presidents find Congress harder to influence than did their predecessors in the White House. Members of Congress are more independent. And with the weakening of strict seniority rules wielded by strong parties, coordinating the legislative process was more difficult for congressional party leaders until the House reforms of the 104th Congress that centralized power with the Republican leadership.

Although Congress created new ways of checking presidential power in the 1970s, ultimately legislative-executive relationships are not zero-sum games. If one branch gains power, the other does not necessarily lose it. The expansion of the federal government since World War II has given vast new power to both branches. Events and public policy issues contribute to the policymaking power of both the president and Congress. The war on drugs, environmental concerns, the savings and loan crisis, Desert Storm, homeland security, the war in Iraq, and continuing budget deficits have all led to new administrative (and legislative) powers expanding the scope of both branches. Even these crises, however, are not enough to reduce the rivalry between the two institutions.

The decentralization and fragmentation of power within Congress was dramatically altered as a result of the 1994 election. The Speaker, the only structural feature of the House dictated by the Constitution, had significant power before Speaker Gingrich expanded that power even more. Gingrich appointed the committee chairs and increased his influence over committee assignments, placing freshmen on the Ways and Means, Appropriations, Rules, and Commerce committees. Of the eleven Republican openings on the Appropriations Committee, Speaker Gingrich appointed nine freshmen, thus assuring cohesion and loyalty from the new Republicans in the House. Gingrich's control over committee assignments for freshmen and over the selection of chairs was a dramatic break from the decentralized and more democratic House of the last twenty years. He abolished proxy voting in committees, which limited the power of committee chairs. He reduced committee staffing, abolished independent subcommittee staff, and placed six-year term limits on committee chairs, thus reducing the power of the chairs and increasing the power of the leadership. Gingrich, with the support of the Republican Conference, also limited committee assignments and restructured the committee system generally. All of these reforms helped to centralize power in the speakership. Under the reformed House of Representatives, Speaker Gingrich gained substantial power to control the policy agenda using key provisions in the GOP Contract with America. He was able to overshadow President Clinton (and the Senate) and pass far-reaching legislation that projected a balanced budget in seven years, cut taxes, cut back spending on Medicare, Medicaid, and welfare, and decentralized federal government, sending more programs and money to the states. Republican Party dominance of the House and Senate and internal change in the House power structure fundamentally changed the relationship with the president in 1995.[28] However, after the shutdown of government as a result of a conflict over the budget in 1995, the committee chairs and members reasserted themselves in the House, and the normal decentralized system of policy making was reestablished. The power of the committee and subcommittee chairs became the locus of decision making, and President Clinton had to build coalitions in a highly fragmented, individualistic House for the next five years of his administration, but that changed dramatically in 2001, after the election of President George W. Bush.

The House Republican leadership has continued to transform the organization and processes of the House. That has helped President Bush achieve his legislative successes under unified party government. There has been a greater concentration of power in the hands of House leaders. There is an increasing use of the House rules to deny the minority a full debate or votes on its views. There is a disintegration of the committee process in the House. There is a heavy reliance on riders to the appropriations bills as a way to act on significant policy issues. There has been an abuse of the conference committee by the majority party. There has been an unwillingness of Congress to make thorough use of its oversight powers to keep the president in check. There has been a breakdown in the budget process, passing large omnibus spending bills well after the start of the fiscal year (October 1).[29] There has been a continued increase in polarization and lack of comity and civility in the House and Senate.[30] All of these trends have helped President Bush dominate Congress on defense and national security policy (e.g., Iraq war, intelligence reform, and homeland security policy) and on many domestic issues (tax cuts, education reform, Medicare prescription drug legislation). The Imperial Presidency was dormant from the late 1970s through the Clinton administration, but it returned with President Bush's election in 2000 and has been assisted by the Republican House and Senate leadership and unified party government.

INTEREST GROUPS AND PLURALISM

Passage of the 2003 Medicare prescription drug bill was dependent upon the strong support of three major associations, the AARP, the pharmaceutical companies, and the health insurance companies of America. The battle to reform Social Security is also directly linked to the battle of special interests in the United States, the AARP (and associated groups), and the U.S. Chamber of Commerce–National Association of Manufacturers coalition (and other association allies). Medicare and Social Security reform are examples of the importance of organized interest groups in the relationship between the president and Congress. Without the help of well-organized groups, the president and Congress cannot easily enact legislation. Pluralism, group-based politics, limits the power of the president and Congress to pursue their own agendas and thereby increases the competition between them. Policy-making gridlock often comes from competition among organized interests in society, not from divided party control of government. Deadlock over Superfund, the multiyear battle over the energy bill, conflict over the transportation bill of 2005, delay in passing the annual budget, the refusal by appropriators to fully fund authorization bills, and the tendency toward government by continuing resolution are all examples of deadlock among groups. As more people are organized (there are over 140,000 associations in the United States), as the political process is opened to more groups and classes than ever before, and as the demands and needs of those competing interests are weighed and mediated in the political process, the power of the president and Congress to control the policy agenda is reduced. The constitutional First Amendment rights, especially freedom of speech, freedom of assembly, freedom of the press, and freedom to petition government for grievances, are the foundation of pluralism in U.S. politics. The decay of political party organizations in the last thirty years in the United States has helped the growth of pluralism.[31] As political parties have lost power to recruit and elect candidates who are loyal to party leaders in government, interest groups have gained political power. The United States is experiencing "hyperpluralism," or extreme competition among groups that makes it almost impossible to define the public good in terms of anything other than the collection of special, narrow interests.[32] Hyperpluralism contributes fundamentally to the rivalry between the president and Congress and often leads to deadlock between the two branches of government (as with the shutdown of government over the fiscal year 1996 budget) by making it difficult to make the necessary compromises between the national interests of the president and the parochial interests of members of Congress.[33]

CONCLUSIONS AND OVERVIEW OF THE BOOK

Organization theorists suggest that conflict produces incentives for organizations to centralize decision-making power.[34] When an organization is threatened, a premium is placed on efficiency, effectiveness, and cohesiveness in setting strategy. After forty years of Democratic control and two years of con-flict from the Clinton White House, the House Republicans centralized their decision-making power structure (especially in the House of Representatives) in unprecedented ways. The House Republican centralization of decision making, starting in the 104th Congress, reduced individualism and brought about a more efficient, disciplined, and cohesive institution in its battle with President Clinton, and more coordination with President Bush in the 108th and 109th Congresses.

Threatened by a unified Republican House and Republican Senate, Presi-dent Clinton also reorganized and centralized his White House staff through Leon Panetta, his chief of staff. He simplified his policy agenda and built a more tightly knit and effective legislative affairs operation. Faced with a Democratic majority in the House in the 1980s, then minority whip Newt Gingrich helped to build a cohesive, centralized, and efficient opposition that was eventually used as a majority party organization against President Clinton and the congressional Democrats in 1995.

Intense rivalry between the president and Congress is inevitable in an electoral system that can produce divided party control of the two branches. Cooperation may be more likely when both the president and Congress are of the same party; however, it is not guaranteed. Because of the wide range of views within a party, unified government is no safeguard against conflict, as was shown with President Clinton and the congressional Democratic Party in 1993 and 1994 and the relationship of Bush with Congress (espe-cially the Senate) in 2005. Partisanship may also serve to move legislation. The give-and-take between national and local representation, deliberation and efficiency, openness and accountability, specific interests and the "public good" ensures a certain amount of confrontation between Congress and the president. The relationship between the president and Congress is shaped by an amalgam of factors: constitutional design, different electoral motivations and constituencies, different terms of office, weak political parties, divided party control of government, ongoing competition for power, and pluralism. Although the rivalry and conflict between Congress and the president are inherent in our system of government, presidents must build support in Con-gress, and members must seek assistance from the White House. To succeed in office, every president must surmount the constitutional and political obstacles to pass his legislative program and establish a working relationship with Congress.

The separation of powers and the division of political control between presidents and Congresses do not present an insurmountable barrier to good public policy making. Presidents need to lead both public opinion and a con-sensus among the policy communities in Congress to solve the problems that are so readily visible. Overcoming divided government, changing public opinion, building consensus, keeping party discipline, and establishing the nation's policy priorities calls for leadership from the president or from inside Congress. Congress and the president must work together. Unified partisan control of both branches of government does not guarantee cooperation, as President George W. Bush found out early in his administration. Divided government does not guarantee conflict, but it does make governing more difficult. Governing calls for bargaining, accommodation, and compromise by Congress and the president, which are the basis of our "separated" and pluralistic system of government.[35]

The chapters in this book present a balance of views between presidential and congressional scholars. This book presents no one viewpoint, no one dominant ideology for or against Congress or the presidency. Some contributors believe the system is working well, and others believe reform is badly needed. Some argue that Congress needs to assert more power to check the president, and others conclude the relationship between Congress and the president is working well and as designed in our Constitution. The following chapters address the most important question about the relationship between the president and Congress. Taking a variety of approaches, what are the root causes of their rivalry and their cooperation? Political scientists, legal scholars, historians, journalists, former White House and Capitol Hill staff, and former members of Congress all contribute. Each author brings unique experiences, methodologies, viewpoints, and theoretical backgrounds to the study of the relationship between Congress and the president.

In chapter 2, "Partisan Polarization, Politics, and the Presidency: Structural Sources of Conflict," James P. Pfiffner argues that relations between the president and Congress have recently become even more polarized and combative. In this chapter, Pfiffner describes the structural sources for the highly partisan and volatile politics of the Clinton and Bush presidencies. The factors leading to the recent increase in polarization between Congress and the president include the fact that the South is no longer the undisputed territory of Democrats and the increased frequency of divided government. He further shows how contemporary presidents do not enjoy the ideological sympathies of some members of the opposing party. Political parties that are more homogeneous—"Rockefeller Republicans" and "Boll Weevils"—are a thing of the past. As a result, presidents find it difficult to build and maintain the support of members from the opposing party for their legislative agenda. Filibusters have also increased, as have presidential threats to veto. Pfiffner argues that all these factors contribute to the contentious relationship between the president and Congress. He also documents a decline in civility in both chambers since the 1970s and how this affects congressional-presidential relations. Given the continuing reality of predictably safe seats in the House, the polarization in Congress is not likely to go away soon. All these factors leave presidents with no natural coalition partners in the middle in the Congress. Presidents often need to cobble together a fluid coalition of policy partners in Congress but cannot count on their own party's support or crossover support from members of the opposing party. Pfiffner concludes that despite the 2004 reelection of President Bush and continued control of Congress by the Republicans, relations between the two branches are likely to continue to be difficult in the second term. With President Bush's continued push for conservative domestic policies and an aggressive foreign policy, Democrats will be fighting a rearguard action (especially in the Senate) and will attempt to check Bush's legislative agenda.

Presidential scholar Stephen J. Wayne, in chapter 3, "Presidential Leadership of Congress: Structures and Strategies," emphasizes the fact that the constitutional design as set by the Framers assigns the president little role in legislating. The Framers of the Constitution did not expect the president to be chief legislator. However, the president's legislative role has increased steadily since Jefferson and Jackson were presidents. Contemporary presidents maintain "public relation teams" and seemingly try to influence legislative activity at every turn. In this chapter Professor Wayne uncovers why this change occurred. He first provides a historical description of how and why presidents first began to enter the legislative arena. He argues that nineteenth-century presidents began to legislate through members of Congress. They also used their veto power, and threats of vetoes, to influence congressional activity. As the twentieth century progressed, presidents went even further into the legislative arena. They developed a two-track agenda for influencing legislation. Major policy decisions received presidential attention, while OMB and executive agencies handled more minor legislative activity. Wayne points out that the presidents since Reagan have most dramatically moved away from the Framers' intent. Chiefs of staff now focus almost exclusively on the legislative agenda, policy directors have cabinet-level status, and the press is regularly used by presidents and their operatives to influence legislative activity. Presidents seek to sway public opinion and define legislative issues through sophisticated, permanent public relation teams centered in the White House. These teams use polling, focus groups, and the press to strategically set priorities, cycle issues, and package proposals in ways most likely to ensure legislative success. This ongoing public relations campaign within the White House stands in contrast to the specified legislative role for the president. Wayne describes how President George W. Bush (unlike his father) used the public relations initiative and the permanent campaign in an inextricably related way to achieve his legislative policy goals. The presidential public relations campaigns helped the president achieve his legislative goals by bringing pressure on lawmakers from the grass-roots and by targeting appeals to groups that were more responsive to them and by placing the burden of proof on Congress for his foreign policy initiatives. To be successful, modern presidents must make their pressure on Congress an extension of a successful election campaign. Wayne concludes that election campaigning and successful governing are closely linked in American politics, which has major ramifications for presidential and congressional rivalry.

Chapter 4, "The Impact of Campaigns on Presidential-Congressional Relations," written by journalist Richard E. Cohen, focuses on the skills needed to campaign effectively for the presidency and the impact of the campaign on governing. He argues they are not the same skills that allow presidents to legislate effectively. Although this is well known, Cohen, a prominent writer for *National Journal* who has followed many presidential candidates and covered several presidents in the White House, suggests that campaigns do have lasting effects for a president's legislative success. Candidate behavior and election results create the climate in Congress that governs the president's legislative possibilities. Using the experiences of the modern presidents and, particularly, the events surrounding the elections in 2000 and 2004, Cohen argues that inclusive candidates with large election majorities experience the most success with Congress. An overriding factor in Bush's 2000 and 2004 elections that carried over to his legislative agenda was that members of Congress were grateful that he helped them to maintain and expand their congressional majorities. That helped to explain why Bush's policy proposals had broad and solid support within his party, even when some lawmakers privately had misgivings about the potential political risk of the policies being advocated. Cohen maintains that new presidents are best positioned to gain acceptance of their legislative agenda when they enjoy clear mandates, demonstrate inclusion and agreement with a substantial number of members of Congress throughout the campaign, and articulate a clear legislative agenda throughout the campaign. When these presidents "hit the ground running" at the onset of their presidency, Congress is most likely to respond favorably. He also argues that presidents who do not enjoy strong mandates, those who run against Congress, and those who do not articulate a clear legislative agenda are not successful and fail when they take proactive legislative agendas, as shown with Presidents Carter and Clinton. The most important lesson for presidential legislative agenda setting is that presidents must reach out to lawmakers and have a well-planned strategy, theme, and political message in campaigns as well as in governing. Above all they must be willing to adapt to the political realities and unanticipated complications that have faced all presidents in their relationship with Congress.

In Chapter 5, "Successful Influence: Managing Legislative Affairs in the Twenty-First Century," two former senior-level White House aides, contemporary lobbyists, and political scientists, one Republican, Gary Andres, and one Democrat, Patrick Griffin, use their own experiences to critique existing conceptualizations of presidential "success" and "influence." From their many years of experience in the White House and on the Hill, they argue that most existing analyses of presidential success with Congress fail to realize the importance of four factors. First, presidents alone cannot drive the legislative agenda; Congress influences presidential behavior just as the president influences congressional behavior. Second, presidents are both endogenous and exogenous forces in the legislative process. Third, contextual factors matter so much that the influence of a president is not constant. Fourth, institutional considerations outside of the president's control are important factors governing the relationship between Congress and a president. Andres and Griffin note that most considerations of this relationship are outcome centered, like analyzing roll-call votes or whether a president can maintain and/or build legislative coalitions. These measures obscure the strategies effective presidents can use to shape legislative outcomes. They are not often used in the White House. From their practical experience with hundreds of legislative battles between the White House and the Hill, they highlight the most important factors in understanding presidential success in Congress. They raise questions about the dynamic relationship between the branches and conclude that whether presidents are successful in their relations with Congress should be evaluated using the broader criteria they propose in the chapter.

Congressional scholar Roger H. Davidson, in chapter 6, "The Presidency and Congressional Time," traces the development of strong congressional party leadership within the House and Senate, its ebb and flow in both chambers, and what the varying levels of power accorded to party leaders has meant for relations between Congress and the president. By taking the viewpoint of Capitol Hill rather than the Oval Office, he offers a useful and nonconventional perspective of congressional-presidential relations. Davidson shows how strong party leadership saw its zenith in the late nineteenth and early twentieth centuries, the structural and partisan factors that led to its erosion, and the gradual reemergence of strong party leadership in the 1970s. On the Senate side, strong party leadership emerged roughly during the same period. Davidson argues that the increased prominence and power of party leaders, especially since the 1950s, can be traced directly to the need for Senate leaders to confer with activist presidents and to help them manage their legislative agenda. He analyzes legislative productivity and presidential-congressional relations over time, in four distinct periods: the bipartisan conservative era (1937–1964), the liberal activist party government era (1965–1978), the postreform era (1979–1992), and the conservative party government era (1995–present). Davidson concludes his analysis by stating that legislative productivity is not always linked with the tenure of individual presidents and is less determined by party control than one would think. Davidson argues that party control is an incomplete guide to legislative activity and productivity, thus casting doubt on the assumption of many observers that unified party control raises legislative output and divided government leads to stalemate.

Richard S. Conley adds a different perspective on unified and divided party control of government in chapter 7, "The Legislative Presidency in Political Time: Party Control and Presidential-Congressional Relations." He analyzes how party control of the Congress and the presidency since 1953 has influenced both the president's legislative priorities and the relationship between the White House and the Congress. In defining "eras" of party unity and reform, Conley helps us to better understand presidential legislative successes and failures. More specifically, this chapter identifies how ideological agendas throughout history have contributed to the advancement of legislative priorities from presidents who have shared and differed in party identification from peers in Congress and what specific benefits resulted from such collaboration or opposition. In contrast to Davidson, Conley provides evidence to show why party control of the presidency, the House, and the Senate matters to the legislative presidency. He concludes that divided government is a much greater challenge to presidents in the postreform party unity era. Conley also shows that President George W. Bush's electoral politics in 2000 and 2004 have had a direct impact on the success of his legislative agenda, showing the importance of party control of Congress and the presidency.

Chapter 8, "The Institutional Context of Veto Bargaining," by C. Lawrence Evans and Stephen Ng, analyzes the power of the presidential veto in legislative bargaining, a central feature of the American constitutional system of separation of powers. They answer several important questions about the role of the veto in presidential-congressional relations. They describe the process through which veto threats are formulated within the executive branch, the different forms they take, and the linkages that exist between presidential signals and the agendas of the congressional party leadership. They clearly show that veto threats decline sharply when the same party controls both branches. Unified government is less useful as a political strategy, as shown with President Bush's relationship with the 108th and 109th

Congresses. Evans and Ng clearly show how the internal characteristics of Congress and the executive branch condition how these branches bargain with each other using the veto. Their analysis explains the variance in intensity and ambiguity of veto threats over time. They also describe the impact of the threat of veto on legislative strategy.

Budgets are not just numbers and program priorities; they are politics and reveal a great deal about the relationship between the Congress and the president. In chapter 9, "Politics of the Federal Budget Process," Leon E. Panetta, former White House chief of staff, director of OMB, and chairman of the House Budget Committee, draws on his experiences and knowledge to explain the political relationship between the White House and Congress in the federal budgetary process. He analyzes the role of the executive and legislative branches in budgeting. He describes the time each branch uses to act on budgetary issues and reveals the considerable differences in style when it comes to budgetary politics. The actions of executive branch offices and the White House are predictable, and the president is always the ultimate arbiter. Congress is different. There is no central authority; each member tries to get their pet projects through and influence the process. As a result, congressional action surrounding the budget is less detailed and more unpredictable. With these broad differences delineated, Panetta offers a temporal discussion of budget development and implementation, noting the relative strength of presidents and Congress at each stage. This chapter pays particular attention to how the budgetary process has been shaped by deficit politics over the last twenty years. He concludes with a discussion of budgetary politics in an era of deficits. Panetta argues that the battle over budgets has become more contentious in this era and highlights a number of factors that contribute to this bitterness. He also argues that the budget process is only effective if those involved are willing to take the risks necessary to make it work. Presidents and the Congress have sought many agreements and reforms to strengthen their ability to discipline spending and establish priorities, but in the end, the process cannot work unless leaders are willing to lead. Panetta concludes by stating the budget process is the essence of our democracy.

In chapter 10, "Ending a Transatlantic Trade War: The Art of Coalition Building on Capitol Hill," Mark J. Oleszek and Walter J. Oleszek focus on the diverse strategies used to build support for the Foreign Sales Corporation/ Extraterritorial Income Act (FSC/ETI) in the 107th and 108th Congresses. They analyze the dynamics of the legislative process in the House, Senate, and conference committee stages. Through this case study of the passage of FSC/ETI, the Oleszeks show the importance of the artful use of political and procedural choices to achieve success. They examine the "three-sided legislative game" of the House, the Senate, and the president and reveal the complexities and uncertainties of lawmaking. By describing and evaluating the politics of passage of one measure, they show the importance of legislative skill, constituency and electoral interests, pragmatism, lobbyists, deadlines, and the president.

In chapter 11, "The Making of U.S. Foreign Policy: The Roles of the President and Congress over Four Decades," the Honorable Lee H. Hamilton evaluates the role of the president and Congress in foreign policy decisions. As a former member of Congress (from 1965 to 1998), former chair of the House Select Committee on Intelligence and chair of the Foreign Affairs Committee, and his recent work as vice chairman of the 9/11 Commission, Hamilton uses his extensive experience in foreign and defense policy making on the Hill to show how the view that the president dominates all foreign policy making must be revised. He argues that presidents are still the chief actor when it comes to foreign policy making but that their dominance is no longer uncontested. Vietnam, Watergate, and the end of the Cold War fundamentally changed the relationship between Congress and the president in foreign policy. Vietnam and Watergate made a mass public less trustful of presidents and, especially, less trustful of presidents on matters of foreign policy. The end of the Cold War made international threats and objectives less clear-cut, and this undermined the president's dominance of foreign policy. As the issues and international actors changed, members of Congress, interest groups, ethnic constituencies within the United States, and others all aimed to shape the American foreign policy objectives. Presidents are also forced to deal with more executive agencies that take an interest in foreign policy and an "information revolution" that enabled ordinary citizens and politicians to have increased access to and understanding of foreign policy. Hamilton also describes how the diversity and individualism of members of Congress has led the institution to be less bashful when it comes to foreign policy making. Hamilton concludes his chapter with a critique of how Congress has comported itself in foreign policy and offers a list of suggestions for how the president and Congress should behave when it comes to foreign policy making. He advocates a relationship between the branches and with the key interests outside government based on consultation as the best way to create sound foreign policy. Hamilton agues that from the Cold War to the current threat of Islamic extremists, the strongest foreign policies of our nation have been the product of a strong collaborative relationship between presidents and Congress in dialogue with the American people.

In the wake of the horrific attacks upon the United States on September 11, 2001, members of Congress were asked to stand side by side with the commander in chief in his defense of our great nation. In the days that followed the attacks of September 11, 2001, our nation learned much more about the mission carried out by al Qaeda terrorists who sought to destroy our society's collective way of life and the individual lives of thousands of innocent civilians in the process. What we did not know during the months that followed was that our government would respond quickly to combat the terrorists while also establishing an agenda to further develop the "war on terror" in countries that had little or no connection with the horrific attacks on our homeland. As a complement to Hamilton's chapter on the role of Congress and the president in foreign policy making, Louis Fisher, in chapter 12, "Justifying War against Iraq," evaluates the intelligence and justifications (e.g., the Iraq link to al Qaeda, nuclear weapons program, chemical and biological weapons, unmanned aerial vehicles, and other supposed threats) used by President Bush and his administration for military operations in Iraq starting on March 19, 2003. Fisher finds fault with the Bush administration for making claims of dire threats from Iraq with little evidence. He also analyzes the compliance that members of Congress provided the president in response to his request for trust and support in prosecuting terror in the wake of 9/11 and the questionable intelligence claims that the administration made to justify invading Iraq. Fisher is critical of the Congress and its committees for being unable to see through the "thinness of claims made by executive officials" and for not demanding more persuasive evidence. He calls for the restoration of better democratic checks on the executive from Congress, especially now that the risk of acting on erroneous intelligence is especially grave because the United States has made explicit the legitimacy of preemptive war. Fisher makes a strong case for the need for Congress to discharge its institutional duties of lawmaking, oversight, and deliberation while reasserting needed checks and balances on the executive.

NOTES

1. James A. Thurber, "Thunder from the Right: Observations about the Elections," *Public Manager* (Winter 1994–1995): 13–16.

2. On September 27, 1994, Republican congressional candidates signed the Contract with America, pledging that if elected they would support changes in congressional procedures and bring votes in the House on a series of proposals such as a balanced budget amendment, a line-item veto, and term limits for members of Congress. For more on the Contract with America, see Ed Gillespie and Bob Schellhas, eds., *Contract with America* (New York: Times Books, 1994).

3. For more on the 1992 elections, see Michael Nelson, ed., *The Elections of 1992* (Washington, DC: CQ Press, 1993).

4. Beth Donovan, "Maverick Chairman Forgiven as Clinton Reworks Bill," *Congressional Quarterly Weekly Report*, June 12, 1993, 1251–52.

5. Erwin C. Hargrove, "The Presidency: George Bush and the Cycle of Politics and Policy," in *The Elections of 1988*, ed. Michael Nelson (Washington, DC: CQ Press, 1989), 175.

6. Quoted in James A. Barnes, "Political Focus," *National Journal*, February 11, 1989, 377.

7. For a description of presidential-congressional policy battles, see Lance T. LeLoup and Steven A. Shull, *Congress and the President: The Policy Connection* (Belmont, CA: Wadsworth, 1993).

8. See Joseph J. Schatz, "With a Deft and Light Touch, Bush Finds Ways to Win," *CQ Weekly*, December 11, 2004, 2900–2905.

9. Schatz, "Bush Finds Ways to Win," 2901.

10. Arthur M. Schlesinger Jr. and Alfred De Grazia, *Congress and the Presidency: Their Role in Modern Times* (Washington, DC: American Enterprise Institute, 1976), 1.

11. See James A. Thurber, "Congress and the Constitution: Two Hundred Years of Stability and Change," in *Reflections on the Constitution*, ed. Richard Maidment (Manchester, UK: University of Manchester Press, 1989), 51–75.

12. For this constitutional basis of conflict, see Richard E. Neustadt, *Presidential Power and the Modern Presidents: The Politics of Leadership from Roosevelt to Reagan* (New York: Free Press, 1990); James L. Sundquist, *The Decline and Resurgence of Congress* (Washington, DC: Brookings Institution, 1981); Steven A. Shull, *Domestic Policy Formation: Presidential-Congressional Partnership?* (Westport, CT: Greenwood Press, 1983); Michael L. Mezey, *Congress, the President, and Public Policy* (Boulder, CO: Westview, 1985); Louis Fisher, *Constitutional Conflicts between Congress and the President*, 4th ed. rev. (Lawrence: University of Kansas, 1996); Louis Fisher, *The Politics of Shared Power: Congress and the Executive* (Washington, DC: CQ Press, 1993); Charles O. Jones, *The Presidency in a Separated System* (Washington, DC: Brookings Institution, 1994); Charles O. Jones, *Separate but Equal Branches: Congress and the Presidency* (New York: Chatham House, 1999); Charles O. Jones, *Clinton and Congress: Risk, Restoration, and Reelection* (Norman: University of Oklahoma Press, 1999).

13. A pocket veto is the act of the president in withholding his approval of a bill after Congress has adjourned. See Harold W. Stanley and Richard G. Niemi, *Vital Statistics on American Politics*, 5th ed. (Washington, DC: CQ Press, 1995), 258. For vetoes and overrides from the 80th to the 103rd Congresses (1947–1994), see Norman J. Ornstein, Thomas E. Mann, and Michael J. Malbin, *Vital Statistics on Congress, 1995–1996* (Washington, DC: Congressional Quarterly, 1996), 167.

14. Todd S. Purdum, "President Warns Congress to Drop Some Budget Cuts," *New York Times*, October 29, 1995, 30.

15. See Jones, *Presidency in a Separated System*.

16. See George C. Edwards III, *Presidential Influence in Congress* (San Francisco: Freeman, 1980); and Cecil V. Crabb Jr., and Pat M. Holt, *Invitation to Struggle: Congress, the President, and Foreign Policy*, 4th ed. (Washington, DC: CQ Press, 1992).

17. James Madison, *Federalist* no. 46, in *The Federalist Papers*, ed. Clinton Rossiter (New York: New American Library, 1961), 296.

18. See Stephen Wayne, *The Legislative Presidency* (New York: Harper & Row, 1978).

19. David R. Mayhew, *Congress: The Electoral Connection* (New Haven: Yale University Press, 1974).

20. Thomas E. Mann, "Breaking the Political Impasse," in *Setting National Priorities: Policy for the Nineties*, ed. Henry J. Aaron (Washington, DC: Brookings Institution, 1990), 302.

21. On divided party control of government, see David R. Mayhew, *Divided We Govern: Party Control, Lawmaking, and Investigations, 1946–1990* (New Haven: Yale University Press, 1991); James A. Thurber, ed., *Divided Democracy: Cooperation and Conflict between the President and Congress* (Washington, DC: CQ Press, 1991); and Gary C. Jacobson, *The Electoral Origins of Divided Government* (Boulder, CO.: Westview, 1990).

22. Ornstein, Mann, and Malbin, *Vital Statistics*, 49.

23. Nelson Polsby quoted in *Congress and the Nation*, vol. 7, 1985–1988 (Washington, DC: Congressional Quarterly, 1990), 21–22.

24. Mayhew, *Divided We Govern*, 198.

25. For more on Speaker Cannon, see Ronald M. Peters, *The American Speakership: The Office in Historical Perspective* (Baltimore: Johns Hopkins University Press, 1990).

26. See Stephen J. Wayne, "Great Expectations: What People Want from Presidents," in *Rethinking the Presidency*, ed. Thomas E. Cronin (Boston: Little, Brown, 1982), 185–99; and Glen R. Parker, "Some Themes in Congressional Opportunity," *American Journal of Political Science* 21 (February 1977): 93–119.

27. See Committee on the Constitutional System, *A Bicentennial Analysis of the American Political Structure* (Washington, DC: Committee on the Constitutional System, 1987).

28. James A. Thurber, "The 104th Congress Is Fast and Efficient, but at What Cost?" *Roll Call*, March 4, 1995, 16; and James A. Thurber, "Republican Centralization of the Congressional Budget Process, *Extensions of Remarks*, December 1995.

29. James A. Thurber, "Twenty-Five Years of Deficit and Conflict: Partisan Roles in Congressional Budget Reform," in *New Majority or Old Minority: The Impact of Republicans in Congress*, ed. Nicole C. Rae and Colton Campbell (Lanham, MD.: Rowman & Littlefield, 1999).

30. Richard E. Cohen, Kirk Victor, and David Bauman, "The State of Congress," *National Journal*, January 10, 2004, 83–105.

31. See Joel H. Sibley, "The Rise and Fall of American Political Parties," in *The Parties Respond: Changes in American Parties and Campaigns*, ed. L. Sandy Maisel (Boulder, CO: Westview, 1994), 3–18.

32. James A. Thurber, "Political Power and Policy Subsystems in American Politics," in *Agenda for Excellence: Administering the State*, ed. B. Guy Peters and Bert A. Rockman (Chatham, NJ.: Chatham House, 1996), 76–104.

33. See Jonathan Rauch, *Demosclerosis* (New York: Times Books, 1994).

34. See James G. March and Herbert A. Simon, *Organizations* (New York: John Wiley & Sons, 1958).

35. See Jones, *Presidency in a Separated System*.

2

Partisan Polarization, Politics, and the Presidency: Structural Sources of Conflict

James P. Pfiffner

In his campaign for the presidency in the 2000 election, George W. Bush promised that he would work closely with Congress and the Democrats and tone down the corrosive partisan rhetoric that had come to characterize Washington in the last years of the twentieth century. After a very close election in which Bush narrowly won the presidency while trailing the Democratic candidate by half a million votes, many expected him to take a conciliatory approach to Democrats in Congress and seek out moderates of both parties to forge an agenda in the middle of the political spectrum.

But that is not what happened. Arguing that political capital had to be spent rather than conserved, Bush put forward a conservative policy agenda and won some impressive victories.[1] Just when his momentum began to lag in late summer of 2001, terrorists struck New York and Washington. The atrocities of 9/11 transformed the political landscape and presented Bush with a country unified under his leadership and broad international support for the United States. Yet three years later as he ran for reelection, the nation was deeply divided over his presidency and the war in Iraq. Although much of the political division between the parties in Congress and among partisans in the electorate could be attributed to disagreement over President Bush's policies, the roots of the divisive partisan politics of the Bush presidency lay in political developments in the preceding four decades. This chapter will examine the roots of polarization in American politics that so poisoned relations between Democrats and Republicans in Congress and affected cooperation between the president and Congress in the beginning years of the twenty-first century.

The first section of this essay will examine the roots of the highly volatile politics of the Clinton and Bush years in the structural underpinnings of political change in the 1960s and 1970s. It will address first the breakup of the "solid South" and its effects on the distribution of power in Congress. It will then examine the consequences of these structural underpinnings in the increasingly polarized behavior in Congress over the past several decades. Voting in Congress has become more partisan; the use of delaying tactics such as the filibuster has become more common; and the level of civility has declined. Finally, it will look at some of the policy and partisan battles between President Clinton and Congress and the correspondingly bitter relations between the parties that characterized President Bush's first term in office. The paper will conclude that, despite the reelection of President Bush and the continued Republican control of Congress, relations between the branches are likely to continue to be rocky in the second term of President George W. Bush.

THE CAUSES OF CONGRESSIONAL POLARIZATION

In trying to explain the vast changes that occurred in Congress in the latter half of the century—from a Democratic-dominated institution with significant overlap between the parties to an ideological polarized battleground with virtually no middle ground—we can turn to Nelson Polsby, who argues that it all started with air-conditioning. Though this claim might seem whimsical, his line of reasoning and evidence present a plausible and often compelling explanation of change in Congress.[2] It goes like this.

The development of affordable residential air-conditioning in the South from the 1950s to the 1980s led to the migration of whites from the North to southern cities and suburbs. Many of these immigrants brought with them Republican voting habits. From the 1960s to the 1980s, approximately 40 to 50 percent of southern Republicans were born outside of the South.[3]

Along with general urbanization in the South and black migration to the North, the partisan complexion of the South began to change. The Republican Party was becoming a viable political party and beginning to attract more voters.[4] Partisan realignment in the South was further encouraged by the Civil Rights Act of 1964 and the Voting Rights Act of 1965, both of which increased the number of black voters, who voted overwhelmingly Democratic.[5]

Conservative whites began to identify with the Republican Party and to send more Republican representatives to Congress. The creation of majority-minority districts concentrated more liberal blacks in districts, while more conservative whites ended up in districts that voted Republican. The result of this realignment was that the Democratic Party in Congress lost its "Dixiecrat" members (conservative southern Democrats) and became more homogeneously liberal.[6] The conservative coalition, which had been thwarting Democratic presidents since FDR, began to decline in importance; the conservative southerners were now in the Republican Party.

The increasing liberal consensus among the Democrats in Congress led the Democratic caucus in the House to become more cohesive and, through control of committee membership, assert its liberal policy views more effectively (e.g., on civil rights, old-age assistance, health care, housing, and other federal programs). According to David E. Price, Democratic representative from North Carolina,

> Revitalizing the House Democratic Caucus proved necessary in order to rewrite the rules, depose recalcitrant chairmen, and otherwise effect the desired transfer of power. The leadership, moreover, was the only available counterweight to conservative bastions like the House Rules and Ways and Means Committees. Therefore, two key early reforms removed the committee-assignment function from Ways and Means Democrats and placed it in a leadership-dominated Steering and Policy Committee and gave the Speaker the power to nominate the chair and the Democratic members of the Rules Committee.[7]

The number of Democrats in the House began to increase in 1958, and particularly in the Democratic landslides in 1964 and 1974. In order for the Democratic caucus to gain more effective policy control, more power was delegated to its leadership in the 1970s and 1980s.[8] As the Democrats in the House became more ideologically similar, their leadership became more assertive in the use of parliamentary tactics that evoked the ire of Republicans by denying them procedural rights in ways that were perceived as unfair.[9] Newt Gingrich led the outraged Republicans in the House to develop Republican candidates, particularly in the South, and orchestrate the development of Republican candidates, which culminated in the 1994 election landslide that put the Republicans in charge of Congress for the first time in forty years.[10]

Thus it was that the introduction of air-conditioning in the South led to Republican domination of southern congressional delegations, which led to a more homogeneous, liberal Democratic Party in Congress, which led to more polarized parties and finally to the Republican takeover of Congress.[11] This polarization was exacerbated and perpetuated by bipartisan gerrymandering that reinforced the polarizing trend.

Redistricting, among other factors, has led to an increasing proportion of safe seats, with fewer congressional districts "in play," that is, that might be won by either party. According to Gary Jacobson's analysis, the number of safe seats increased significantly between 1992 and 2002: Democrats' safe seats increased from 142 to 158, and Republicans' safe seats increased from 139 to 198.[12] Thus the total number of safe seats was 356 of 435, but the number of House races that were actually competitive were many fewer than that.[13] In the 2004 elections, 83 percent of House races were won by margins of 20 percent or more, and 95 percent of districts were won by more than 10 percent. Only seven incumbents were defeated, and four of those were in recently redistricted Texas. Overall, Republicans gained five seats in Texas alone. Excluding Texas, the Democrats picked up four seats and the Republicans two.[14]

Redistricting, from the 1970s through 2004 in the South and elsewhere, led to safer districts, which, along with the advantages of incumbency, led to the election of more liberal Democrats and more conservative Republicans. If congressional districts are competitive, with elections won and lost by small margins, candidates must move to the middle of the ideological spectrum to try to capture a majority of votes. But safe seats put moderate candidates of both parties at a disadvantage. Turnout for primary elections is low, and most of those who actually vote are committed partisans, that is, true believers who hold more extreme views than most voters in their parties. Thus in order to get nominated and then to remain in office, members must please their respective wings or be outflanked by more extreme candidates. Congressman Jim Leach (R-Iowa) explains the problem this way:

> A little less than four hundred seats are totally safe, which means that there is competition between Democrats and Republicans only in about ten or fifteen per cent of the seats. So the important question is who controls the safe seats. Currently, about a third of the over-all population is Democrat, a third is Republican, and a third is no party [independent]. If you ask yourself some mathematical questions, what is a half of a third?—one-sixth. That's who decides the nominee in each district. But only a fourth participates in primaries. What's a fourth of a sixth? A twenty-fourth. So it's one twenty-fourth of the population that controls the seat in each party.[15]

This gradual polarization of Congress over several decades was caused mostly by members being replaced by less moderate candidates in their seats, but some of the changes were individual members changing their own ideological perspectives and becoming less moderate in order to head off a challenge in the primaries.[16] As Representative Leach put it, "It's much more likely that an incumbent will lose a primary than he will a general election. So redistricting has made Congress a more partisan, more polarized place."[17]

Once candidates are in office, the advantages of incumbency help keep the more extreme members in office for longer periods of time. But even more important than advantages for individual incumbents (e.g., name recognition, media coverage, travel to the district, raising money, etc.) is the advantage gained through safe partisan majorities of congressional districts ensured through skillful drawing of district boundaries (gerrymandering).[18] Thus the advantages of incumbents who sought reelection, always considerable, have become even more effective. From 1984 to 1990 House members seeking reelection were successful 97 percent of the time, and in 2002, 98 percent were successful. Senators were a bit more vulnerable, but still quite successful, winning 86 percent of bids for reelection from 1982 to 2003 and 95 percent in 1996.[19] In 2004, aside from the redistricted Texas, 99 percent of House incumbents won reelection, with only three incumbents being defeated.[20]

Some scholars have argued that the election of more extreme partisans to Congress was caused by voters who had first become more polarized.[21] But Morris Fiorina in his book *Culture War?* argues that although political elites in the United States (party activists, members of Congress, etc.) are ideologically polarized, the vast majority of citizens in the country are not.[22] Recent presidential elections have been decided by very small margins, and the total vote for Congress has been evenly divided, but this does not mean that voters are *deeply* divided, only that they are *evenly* divided.

After the 2000 election the media featured colored maps of the country that indicated states carried by George W. Bush as red and those carried by Al Gore as blue. The broad swaths of red and blue seemed to show a country deeply divided, but many of the states were won by very small margins. A comparison of the red states with blue states shows very little ideological difference among voters, 30 percent of whom place themselves in the middle of a seven-point political spectrum, and a third of the voters considered themselves independents or not affiliated with the Democrats or Republicans.[23] Fiorina concludes that "it is not voters who have polarized, but the candidates they are asked to choose between."[24]

Even on the hot-button issue of abortion, public attitudes are not more polarized than they were thirty years ago when the Supreme Court decision on *Roe v. Wade* made abortion legal in the United States. The gap between Republicans and Democrats is significant, but relatively small.[25] And although there is a gender gap on many political and policy issues, there is very little difference between men's and women's attitudes about abortion. Fiorina concludes that with respect to abortion there is "a gender gap among high level political activists that is not apparent among ordinary Americans, and minimal partisan disagreement about the issue at the mass level contrasted with vitriolic conflict at the elite level."[26] Similarly, on the volatile issue of homosexuality, attitudes in the United States have been more accepting in recent years, and the differences among partisans are different but not drastically so. Fiorina concludes that, overall, Americans "look moderate, centrist, nuanced, ambivalent—choose your term—rather than extreme, polarized, unconditional, dogmatic."[27]

The overall argument here is that political parties and political elites more broadly are much more polarized in the early years of the twenty-first century than several decades ago. But that polarization was not caused by a polarized electorate. Rather, voters are generally centrist, as they have been at least since the middle of the twentieth century, but they must choose between candidates who are more extreme than they are. According to Fiorina, "Even if they still are centrists, voters can choose only among the candidates who appear on the ballot and vote only on the basis of the issues that are debated. Elites nominate candidates and set the agenda, and voters respond."[28] There is "little reason to believe that elites are following voters. Rather, they are imposing their own agendas on the electorate."[29] To oversimplify, instead of voters choosing their candidates, candidates choose their voters (through gerrymandered redistricting).

In addition to the genuine polarization of elites (partisans and officeholders), Fiorina attributes the broad perception of polarization of the electorate in the country to an explosion of advocacy among those who are most committed to their political causes combined with more media attention to the conflict generated by extremists on both sides of volatile issues. The question of polarization in the 2004 election will be addressed in the conclusion.

We have examined the partisan changes that began in the South and the resulting polarization in Congress; the following section will analyze the consequences of that partisan polarization in the behavior of individuals and political parties in Congress.

THE CONSEQUENCES OF STRUCTURAL CHANGE: PARTISAN POLARIZATION IN CONGRESS

The consequences of partisan realignment in the South and more committed partisans in Congress have been the collapse of the moderates in Congress, which has in turn led to policy stalemate and the decline of civility.

The next section will present evidence that Congress is indeed much more polarized than it was in the middle years of the twentieth century (though comparable to polarization in the late nineteenth century). This polarization will then be linked to increasing problems of policy gridlock or stalemate. The second section will note some dimensions of the decline in civility, which has made Congress a less congenial place to work and has led some eminent moderate legislators to retire rather than continue in office.

The Waning Center

In the middle of the twentieth century the two political parties in Congress were not ideologically monolithic. That is, each party had a significant number of members who were ideologically sympathetic to the other party. The Democratic Party contained a strong conservative wing of members, the southern "Boll Weevils," who often voted with the conservative Republicans. The Republican Party contained a noticeable number of moderates, mostly from the Northeast, the "Rockefeller Republicans," who would often vote with the Democrats. These cross-pressured members of Congress made up between one-fifth and one-third of each house of Congress from 1950 to the mid-1980s.[30]

In the last fifteen years of the twentieth century the cross-pressured members of each party all but disappeared. Bond and Fleisher have calculated the number of liberal Republicans and conservative Democrats in Congress from the 1950s through the 1990s and have documented their decline. The number of conservative Democrats in the House has decreased from a high of 91 in 1965–1966 to a low of 11 in 1995–1996. In the Senate the high of 22 in the early 1960s was reduced to zero in 1995–1996. Liberal Republicans similarly fell from a high of 35 in the early 1970s to a low of 1 in 1993–1994 in the House, and a high of 14 in 1973–1974 to a low of 2 in 1995–1996 in the Senate.[31] This disappearance of the middle is a convincing demonstration of ideological polarization in Congress.

Sarah Binder has also found that the area of ideological overlap between the two parties in Congress has drastically decreased from a relatively high level of overlap in 1970 to "virtually no ideological common ground shared by the two parties."[32] The *National Journal* developed its own ideological scale of liberal and conservative voting and has calculated individual scores for members of Congress. Since 1981, most House Democrats would be on the liberal end of the spectrum and most Republicans on the right. There was always a number of members of each party whose voting record put them in the middle, overlapping ideological space. In 1999, however, only two Republicans and two Democrats shared the middle ground.

Up to the mid-1990s the Senate had a middle group of ten to seventeen centrists from both parties who often voted with the opposite party. But in

1999, for the first time since the *National Journal* began calculating the scores in 1981, all of the Republicans had a score to the right of the most conservative Democrat, and all of the Democrats had a score to the left of the most liberal Republican.[33] The polarization in the Senate was exacerbated in 1996 by the retirement of fourteen Senate moderates who contributed significantly to the civility of the Senate and who could reach across party lines in policy deliberations, among them Republicans Alan Simpson (WY) and Hank Brown (CO) and Democrats Sam Nunn (GA) and Bill Bradley (NJ).[34]

What the above data mean in a practical sense is that each of the political parties in Congress is more ideologically homogeneous and that there is greater ideological distance between the two parties. Thus there is less need to compromise in a moderate direction when reaching a consensus within each party. And it is correspondingly more difficult to bridge the ideological gap between the contrasting perspectives of the two parties. Finding middle ground where compromise is possible becomes much more difficult. It is more likely that votes will be set up to highlight partisan differences and used for rhetorical and electoral purposes rather than to arrive at compromise policies.[35]

Another measure of partisan conflict that reflects the polarization in Congress is the "party vote," in which a majority of one party opposes a majority of the other party in a roll-call vote. This measure of polarization has been increasing in recent years, especially in the House. From 1955 to 1965 the percentage of votes in the House that were party votes averaged 49 percent; from 1967 to 1982 the percentage was 36 percent. But after 1982 it began to climb, and in the 1990s, it reached 64 percent for the 103rd Congress.[36] Party voting reached a record 73.2 percent in 1995.[37] Senate scores on party voting roughly paralleled those in the House, though at slightly lower levels, reaching a Senate record of 68.8 percent in 1995.[38] Party-unity scores, in which members of the two parties vote with their majorities on party-line votes, also increased to unusually high levels.[39]

Partisan differences in the Senate are often registered by the threat of members of the minority party to filibuster. The filibuster is a time-honored convention (formalized in Rule XXII) in which any member (or members) can hold the floor as long as he or she wants in order to delay the consideration of legislation. Before the 1970s the filibuster was used occasionally when senators felt strongly about an issue and were willing to block Senate business in order to achieve their goals. In the 1950s filibusters were occasionally used to keep the majority from enacting civil rights legislation. In the early decades of the twentieth century use of the filibuster would occasionally peak at ten per Congress, but in the 1980s and 1990s the use of the filibuster exploded to twenty-five or thirty per Congress.[40] The increased use of the filibuster and other dilatory tactics, such as "holds" on nominations, has amounted to a "parliamentary arms race" in which each side is willing to use the extreme tactic because the other side has used it against them.[41]

In addition to actual filibusters, the mere threat of a filibuster can slow the legislative process. As Barbara Sinclair has calculated, threats to filibuster major legislation have increased significantly in the past three decades. Presidential threats to veto bills also have increased sharply in the 1990s, from 15 to 25 percent in the 1970s to 60 to 69 percent in the late 1990s.[42] Binder found that in the 103rd and 104th Congresses either an actual filibuster or the threat of one affected almost 20 percent of all items on the congressional agenda and 40 percent of the most important issues.[43]

One consequence of the polarization documented above is that Congress is less able to legislate in order to deal with pressing policy issues. The farther apart the two parties are ideologically (polarization), the less likely they are to be able to find common ground to pass laws. And often, the parties would rather have an issue to debate than compromise and accept half a loaf.[44]

According to her systematic comparisons of the ratio of actual laws enacted to important issues considered by the political system, two dimensions of polarization outweighed even the effect of divided government: the ideological gap between the parties and the ideological distance between the two houses of Congress. Thus if one is concerned with the problem of "gridlock" (which she defines as "the share of salient issues on the nation's agenda left in limbo at the close of each Congress"), ideological polarization in Congress is even more important than divided government (when the president's party does not control both houses of Congress).[45]

From this rather abstract discussion of the consequences of polarization, we now turn to the more human consequences: the decline of civility in Congress.

The Decline of Civility

The traditional norms of courtesy, reciprocity, and comity that marked the 1950s and 1960s in Congress began to break down in the 1970s.[46] Reflecting broader divisions in U.S. politics over the Vietnam War and Watergate, life in Congress became more contentious. Legislative language had traditionally been marked by overly elaborate politeness in order to manage partisan and sometimes personal conflict. But instances of harsh language and incivility became more common and more partisan in the 1970s and 1980s. In the House the Republicans felt increasingly suppressed by the majority Democrats through the rules of debate and legislative scheduling and, under the leadership of Newt Gingrich, began to use obstructionist tactics to clog up the legislative process.[47] The predictable Democratic response was to tighten up the rules even more to deal with disruptive tactics. After Republicans took control of Congress in 1994, relations between the parties continued to deteriorate.

Even the usually more decorous Senate suffered from declining civility. In the early 1980s Sen. Joseph Biden remarked, "There's much less civility than when I came there ten years ago. There aren't as many nice people as there were before. . . . Ten years ago you didn't have people calling each other sons of bitches and vowing to get at each other."[48]

Scholars David Brady and Morris Fiorina summarize the political context:

> In a context in which members themselves have stronger and more distinct policy preferences, where they scarcely know each other personally because every spare moment is spent fund-raising or cultivating constituents, where interest groups monitor every word a member speaks and levy harsh attacks upon the slightest deviation from group orthodoxy, where the media provide coverage in direct proportion to the negativity and conflict contained in one's messages, where money is desperately needed and is best raised by scaring the bejesus out of people, is it any wonder that comity and courtesy are among the first casualties?[49]

Near the end of the 106th Congress, even the leadership in both houses was not able to restrain the harsh feelings that had been building up. Speaker of the House J. Dennis Hastert, who had taken over the speakership at the beginning of the 106th Congress, had a reputation (in contrast to his predecessor, Newt Gingrich) as a mild-mannered and workmanlike legislator who was more concerned with making deals and legislating than making symbolic points through hostile rhetoric. Yet one year into his speakership, the level of hostility between Hastert and Minority Leader Richard Gephardt was quite high.

The two leaders seldom talked with each other, even on necessary procedural issues, and they held each other in contempt. According to Gephardt, "Frankly, the relationship is really no different than it was with Newt Gingrich. . . . Their definition of bipartisanship is, 'My way or the highway.'"[50] According to Hastert, Gephardt's "sole purpose is to try to make this House fail."[51] Hastert went so far as to campaign in Gephardt's district for his Republican challenger in the 2000 election campaign, a very unusual breach of the usual House leadership decorum.[52]

The Senate was not spared the leadership animosities that plagued the House in 2000. Senate Majority Leader Trent Lott and Minority Leader Tom Daschle became particularly bitter in the second session of the 106th Congress as the Senate struggled with passing legislation during an election year. In early June 2000 Majority Leader Lott complained, "The last couple of weeks before we went out have been the most obstructionist I've ever seen them."[53] According to Daschle, "No Majority Leader in history has attempted to constrain the Senate debate as aggressively as Senator Lott has chosen to do," and it amounted to "a Senate version of dictatorship that I think is unacceptable."[54] Lott replied, "I have to go on the record saying I do believe I have been maligned unfairly. . . . [T]o come in here and think we have to have a right to offer non-germane amendments to every appropriations bill that comes through, and then criticize us for not getting our work done—Oh, boy, that is really smart, really smart."[55]

From the perspective of the Democrats, the Republican majority was refusing to confirm the nominees of President Clinton and was preventing them from offering amendments to legislation so they could have their priorities voted upon. From the perspective of the Republicans, the Democrats were trying to obstruct the flow of legislation with their amendments so that they could blame the Republicans for being a "do-nothing Congress" in the election campaign. The unusual personal bitterness and intemperate language reflected election-year politics in which much was at stake, but it also was a product of the polarization of the Congress over the past several decades.

The decline in civility that marked the end of the 1990s continued into the early twenty-first century, as the polarized politics of the era continued to erode the relatively more decorous times of the mid–twentieth century. With the narrow Republican control of the Senate at stake, Majority Leader Bill Frist of Tennessee decided to go to South Dakota to campaign against Minority Leader Tom Daschle. Such personal campaigning by the Senate majority leader in the minority leader's home state was unprecedented in the twentieth century and highlighted the animosity that marked the polarization in Congress.[56] Frist was successful when Daschle lost his bid for reelection in 2004.

On the floor of the Senate, the personal animosity resulting from the polarization was illustrated when Vice President Cheney publicly said to Democratic senator Patrick Leahy, "Fuck yourself." Although such insults are common among politicians (and nonpoliticians), they are most often expressed in private. This particular insult was particularly egregious because it was not a comment about a third party but stated directly to the person insulted; it was not private, but public; it was said on the floor of Congress; and it was said publicly by the president of the Senate, the vice president of the United States. In explaining his remark, the vice president did not address a substantive difference between the two men, but said that it correctly expressed his feelings: "I expressed myself forcefully, felt better after I had done it."[57]

Democrats in 2004 also complained that Republicans systematically

excluded them from important conference committee negotiations between
the two houses and that the procedural rules were used against them in ways
that exceeded the Democrats' partisan use of procedures in the later years of
their domination of Congress. Republican senator John McCain commented
on the partisanship of the procedural battles, "The Republicans had better
hope that the Democrats never regain the majority."[58] House Democrats also
broke an unwritten seven-year truce on ethics charges in the House when
they charged majority leader Tom DeLay with improprieties with regard to
the 2002 redistricting of Texas that gained the Republicans several seats and
his tactics in winning votes on a close Medicare vote in 2003.[59]

Former Tennessee senator and Republican National Committee chair William Brock attributed the incivility, with "less dialogue, less comity, and
more partisanship," to safe districts and the resulting polarized politics.

> Consistently now in general elections, well over 90 percent of congressional races
> are virtually uncontested. . . . If a candidate need talk only to those who are most
> fervent in support of the party, he or she doesn't have to listen to, or even speak to,
> people at the center, much less those of the other party. . . . We're increasingly
> moving to a political system that looks, and feels, like a political barbell: one where
> all the weight is at the ends of the spectrum, leaving those in the center with little
> voice or opportunity for impact.[60]

PRESIDENT AND CONGRESS IN AN
ERA OF POLARIZED POLITICS

The Clinton era was a contentious time for relations between the president
and Congress. At one level the conflict reflected a personal rivalry between
Bill Clinton and Newt Gingrich. Clinton, a self-described "New Democrat,"
pulled the Democratic Party in a more moderate direction and "captured"
some issues from the Republicans: for example, support for crime control,
fiscal prudence, and family values (at least in rhetoric). Gingrich, on the
other side, had led the Republicans from the wilderness of minority status to
the promised land of majority control of Congress and sought to dismantle
much of the liberal "Great Society" legislation that Democrats had passed
in the 1960s.

President Bush campaigned for the presidency in 2000 as a moderate,
"compassionate conservative." Once in office he pursued a conservative policy agenda and enjoyed widespread political support after the 9/11 terrorist
attacks. But his decision to invade and occupy Iraq led to a divided country
and a contentious campaign for the presidency in 2004. This section will
examine the polarized politics of the Clinton and Bush presidencies.

President Clinton and Congress: A Mixed Record

In the 103rd Congress (1993–1995) the Democrats still held a majority in Congress and had high hopes that they would achieve a positive policy record that would mark a resurgence of Democratic hegemony after twelve years of Republican control of the presidency.[61] But the dream was not to come true. Clinton's first major policy push was for deficit reduction, which he won with no Republican votes, but which was bitter medicine for congressional Democrats who would rather have pushed new programs. Then Clinton's big initiative for universal health care coverage was defeated by the Republicans in 1994. The huge and complex plan favored by the administration was framed by the Republicans as more "big government" and too costly. In 1994 the Republicans were able to use the Clinton record to "nationalize" the midterm congressional elections and take control of Congress for the first time in forty years.

The Gingrich-led Republican victory was so overwhelming that at the beginning of the 104th Congress they were able to push the Contract with America agenda through the House in the spring of 1995 and roll over the Democrats in doing so. The national agenda was so dominated by the Republican contract that on April 18, 1995, President Clinton had to argue that he was "relevant" to the policy process. "The President is relevant. . . . The Constitution gives me relevance; the power of our ideas gives me relevance; the record we have built up over the last two years and the things we're trying to do give me relevance."[62] But when many of the contract proposals foundered in the Senate, the Republicans decided to build into the appropriations process provisions that would go far beyond the contract in trying to severely reduce many of the government programs of which they disapproved. They wanted to abolish three cabinet departments and cut back severely programs in education, environmental protection, Medicare, and Medicaid, as well as eliminate smaller programs such as the National Endowments for the Arts and Humanities.

These priorities were packaged in omnibus legislation in the fall of 1995, and President Clinton vetoed the bills several times. When the Republicans did not change the provisions, much of the government was shut down for lack of appropriations. When it became clear that the public saw the Republican Congress rather than President Clinton as responsible for the shutdown, Robert Dole, who was running for president, convinced Congress to pass appropriations bills and negotiate the budget bills. Clinton was reelected in 1996, and the Republicans retained control of Congress by narrow margins.[63]

The 105th Congress (1998–1999) began with Clinton's plans to propose a number of "small bore" policy proposals that would be acceptable across the political spectrum, but in late January the Monica Lewinsky scandal hit. The rest of the spring was dominated by the efforts of Kenneth Starr to investigate the scandal, and the fall was dominated by the bitterly partisan battle to impeach the president. Many Democrats and moderate Republicans would have preferred to condemn the president's behavior rather than impeaching him and trying to remove him from office. The key to President Clinton's impeachment was the ability of the House Republican leadership to invoke party discipline to prevent a vote on censoring the president. The articles of impeachment passed on party-line votes, with only a few members from each party defecting on the two articles that were adopted.

The 106th Congress began with the Senate trial of the president and its decision not to remove him from office. The rest of the session was taken up with the aftermath of the impeachment trial and partisan battles over policy priorities. The second session began in an election year (2000) and was not marked by major policy victories or an impressive legislative record. Each party was more concerned with its efforts to prevail and win a slim majority in the fall elections. Even issues with broad bipartisan support were not able to be passed in the corrosive atmosphere. Representative Jim McDermott (D-WA) characterized the 106th: "Everything was crafted on their side to win the election. And everything we tried to do was [to] derail them from winning the election. . . . It was the most unproductive public policy year[s] I've spent in my life." Senator John Breaux (D-LA) put it this way, "We've entered into a pattern of blaming each other for failure. People were actually in some cases afraid to compromise because they would lose the issue. On both sides."[64]

As bitter as the battles between Clinton and Gingrich were, the argument of this essay is that the fundamental causes of the partisan battles that dominated the four Congresses of the Clinton era have been driven by the polarization of Congress rather than by the personalities of the two men. The structural underpinnings of polarization lie in the demise of the solid South and the division of Congress, especially in the House, into a more conservative Republican Party and a more liberal Democratic Party (recognizing that the whole political spectrum shifted in a conservative direction in the 1980s just as it shifted in a more liberal direction in the 1960s). This polarization, as documented earlier in the essay, has led to a more contentious atmosphere in Congress, with more party voting and use of obstructionist tactics in both the House and the Senate. It has also led to greater use of the veto by the president.

Partisan conflict and battles between the president and Congress, however, do not mean that no important legislation gets passed. Stalemate is a relative term, and the government keeps operating (even during a shutdown) during intensely partisan periods. Thus President Clinton and Congress were able to pass a number of important policy initiatives. In 1993 President Clinton fought for congressional approval of the North American Free Trade Act (NAFTA). But he was able to get it passed only by knitting together a coalition of more Republicans than Democrats, and he was opposed by Majority Leader David Bonnier in the House. Democrats in Congress were not pleased that Clinton backed the Bush-initiated NAFTA legislation, but free trade was a Clinton New Democrat issue.

Similarly, President Clinton decided to sign the Republican welfare reform bill in the summer of 1996, despite opposition of the Democrats in Congress (and some in his own administration). While Clinton thought the bill was too harsh, it did move in the direction he favored. But it was also an election year, and Clinton did not want to give Republicans the issue of arguing that he vetoed three welfare bills after promising to "end welfare as we know it."

In 1997 President Clinton and the Republican Congress were able to compromise in order to come to an agreement that would balance the budget within five years. This impressive agreement was achieved by the willingness of each side to set aside partisan warfare and negotiate an outcome in which each side could claim victory. The 1997 deal was followed by a fiscal year 1998 budget that was actually balanced—four years earlier than had been projected.[65] The surplus in fiscal year 2000 was more than $200 billion, and surpluses continued in 1999, 2000, and 2001. This historic turnaround was based on the groundwork laid by Presidents Bush in 1990 and Clinton in 1993 with their deficit-reducing agreements and spending constraints. But it was made possible by a booming economy and historically high stock market.[66]

In the spring and summer of 2000 President Clinton was able to work with Republicans in Congress to win approval of permanent normal trade relations with China. In the House more than twice as many Republicans as Democrats supported the measure, echoing the coalition that passed NAFTA in 1993. The above policy achievements were possible only through bipartisan cooperation and the willingness to share credit. But such cross-party victories have been unusual; the primary pattern has been one of partisan rancor and stalemate.

President Bush and Congress: Winning the Big Battles

President Bush's first term can be divided into three periods: (1) pre-9/11 conservative policy agenda, (2) the unified response to 9/11 and the war in Afghanistan, and (3) the divisive campaign for war in Iraq and its aftermath.

During the presidential campaign of 2000 candidate Bush set a moderate tone by asserting that he was a "compassionate conservative" and advocating educational proposals that often appealed to Democratic voters. He promised to "change the tone" in Washington by taking a bipartisan approach to governing, as he had in Texas. While arguing for more defense spending and a national missile defense, privatizing part of Social Security, and a large tax cut, the emphasis was not on the more conservative aspects of his policy agenda.

In his first weeks in office he followed up on his promise to change the tone in Washington by meeting with a large number of members of Congress, many of them Democrats. He even attended caucus meetings of the Democrats in the House and the Senate to show that he was willing to communicate with the opposition. In his initial policy agenda, however, he pursued a conservative agenda that appealed to his Republican base in the House of Representatives and the electorate.

In January 2001 Republicans controlled both houses of Congress and the presidency for the first time since the beginning of the Eisenhower administration, but their control of Congress was narrow, with a 221–212 margin (with two independents). President Bush's first and largest legislative initiative was to propose a large tax cut, as he had promised in the campaign. The administration's proposal was for a $1.6 trillion cut over ten years that included reducing the top brackets, eliminating the estate tax, reducing the marriage penalty, and increasing child credits. Democrats argued that most of the benefits would go to the relatively well-off and that the overall size of the reduction in revenues would threaten the projected surpluses; they favored a smaller cut that was targeted at lower income levels. The House passed Bush's plan, but the Senate held out for a smaller cut. After negotiations, the Senate went along with the House to vote for a $1.35 trillion cut, an important policy victory for the president.

In another of Bush's top priorities he established by executive action a White House Office of Faith-Based Initiatives to facilitate the use of federal funds for social purposes, to be administered by faith-based organizations. He proposed privatizing part of the Social Security system by setting aside a portion of contributions to the system for private investment in personal retirement accounts. Although much of his education agenda was endorsed by Democrats, Bush favored the creation of vouchers allowing public funds to be used by parents to send their children to private schools. A version of his education plan, without vouchers, was passed by Congress in the late fall of 2001.

In the late spring of 2001 the president had won an important victory in his large tax cut and was turning to his other priorities when his political power was dealt a blow. Senator James Jeffords, a third-term Republican from

Vermont, had been a moderate, but loyal Republican. But he had felt increasingly out of place in the conservative Republican Party of the 1990s.

So in the middle of the first session of the 107th Congress, party control of the Senate shifted from the Republicans to the Democrats. With the fifty-fifty split after the election, the Republicans could count on a tie-breaking vote from the vice president. But with the Democrats controlling fifty-one votes to the Republicans' forty-nine, control of the Senate agenda, along with chairmanships of all the committees, went to the Democrats, who would not be as sympathetic to President Bush's priorities.

Thus in the summer of 2001 the Bush administration began to recalibrate its policy priorities to adjust to Democratic control in the Senate and looked forward to some difficult policy battles in the fall. Then came the terrorist attacks that transformed the Bush presidency and the nation's priorities.

The terrorist attacks on the World Trade Towers and the Pentagon created a surge of public unity that gave President Bush unprecedented public support and a compliant Congress willing to support the administration's war on terrorism. The first and most important political effect of the terrorist bombings of September 11 was a huge jump in public approval of President Bush. In the September 7–10 Gallup poll public approval of the president stood at 51 percent; the next poll, on September 14–15 registered 86 percent approval—a 35 percent jump virtually overnight.

Congress quickly passed a bill providing $40 billion in emergency appropriations for military action, beefing up domestic security, and rebuilding New York City. Congress also passed antiterrorism measures proposed by Attorney General John Ashcroft with broad, bipartisan support. The legislation, which was passed by Congress in mid-October and signed by the president later in the month, was entitled the "Uniting and Strengthening America by Providing Appropriate Tools Required to Intercept and Obstruct Terrorism Act of 2001," or more briefly the "USA Patriot Act." Congress also passed provisions expanding government powers on wiretapping, computer surveillance, and money laundering. Attorney General Ashcroft also issued an order allowing officials to listen in on attorney-client communications for suspects who might be terrorists.

The administration also asked for and got sweeping authority to pursue an international war on terrorism. On September 14 Congress passed a joint resolution giving President Bush broad discretion in his direction of the military response to the terrorist attacks. The grant of power was sweeping in that it allowed the president to decide as "he determines" which "nations, organizations, or persons" United States forces may attack.

The president used his authority to attack the Taliban regime in Afghanistan, which had harbored the al Qaeda terrorists. U.S. ground forces, cooperating with the Northern Alliance, began attacking Taliban forces, and the tide turned in favor of the United States in mid-November, with Kabul falling to the Northern Alliance on November 13. In early December allied forces took control of Kandahar, and a coalition of Afghan forces took official control of the country by the end of the year.

The partisan unity that marked the administration's immediate reaction to the 9/11 attacks and the war in Afghanistan began to erode as the administration's plans for war in Iraq came to be debated in 2002. As the war in Afghanistan went on and Osama bin Laden was being pursued, secret planning was underway for war with Iraq. In late 2001 President Bush asked Secretary of Defense Rumsfeld to begin detailed planning for an attack on Iraq, and Gen. Tommy Franks presented his first formal plans on December 4, 2001. After several more iterations, Franks presented the refined operation plans to President Bush on February 7, 2002.[67]

In his 2002 State of the Union address, the president announced that the United States would oppose the "axis of evil" countries: Iraq, Iran, and North Korea. The seriousness of this announcement was not fully appreciated, even when in the spring the administration began talking about "regime change" in Iraq.

In the summer of 2002, talk about war with Iraq was becoming more widespread, and members of the officer corps, especially the army, began to voice reservations about the wisdom of attacking Iraq. Even Brent Scowcroft and James A. Baker, both members of the president's father's administration, wrote op-ed pieces arguing that war with Iraq was not wise.[68] In August Vice President Cheney began the political campaign for war with a speech that charged that Saddam Hussein was nearing the acquisition of a nuclear capacity as well as possessing chemical and biological weapons that he was planning to use against the United States.

In the fall of 2002 President Bush decided to go to the United Nations for a resolution demanding that Saddam disclose his weapons of mass destruction. He then went to Congress for a resolution giving him authority to take the country to war with Saddam. The president framed the issue as the necessity of standing up to Saddam Hussein and backing the president in his attempt to get Saddam to back down. With an eye to the upcoming 2002 elections, the implication was that if Democrats in Congress did not support the president, they would be attacked in the campaign as weak on national security. The final resolution passed Congress by large margins in the House and Senate.

After the administration convinced Congress to give the president authority to attack Iraq, Colin Powell and U.S. diplomats went to work building a coalition to convince the UN Security Council to pass a new resolution on

Iraq. After much negotiation the Security Council agreed on a strongly worded, unanimous resolution. Resolution 1441 gave Iraq one week to prom- ise to comply with it and until February 21, 2003, at the latest for the UN inspectors to report back on Iraq's compliance.

The UN weapons inspectors searched Iraq with seeming carte blanche and surprise visits to sites of possible weapons manufacture but by late January had found no "smoking gun." Chief UN inspector Hans Blix said that he needed more time to do a thorough job. But as the initial reporting date for the UN inspectors (January 27, 2003) approached, President Bush became increasingly impatient with the inability of the UN inspection team to locate evidence of Iraq's weapons of mass destruction.

In his State of the Union address on January 28, 2003, President Bush said that the UN had given Saddam Hussein his "final chance to disarm." On March 19 U.S. forces attacked Saddam and after three weeks had prevailed over Saddam's forces in the battle for Baghdad. In the immediate aftermath of the U.S. victory, looting and general disorder prevailed, and U.S. forces began to restore order and to rebuild the infrastructure of Iraq. But in the summer of 2003 insurgents began to use guerilla tactics to attack U.S. forces and disrupt the rebuilding of the country, and intensive searches by U.S. forces did not lead to the discovery of any of the weapons of mass destruction that Saddam had been thought to have.

In 2004 Democrats criticized the administration for what they considered the rush to war without full UN support and for not giving the UN inspec- tors time enough to complete their job. As attacks against U.S. forces increased in frequency and intensity, the president's policy in Iraq became the major issue in the 2004 presidential election.

The Bush administration's record with Congress was characterized by suc- cess on national security matters but difficulty, particularly in the Senate, on domestic policy. Overall in domestic policy the Bush administration won some significant victories, particularly the series of tax cuts that amounted to almost $2 trillion over ten years. It also succeeded in passing the signifi- cant No Child Left Behind education program in 2001 and the Medicare drug benefit in 2003. But in many areas of domestic policy, Democrats, par- ticularly in the Senate, were successful in frustrating the policy goals of the Bush administration and Republicans in Congress. Congress did not pass major changes in the administration's faith-based initiative, approve oil dril- ling in the Arctic National Wildlife Refuge, approve tort reform, or take up Social Security privatization.

The Bush overall success rate with Congress was quite high in terms of the CQ box score, with the president achieving 87 percent success ratings in 2001 and 2002 and 78 percent in 2003.[69] But just as in the Clinton administration in its first two years, the scores seemed to indicate more success than the reality, at least in domestic policy. The majority party in Congress was able to schedule votes to maximize victories and avoid votes on measures that would not be successful.

CONCLUSION

The presidential campaign in 2004 seemed to raise the level of partisan conflict to unusually high levels. Attack ads from both sides, both official campaign ads and "independent" ads, swamped the swing states in the weeks before the November 2 election. While the rest of the country did not get the same attention from candidates or their hired guns, partisan feelings among activists were just as high as in the swing states. The country seemed to be polarized between the reds (Republicans) and the blues (Democrats). One indicator that was taken to demonstrate polarization during the 2004 election was evidence that most voters had made up their minds relatively early. By July of 2004, 79 percent of voters had decided they would vote for either Bush or Kerry (compared with 64 percent in 2000), leaving fewer undecided voters than in most presidential elections.[70] The outcome of the 2004 election was a replay in its relatively close margins (though with a clear and undisputed outcome), but the campaign was vastly more contentious.

The difference between the 2000 election and the 2004 election was the political perception of George W. Bush. In 2000 he was in the middle of the spectrum with Democrat Al Gore, and the electorate did not see large ideological differences between them. Bush was for tax cuts, a "humble" foreign policy, education reform, and a strong defense. Gore was more liberal on environment, more fiscally conservative, and less friendly to big business. The consequences of either one being elected did not seem drastic, and many noncommitted voters were ambivalent.

In contrast, the choice in the 2004 election was much more stark. President Bush had governed from the right, with large tax cuts, business-friendly environmental policies, proposals to partially privatize Social Security, and his proposal for a constitutional amendment to prevent states from allowing gay marriage. But most importantly, he had pursued war with Iraq based on questionable claims of WMD and a purported link between al Qaeda and Saddam Hussein. The subsequent occupation was difficult, and there was no clear exit strategy in the fall of 2004. Thus the choice for voters in 2004 was stark. Despite Democrat John Kerry's commitment to maintain the U.S. presence in Iraq, it was clear to voters that he would pursue a distinctly different and more "internationalist" foreign policy.

In most presidential elections a large portion of voters are in the middle of the political spectrum, and presidential candidates must move to the center in order to capture enough votes to win. Candidates often appeal to their party's base in the primaries, because turnout in the primaries is limited to those strongly committed to the party. But candidates usually must then move back to the middle of the spectrum in order to appeal to the general electorate, which is not as polarized as the party base. Thus in most presidential elections, for example, in 1988, 1992, 1996, and 2000, the candidates were perceived to be in the middle of the spectrum. But in 2004 the gap in approval of the president between Democrats and Republicans, at 74 percent, was larger than it had been since the measure had been taken. That is, Republican approval of President Bush was near 90 percent and Democratic approval was near 15 percent.[71]

How can we explain the deep cleavage between Democratic and Republican support for President Bush? Democrats and Republicans were polarized over President Bush's policies, but independents and other moderate voters were not as polarized as the committed partisans in the electorate. This is consistent with Fiorina's conclusion of no *increasing* polarization among most of the electorate over the past several decades. There were, however, important differences between the identifiers with both parties, but the differences were not extremely deep or increasing, except for party activists.

Many voters felt strongly about the choices they faced in the 2004 election. But the primary cause of their strong feelings was the choice they were presented with: a continuation of President Bush's approach to domestic and foreign policy or a change to a Democratic alternative. It is entirely possible that they would have preferred a more moderate set of options for the 2004 election. The aftereffects of 9/11 also contributed to the election of President Bush for a second term and the strong feelings of many Democrats that the war in Iraq did not make the country safer.

Given the continuing reality of predictably safe seats, the polarization in Congress is not likely to go away soon. Similarly, the relatively narrow margins between the parties in Congress (eleven seats in the Senate and thirty seats in the House for the 109th Congress) are likely to remain, as is the domination of Congress by the Republican Party. According to Gary Jacobson's analysis, Democratic voters are more tightly packed into districts that are quite safely Democratic, while Republican voters are distributed more effectively for electing Republicans from safe but not overwhelmingly Republican districts: "53 percent of the Gore majority districts have more than 60 percent Gore voters, whereas only 41 percent of the Bush majority districts have more than 60 percent Bush voters." Thus, Jacobson concludes, the next several election cycles will see "uphill struggles for the Democrats, fought with enormous intensity in a handful of districts, while the great majority of races go effectively uncontested."[72] Similarly, Republicans have an advantage in the Senate, though less so than the House. Democrats tend to win more votes in more populous states, and Republicans tend to do better in more rural states. In 2000 Bush won fifteen of the twenty states with the least population, and Al Gore won six of the nine states with the largest populations.[73]

All of this means that the contentious politics of the first Bush term will continue, with the president pushing for conservative domestic policies and a continued aggressive foreign policy and Democrats in Congress fighting a rearguard action, particularly in the Senate, in attempts to thwart many of his policies.

NOTES

1. See James P. Pfiffner, "The Transformation of the Bush Presidency," in *Understanding the Presidency*, James P. Pfiffner and Roger H. Davidson, 3rd ed. (New York: Longman, 2004), 453–71.

2. Nelson Polsby, *How Congress Evolves: Social Bases of Institutional Change* (New York: Oxford University Press, 2004).

3. Polsby, *How Congress Evolves*, 87–93.

4. Polsby, *How Congress Evolves*, 80–94.

5. For analyses of the changing electoral makeup of the South and the partisan implications, see Earl Black and Merle Black, *The Vital South* (Cambridge, MA: Harvard University Press, 1992); Bruce Oppenheimer, "The Importance of Elections in a Strong Congressional Party Era" in *Do Elections Matter?* ed. Benjamin Ginsberg and Alan Stone (Armonk, NY: M. W. Sharpe, 1996); Gary Jacobson, "The 1994 House Elections in Perspective," in *Midterm: The Elections of 1994 in Perspective*, ed. Philip A. Klinker (Boulder, CO: Westview, 1996); Gary C. Jacobson, "Reversal of Fortune: The Transformation of U.S. House Elections in the 1990s," paper delivered at the Midwest Political Science Meeting, Chicago, April 10–12, 1997; Paul Frymer, "The 1994 Electoral Aftershock: Dealignment or Realignment in the South," in *Midterm: The Elections of 1994 in Context*, ed. Philip Klinker (Boulder, CO: Westview, 1996); Lawrence C. Dodd and Bruce I. Oppenheimer, "Revolution in the House: Testing the Limits of Party Government," in *Congress Reconsidered* (Washington, DC: CQ Press, 1997), 29–60; and Lawrence C. Dodd and Bruce I. Oppenheimer, "Congress and the Emerging Order: Conditional Party Government or Constructive Partisanship?" in *Congress Reconsidered*, 371–89.

6. Polsby, *How Congress Evolves*, 94.

7. David E. Price, "House Democrats under Republican Rule," *Miller Center Report* 20, no. 1 (Spring/Summer 2004): 21.

8. Polsby, *How Congress Evolves*, 80, 150.

9. See Burdett A. Loomis and Wendy J. Schiller, *The Contemporary Congress*, 4th ed. (Belmont, CA: 2004), 150–60.

10. For an analysis of the 1994 elections and the 104th Congress, see James P. Pfiffner, "President Clinton, Newt Gingrich, and the 104th Congress" in *On Parties: Essays Honoring Austin Ranney*, ed. Nelson W. Polsby and Raymond E. Wolfinger (Berkeley, CA: Institute of Governmental Studies Press, 2000), 135–68.

11. Polsby puts it this way, "Air conditioning (plus other things) caused the population of the southern states to change [which] changed the political parties of the South [which] changed the composition and in due course the performance of the U.S. House of Representatives leading first to its liberalization and later to its transformation into an arena of sharp partisanship, visible among both Democrats and Republicans." *How Congress Evolves*, 3.

12. Gary C. Jacobson, *The Politics of Congressional Elections*, 6th ed. (New York: Longman, 2004), 252.

13. Charlie Cook, "Value of Incumbency Seems to Be Growing," *National Journal*, March 20, 2004, 906.

14. These data do not include two seats that were subject to runoff elections. Ordinarily, states redistrict themselves following each decennial census. But Rep. Tom DeLay engineered a redistricting in Texas after the 2002 elections that forced seven incumbent Democrats out of office (four in general elections, one retirement, and two losing in primaries). See Jennifer Mock, "Texas 'Firewall' Strategy for House Pays Off with Five-Seat GOP Pickup," *CQToday*, November 4, 2004, 15; David S. Broder, "No Vote Necessary," *Washington Post*, November 11, 2004, A37; Editorial, "Scandal in the House," *Washington Post*, November 4, 2004, A24.

15. Quoted in Jeffrey Toobin, "The Great Election Grab," *New Yorker*, December 8, 2003, 76.

16. See Gary C. Jacobson, "Explaining the Ideological Polarization of the Congressional Parties since the 1970s," in *Parties, Procedure and Policy Choice: A History of Congress*, ed. David Brady and Mathew McCubbins (Stanford, CA: Stanford University Press, forthcoming), draft of June 2004, p. 10–12. For an argument that individual shifts in ideology contributed to the overall shift, see Sean M. Theriault, "The Case of the Vanishing Moderates: Party Polarization in the Modern Congress," manuscript, University of Texas, Austin.

17. Quoted in Toobin, "The Great Election Grab," p. 76.

18. Bruce Oppenheimer argues that individual incumbency advantage has been decreasing and that very high reelection rates of House incumbents is primarily due to the partisan loading of districts. See "Deep Red and Blue Congressional Districts: The Causes and Consequences of Declining Party Competitiveness," in *Congress Reconsidered*, 8th ed., ed. Lawrence Dodd and Bruce Oppenheimer (Washington, DC: Congressional Quarterly, 2005), 135–58.

19. Loomis and Schiller, *Contemporary Congress*, 66.

20. In Florida, if an incumbent is not opposed, his or her name does not appear on the ballot. Thus the candidate is "automatically reinstated in Washington" without any constituent having to cast a ballot in his or her favor. Broder, "No Vote Necessary," A37.

21. See Jacobson, *The Politics of Congressional Elections*, 236–43.

22. Morris Fiorina, *Culture War? The Myth of a Polarized America*. (New York: Longman, 2005).

23. Based on data from the National Election Studies at the University of Michigan. Fiorina, *Culture War?* 23, 28, 43.

24. Fiorina, *Culture War?* 49.

25. Fiorina, *Culture War?* 60.

26. Fiorina, *Culture War?* 79.

27. Fiorina, *Culture War?* 92, 95.

28. Fiorina, *Culture War?* 114.

29. Fiorina, *Culture War?* 130.

30. Jon R. Bond and Richard Fleisher, "The Disappearing Middle and the President's Quest for Votes in Congress," *PRG Report* (Fall 1999): 6.

31. Bond and Fleisher, "The Disappearing Middle," 7. The authors calculate their ideological scores from the rankings of liberal and conservative groups, Americans for Democratic Action (liberal) and American Conservative Union (conservative).

32. Sarah Binder, *Stalemate: Causes and Consequences of Legislative Gridlock* (Washington, DC: Brookings, 2003), 24, 66.

33. Richard E. Cohen, "A Congress Divided," *National Journal*, February 26, 2000, 4. The *National Journal* calculates its own liberal-conservative scores for members of Congress.

34. Burdett A. Loomis, "Civility and Deliberation: A Linked Pair," in *Esteemed Colleagues: Civility and Deliberation in the U.S. Senate*, ed. Burdett A. Loomis (Washington, DC: Brookings, 2000), 9.

35. On the decrease of the number of moderates in Congress, see also Binder, "Going Nowhere," APSR, 526.

36. See Sinclair, "Transformational Leader or Faithful Agent?" 5; and CQ *Weekly Reports*, January 27, 1996, 199.

37. It was the highest since CQ began keeping the data in 1954, CQ *Weekly Reports*, January 27, 1996, 199. According to John Owens's calculations, party voting was the highest since 1905–1906. See John Owens, "The Return of Party Government in the U.S. House of Representatives: Central Leadership—Committee Relations in the 104th Congress," *British Journal of Political Science* 27 (1997): 265.

38. See Richard Fleisher and Jon Bond, "Congress and the President in a Partisan Era," in *Polarized Politics*, ed. Richard Fleisher and Jon Bond (Washington: CQ Press, 2000), 4. Party unity voting fell off slightly from 2001 to 2004 because of consensual voting on homeland security issues in response to the terrorist attacks of 2001. Jacobson, *The Politics of Congressional Elections*, 231.

39. Sinclair, "Transformational Leader or Faithful Agent?" 5.

40. Richard E. Cohen, "Crackup of the Committees," *National Journal*, July 31, 1999, 2212. See also Sarah A. Binder and Steven S. Smith, *Politics or Principle?* (Washington: Brookings, 1997), 10.

41. Binder and Smith, *Politics or Principle?* 16.

42. Barbara Sinclair, "Hostile Partners: The President, Congress, and Lawmaking in the Partisan 1990s," in Bond and Fleisher, *Polarized Politics*, 145.

43. Binder, *Stalemate*, 93.

44. Binder, *Stalemate*, 58.

45. Sarah A. Binder, "Going Nowhere: A Gridlocked Congress?" *Brookings Review* (Winter 2000): 17.

46. See Eric M. Uslaner, *The Decline of Comity in Congress* (Ann Arbor: University of Michigan Press, 1993).

47. Eric M. Uslaner, "Is the Senate More Civil than the House?" in *Esteemed Colleagues: Civility and Deliberation in the U.S. Senate*, ed. Burdett A. Loomis (Washington, DC: Brookings, 2000), 32–55.

48. Uslaner, "Is the Senate More Civil than the House?" 39.

49. David Brady and Morris Fiorina, "Congress in the Era of the Permanent Campaign," in *The Permanent Campaign and Its Future*, ed. Norman Ornstein and Thomas Mann (Washington, DC: Brookings-AEI, 2000), 147.

50. Eric Planin and Juliet Eilperin, "No Love Lost for Hastert, Gephardt," *Washington Post*, March 20, 2000, A4.

51. Karen Foerstel, "Hastert and the Limits of Persuasion," *CQ Weekly*, September 30, 2000, 2252.

52. Karen Foerstel, "Hastert and the Limits of Persuasion," *CQ Weekly*, September 30, 2000, 2252.

53. Lizette Albarez and Eric Schmitt, "Undignified and Screaming, Senate Seeks to Right Itself," *New York Times*, June 7, 2000, A26.

54. David Baumann, "The Collapse of the Senate," *National Journal*, June 3, 2000, 1758.

55. Erich Schmitt, "When Senators Attack: 'Why, I Oughta . . .'" *New York Times*, June 11, 2000, WK7.

56. Carl Hulse, "A Longtime Courtesy Loses in the Closely Split Senate," *New York Times*, April 24, 2004, A7; Sheryl Gay Stolberg, "Daschle Has Race on His Hands and Interloper on His Turf," *New York Times*, May 23, 2004, 18.

57. Dana Milbank and Helen Dewar, "Cheney Defends Use of Four-Letter Word," *Washington Post*, June 26, 2004, A4.

58. Charles Babington, "Hey, They're Taking Slash-and-Burn to Extremes!" *Washington Post*, December 21, 2003, B1, B4.

59. Charles Babington, "DeLay to Be Subject of Ethics Complaint," *Washington Post*, June 15, 2004, A5.

60. William E. Brock, "A Recipe for Incivility," *Washington Post*, June 27, 2004, B7.

61. See James P. Pfiffner, "President Clinton and the 103rd Congress: Winning Battles and Losing Wars," in *Rivals for Power: Presidential-Congressional Relations*, 2d ed., ed. James Thurber (Washington, DC: CQ Press, 1996), 170–90.

62. Quoted in Joe Klein, "Eight Years: Bill Clinton and the Politics of Persistence," *New Yorker*, October 16 & 23, 2000, 209.

63. For an analysis of the shutdown and the partisan battles surrounding it, see James P. Pfiffner, "President Clinton, Newt Gingrich, and the 104th Congress," in *On Parties: Essays Honoring Austin Ranney*, ed. Nelson W. Polsby and Raymond E. Wolfinger (Berkeley, CA: Institute of Governmental Studies, 1999), 135–68.

64. Quotes in Andrew Taylor, "Symbolism and Stalemate Closing Out 106th Congress," in *CQ Weekly Report*, October 28, 2000, 2519, 2521. See also "An Ineffectual Congress," *New York Times*, editorial, November 1, 2000, A30.

65. See Allan Schick, *The Federal Budget: Politics, Policy, Process* (Washington, DC: Brookings, 2000), 26–30.

66. See Louis Uchitelle, "Taxes, the Market and Luck Underlie the Budget Surplus," *New York Times*, October 20, 2000, 1.

67. Bob Woodward, *Plan of Attack* (New York: Simon & Schuster, 2004), 77, 80, 96,

98. In the spring of 2002, President Bush said several times in news conferences, "I have no war plans on my desk." Woodward, *Plan of Attack*, 120, 127.

68. For a detailed analysis of President Bush's public campaign for war in Iraq, see James P. Pfiffner, "Did President Bush Mislead the Country in his Arguments for War with Iraq?" *Presidential Studies Quarterly* 34, no. 1 (March 2004): 25–46.

69. *CQ Weekly*, January 3, 2004, 53.

70. Robin Toner, "Voters Are Very Settled, Intense, and Partisan, and It's Only July," *New York Times*, July 25, 2004, 1, 12.

71. Toner, "Voters Are Very Settled."

72. Jacobson, *The Politics of Congressional Elections*, 251.

73. Gary C. Jacobson, *The Politics of Congressional Elections*, 6th ed. (NY: Longman, 2004), p. 253.

3

Presidential Leadership of Congress: Structures and Strategies

Stephen J. Wayne

THE CONSTITUTIONAL DESIGN

The Framers of the American Constitution did not expect or want the president to be chief legislator. They did not expect the president to set Congress's policy agenda except in times of crisis, particularly in situations in which Congress was not in session. The emergency triggering mechanism devised by the delegates gave the president the authority to call a special session, provide the Congress with the information it needed on the state of the union, and then, if the president thought it was desirable, recommend necessary and expedient legislation.

Nor did the Framers anticipate or want the president to be the principal domestic policy maker, although in conjunction with the Senate, the chief executive was given responsibility to formulate treaties and alliances and thereby participate in the making of foreign policy. But Congress had a role here as well: to enact any implementing legislation including appropriations.

The veto power, a traditional executive prerogative and the president's only other legislative weapon, was intended primarily as a defensive check on a Congress that intruded into the executive's sphere of authority or a device the president could use to negate unwise and ill-conceived legislation. It was not intended as a tool for imposing a presidential policy judgment on the legislature. In *Federalist 73*, Hamilton writes: "The primary inducement to conferring the power in question [the veto power] upon the Executive is, to enable him to defend himself; the secondary one is to increase the chances in favor of the community against the passing of bad laws through haste, inadvertence, or design." [1] As a hedge against misuse by the president, an overwhelming majority in Congress, a minimum of two-thirds of each house, could override the veto. In this sense, a unified Congress had the last word.

Legislative draftsman, congressional lobbyist, coalition builder, both inside and outside the government—there is little indication that the Framers expected or wanted the president to assume any of these roles on a regular basis. In fact, there is much more indication that they did not. The policy-making authority of the national government appears in the same constitutional article which gives the Congress, "*all legislative powers herein granted.*" Although a president could affect the legislature's exercise of its authority through information, recommendations, and as a final resort, the veto, the executive could not assume legislative powers by virtue of any inherent or implied constitutional grant.

Nor did the concept of separation of powers anticipate a major, ongoing legislative role for the president beyond the sharing of the appointment and treaty-making powers with the Senate. George Washington, chair of the Constitutional Convention, had limited contact with Congress and much of it was formal: his State of the Union addresses, several dinners and events in which members of Congress were present, and three legislative proposals submitted to Congress. [2] Washington even refused a House committee's request for his advice on the grounds that it would violate the constitutional separation.

As far as lobbyist and coalition builder are concerned, there was no expectation and no formal or informal authority by which the president should or could exercise these roles. The debate over presidential selection suggests that Framers were fearful of demagogues, equated popular leadership with them, and saw the constitutional structure as a hedge against a plebiscitary president. Going public was viewed as undesirable, even dangerous. [3]

The good news is that the Constitution and the framework it established are alive and well. The bad news is that this framework inhibits presidential leadership of Congress in an era when the public, press, and to some extent the Congress itself expects and wants that leadership. [4] Herein lies the president's legislative leadership dilemma.

THE NINETEENTH CENTURY: EXERCISING INFORMAL INFLUENCE

Despite the constitutional investiture of legislative powers to the Congress, the president's legislative role has increased. Jefferson and Jackson used their party leadership to influence Congress. Jefferson met informally with his partisans, had two of his cabinet members, James Madison and Albert Gallatin, attend congressional caucus meetings, used the appointment process to satisfy some members of Congress's personnel requests, and engaged in social lobbying. Jackson, too, exerted partisan influence in Congress, but he also threatened and used the veto to get his way. He exercised twelve vetoes, two more than all his predecessors combined. By doing so, he opened up the veto as an instrument of presidential power.

Lincoln, too, enhanced the president's legislative role, but he did so in times of crisis. So his actions, which included the first bill actually drafted in the White House and sent to Congress as well as emergency measures that he initiated on his own, were not seen initially as precedents by those who followed him in office. In fact, by the end of the nineteenth century the conventional wisdom, as described by Professor Woodrow Wilson, was that ours was a *Congressional Government*.[5] Wilson saw the president's legislative powers as no greater than his prerogative of the veto.

THE TWENTIETH CENTURY

The President as Policy Initiator

The policy initiatives of Theodore Roosevelt, his Square Deal program, and later, Woodrow Wilson himself, his New Freedoms program, had much to do with modifying Wilson's initial view of the balance between Congress and the president. But so did the consequences of World War I, particularly budget deficits at home and a larger international role abroad. Although the Senate rejected the Versailles Treaty and League of Nations, it could not prevent future presidents from assuming a more active policy-making role in foreign affairs if they chose to do so, a role which the Supreme Court acknowledged they had the power to exercise in 1936.[6] Legislators did turn to the president for imposing fiscal responsibility. The enactment of the Budget and Accounting Act of 1921 made it a presidential responsibility to provide Congress with an annual executive branch budget.

Franklin Roosevelt's new economic initiatives,[7] his lobbying of Congress, and his public appeals added a new dimension to presidential leadership of Congress while the Executive Office of the President provided an institutional structure to facilitate the president's expanded legislative presence.[8] Both Truman and Eisenhower continued these roles, also depending on units in the new Executive Office to perform them. Truman converted the State of the Union message into an annual agenda-setter for Congress and political address to the country. Eisenhower created the first White House legislative affairs office to explain his program to members of Congress, and later, after the Democrats gained control of both houses, to dissuade them from enacting proposals he opposed.[9]

Kennedy and Johnson expanded the president's domestic policy-making sphere to include civil rights and social welfare legislation. They also created policy staffs in the White House to develop priority policy initiatives. Outside task forces generated ideas which were "staffed out" by executive branch personnel under the coordination of the White House while an expanded congressional legislative operation, working out of the East Wing of the White House, pushed these initiatives on Capitol Hill. In coordination with the Democratic leadership, the White House liaison staff counted heads, twisted arms, and involved the president with committee chairs and other critical members of Congress.[10]

Prioritizing Legislative Proposals

In effect a two-track legislative system was created, with priority legislation on track one, initiated, coordinated, and pushed by the White House, and less important legislation on track two, initiated by the departments, coordinated by the Bureau of the Budget, and monitored by the departments' legislative affairs offices. There was considerable presidential involvement in track-one lobbying activities. Johnson, especially, enjoyed the give-and-take of legislative relations and, according to most reports, was very good at it.[11]

Whether Johnson's civil rights and Great Society programs were enacted primarily because of the president's legislative skills, the Democrats' overwhelming majority in both houses, and/or public support is difficult to determine. It is clear, however, that the structure of power in Congress in the 1960s, the committee system, controlled by southern Democrats, Johnson's personal relations with them, and the closed-door style of decision making facilitated presidents' influence in a way that today's more decentralized, more individualistic, more public congressional decision-making process, particularly the opening of markup sessions to full public view, does not.

From the perspective of the president's legislative goals and operations, the Nixon-Ford presidency was transitional. The White House, enlarged and more centrally managed, particularly under Nixon, continued to have its policy staffs develop, coordinate, and oversee track-one legislation. A more politicized, management-oriented, and newly named and structured Office of Management and Budget ran the executive clearance processes. The liaison operation continued in much the same manner as it had during previous Democratic administrations.

Differentiating Executive Responsibilities

The centralization of policy making and legislative liaison in the White House permitted the administration in power to focus its efforts on major priorities, track one, while the Office of Management and Budget coordinated and monitored track two, with the executive departments and agencies expected to shoulder the principal burden of policy formulation, congressional liaison, and, if successful on the Hill, with implementation.

During the Ford administration, the person who functioned as head of White House operations did not, as a general matter, get involved with congressional matters. Although Donald Rumsfeld had served in Congress, and his deputy and later White House successor, Dick Cheney, had worked on the Hill, neither played a major legislative role in their capacity as chief of staff.

Carter's refusal to designate a chief of staff at the beginning of his term in office, combined with his personal reluctance to lobby members of Congress, left legislative liaison initially to Frank Moore, a non-Washingtonian who had few congressional contacts and a very small staff. Hamilton Jordan, the president's de facto assistant, functioned briefly as a contact person between the president-elect, and later the White House, and the congressional leadership. But relations were chilly. From the perspective of the Democratic leadership, Jordan's "holier than thou" attitude combined with his and the president's refusal to do politics as usual got Carter's congressional relations off to a very poor start.[12]

Jordan did get involved with the ratification of the Panama Canal Treaty. He was instrumental in organizing and operating an administration task force from his office that coordinated a public education campaign in accordance with the administration's lobbying effort in the Senate. The task force operation was eventually institutionalized by Carter in the form of a public liaison office that organized interest and community groups in support of the president's legislative initiatives on a range of policy issues.

The chief of staff's involvement in legislative relations, however, remained ad hoc until Carter restructured his White House in 1979 and placed Hamilton Jordan in charge. One of Jordan's principal responsibilities was to improve the administration's relations with Congress. He tried to do so but did not have much success. By then, even Democratic members of Congress were leery about getting too close to the White House, and Jordan became increasingly involved with the president's reelection campaign.[13]

THE CONTEMPORARY PRESIDENCY

Coordination in the White House [14]

James Baker III, Reagan's first chief of staff, was heavily involved in the formulation and promotion of the president's legislative policy initiatives. Throughout Reagan's first term, Baker ran a legislative strategy group out of his own office to monitor and move the administration's program on Capitol Hill. In addition to the chief of staff, the group included one of Baker's deputies, the policy director from the appropriate cabinet council, the head of congressional liaison, and the president's chief political adviser. Meetings, which occurred almost daily, were designed to coordinate the administration's contacts with members of Congress, involving cabinet members as needed, and linking these efforts with the administration's outreach and public relations activities, which were occurring simultaneously. Baker also made it a practice to stay in close touch with the congressional leadership. He also promoted the president's program in his daily contacts with the press, with whom he would speak regularly on an *off-the-record basis*.[15] Routine legislative matters continued to be handled by the congressional liaison staff and their departmental counterparts.

Donald Regan, Baker's successor as chief of staff, had poorer relations with Congress and limited patience for negotiating with the Republican leadership. Nonetheless, he tried to keep his hands in an array of legislative matters. Regan's penchant for tightly filtering congressional input to the Oval Office proved to be his downfall. Frustrated members of Congress who could not reach the president because of Regan and his aides took a back channel to the Oval Office in the form of anonymous leaks to the press, which undercut and infuriated Regan and quickly reduced even further his tolerance for dealing with Congress. The result was a chilly relationship, which lasted until a new chief of staff, Howard Baker, was named. Baker and his deputy and later successor, Ken Duberstein, both had extensive congressional experience, many contacts with members and their aides, and were well liked, so relations improved even though both houses of Congress were controlled by the Democrats.

George H. W. Bush was not as successful in dealing with Congress. Part of the reason stemmed from his lack of a comprehensive legislative agenda and his focus on foreign affairs. But part also stemmed from chief of staff problems. As in the Reagan White House, Bush's top aides, including chief of staff John Sununu, were heavily involved in legislative matters that affected the president's initiatives on the budget, education, and the environment. According to one senior official who was also involved in these issues, "Sununu got right down into the weeds with the Clean Air Act. He participated in practically every aspect of the policy from interagency lobbying to lobbying the Congress."[16] Similarly, he was also a major participant in the deficit-reduction compromise that forced Bush to recant his "read my lips, no new taxes" pledge. In fact, Sununu's interest in the domestic agenda and role in congressional negotiations was so great that a high White House official noted sarcastically, "We had to remind him [Sununu] of the cabinet's role in the domestic arena."[17]

But Sununu developed a congressional problem similar to Regan's. He antagonized members of Congress, who perceived him as abrasive, condescending, and intolerant.

After Sununu fell from presidential grace, he was replaced by Sam Skinner, secretary of transportation. Having little congressional experience of his own and lacking a close relationship with the president, Skinner had difficulty mediating between Congress and the president. W. Henson Moore, a former member of Congress and Skinner's deputy, became in practice the principal White House liaison, particularly for Republicans who knew him from his days on the Hill.[18] After the Persian Gulf War ended, however, Bush's relations with Congress deteriorated. Skinner and Moore were replaced by James Baker, who was forced to focus almost entirely on the president's reelection campaign, not congressional affairs as he had during the Reagan administration.

Despite the difficulties Bush's chiefs of staff encountered in their dealings with Congress, members continued to look to them, not the head of the liaison office, as the principal go-between with the president on the priority issues. Congress's go-to-the-top orientation presented a problem in the early months of the Clinton administration because of the disorder in the White House. In addition to the president, who was heavily involved in policy formulation and promotion, chief of staff Mac McLarty, communications director George Stephanopoulos, liaison chief Robert Paster, economic adviser Robert Rubin, treasury secretary Lloyd Bentsen, and vice president Al Gore also participated in congressional negotiations on the economic stimulus and deficit reduction plans, sometimes working at cross-purposes with one another.

It was not until the defeat of the economic stimulus bill by a Senate filibuster that the White House tried to impose order on its legislative operations. Bentsen was designated as the principal point man to deal with the House and Senate tax committees on the deficit-reduction bill, assistant treasury secretary Robert Altman was put in charge of a "war room" to forge and promote a coherent public position while Clinton continued to engage in behind-the-scenes lobbying. The president attributed the defeat of his economic stimulus bill in the Senate to his delegation of Sen. Robert Byrd as floor leader for the bill. According to David Gergen, the lesson Clinton learned from this experience was to keep control himself and get the bills through on his own.[19] On the other hand, Clinton's negotiating style encouraged members of Congress, especially Democrats, to feign opposition or being undecided in order to gain favors from the White House. According to Treasury Secretary Bentsen, "Clinton had made it too desirable for congressmen to hold out, to appear to make up their minds in the end game when they had maximum leverage. Clinton needs more discipline and should not keep paying off the holdouts."[20]

The legislative affairs office lost credibility during this period. It was clear that Paster was not speaking for the president and his efforts were being undercut by the activities of other White House aides. As a consequence, end runs were encouraged; partisan support in Congress for the president's policy proposals weakened. The president's reputation suffered.[21] Rolling Clinton continued to be the most popular sport on Capitol Hill. In fact, it assumed bipartisan dimensions, one of the few times that Democratic and Republican members of Congress seemed to have a common political objective.

In the late spring of 1994, Clinton began the restructuring of his White House operation with the appointment of Leon Panetta as chief of staff. Panetta attempted to impose order on the administration's relations with Congress. He personally played a key role in negotiations with the congressional leadership, especially on budget matters, which were salient from 1995 to the end of Clinton's second term. Panetta described his contact in the following way:

> I knew most of the players up there. I would go up and brief our caucus. . . . I would go to their luncheons. I would go to their meetings. Usually we tried to tie it to major issues [and votes] that were coming up so that we could make the case for why they should support the administration.[22]

Panetta was also conscious of the need to coordinate his activities with the legislative affairs office. "I had to be very careful that I didn't just go out there and do it on my own without coordinating with the people who had a responsibility. And they also had a lot of responsibility to come up with a lot of the backup material . . . they had a responsibility to provide all the material and supporting documents every time we developed policy."[23]

But Clinton continued to stay heavily involved in legislative matters. He used the White House to lobby legislators in order to maximize his persuasive advantage. Panetta noted,

> If you bring a member down to the White House into the Oval Office, one on one with the president, it's a much more effective way to lobby a member than to have your presidential assistant for legislative affairs go up there or even the Secretary of State go up there. It's just much more powerful . . . and there's the ambiance. There aren't a lot of people who tell the president to go to Hell when they are in the Oval Office.[24]

Besides, he added, "the people that come down from the Hill . . . always like to be able to ride up there and have the press see them walk into the West Wing. So if you want to give the meeting a higher profile . . . you usually have it at the White House. If you want to low key it and really talk business, I found that it was just much better for me to go up to the Hill."[25]

Panetta's successors, chiefs of staff Erskine Bowles and John Podesta, operated in much the same manner. They too engaged in negotiations with the congressional leadership; they too served as spokesmen for the administration; they too coordinated the president's legislative operation on major initiatives, continuing the practice of recent administrations of centralizing control of the legislative operation on major policy issues in the White House at or near the Oval Office.

The administration of George W. Bush began with a sizable legislative agenda that included tax relief, education reform, a military buildup, a national energy policy, and the president's faith-based initiative. In the first six months only one of these goals was achieved, a major tax reduction. And it was obtained at a high cost; it contributed to the defection of Sen. James Jeffords from the Republican Party.

President Bush initially planned to maintain a light hand and cooperative attitude toward Congress, much as he had done as governor toward the Democratic-controlled Texas state legislature. In the aftermath of his controversial, nonplurality victory in the 2000 election, such an approach seemed to be merited. However, the conservative House and more moderate Senate were too far apart ideologically for the White House to find common ground on most of the president's legislative initiatives. Of them, only education reform was enacted during the administration's first year in office, a product of the national unity that the terrorist attacks and the administration's reaction to them produced.

Bush's initial domestic agenda became a casualty of September 11, 2001. Fear of terrorism replaced myriad economic and social issues as the focus of administration action and public attention. The legislative components of the administration's response to the attacks were enacted mostly in accord with the president's wishes. During the remainder of 2001 and the beginning of 2002, Congress played follow the leader, partisanship was muted, and the country unified. Only in the creation of a Department of Homeland Security did partisanship divide the Congress and delay the legislation. The Republican victory in the 2002 midterm elections broke the stalemate on the new department and a program to indemnify insurance companies in the event of another terrorist attack. The president had gotten what he wanted.

Bush continued to emphasize national security concerns throughout the next two years. With the exception of reforming the Medicare system, most of the policy initiatives enacted into law during this period emanated from the Republican Congress, not the Republican White House. The president was not heavily involved in lobbying; the vice president was, however. Cheney became the principal link to the Republicans in Congress. He regularly attended their policy caucuses. During the 108th Congress, changes in the composition of Bush's liaison staff, a new Senate leader, and tight domestic budgets reduced the administration's incentives and decreased its ability to influence domestic and economic public policy outcomes.

The president's reelection and the Republican gains in Congress, however, raised the legislative ante for Bush's second term. The president's claim that he earned the political capital from the election, combined with his expansive policy agenda—maintaining the tax cuts and reforming the tax system, privatizing part of Social Security, enacting Patriot II—plus the initiatives left over from the previous Congress—tort reform, an energy policy, bankruptcy and telecommunications legislation—all suggested an active legislative presidency for George W. Bush's remaining years in office. But the administration's difficulties with the lame-duck session of the 108th Congress questioned whether the president and his advisers were really up to the task.

Not only did the administration have to accept an omnibus spending bill that exceeded the president's budget, replete with hundreds of earmarks for members of Congress's pet projects, but it was also embarrassed by Republican opposition to a bill establishing a national intelligence director.

Pressured by the 9/11 Commission and victims' relatives who formed a Family Steering Committee, the president went on record in favor of the commission's recommendation to establish a national intelligence director with budget and personnel authority over the other major intelligence agencies.[26] He did so to avoid intelligence becoming an issue in the 2004 elections. Republicans who opposed the legislation, however, sensed that the president's support was lukewarm, a campaign necessity, not a personal endorsement. As a consequence, the powerful chairs of the House Armed

Services and Judiciary committees opposed a compromise bill that House and Senate conferees had negotiated during the fall of 2004.

With a majority of the majority objecting to the legislation, Speaker Hastert refused to bring it to the floor of the House. The Speaker's position, only to vote on measures supported by a majority of House Republicans, embarrassed the White House on this issue and frightened them on future ones. The tactic, designed to ensure that the conservative Republican majority's policy orientation would prevail on House votes and that Hastert would continue to receive the backing of a majority of his party, placed the administration in an ideological straitjacket and gave House conservatives, in effect, a veto over presidential policy. The "majority of the majority" rule, if implemented, would have made bipartisan coalitions on controversial measures less likely, thereby diminishing the administration's chances for achieving its ambitious policy agenda. The president was in a bind. By his decision not to move the legislation, Hastert had gotten the White House's undivided attention.

Presidential aides quickly went into action. With Vice President Cheney leading the charge, White House negotiators worked out a compromise with House and Senate Republican leaders in which the bill's language was modified to meet the objections of one of the principal opponents, Representative Duncan Hunter, chair of the House Armed Services Committee.[27] An attempt to mollify the other Republican chair failed, but sufficient GOP support had been garnered by White House pressures and the change in wording to move the legislation to a vote. The episode, like a shot across the bow, awakened the administration to the realities of dealing with Congress, even a Republican Congress. Republican support could not be taken for granted.

The lessons for the administration were clear:

1. It is necessary to state presidential priorities and positions clearly and unequivocally. Ambiguity permits members of Congress to pursue their own policy preferences with less fear of reprisal. In the case of the intelligence bill, the president's inattention to the matter was seen by interested parties, particularly the military and their congressional supporters, as a sign that Bush did not really care about the details of the legislation and, perhaps, did not really support the bill. Some opponents even suggested that they were doing him a favor by opposing it. The president had lost his persuasive advantage by his failure to clarify his position, indicate the priority he attached to the bill, and communicate directly with the Republican leadership on this matter.

2. Political capital is not a commodity that presidents can put aside for safekeeping. It must be earned, worked, and employed skillfully, not

assumed, overused, or underutilized, for it to be a valuable resource for influencing congressional deliberations and policy outcomes. The successful use of political capital, however, can generate more capital down the road. In the case of the intelligence bill, President Bush's principal mistake was to assume Republicans would naturally defer to his public utterances, an assumption that turned out to be incorrect.

3. There are built-in institutional rivalries that make presidential-congressional relations tenuous at best, even during conditions of unified government. Similarly, the parochial behavior that members of Congress manifest on a regular basis is a perpetual hurdle that presidents have to overcome in their pursuit of national policy goals. In a "politics as usual" environment, the diversity of American society is more apt to be reflected in divisions within Congress than in a consensus on policy. The burden rests with the president and his aides to build that consensus.

STRATEGIES FOR A SUCCESSFUL LEGISLATIVE PRESIDENCY

Emphasizing National Goals

One way for presidents to overcome congressional parochialism is to define the issue in national terms. Reducing the budget deficit by holding the line on domestic spending is the tactic that Presidents George H. W. Bush, Bill Clinton, and George W. Bush used to curb members of Congress's appetites for earmarking money for their pet projects. These presidents were only partially successful in achieving their objectives. Keeping the Medicare and Social Security systems solvent for future generations is another generic appeal that presidents have made to justify proposals to modify revenues or maximize benefits.

Another tactic that presidents have used for building congressional support is to establish a blue-ribbon commission, task force, or White House conference to bring attention to a problem and make recommendations for its solution. Bush's economic summit following his reelection is a case in point. Experts invited to the two-day conference were instructed to examine the tax structure, Social Security, and deficit reduction and suggest programmatic changes that would help the president achieve his goals of simplifying the tax code, privatizing part of Social Security, and reducing the deficit by half during his second term.

Stressing the "Crisis" Component

Presidential influence is enhanced in times of peril. Members of Congress, much like the general public, tend to support the country's leader and unifying figure, the president, during crises. The amount of support and its duration are often dependent on the magnitude of the problem and its impact on society.

President George W. Bush benefited from this "rally round the flag" effect in dealing with Congress following the terrorist attacks and throughout his first term. Bush used his bully pulpit to articulate and reinforce the administration's antiterrorism crusade. During this period from September 11, 2001, to the end of the president's first term, legislation that pertained to national and homeland security received more attention and congressional backing than it would have in a "politics as usual" situation. The crisis atmosphere enhanced the president's influence and enabled him to get his way. Congress enacted most of the items on his national and homeland security agendas: These included measures enacted during the regular sessions of the 107th Congress:

- A Use of Force Resolution authorizing the president to use force to bring the terrorists and those who harbor them to justice
- A supplemental spending bill ($40 billion) to help recovery from the attacks, enhance national security, and provide moneys in anticipation of a military response
- Airline bailout ($15 billion)
- Antiterrorism legislation, the USA Patriot Act, that provided expanded surveillance and enforcement powers for the federal government
- Aviation security, the creation of the Transportation Security Agency
- A $46 billion increase in the Defense Department's budget

The lame-duck session of the 107th Congress:

- Creation of the Department of Homeland Security
- Enactment of legislation indemnifying insurance companies against losses in another terrorist attack

The first session of the 108th Congress:

- Enactment of a resolution authorizing the president to use force, if necessary, in Iraq

- Supplementary spending bills to support the military efforts and subsequent peacekeeping activities in Afghanistan and Iraq

Presidents have frequently defined problems in crisis terms to enhance backing for their legislative proposals. Lyndon Johnson's War on Poverty, Jimmy Carter's energy crisis, Bill Clinton's health care reforms, and George W. Bush's partial privatization of Social Security are four such examples. Similarly, presidents tend to prolong the crisis atmosphere to maximize their support. Through terrorism alerts, announcements of extra security measures, and media coverage of terrorist activities around the world, the Bush administration successfully kept the terrorism issue front and center throughout the president's first term. Over time, as the crisis fades, if the objectives are not achieved, or if the cost becomes too high, presidential influence is apt to decrease.

Much of the presidents' power in declaring and extending crises comes from maximizing the symbolism and voice of the office. The public relations dimension of the modern presidency has been an important instrument of presidential power, or at least presidents have thought it to be. In the words of Lyndon Johnson, "Presidential popularity is a major source of strength in gaining cooperation from Congress."[28] Richard Nixon put it this way: "No leader survives simply by doing well. A leader survives when people have confidence in him when he is not doing well."[29] Presidents and their advisers believe that being popular encourages members of Congress to support the president; low popularity does not.

These beliefs, for the most part, have been reinforced by the political science literature on presidential power. In his seminal work, Richard E. Neustadt argued that presidential prestige contributed to presidential power to bargain successfully with members of the Washington community.[30] Samuel Kernell noted in his revision of Neustadt's thesis, "Going public becomes the preferred course when protocoalitions are weak, when individual politicians are susceptible to public pressures, and when politicians in the White House appreciate the requirements of television better than the needs of committee chairs."[31] George Edwards, another presidential scholar, was less optimistic about presidential popularity impacting on congressional decision making. He wrote, "The impact of public approval for the president on congressional support for the president occurs at the margins, within the confines of other influences. . . . Approval gives a president leverage, but not control."[32] In a more recent study, this one focusing on presidential attempts to affect public opinion on policy issues, Edwards found little evidence that presidents, even those who are judged to be effective communicators, can change public opinion very much. He concluded,

Chief executives are not directors who lead the public where it otherwise refuses to go. . . . Instead, presidents are facilitators who reflect, and may intensify, widely held views. In the process, they may endow the views of their supporters with structure and purpose, and exploit opportunities in their environment to accomplish their joint goals.[33]

Despite Edwards's finding, contemporary presidents and their advisers have increasingly emphasized the public dimensions of their office to enhance their influence with Congress, their popularity, their reelectability, and their place in history. They have done so by creating "PR" offices in the White House, appointing media experts to advise them, and spending a greater portion of their time out of the White House on the road, in full public view.

The White House's Public Relations Operation

The development of institutional mechanisms in the White House to build public support began during the Nixon administration, when an office of communications was established. That office tried to control or at least monitor the flow of information into and out of the White House. Nixon was also the first president to appoint a liaison to business and labor. He saw these outreach efforts as essential to leverage the Democratic Congress, buttress the administration against its real and imagined political enemies, and provide a broad constituency on which to build his reelection campaign.

The communications office, business and labor liaison, and a more coordinated media operation worked in tandem with one another to build support for the president's legislative priorities, both domestic and foreign. This institutional structure, based in the White House, provided the president with a mechanism for "going public."[34] However, continuing public divisions over the Vietnam War and the events of Watergate prevented the Nixon administration from reaping the benefits of these outreach activities in the president's abbreviated second term.

Nonetheless, the foundation had been set. And the communications technology was available. The representational expansion of the Washington political community, with its proliferation of single-issue interest groups, weaker political parties, and partisan division between the White House and Congress for much of the period from 1968 to 2002, provided incentives for presidents to try to reach beyond Congress to influence it.

Ford and Carter, however, took limited forays into the public arena. Ford was deterred by Watergate, his pardon of Nixon, and his own unpolished speaking style. He went public when he had to do so: when he became president; when he pardoned Nixon; and when he campaigned for election in 1976. Similarly, Jimmy Carter never developed a strong public persona. His halting manner of speaking, desire to downplay the pomp and majesty of the office in the light of Johnson and Nixon's imperial presidency, and unease with Washington, especially the White House press corps, led him to deemphasize the public dimensions of his presidency as much as possible.

Both presidents also had difficulty leading Congress. Although these difficulties may have been exacerbated by their communication deficiencies and their low public approval, changes within the political and institutional environment also worked to inhibit their leadership. Congress had decentralized power; powerful single interests had organized, professionalized, and proliferated; parties had become weaker; and the press was more critical. All of these developments worked to inhibit presidential leadership of Congress.

Ford's problems were primarily due to partisan politics; in the aftermath of Watergate, the Democrats increased their congressional majorities and were looking forward to the 1976 election. They did not want to help a Republican get elected by virtue of his legislative successes.

Carter's failings were more personal: his refusal to play the game of politics, his unwillingness to lobby individual members of Congress, and his introduction of too many new programs six months into his presidency. These shortcomings, well publicized by the news media, forced the Carter administration to modify the ways it dealt with Congress. Not only did the coordination of key legislative lobbying become more centralized in the White House, but outreach activities were expanded. By 1978, the Carter White House had two additional liaison offices concerned directly or indirectly with Congress: the public liaison office, which linked and coordinated interest group activity for the president, and the intergovernmental affairs office, which had a similar mission for and with state and local governments. A political affairs office was added during the Reagan administration to help mobilize partisan support for the president.

Creating a Permanent Presidential Campaign

The people who advised Ronald Reagan understood the lessons of Ford and Carter's legislative experiences. Setting priorities, cycling issues, packaging proposals, and going both inside and outside simultaneously were seen as key to the president's policy successes. Moreover, Reagan needed to adopt a hands-on style for selling his policy, even though he had not utilized a hands-on approach for making it.

To achieve these objectives, the Reagan White House brought in skilled media managers to develop and implement a communications strategy.

Michael Deaver, deputy chief of staff, oversaw the operation and was the key aide for coordinating the public relations campaign with the administration's other legislative activities on major presidential priorities.

Using the president as the key salesman, the Reagan PR campaigns consisted of speeches, travels, and appearances before organized groups, all choreographed for television. The objective was to mount a dual campaign in pictures and words that the news networks would feel compelled to air. Much preparation and coordination characterized these campaigns. Here's how Kernell describes the components of the Reagan media-oriented operation:

> Polls were taken; speeches incorporating the resulting insights were drafted; the press was briefed, either directly or via leaks. Meanwhile in the field, the ultimate recipients of the president's message, members of Congress, were softened up by presidential travel into their states and districts and by grass-root lobbying campaigns, initiated and orchestrated by the White House but including the RNC [Republican National Committee] and sympathetic business organizations.[35]

Major speeches were timed to coincide with key votes. Prior to the speeches, the public liaison office working with outside groups such as the Business Roundtable would establish telephone banks that went into action the moment the speech ended. By generating a seemingly spontaneous and favorable public response and by doing so on a constituency-by-constituency basis, the White House was able to provide Democrats with political cover to support the president.

The Reagan model has set the tone for today's public, legislative presidency even though George H. W. Bush, Reagan's successor, was much less desirous of conducting a permanent PR campaign. Lacking Reagan's skills and confidence as a communicator and critical of his predecessor's scripted presidency, Bush downplayed the president's public role and sought to govern in the old bargaining environment of the pretelevision age. Although the president's numerous trips abroad, his diplomatic initiatives, his administration's responses to international humanitarian crises, and his use of force in Panama and the Persian Gulf commanded public attention and worked to his advantage, his inaction during the economic recession combined with the news media's continuing emphasis on the poor economic conditions led the public to reappraise his leadership negatively. With Democrats controlling both houses of Congress, conservatives angry with the administration's economic policies, the 1992 campaign underway with two candidates, Bill Clinton and Ross Perot, both criticizing Bush, and with the economy in recession, the White House was unable to mount a public campaign on the president's behalf. The die was cast. The public had lost confidence in the president.

The Carter Experience: It Is Harder to Play Offense
Than Defense with Congress

Clinton should have learned from the experiences of Ford, Carter, and Bush. At the beginning of his presidency, he claimed to be following Reagan's legislative strategy, but his fragile political mandate (he was elected with only 43 percent of the vote), his own inexperience, magnified by his White House's blunders, the administration's circumvention of the White House press corps, and the diverse and oft conflicting economic policy proposals that were made or leaked to the press indicated a presidency in chaos and a White House that lacked central coordination.

The president's first two legislative priorities suffered as a consequence. His economic stimulus bill was defeated by a Senate filibuster, and his deficit-reduction plan was significantly and publicly modified before it passed the Democratically controlled Congress by the narrowest of margins, two votes in the House and one vote in the Senate, that of the vice president, who broke the tie. Although the administration did have some legislative successes in its first year, the North American Free Trade Agreement (NAFTA) being the most noteworthy, most of the policy achievements resulted from Democratic congressional initiatives that the president supported, not the other way around.

Although Clinton managed to gain approval for NAFTA, he paid a heavy price for his arm-twisting and political trading. In order to secure sufficient Democratic support to ensure the bill's passage, Clinton and his legislative aides literally had to go door to door in the House, making promises to on-the-fence Democrats. In some cases, exemptions from the treaty for crops grown in their districts were made; in others, financial help was pledged for the next election cycle. The horse trading, accompanied by a public relations campaign, concluded with a 234-200 vote in favor of the agreement. In the end, 102 Democrats voted with the president despite opposition from many of their key constituents: organized labor, public interest, and environmental groups. But Clinton's legislative reputation was tarnished in the process, particularly among those who were associated with the liberal wing of his party. His attempt to placate this wing by holding fast to the major components of the administration's health care reform package contributed to the latter's defeat.

The second year of Clinton's legislative presidency, marred by the demise of health care reform and the subsequent Republican takeover of Congress, forced the administration to reinvent itself, the president to change his policy priorities and positions, and the White House to modify the way it did business with Congress. Instead of setting the congressional agenda, the president was forced to react to the Republicans' Contract with America. Instead of operating as head of government, the president was forced into the role of head of state, a role in which public relations are emphasized. Instead of continuing to focus on domestic policy, the president turned to foreign affairs. In making these adjustments, as painful as they were, Clinton and his aides finally figured out how to use the president's bully pulpit, presidential seal, and White House communications office to better advantage. What followed was a public relations extravaganza, as calculated and as orchestrated as Reagan's, but one that was very different.

Whereas the Reagan White House used its outreach and public relations to build support for the president's congressional initiatives, the Clinton White House used them to build support for the president's legislative vetoes. Whereas the Reagan White House emphasized the distinctiveness of the president's legislative goals, the need to reverse the course of government, the Clinton White House repositioned the president on Republican issues, claimed the middle ground for itself, and put the president in a position to take credit for legislative successes such as the balanced budget, welfare reform, and incremental health care policies while blaming the Republicans for its legislative failures.

The Reagan and Clinton models were similar in that both used foreign travel to enhance the president's image, particularly in light of the scandals that afflicted both presidents in their second term. Both PR campaigns showed an active and powerful president, thereby countering the allegations that they would be crippled as lame ducks with the opposition party controlling both houses of Congress. Clinton also took advantage of man-made and natural disasters to play the role of crisis manager and empathic leader, a people-oriented president. In short, both White Houses used the public relations presidency to offset their policy weaknesses and enhance presidential images. The public responded with high approval ratings.

The Legislative Presidency of George W. Bush: "It's Terrorism, Stupid"

George W. Bush followed the Reagan and Clinton models. Determined not to repeat his father's mistakes, one of which was to deemphasize public relations, the younger Bush made PR a top priority. Under the leadership of Karen Hughes, Dan Bartlett, and Karl Rove, the White House carefully coordinated policy initiatives with presidential events. The president traveled widely at the beginning of his first term, preaching the faith to whomever would listen.

Prior to the terrorist attacks of September 11, 2001, the White House reported seventy-one presidential statements and news releases and pictures from twenty-one photo ops on its Website. During this period, the president addressed sixty-two groups and gave twenty radio addresses. After 9/11, it was more of the same except the focus of the public presidency turned to national and homeland security. Of the 223 presidential statements and press releases, forty photo ops, and twelve radio addresses that occurred between September 11, 2001, and December 31, 2002, more than half dealt with terrorism at home or abroad. With domestic policies a lower priority, the president met with fewer outside groups than he did in the previous period.[36]

The public relations initiative continued through the president's first term, merging with the successful reelection campaign in 2004. The focus remained on terrorism and its threat to the United States. Policy toward Iraq was front and center beginning in the fall of 2002. In all, there were ninety-five speeches and statements on Iraq by the president, many to military groups, plus press conferences, radio addresses, and other presidential events. In contrast, only a few domestic concerns, such as Medicare and tort reform, made it onto the White House's PR calendar of events. For Bush, the issue was terrorism, pure and simple. Congress responded accordingly; it enacted the president's national security legislative agenda in the form and with the content he desired (see pp. 71–72).

The Permanent Campaign as an Instrument of the Legislative Presidency

The Clinton and George W. Bush administrations both indicate how the permanent campaign and public relations agenda have become inextricably interrelated. In 1995, a new team of political operatives joined with ongoing White House staff to recast Clinton as a plebiscitary president. With the pulse of the public measured by continuous polling, the administration repositioned itself within the political center and used its presidential podium to cast the congressional Republicans as extreme and mean-spirited and to stereotype their policy orientation as one that was designed to benefit the rich. Focus groups were used to capture emotionally laden words and phrases while presidential travels, meetings, and events highlighted the active, publicly oriented Clinton presidency.

Much of the White House–generated public activity was intended to benefit Clinton politically, to set the stage for his reelection, maintain his high approval ratings, and shield him from personal scandal. Occasionally, however, public campaigns were designed to help the president with legislative policy goals. Clinton had attributed the defeat of his health-care initiative, and later, fast-track authority, to the administration's failure to mount and maintain a successful public relations campaign for these issues, while in the case of health care, opponents of the Clinton plan, such as the Health Insurance Association of America, spent in excess of $13 million on advertising to defeat his plan. Obviously there were other factors that contributed to their defeat, but the president saw public relations as the key variable.[37] The lessons of these failures were not lost on the administration.

George W. Bush followed the Clinton strategy. On a political level, he raised money to deter a primary opponent, respond to Democratic criticism, and put himself into position to mount his reelection in the spring of 2004. On a policy level, he articulated his terrorism theme, defended his Iraqi policy, and took advantage of social issues on gay marriage, abortion, and religion to energize his Christian Coalition base. Throughout this public relations campaign, Bush and his communication advisers emphasized those character attributes that coincided with the public's image of strong presidential leadership: strength, courage, conviction, consistency, and vision based on moral values. For a person who entered office with an underwhelming leadership image, the president had come full circle.

Are administrations correct in believing that major public relations campaigns are part and parcel of today's legislative presidency? Can presidents actually change public opinion? Can they build support in the public arena that enhances their legislative influence and contributes to a successful policy outcome? Despite the findings of George Edwards and others that presidential influence in Congress is marginal at best, most contemporary White Houses see their public dimension as an essential component of presidential power, a key ingredient in exercising presidential leadership.[38]

Presidential public relations campaigns are important for several reasons:

1. They signify to Congress the high priority that the president attaches to an issue. Members of Congress cannot mistake it for just another vote or just another policy on which the president has taken a position.
2. They bring issues to the attention of more people than would otherwise be the case, thereby upping the ante for members of Congress.
3. They enable a president to use his bully pulpit to advantage, to set the agenda, define the issues, and even target appeals to groups that are likely to be more responsive to them. The other side is usually unable to argue as loudly and clearly because it lacks the reach and status of the president's pulpit.
4. In the area of foreign policy, the president maximizes his advantage by going public because it puts the burden of proof on those who would go against the president in an arena in which he is expected to lead.

The negative side of going public, however, is that compromise may be made more difficult, electoral calculations become more salient, and interest group participation may unleash forces that an administration cannot control, as was the case with Clinton's health care reform and George W. Bush's support of a national intelligence director.

Going public raises the stakes and makes defeat more politically, and perhaps psychologically, devastating. It also may impede compromise by solidifying positions, heightening rhetoric, personalizing issues, and increasing incivility, thereby making relations with members of Congress more difficult in the future. Nasty rhetoric can burn bridges that presidents may have to cross later on.

But it is easy, easier than engaging in hard bargaining. It is merely an extension of a successful election campaign. It accords with public expectations. It feeds the news media, often diverting their attention from less positive pictures and events. Presidents become actors; they read scripts; they speak to friendly groups and crowds, carefully selected by the White House, to provide a supportive environment and a sympathetic hearing. The event is choreographed for television; the president speaks behind the seal; the audience responds positively. Even if the president's remarks do not change public opinion, even if Congress is not moved to respond as the president desires, the president still gets a favorable sound bite, a good picture, and probably an inflated ego. The benefits outweigh the costs—at least that is what most White Houses believe.

NOTES

1. Alexander Hamilton, *Federalist* no. 73, in *The Federalist* (New York: Modern Library, 2001), 477.

2. Louis Fisher, *The Politics of Shared Power* (Washington, DC: Congressional Quarterly, 1993), 18, 29.

3. See Jeffrey K. Tulis, *The Rhetorical Presidency* (Princeton, NJ: Princeton University Press, 1987), 25–49.

4. Charles O. Jones in his book *The Presidency in a Separated System* (Washington, DC: Brookings Institution, 1994) draws the opposite conclusion: it is good news that the Constitution constrains the president's legislative leadership but bad news that the public, Congress, and the president do not understand, much less appreciate, a more constrained presidential role.

5. Woodrow Wilson, *Congressional Government* (New York: Meridan Books, 1885).

6. In *United States v. Curtiss Wright Corporation* (299 U.S. 304, 1936) the Supreme Court acknowledged the president as "sole organ of the federal government in the field of international relations" with constitutionally based "plenary and exclusive power" within the realm of foreign affairs.

7. In the first phase of the New Deal, Roosevelt submitted to Congress an emergency banking bill, the Truth in Security Act, the Agricultural Adjustment Act, the National Industrial Recovery Act, and the Federal Deposit Insurance Corporation Act, to name but some of his initiatives to deal with the exigencies of the Great Depression. In the second phase, from 1934 to 1936, Roosevelt got a Democratic Congress to enact the Wagner Act, the Social Security Act, and the Soil Conservation and Domestic Allotments Act, as well as the National Labor Relations Act. New bureaucracies were also created to implement this legislation and provide for ongoing regulatory activities.

8. It was during this period that the legislative clearance and enrolled bill processes were established by the Bureau of the Budget to coordinate and control the executive departments and agencies. See Stephen J. Wayne, *The Legislative Presidency* (New York: Harper & Row, 1978), 70–107.

9. Wayne, *Legislative Presidency*, 41–42.

10. The liaison office also began to service members' constituency needs, thereby necessitating an increase in size.

11. However, George C. Edwards III found that Johnson's legislative success on the whole (as measured by the percent of legislative support he received on all bills in which he took a public position) was not much greater than Carter's even though Carter was seen as a much less effective legislator by Congress, the press, and the public. As a consequence, Edwards contends that legislative skills are overrated as an instrument of presidential power. They do not have a systemic effect on increasing congressional support for the president, although he admits that in individual cases they may matter. See George C. Edwards III, *At the Margins* (New Haven, CT: Yale University Press, 1989), 176–89.

I contend that Edwards's methodological assumptions and his aggregate analysis of roll-call voting patterns force these conclusions. For a discussion of the limitation of this type of analysis of presidential influence in Congress, see the author's response in his book *The Legislative Presidency* (New York: Harper & Row, 1978), 168–72.

12. Speaker Tip O'Neill derisively referred to Jordan as Hamilton Jerkin and refused to have anything to do with him after a much publicized incident in which Jordan cavalierly refused to satisfy the Speaker's request for seats to inaugural activities.

13. Charles O. Jones, *The Trusteeship Presidency* (Baton Rouge: Louisiana State University Press, 1988), 114.

14. The description of the role of the chief of staff's office in legislative policy making is based in large part on interviews conducted by Martha Kumar for the Presidency Research Groups's Transition Project. Interviewees were promised that there would be no quotation with attribution unless and until they consented to allow their interviews to become part of the public record. Accordingly, I have identified only those officials who have provided that consent and did so at the time this chapter was written.

15. Interview, Presidency Research Group's Transition Project.

16. Interview, Presidency Research Group's Transition Project.

17. Interview, Presidency Research Group's Transition Project.

18. W. Henson Moore, interview, October 15, 1999.

19. David Gergen, *Eyewitness to Power* (New York: Simon & Schuster, 2000), 278.

20. Gergen, *Eyewitness to Power*, 297.

21. Although an amended deficit-reduction bill was finally enacted, the cost, measured in terms of the president's relations with Congress, was very high. House Democrats,

forced to vote in favor of a BTU tax, were livid when the administration backed off it in the Senate. Democratic divisions in the Senate, heightened by the deficit-reduction negotiations and debate, exploded into full public view. Clinton's relationships with Senator Boren, Kerrey, Moynihan, and Shelby turned into personal animosities that lasted well through the administration.

22. Leon Panetta, interview, May 4, 2000, Presidency Research Group's Transition Project.

23. Panetta, interview. Panetta added, "Anytime I was dealing with something on Capitol Hill, I would normally call that person (the president's assistant for legislative affairs) into my office so that they would know what I was doing and were supportive of it."

24. Panetta, interview.

25. Panetta, interview.

26. Dana Milbank, "Two Mothers Helped Move Mountain on Post-9/11 Bill," *Washington Post*, December 9, 2004, A1, A4.

27. Walter Pincus, "Intelligence Bill Clears Congress," *Washington Post*, December 9, 2004, A4, A5.

28. Lyndon Johnson, *The Vantage Point: Perspectives of the Presidency, 1963–1969* (New York: Popular Library, 1971), 443.

29. Richard M. Nixon, *In the Arena: A Memoir of Victory, Defeat, and Renewal* (New York: Simon & Schuster, 1990), 282.

30. Richard E. Neustadt, *Presidential Power and the Modern Presidents* (New York: Free Press, 1990), 29–49.

31. For an extended discussion of the ongoing public phenomenon, see Samuel Kernell, *Going Public*, 3rd ed. (Washington, DC: Congressional Quarterly, 1997).

32. George C. Edwards III, *At the Margins* (New Haven, CT: Yale University Press, 1989), 113.

33. George C. Edwards III, *On Deaf Ears* (New Haven, CT: Yale University Press, 2003), 74.

34. Kernell, *Going Public*, 57.

35. Kernell, *Going Public*, 169–70.

36. White House archives, www.whitehouse.gov.

37. Health care reform lost in part because the administration did not mount a coordinated effort. A separate health care group, which did not include most of the president's principal West Wing aides, managed the bill and oversaw the public relations campaign. Although President Clinton delivered a major address on health care before Congress in September 1993, the actual legislation did not arrive until almost one month later. The bill, large and complex, made it difficult to sell but easy to attack. Meanwhile, as the president's focus was diverted by foreign policy matters, Mrs. Clinton became the public advocate and major critic of those industries that opposed the bill. Her involvement, her advocacy, and her criticism made compromise difficult. No single person coordinated the administration's campaign as the opposition to the plan mounted, the Harry and Louise ads were aired, and Congress was increasingly divided over various health care proposals. With the opponents of the plan spending heavily to defeat it, with the administration unable to organize a counterattack, with the 1994 election approaching and the Republicans seeing the demise of health care as the road to their electoral success, the proposal died on the floor of Congress and, with it, Democratic control of both houses.

The fast-track problem was also magnified by the absence of a public relations campaign amid the bitter politics of the Monica Lewinsky affair. The administration claimed that it was surprised by events that brought the legislation to the floor of the Senate earlier than expected. Without the time to mount a full-scale public relations campaign, the president was forced to lobby for the bill, mostly behind closed doors. Because he had forced many reluctant Democrats to vote for NAFTA against their own best political judgment, Clinton let it be known that he would not do so for fast track. This concession weakened his position; he could not gain sufficient votes by simply making deals. Besides, the publicizing of such deals by those who benefited from them made the president look like he was buying votes, an undesirable public perception.

38. See also George C. Edwards III and Andrew Barrett, "Presidential Agenda Setting in Congress," in *Polarized Politics*, ed. Jon R. Bond and Richard Fleisher (Washington, DC: Congressional Quarterly, 2000), 109–33; Barbara Sinclair, "Hostile Partners: The President, Congress, and Lawmaking in the Partisan 1990s," in Bond and Fleisher, *Polarized Politics*, 134–53.

4

The Impact of Campaigns on Presidential-Congressional Relations

Richard E. Cohen

President Bush didn't take long to draw the connection between his reelection and his agenda for the next four years. "Let me put it to you this way: I earned capital in the campaign, political capital, and now I intend to spend it," Bush responded when asked about his second-term plans during a White House press conference less than twenty-four hours after John Kerry's concession speech. "I'm going to spend it for what I told the people I'd spend it on, which is—you've heard the agenda: Social Security and tax reform, moving this economy forward, education, fighting and winning the war on terror."

Although the president had provided few specifics of his domestic policy proposals during the campaign, his general goals were not surprising to those who had been listening closely. What was more striking, however, was his bold approach. In the past half century, second-term presidents typically have conveyed a sense of continuity, not major new initiatives. But several factors—ranging from his personal style to the election results—have created an unusual sequencing in Bush's presidential agenda setting. His larger electoral majority plus unprecedented gains by House and Senate Republicans in the 2004 election—on top of their similar, albeit narrow, increases in the midterm election two years earlier—have given Bush an opportunity for two fresh starts following his razor-thin Electoral College victory in 2000. With the additional political turmoil that followed the September 2001 terror attacks on New York and the Pentagon, plus Bush's subsequent military campaigns to overthrow the regimes in Afghanistan and Iraq, he seemingly has turned political dynamics upside down by seeking to exploit his increasing political capital the longer he has been in the White House.

Presidential exercise of power is closely monitored on Capitol Hill, of course. Elections and governing naturally are related in a democracy. In recent decades, however, how our presidents attempt to shape policy once they are in office has become more distant from the skills and rhetoric necessary for presidents to win office. Various factors have been responsible for this dissonance: Campaigns have become theatrical exercises that are less relevant to the affairs of state. Plus, legislating has become so much more complex that even the most skillful politicians have encountered more obstacles to success. More to the point, some recent presidential campaigns appear to have lost sight of the fact that elections—and the mandates that may result—have consequences for what follows in the political system.

For most of the past century, a major element for judging presidents' success after they have been elected has been their ability to work with Congress and achieve policy changes. And yet, students of this relationship—including scholars, journalists, and other observers of Washington's sausage making—have typically paid scant attention to the connection between how presidents win office and how they fare legislatively. But a review of the link between presidential candidates since 1960 and their subsequent accomplishments reveals clear predictors of the electoral victors' legislative prospects.

Some conclusions are intuitively logical:

1. The more comprehensive and specific the candidate's agenda with the voters, the stronger his position in dealing with Congress following the election.
2. The greater the winning candidate's electoral mandate from the voters, the more likely that he scores significant legislative achievements.
3. The more closely the eventual president has worked with congressional allies during his campaign, the more likely that he secures a positive relationship to work with them in office.

In short, inclusive candidates and big election winners become inclusive presidents and skillful legislators in office.

Compared to some of his recent predecessors, George W. Bush has not had the benefit of overwhelming victories. His narrow 51%-48% win in the November 2004 popular vote, plus an Electoral College outcome that would have been reversed if John Kerry had taken Ohio or Florida, was balanced by Bush's strong showing in the nation's heartland and his contribution to the more impressive congressional Republican gains. But his aggressive moves following these mixed results revealed that he and his advisers were acutely aware of their strategic opportunities plus the challenges and limitations that they faced.

There are additional factors, of course, that determine the course that presidents have pursued, plus their success. With presidential candidates of both parties increasingly running as outsiders who win office by distancing themselves from Washington and its political establishment, some have found it more difficult to effectively exercise the perquisites of their office. For that matter, some presidential candidates succeed in their campaigns without devoting much attention to a legislative agenda, or they decide to focus on foreign policy after taking office. In such cases, not surprisingly, their dealings with Congress inevitably have become more limited than would otherwise be the case.

As the first Republican president in the modern political era who has been bolstered by his party's control of both the House and Senate at the start of his second term, Bush sought to take advantage of an unfamiliar governing model. "Recent second terms have been dominated by impeachment [of presidents Nixon and Clinton] and the Iran-contra problems [of Reagan]," Lee Rawls, the chief of staff to Senate Majority Leader Bill Frist, told a postelection seminar sponsored by the Woodrow Wilson International Center for Scholars in Washington. "The contrast is that in all those cases there was not a unified government. . . . The minority party had attack machinery available." Republicans undoubtedly welcomed and planned to exploit that significant contrast. In addition, Bush's leadership style has been designed to maximize partisan advantage. "Bush is in a sense the fruition of Reagan," Bill Keller of the *New York Times* wrote during his first term. "He has adapted Reagan's ideas to new times, and found some language in which to market them."[1]

Bush's two elections plus the two prior campaign victories by Bill Clinton were reminders that it's the exception, rather than the rule, for sweeping legislative mandates to emerge from an election. As this chapter describes, only two campaigns since 1960 have yielded a clarion call for action. In each of those cases, the president took advantage of that opportunity in Congress and scored major legislative triumphs that had lasting national impact. Significantly, however, the period of those Capitol Hill successes was of limited duration. In less than a year, the White House and Congress returned to slogging as usual.

With a Republican president in the best position to deliver results from Congress in more than seventy-five years as Bush began his second term, both friends and foes were aware that the public typically holds a party accountable in such a situation. Whether or not Republicans were prepared to follow Bush's leadership, they may have few excuses for inaction. "There's accountability and there are constraints on the presidency, as there should be in any system," Bush pointedly said in his postelection press conference. But he added, "The people made it clear what they wanted, now let's work together."

MEASURING A CANDIDATE'S LEGISLATIVE AGENDA

The two presidents who achieved short-term mastery in moving their agenda through Congress were Lyndon B. Johnson in 1965 and Ronald Reagan in 1981. To be sure, there were marked differences between them. One was a liberal Democrat and a proven Capitol Hill wheeler-dealer; the other, a conservative Republican and a self-styled political outsider. Johnson was working with huge Democratic majorities in both the House and Senate—slightly more than two-thirds control in each case, the largest majorities since Franklin Roosevelt's New Deal. Reagan, on the other hand, had only a narrow Republican majority in the Senate, and he had to work with a House that was nominally under Democratic control. But the similarities in the election campaigns of those two successful presidents were far more important to their legislative prospects.

First, each defined clear-cut objectives for his presidency. Johnson ran in 1964 with promises of the "Great Society," an unprecedented expansion of federal programs to assist the public during good economic times. For the poor, he offered urban renewal and expanded federal housing. For racial minorities, he promised to build on the 1964 Civil Rights Act with what became the Voting Rights Act, which guarantees every citizen's political franchise. For the broad middle class, the goals were federal aid to education and medical care for the aged—which ultimately became the centerpiece of Johnson's legacy. Reagan's promises in the 1980 campaign were very different but equally comprehensive. Chief among them was an across-the-board tax cut of 10 percent for each of the next three years. But he also made less specific promises to scale back the federal role in daily lives, both through less government spending and through less regulation.

Second, in each case, members of the president's party on Capitol Hill had defined and promoted the ideas extensively for years. What became the Medicare program had been the topic of liberal Democrats' promises for many years and of unsuccessful legislative efforts under President John F. Kennedy. Prior to the 1964 election, however, Democrats lacked the congressional votes to achieve their goal. Reagan's tax cut originally was known as "Kemp-Roth." Representative Jack Kemp of New York and Senator William Roth of Delaware, its two hard-charging proponents, had convinced many initially reluctant Republicans to sign on during the late 1970s; but with Democrats holding firm House and Senate majorities at the time, the tax plan had no chance of passage before the 1980 election, even with the preponderance of Republican support.

Third, both Johnson and Reagan in those campaigns scored huge electoral victories, which transcended their own contests. LBJ won 61 percent of the popular vote against Barry Goldwater and carried 486 electoral votes, losing only five states in the Deep South and Goldwater's home of Arizona. In 1980, Reagan won 51 percent of the popular vote against President Jimmy Carter, who won 41 percent, and independent John Anderson, with 7 percent; Reagan won 489 electoral votes and all but six states scattered across the nation. Equally significantly, Democrats in 1964 gained thirty-six House seats and two Senate seats—giving Johnson firm control on Capitol Hill; Republicans in 1980 won thirty-three House seats and twelve Senate seats— yielding their first Senate majority in twenty-six years—and left many conservative Democrats reluctant to buck Reagan's legislative initiatives. In each case, members of the president's party overwhelmingly fell in line behind his agenda.

Other presidential candidates have prevailed in a variety of different circumstances. In some cases, the victories were personal mandates, rather than calls for a sweeping policy agenda or a clearly partisan mandate. In 1960, for example, John F. Kennedy promised a "New Frontier." But his victory, though an important political turning point, was largely a matter of style. He wanted to inject renewed vigor in Washington more than he sought to propose an endless string of new programs. As was the case with other presidents during that era, he and the nation also became consumed by Cold War conflicts around the world, leaving less time for domestic issues. Jimmy Carter succeeded in his 1976 campaign on his promise to restore integrity in government in the wake of President Richard Nixon's 1974 resignation amid the Watergate scandal. Carter, who had little background in Washington, defeated several senior congressional Democrats to win the presidential nomination. Even though Democrats retained large House and Senate majorities following his election, and the "conservative coalition" had all but disappeared from Congress, they struggled with Carter throughout his presidency.

Other presidents have won election on nonlegislative issues. Nixon's 1968 victory was based largely on his unspecified pledges to end the Vietnam War, which had badly divided the nation. With Democrats retaining firm control of Congress, Nixon did not offer a campaign agenda to make significant changes in Johnson's recently enacted domestic program. Winning only 43 percent of the vote in the three-way contest with Democrat Hubert Humphrey and George Wallace, Nixon was not positioned for major legislative initiatives.

As for Nixon's 1972 reelection, in which he swept forty-nine states, that too was largely a personal triumph, which was not accompanied by a broad party manifesto or by significant changes in the Democrats' congressional majority. (Plus, Nixon would soon become entangled in the Watergate scandal.) Likewise, when Reagan won reelection with forty-nine states in 1984, his campaign theme was a nonpartisan evocation of "Morning in America"; as it turned out, his chief legislative initiative in his second term was tax reform, which had a bipartisan genealogy. In their landslide reelections, neither Nixon nor Reagan emphasized his cooperation during the prior four years with congressional Republicans, nor extended himself to ensure their election success. In both 1972 and 1984, ironically, Republicans won about a dozen House seats and actually lost two Senate seats.

The 1988 and 1992 elections meshed the policy and personal approaches. Neither produced a resounding political victory. In the former, Vice President George Bush carefully sought to distance himself from Reagan without disavowing his leadership and broad goals of the previous eight years ("Read my lips, no new taxes!"). Bush used both policy proposals (environment and education, for example) and personal style ("kinder and gentler") to draw those contrasts. His approach, which implicitly acknowledged the likelihood that Democrats would retain their House and Senate majorities, gave him a less than overwhelming 53 percent of the popular vote. In challenging Bush four years later, Bill Clinton used stylistic points ("the man from Hope," with a focus on "the economy, stupid") to underline how he would offer more vigorous policies than the incumbent. But neither Clinton nor congressional Democrats during the campaign were specific on their budget or health care proposals, which eventually brought major political headaches for both him and the party. The winners in the 1988 and 1992 elections received sizable Electoral College majorities, but that factor subsequently proved insignificant, especially with the modest congressional changes in each case.

Clinton's 1992 campaign had some similarities to Carter's in 1976: the southern governor running as a political outsider to defeat a Republican president while keeping his distance from the Democrat-controlled Congress. In contrast to Carter, Clinton had more interest and background in federal policy debates. But his victory was hampered by the fact that he won only 43 percent of the vote in the three-way race that included independent Ross Perot; and Clinton entered office with notably fewer congressional Democrats (258 in the House, 57 in the Senate) than Carter had when he took office (292 in the House, 62 in the Senate).

In his 1996 reelection, Clinton's success was substantially based on his skill in running *against* the Republican-controlled Congress that had been led by his campaign opponent, former Senate Majority Leader Robert Dole and by still controversial House Speaker Newt Gingrich. Running as a "New Democrat," whose support of welfare reform and a balanced budget was not enthusiastically embraced throughout his party and created what was termed "triangulation," Clinton's victory was more personal than partisan. Despite a major effort, Democrats failed in their goal of regaining House control.

When George W. Bush won his first term, he set a relatively limited agenda for Congress, and he was mostly successful in achieving it. His campaign's two chief legislative priorities were cuts in individual income tax rates plus reform of federal aid for elementary and secondary education, which Republicans termed the "No Child Left Behind Act." The limited policy discussion during the 2000 campaign reflected that the nation and its elected representatives lacked agreement on a compelling set of new national priorities and appeared content to maintain the status quo. In contrast to some previous elections, in which there was an obvious demand for either an increase in federal programs or a decrease in spending and taxes, the relative "peace and prosperity" at the start of the twenty-first century produced an election without a call for obvious new policy directions. Although Bush discussed during the campaign the need for Medicare and Social Security reform, he ultimately deferred legislative action on those issues for two and four years, respectively. So, too, neither Democrats nor Republicans in Congress had prepared a broad set of initiatives for their party's candidate to embrace. Those factors added to the limited political mandate that appeared to flow from the 2000 election, even apart from the extraordinarily narrow outcome of both the Bush-Gore contest and the battles for House and Senate control.

This brief history of the eleven presidential campaigns from 1960 to 2000 demonstrates the significance for governance of how the candidates posture themselves as the nation's prospective chief policy advocates and legislative agenda setters, both before and after an election. Indeed, even though many presidential campaigns have been thin in their discussion of policy, they have provided the chief focal point for a broad discussion of issues. (When they subsequently seek to take legislative action on controversial proposals that were not discussed, or even were rejected, during their campaigns, presidents usually are inviting trouble; Carter's calls to limit energy consumption, Reagan's 1981 proposal to revise Social Security benefits, Bush's approval of the 1990 tax increase in contravention of his "no new taxes" campaign pledge, plus Clinton's complex 1993 health care reform plan are examples.) Although presidents must recognize limits in how much they can affect the actual drafting of legislation, as will be discussed in the following section, they have gained a unique role in determining what topics will be the focus of national debate and action. That role has evolved significantly since the Founding Fathers drafted the Constitution and envisioned the president mainly as the chief executive.

In addition, it has become clear during the past century that only the president has the political standing and leadership authority in our representative democracy to define the national agenda and advocate it from his bully pulpit. Notwithstanding Gingrich's limited success in supplanting Clinton in setting the policy agenda following the 1994 election, in which House Republicans made their Contract with America the national political focus, the ensuing two years demonstrated that the president's veto power and his ability to command the executive branch with a single voice gave him huge advantages in dealing with a Congress led by the opposite party. Even strong Democratic congressional leaders who have been in the majority, such as House Speaker Jim Wright plus Senate Majority Leader George Mitchell (and Tom Daschle's brief tenure as majority leader), were mostly reactive in seeking to urge—or thwart—presidential initiatives. And as the tenures of Speaker J. Dennis Hastert and Senate Majority Leader Bill Frist have shown, legislative leaders acting on behalf of a president whose party controls Congress typically, and most usefully, play a subservient role on behalf of the president's agenda.

A notable feature of this review has been the limited campaign agenda of presidents seeking reelection. In her review of the contrasts between the first- and second-term bids of both Reagan and Clinton, government and politics professor Colleen Shogan of George Mason University concluded that "neither pushed forward [in his reelection campaign] a policy agenda that aggressively pursued innovative ideas or concepts."[2] With each entering his second term as a "lame duck" under the Twenty-second Amendment to the Constitution, Shogan concluded, those cases demonstrated that "power dissipates over time, and opportunities for legislative reform diminish." Likewise, New York University public service professor Paul C. Light wrote a month before the 2004 election, "Second terms generally produce fewer proposals, especially following closer elections, which suggest that the nation may have seen the high point of the Bush domestic agenda already."[3] Neither scholar appeared to give much credence to the prospect of a Bush-style rejuvenated second term.

A PRESIDENT'S FIRST-YEAR
DEALINGS WITH CONGRESS

When a president emerges from an election with a clear mandate from the voters and has shown agreement with a substantial number of congressional lawmakers on key issues, those logically are the ideal circumstances for seeking speedy legislative action. Although success is not guaranteed, such a step gives strong momentum to a presidency. Although the significance of political honeymoons probably has been overblown in any case, it's also true that delay hardly strengthens a president's hand with Congress.

In the initial weeks and months following a convincing victory, a new president typically will meet with his party's congressional leaders—both during the transition period and soon after the inauguration—and will agree on a clear set of objectives, usually in a limited number of areas. Then, they move to achieve those goals; this period was once known as the "first hundred days" but more recently has become a six-month legislative blitz leading to the August recess. After that period, business as usual typically begins to settle in, especially among House members, who become less receptive to presidential entreaties as they prepare for the midterm election.

The most successful practitioners of the intensive early start, not surprisingly, were Johnson and Reagan, with their sweeping campaign agendas and convincing electoral mandates. Despite their contrasting styles, each showed the political wisdom of moving quickly after his election to implement his campaign agenda.

Johnson proposed a laundry list of social and economic development legislation and remained personally engaged in keeping the pressure on his Democratic allies—both his longtime colleagues from the House and Senate and the many freshmen elected on his coattails. For most of 1965, Congress moved at a relentless pace as he virtually dictated the terms of his legislation. With a House majority of 295-140 and Senate control of 68-32, plus some support from moderate Republicans for his programs, the president could not be stopped. "Members of Congress were like mere stage props for LBJ's initiatives, making few changes before returning the finished bills to the president for his signature."[4] The intense pace continued through the October end of the legislative session. But 1966 proved to be a different story as Republicans became more aggressive in counterattacking and Democrats grew concerned about reelection.

In 1981, with Democrats holding a 243–192 majority and still chairing House committees, Reagan and his team were forced to adopt a more indirect route to secure passage of their program. With weaker leverage over day-to-day operations, they essentially circumvented the House Rules Committee—which is typically the House's scheduler and traffic cop—and instead concentrated their efforts on a handful of bills, which they prepared outside the committee process. They were immeasurably aided by the procedures in the 1974 Congressional Budget Act. First, they defined the outlines of their tax and spending goals in the annual budget resolution; then they used the budget "reconciliation" process to achieve their specific objectives for tax cuts (which were reduced slightly to 25 percent over three years) and changes in entitlement programs. In each case, Republican control of the Senate— where their majority of 53–47 was firm—became a useful management device, especially given the occasionally slapdash quality of the legislative drafting by Reagan's House allies. Assisted by occasional timely presidential speeches and private persuasion, Reagan achieved by the August recess the principal legislative goals that defined his presidency. As was the case for Johnson, Reagan's second year was far less active legislatively as his allies grew concerned about the coming election.

In each case, the presidential team's electoral fears proved warranted. House Democrats in 1966 suffered a forty-six-seat loss, with thirty-nine members losing their seats, and many conservative Democrats returned to their more comfortable alliance with resurgent House Republicans. In 1982, Democrats picked up twenty-six seats and regained effective control of the House; in the Senate, Republicans retained their majority until their large freshman class faced the voters in 1986, but the party's loss of the House also reduced the previously iron-clad discipline in the Senate.

Despite their relatively brief legislative dominance and subsequent electoral setbacks, the Johnson and Reagan whirlwinds left major marks on the nation. Most of the Great Society expansion of the federal government withstood not only Nixon but also the conservative victories led by Reagan and Gingrich, none of whom seriously challenged the core of civil rights and Medicare protections. True, some of the "poverty program" did not survive; but, collectively, federal support for low-income groups has grown sizably in other, probably more effective programs and benefits. As for Reagan's tax cuts, opponents sought to reverse them and later criticized their role in creating huge federal deficits during the following decade. But they remained in place. Whether or not there is a link is for others to determine, but it's a fact that the nation experienced only one brief and modest recession during the seventeen years after Reagan's economic program fully took effect.

Other presidents—notably Carter and Clinton—have sought quick legislative starts with Congress, especially when their party was in control. Because they lacked an electoral mandate, however, their results were less impressive. Carter entered office with nearly as many congressional Democrats as did Johnson, but he was poorly positioned to take advantage of the opportunity. He did not have a well-defined agenda, he had few dependable legislative allies, and he had little experience in dealing with Congress. From the start, the Carter team's legislative efforts proved disastrous. They offended the newly elected House Speaker, Thomas P. O'Neill Jr., on matters as mundane as distribution of inauguration tickets. Carter's early economic-stimulus proposal of a $50 rebate for all taxpayers became a laughingstock.

In extended battles on various issues, he ended with a mixed scorecard on economy, energy, and health care proposals, with congressional Democrats frequently fighting each other as well as the White House. Carter's government-reform proposals, such as the independent-counsel statute and tighter financial disclosure rules for federal employees, gained broader legislative support, but their lasting impact was more dubious.

Clinton, too, sought a quick legislative start. With few close allies, he found himself beset with problems within his own party on Capitol Hill. In his early weeks in office, he backed down on a proposal to permit gays in the military, his first two nominees for attorney general were forced to withdraw after they ran into confirmation problems, and his economic-stimulus plan to send dollars to chiefly Democratic constituencies bogged down and eventually became the victim in the Senate of a Republican filibuster and objections by moderate Democrats. But his biggest setback came on his health care reform proposal, which was planned as the centerpiece of his legislative agenda. Lacking a specific proposal from his campaign or from congressional Democrats, Clinton and his White House staff—led by First Lady Hillary Rodham Clinton—spent most of 1993 in an elaborate process to produce a complex proposal that few understood, which was designed to give federal guarantees of medical coverage to all Americans. By the time that House and Senate committees began to work on the proposal, Republican and industry opposition was deep-seated and Democrats were divided on their best legislative approach. With the bill bogged down in the House and Senate amid the election campaign and with no agreement for votes in either chamber, the exercise became a legislative debacle. The chief political result was that Democrats lost the majority in both chambers in the 1994 election and never regained control during Clinton's presidency.

In other cases, presidents have moved cautiously, either because they faced a divided government in which they faced a hostile political environment with the other party controlling Congress or because their own forces held a weak hand. When Kennedy took office in 1961, for example, his limited legislative goals were an acknowledgment of the reality on Capitol Hill. With Republicans having gained twenty-two House seats in the 1960 election, Kennedy was forced to do battle during his presidency with what was termed the "conservative coalition" of Republicans and southern Democrats, especially in the House. Although he was a product of Congress, Kennedy clearly distanced himself from the conservative Democratic chairmen in control of most committees; they largely represented an earlier political generation that was out of sync with the president's New Frontier. And, unlike Johnson, Kennedy had little interest or skill in working the legislative machinery to advance his program.

Nixon's 1968 victory had little to do with domestic policies, and he was reluctant to disrupt Johnson's Great Society achievements. Nixon's presidency witnessed the activist Democratic-controlled Congress's significant expansion of domestic spending and regulation. Nixon's chief initiatives dealt with his politically popular attention to "law and order" issues. That resulted in several major pieces of legislation and, perhaps more importantly, led to major showdowns with the Senate on Supreme Court nominees, two of whom were defeated.

After his 1988 election, Bush was duly warned of the dilemma he faced with Congress when the Democratic-controlled Senate rejected his nomination of John Tower for defense secretary. In addition, the House was consumed that spring by an ethics investigation of Speaker Jim Wright, which was spurred by Republican backbencher Newt Gingrich and led to Wright's resignation under fire in June 1989. The Bush team moved deliberately to prepare and advocate a legislative agenda, with emphasis placed on a capital-gains tax cut and clean-air amendments. Unexpectedly, Congress spent much of the year consumed by what became a successful bipartisan move to repeal a 1988 law to provide catastrophic-insurance coverage to Medicare beneficiaries. Not until 1990 did Bush and Congress begin to seriously engage, chiefly in a budget summit that lasted for months and ultimately led the president to his politically fateful decision to abandon his "no new taxes" pledge.

The political shoes were reversed following the 1996 election when Clinton won a second term but faced a continuation of the Republican-controlled Congress. Once again, ethics conflicts poisoned the climate. The House began the new year with a virtually unanimous vote to reprimand Speaker Gingrich for improprieties in his personal finances. Then, in January 1998, reports of Clinton's dealings with Monica Lewinsky led to an independent-counsel investigation and ultimately to House impeachment, shutting down most serious legislative work for that year. Between those two events, Clinton and the Republican-controlled Congress reached agreement in 1997 on the Balanced Budget Act, which was designed to achieve its goal in 2002. But that deal was chiefly a political cessation of the budget war that dominated the previous two years; in economic terms, it was little more than a ratification of the booming economy, which actually placed the federal budget into surplus in 1998, four years ahead of the once optimistic schedule. In any case, this divided government became a synonym for paralysis.

George W. Bush's approach to Congress had both substantive and stylistic features. Seeking to break Washington's gridlock, he repeatedly said that he was "a uniter, not a divider" and that he wanted to "change the tone" in Washington. He cited his success, as governor, in working across the aisle with the Texas legislature. Notwithstanding his narrow victory, Bush demonstrated bold self-confidence as though he had a strong electoral mandate as he took office. His dealings with Congress during his first year as president were complicated because, in effect, there were three distinct phases. With a quick start, Bush won enactment in 2001 of his two chief domestic priorities: tax cuts and education reform. But his limited honeymoon was abruptly concluded in late May by the surprise decision of Senator Jim Jeffords of Vermont to abandon the Republican Party and join the Democrats (though he technically called himself an independent). That switched Senate control to the Democrats, and the new majority leader, Tom Daschle, moved quickly to place his own imprint on the Senate agenda. But the Daschle interregnum, too, proved to be a brief phase, as the September 11 attacks forced an upheaval of Washington's agenda and operations. Bush moved firmly in control, but with an intensified focus on national security policies, and the immediate economic and homeland ramifications of the terror attacks.

As for the Nixon and Reagan overwhelming reelections, the fact that they scored the biggest margins of any presidential candidates during the past forty years had minimal residual impact and offered the winners little political cover on Capitol Hill. Within months, Nixon was deeply enmeshed in investigations of the Watergate scandal involving the cover-up of a burglary of Democratic headquarters. Two years after Reagan's landslide, Congress launched its extended investigation of the Iran-contra affair concerning the administration's allegedly illegal transfer of funds to rebel forces in Nicaragua. In each case, some members of the president's own party were among his most severe critics.

Would it have mattered if each president had campaigned more actively on behalf of candidates from his own party? Perhaps. But there were two larger factors: (1) the limited congressional Republican gains in 1972 and 1984 meant that there was little political loyalty in his own party for a president who, not coincidentally, became a lame duck on the next day; and (2) with Democrats retaining control of the House in each election (plus the Senate in 1972), the congressional majority felt liberated to respond to the president on their own terms—sometimes with cooperation, often with confrontation.

As this chronology reveals, election results create a climate of expectations in Congress. Successful and cooperative candidates breed successful and cooperative legislating. While it's not quite that simple, of course, most members of Congress are shrewd politicians who are ever mindful of the shifting political winds. Except for those on the ideological extremes, they would rather not have to explain to constituents why they have cast votes against the program of a popular president. Achieving that state of equilibrium is an appropriate presidential goal, though that's easier said than done.

BUSH'S CAMPAIGNS

From his initial quest for the presidency, George W. Bush and his election team appeared to be well aware of and responsive to these political dynamics. In each of his campaigns, he laid out a consistent and well-defined agenda, with a limited set of goals. Bush showed a commitment to his agenda and confidence that he could achieve it. At the center of this approach was his view that the goals were popular with the public and that Congress was eager to break the legislative logjam of the Clinton years and address these national priorities.

Maintaining Republican unity was essential to his legislative success. "Mr. Bush is the GOP nominee largely because of his agenda," *Wall Street Journal* columnist Paul A. Gigot wrote during the 2000 campaign. "Mr. Bush is the Republican who wanted to cut taxes and who realized his party had to compete on education, Social Security and health care."[5] And, with the benefit of experience and a new mandate, that discipline intensified following the 2004 campaign. "GOP actions set the stage for an efficient legislative operation to process Bush administration objectives through Congress and then on to the White House for Bush's signature," the *Boston Globe* reported shortly after his reelection. "Bush also benefits from an unusually friendly Congress, where Republicans will have expanded, comfortable majorities next year. While previous Congresses have served as political counterweights to the White House, the current Congress rarely challenges the administration, Democratic legislators say."[6]

Skeptics warned that he was trying to accomplish more than his election success warranted. Indeed, each of his narrow election wins had obvious limitations. In contrast to the 1964 and 1980 presidential elections, few if any lawmakers felt that they owed their local success to Bush or his coattails. Aside from his education reform in 2001, most Democratic members of Congress opposed the key elements of his domestic agenda: tax cuts plus changes in federal entitlement programs. Another potential limitation was that although Bush regularly discussed his broad themes and priorities in his campaign speeches, he did not divulge specific details. Consequently, his campaigns did not appear to evoke a strong mandate for action.

But there were two overriding factors in Bush's elections, which carried over to his legislative agenda. First, members of his party were grateful that he had helped them to maintain and build their congressional majorities.

The numbers were compelling. The 2004 election resulted in 232 Republicans in the House and fifty-five in the Senate, increases of eleven in the House and five in the Senate since the 2000 election. The totals were the largest to accompany a Republican president since the 1920s. Those results, in turn, helped to explain why his chief policy proposals had enthusiastic and broad support within his party. Even when some lawmakers privately had misgivings about some of the policy details or the potential political risk, most Republicans ultimately followed Bush's leadership; that was shown dramatically by the three-hour House vote in November 2003 for final approval of Medicare reform and prescription drug coverage for seniors. In part, they recalled the disastrous electoral consequences that congressional Democrats suffered when they balked at the agendas of Carter and Clinton.

Of Bush's proposals, his Social Security initiative probably has had the potential for the greatest public impact, though it carried significant political risks. Presidents and candidates generally have kept their distance from the issue, which has been termed the "third rail" in American politics because politicians who touch it pay a big price. But generational pressures to fix the long-term financing shortfalls in the retirement system, plus many younger Americans' desire for greater control of their investments, led Bush to embrace proposals that permit individuals to allocate some of their Social Security funds to personal retirement accounts. Although he discussed his goals in broad terms during the 2000 campaign, he waited until his second term before proceeding. "The Social Security system is safe today, but is in serious danger as we head down the road of the twenty-first century. And this problem has got to be confronted now," he told a White House conference in December 2004. While assuring the elderly that "nothing will change if you're retired or near retirement," he added, "I do believe younger workers ought to be allowed to take some of their own money, some of their own payroll taxes, and on a voluntary basis, set up a personal savings account."

It remained to be seen whether Bush and congressional Republicans could maintain their solidarity and rally behind a specific legislative plan. No doubt, there would be challenges. Even before he was sworn in for a second term, the brief postelection lame-duck session in late 2004 revealed the formidable managerial obstacles that lay ahead. That became most evident when Republicans in the House temporarily rebelled against a carefully crafted package of reforms in the nation's intelligence agencies, including the creation of a national intelligence director who had oversight of Pentagon operations. Although the legislative deal had been blessed by President Bush, Speaker Hastert, and others close to them, many conservatives initially found it too much to swallow. It took another two weeks of private discussions and some modest tinkering with words before a solid majority of House Republicans agreed to go along.

Even in the most positive political circumstances, legislative success requires skill, timing, and some luck. As Republicans prepared for Bush's second term, all sorts of potential stumbling blocks lay before them, including the prospect of bitter battles to fill one or more vacancies on the Supreme Court; internal concerns about continuing criminal investigations in Texas and Washington that might jeopardize House Majority Leader Tom DeLay; the inevitable jockeying among aspirants in both parties for the 2008 presidential nomination, which appeared to include Senate Majority Leader Frist; the uncertainties of the war in Iraq and efforts to establish a representative government for that nation; plus possible new terror threats.

But the most important lesson of the past several decades may be that presidential agenda setting requires a well-planned and consistent political message that can withstand the inevitable bumps in the road and other complications. If the national leader wants to change public policy, he must reach out from the start to the lawmakers whose support will be essential.

NOTES

1. Bill Keller, "The Radical Presidency of George W. Bush; Reagan's Son," *New York Times Magazine*, January 26, 2003, 26.

2. Colleen Shogan, "Presidential Campaigns and the Congressional Agenda: Reagan, Clinton, and Beyond," presented to the Woodrow Wilson International Center for Scholars, Washington, DC, November 22, 2004.

3. Paul C. Light, "Fact Sheet on the President's Domestic Agenda," Washington, DC, Brookings Institution, October 12, 2004.

4. Richard E. Cohen, *Rostenkowski* (Chicago: Ivan R. Dee, 1999), 51.

5. Paul A. Gigot, "Now Bush Has to Win on the Issues," *Wall Street Journal*, September 8, 2000, A18.

6. Susan Milligan, "GOP Preps Stage for Bush Agenda," *Boston Globe*, November 20, 2004, A1.

5

Successful Influence: Managing Legislative Affairs in the Twenty-first Century

Gary Andres and Patrick Griffin

When George W. Bush was sworn in for his second term as president, he joined a unique historical club: the first president reelected whose party gained seats in Congress since Franklin Delano Roosevelt in 1936, and the first Republican to do so since Calvin Coolidge in 1924. Due to these gains, and unlike his father, President George H. W. Bush, who faced Democratic majorities in the House and the Senate and played defense with the opposition, the younger Bush should be more successful in passing his legislative program and influencing lawmakers. Right?

At one level, yes. And major White House legislative victories on tax cuts, Medicare prescription drugs, and education reform (the No Child Left Behind Act) support this conclusion. Yet viewing the task of managing relations with Congress only from the perspective of the president's ability to get his program through the House and Senate is incomplete and understates the complexities of successfully managing the legislative/executive dance.

Few relationships endure more hardships, handshakes, fallings-out, forced reconciliations, screaming, shared accomplishments, deliberate deception, finger-pointing, and honeymoons than that between the American president and the U.S. Congress. How these two institutions "get along"—whether they dance smoothly or step on each other's toes—has broad implications for U.S. public policy making. Nonetheless, understanding concepts like presidential "success" or "influences" must be viewed in a much broader context. We propose a more expansive approach in this chapter and argue that looking narrowly at how much legislation a president muscles through Congress is only one way of measuring successful influence. Comparing FDR and the institutional circumstances he faced in, say, 1932, to Bill Clinton after the Republicans captured congressional majorities in the House and Senate only on the basis of "how much of the president's program Congress adopted" misses a lot of the complexities underlying those relationships and may mask many of Clinton's success as well as FDR's failures.

We also make some suggestions about how to improve White House relations with Congress in the future using some of the insights of academic research on presidential influence as well as our experiences as senior White House aides (Andres worked for both Bush White Houses and Griffin served President Clinton).

A BROADER PERSPECTIVE ON PRESIDENTIAL-CONGRESSIONAL RELATIONS

Many colloquialisms like "The president proposes and Congress disposes" simply do not capture the complexities, nuances, and contours that define presidential-congressional relations. One of the central goals of this chapter is to dispel the common myth that presidents drive the lawmaking process and that "success" and "influence" are based solely on how much of their agendas the chief executives can get the Congress to accept. Already, at this writing after the 2004 presidential election, Mr. Bush is being prejudged on his legislative influence based on his ability to push Congress to adopt his agenda on Social Security reform and tax simplification.

We explicitly reject this view, believing that it is both empirically incorrect and damaging to citizens' expectations about the proper role of the various branches of American government institutions. True, Mr. Bush has some initiatives on which his success should be partially judged. But the president and the Congress are truly "separate institutions, sharing power" and, as the title of this volume accurately states, "rivals for power." Keeping this perspective helps citizens evaluate successful presidential-congressional relations, creating a new realism about what is possible under our system of government.

Conventional wisdom suggests that skillful presidents lead and cajole Congress to produce important public policy outcomes. In the twentieth century, the accomplishments of Franklin Roosevelt, Lyndon Johnson, and the first year of the Reagan administration are noted as examples of "success" or "influence" with Congress. Other presidents, such as Truman, Carter, and

George H. W. Bush, had fewer congressional success stories and are often considered less influential—or perhaps even failures—in the legislative arena.

Analyzing how the Congress "processes" presidential initiatives or agendas is only one narrow piece of the puzzle. There are many other metrics on which to judge success. Many political pundits, journalists, and even academics make the mistake of viewing the persuasive relationship between the president and Congress as only moving in one direction.

But this is only part of the equation.

First, the flow of influence between the president and Congress is both ways, not unidirectional. Edwards and Woods point out that patterns of influence between the public and the president are interactive.[1] That is, the president influences public attitudes, and the public influences the president. *The same is true between the president and Congress.* It is an interactive relationship with patterns of influence flowing both ways.

In other words, when we ask how much the president influences Congress, we must also ask the question in reverse: how successful is the Congress in influencing the president?

In *Legislating Together*, Peterson makes a similar point.[2] He notes that conventional wisdom among the press, public, and scholars about presidential-congressional relations is "president centered." He paints a picture of the president standing before Congress, giving his State of the Union message with his agenda on the line. If the president can convince Congress to pass it, he wins; if not, he loses. It is all about the president, and it is all about passing his agenda—a one-way set of inputs from the president into the Congress to achieve legislative outputs.

Even some informed political elites, like U.S. senators, also hold this president-centered conventional wisdom. During the 1988 presidential campaign, a prominent U.S. senator told the Bush campaign's legislative liaison staff that he would withhold his endorsement of Bush until he heard the candidate's agenda for the first one hundred days. According to the senator, the president's "first one hundred days" represented his "best and only chance" for great potential legislative accomplishments. In reality, Bush's team spent the first hundred days figuring out where the bathrooms were in the White House and how to respond to a barrage of legislation passed by a Democrat majority over the objections of the Republicans. In the modern era, Congress normally spends the first hundred days organizing itself internally and getting its own plans in order, not processing a presidential agenda.

This approach views the president as an "input" trying to exert unidirectional influence and gain success in the form of congressional "outputs," much like any other interest group in the legislative policy-making environment. As we note later, this approach is too limited, because Congress tries to influence the president as much as the president attempts to wield influence over legislators. Presidential-congressional relations are best understood as a two-way street with pressure, influence, success, and failure flowing freely in both directions.

And sometimes this two-way street causes the White House to shift gears somewhere in the middle of the process. Two relatively recent examples make this point. First, most observers agree welfare reform was never a top priority in the Clinton White House, yet congressional Republicans continued to push for this legislation. After rejecting broader legislation that included welfare reform, President Clinton not only signed a modified version of the measure but also shifted strategy to embrace the bill and share in the political credit with the Republicans.

Creating a Department of Homeland Security was a similar example for George W. Bush. After resisting creation of the new department, Mr. Bush pivoted due to continued congressional prodding, signed the legislation, and used its creation as a political benefit in his reelection bid.

Both examples underscore how presidents are not only led by Congress occasionally but can also shift strategies (if they are politically facile and astute) and claim credit for legislative initiatives.

Models of presidential-congressional relations based on a unidirectional influence flow also tend to view presidential success or influence in "constant" as opposed to "dynamic" terms. Jones, for example, notes this shortcoming in extant scholarship and argues for a dynamic approach. He notes that the "strategies of presidents in dealing with Congress will depend on the advantages they have available at any one time. One cannot employ a constant model of an activist president leading a party government. Conditions may encourage the president to work at the margins of president-congressional interaction (for example where he judges that he has an advantage, as with foreign and defense issues)."[3] Again, using the example of the presidency of George W. Bush, his ability to successfully influence Congress on matters related to defense, national security, and homeland security changed dramatically after the 9/11 terrorist attacks on the United States.

By analyzing presidential-congressional relations using some of the insights suggested above, we gain a deeper, richer, and more realistic understanding of how the system works and a better way to gauge "influence and success." Factoring in these variables allows us to analyze presidential-congressional relations from a "pre-outcome" perspective, including the impact of the interactive relationship, institutional and policy variables, and the strategic goals of the actors. The next section of this chapter lays out three "pre-outcome" aspects of presidential-congressional relations that we must appreciate and factor into our models to better understand legislative outputs (or the lack thereof).

Precursors to Outcomes: Three Considerations

Clearly, evaluating success and influence only from the perspective of votes taken, bills signed, or vetoes sustained is the most traditional and obvious way to gauge who is leading and who is following in the dance of legislation between the Congress and the executive branch. While the focus on outcomes is often interesting and relatively easy to measure, it fails to capture the rich and complex dynamics between the branches of government and party leaders that precede each outcome. In other words, to better understand the final product, one needs to step back and consider the context that shaped these outcomes.

We suggest focusing on three: (1) how well the White House manages the process of interacting with Congress, including consultation and communication; (2) the context in which the president finds himself matters (e.g., "success" and "influence" should be defined differently depending on mixed party government environments or when his party possesses large versus small majorities in Congress); (3) success and influence are also dependent on the strategic goals of the White House and congressional actors.

Outcome measures alone rarely provide any insight into the overall strategic goals and objectives of the president or congressional leaders. Nor do they help in understanding how these sets of goals and objectives relate to each other or to the public. For example, a Democratic president along with his party colleagues in the Congress may embrace an opportunity to show how prodigious their legislative capabilities are. They might welcome a "scorecard" evaluation, laundry-listing all the bills they jointly pass and sign into law. In this case, a straight-line evaluation of votes taken, bills passed and signed into law, and vetoes not only would be consistent with the strategic objective of such a presidency but also would likely provide additional perspectives on presidential efforts. However, one could easily imagine a Republican president who campaigned on a platform of a smaller, less active government who, along with his party leaders in the Congress, may want to convince supporters that they are doing more by doing less. With the exception of providing for the national defense and attempting to eliminate Democrat-sponsored programs, their strategic objectives might be to make their role in government as small a target as possible. Using "legislative outcomes" to judge these two presidents may mask which one is truly successful or influential.

Divided government is another scenario in which outcome measures produce an unclear perspective. When party control is split between the branches, each side openly claims that its reason for being in office is to thwart the objectives of the other. What did not happen or how a proposal was watered down before it became a law is a better way to define success in these cases. An extreme example occurred in 1995 when a Republican majority in Congress fought a Democratic president to a legislative draw. No authorizing legislation and no appropriation bills passed the entire year, shutting down the government three times. In the end, Democrats won a "TKO," apparently convincing most of the public that their effort to stop the Republican agenda was more important than having the GOP stop theirs. The only outcome measure was whose message was more convincing in proving the negative.

Outcome measures also fail to capture the influential role that individual members, committee chairs, and leaders have in promoting, shaping, and even killing policy proposals throughout the entire legislative process. This is typically done by offering and withholding critically needed support at crucial times in the process. It is also accomplished by utilizing parliamentary tactics that obstruct or prohibit the legislative process from progressing. The majority party's leaders at the committee and institutional levels also wield enormous influence by being able to set the schedule, agenda, and conditions for proceeding to specific pieces of legislation.

Individual members' motivations vary greatly in their participation in legislative efforts and skirmishes. While members could have considerable impact on specific policies, their positions are typically a reflection of their constituent concerns. On the other hand, committee chairs and party leaders need to factor in not only personal constituent agendas when making decisions that affect legislation but also those of the entire party. Decisions regarding legislative content, when and whether to schedule the legislation, and how and if it might be amended are often worked through as much as possible before the first vote is taken. Outcome measures simply do not begin to reveal the role and influence that the process, context, and strategic goals play in shaping the outcome before the quantification of results.

At this writing, as President Bush is in the first year of his second term, his strategic goals pertaining to outcomes are aimed at specific legislative accomplishments. He wants to pass some version of Social Security reform and tax simplification and change the basic relationship between voters and the government (what some call his "ownership society" initiative.) Mr.

Bush, we believe, would like voters to judge him on outcomes, but he's giving Congress a great deal of discretion in writing the specific measures.

Process, Context, and Strategic Goals

So let us take a step back from outcomes and investigate process, context, and the participants' strategic goals in evaluating presidential success or influence with Congress. For example, what are the tactics used by successful presidents in producing positive outcomes with Congress? Similarly, how do institutional variables like dealing with mixed versus unified party government, the House versus the Senate, and different types of public policy change the ways in which presidents approach Congress? Finally, how do presidential and congressional strategic goals influence the nature of legislative outcomes and relations? Each of these "precursors" to outcomes is a critical variable in achieving a better understanding of the proper role of the president and Congress in U.S. government.

The balance of this chapter analyzes factors that shape outcomes. Focus on these variables helps explain why some presidents produce prodigious legislative accomplishments and others do not. This approach also suggests presidents can have "success" or "influence" with Congress in ways not measured by studying only outcomes. Finally, we focus on more than just the president in this dance. A better starting point is one that accepts the reciprocal nature of the relationship: Congress tries to influence the president as much as, or more than, the president tries to shape Congress. Articulating a broader view of how these two institutions interact, including the challenges, trade-offs, and opportunities, will also lead presidents and their staff to manage the relationship with more success in the future. We hope scholars and pundits will use this model to foster a clearer and more realistic understanding of presidential-congressional relations.

PRECEDING OUTCOMES I: PROCESS— A TAPESTRY OF SUCCESS

The "process" of managing White House–congressional relations has many dimensions. "Success" with Congress is an interwoven tapestry of activity rather than a single strand, such as winning roll-call votes. True legislative success builds an active two-way dialogue between the Congress and the president. Bryce Harlow, who adroitly negotiated the shoals of Congress for Presidents Eisenhower and Nixon, has said, "The president's legislative affairs office creates a bridge across a yawning Constitutional chasm, a chasm fashioned by our power-fearing Fathers to keep the Congress and the President at a safe distance from one another in the interest of human liberty."

Identifying the tools necessary to build this bridge is the subject of the next section. Most of the recommendations apply to the president and the White House legislative affairs staff.

Active Consultation

Presidents who put a strong emphasis on consultation with Congress, communicating often personally or through the staff with legislators, will get high marks and succeed in influencing the House and the Senate. The Clinton team got high marks early on with the Democratic leadership in Congress for consulting and working in concert on a variety of measures during 1993. Their initiatives included proposals on education and environment, the Family and Medical Leave Act, and "motor voter" legislation (two initiatives that President Clinton's predecessor George Bush consistently opposed that now could pass under conditions of unified party government), as well as modest institutional reform proposals regarding campaign finance and lobbying registration. Their agenda also included legislative objectives that began to reposition Democrats as supporting a balanced budget while reducing the size of government and expanding efforts to fight crime.

As is often the case in unified government, the Democrats worked to ensure that their proposals passed without Republican support. The cornerstone of this early agenda was a $500 billion tax increase and spending cut package to reduce the deficit. The measure passed the House by a margin of one, with all Republicans opposing it.

President George W. Bush's legislative strategy in the House has followed a similar path over the past five years. In the Senate, however, as mentioned above, Mr. Bush was also able to secure some Democratic support for most of his major initiatives like tax cuts, Medicare prescription drug legislation, and the No Child Left Behind education bill.

Holding all the Democrats in line for Mr. Clinton, as well as the Republicans for President George W. Bush, on a variety of these initiatives took many hours of consultation and compromise, both by inviting members to the White House and by sending administration personnel to Capitol Hill. Active consultation results in members of Congress believing that someone at the White House is listening and that their views matter. Often just "hearing people out" and being attentive to their views go a long way toward strengthening and creating positive relations with Congress.

Creating a Capitol Hill Presence

Building successful bridges with legislators requires accessibility on the part of the White House staff on Capitol Hill. Both Bush (George H. W. and George W.) administration legislative affairs teams stationed their members in critical places around the Capitol during every roll-call vote in the House and the Senate. This allowed senators and congresspeople to find the staff and vice versa. It helped develop an image of a White House and administration actively engaged with the Congress, listening to members' concerns and complaints, and feeding information back to lawmakers.

Conversely, the Clinton team spent more time early in the administration in internal policy-development meetings in the White House. Soon many on Capitol Hill began to complain that the White House team was "invisible" on the Hill, and complaints about lack of attentiveness began to mount.

David Hobbs, former assistant to the president for legislative affairs in the current Bush administration, was also a former chief of staff to former House majority leader Dick Armey (R-TX) before joining the White House lobbying team in 2001. As a denizen of the House, Hobbs took creating a presence to a new level by literally sitting in the House Republican cloakroom—normally an area restricted to members only—to listen, learn, and cajole. Without floor access most legislative affairs staff don't have that kind of presence. Yet because of Hobbs's unique background in the House, he was "presence personified."

Creating a Hill presence is a key ingredient for the White House to engage daily in the ebb and flow of congressional culture. Presidents who dispatch their staff to talk to legislators in this manner will win high marks from Congress. It is a tactic that requires a large time commitment; Bush and Reagan's legislative affairs teams were on Capitol Hill whenever Congress was in session. Yet it is also a tactic that will result in major dividends in creating an effective two-way dialogue with Congress.

Engaging the Leadership

Fostering a constructive relationship with the congressional leadership—both the president's party and the opposition—is one of the most important tasks in which the White House can invest time and energy. As we discuss later in this chapter, the nature of the relationship with the leadership changes somewhat when the president's party is in the majority compared with when it is in the minority. For now, it is important to note that the president and his staff must cultivate and forge strong relations with the congressional leadership.

In the administration of George H. W. Bush, the president and his staff worked hard cultivating these relationships, meeting with the congressional leadership nearly every week when Congress was in session during the president's four-year term. The president and his staff would organize bipartisan, bicameral meetings twice a month, dedicating the other two monthly meetings to only Republicans from the House and the Senate. Bush consciously tried to convey the impression that he was diligently working with the congressional leadership, listening to their views, and meeting them halfway on any issue he could.

This strategy had mixed results. Often Bush never moved far enough to accommodate the congressional Democratic leadership, and his Republican allies viewed his actions with suspicion. In the mixed party government environment faced by Bush, engaging the leadership seemed to work best when playing defense. In those cases in which he and his staff could rally the GOP leadership to oppose a Democratic initiative, the combination of the Republican leadership whipping its members and the White House working conservative Democrats did result in a few key legislative wins. House passage of a capital gains tax cut and the first authorization of "fast-track" trade-negotiating authority are two primary examples.

The current President Bush faced a completely different situation, at least with the House leadership. Instead of constantly trying to get morsels of information from the majority Democrats about scheduling and agenda, as the first President Bush did between 1989—1992, the current Bush administration spends far less time trying to work with the current House Democrat leadership team. The difference between the two Bush administrations in the amount of time, energy, and contact with the Democrats underscores how differing political and institutional contexts should affect how we evaluate success and influence.

Working with congressional leadership emerges as one of the key tasks of White House staff in any review of process and tactics. It is an important ingredient to any successful legislative strategy. Strong relations with the congressional leadership make every other aspect of relating with the House and the Senate operate more smoothly and efficiently. We discuss some of the nuances of relations with a president's own party leadership versus working with the opposition party later in this chapter.

Addressing Needs and Wants

When Senator Trent Lott was minority whip in the House, he used to admonish President Reagan's White House staff, "You've got to take care of members' needs and wants." This is both a big and a small request, but it is important to take care of those needs and wants that can be taken care of. This may involve a letter from the president, a trip on Air Force One back to the district or state, a change in an administration position, or a signing pen from a piece of legislation recently enacted into law. There is no better way to build a reservoir of goodwill and develop a reputation of responsiveness than by attending to member needs and wants.

M. B. Oglesby, legislative affairs chief for President Reagan, told his staff that responsiveness meant that they should never leave the White House at the end of the day without having returned every phone call. A president can vastly improve his relations with Congress by making it clear that he wants to address member needs and wants. Doing so will pay large dividends when it comes time to spend some political capital—even if it fails to produce active support by the opponents, sometimes it can moderate their attacks.

Nicholas Calio, assistant to the president for legislative affairs for President Bush from 2001 to 2002, used to invite people from the Hill to his office for drinks and sandwiches and then give them private tours of the Oval Office after hours. In the world of politics, that kind of currency carries real value.

Access to the President

Effective leadership and influence with Congress includes staff who can speak clearly and authoritatively for the president. In order to do this, White House staff charged with relations with Congress must have unfettered access to the president. One of the biggest mistakes of any White House staff organization is building too many layers of staff between the president and the personnel that must speak for him. A recurrent theme in our own experience and in research by political scientists, such as Ken Collier in his book *Between the Branches*, is that White House staff who lack easy access to the president are diminished in their effectiveness.

When the legislative affairs staff members lack access to the president, they lose stature and ultimately effectiveness in influencing Congress. One of the best examples of this occurred during the Bush administration and the now infamous 1990 budget agreement in which the president broke his "read my lips, no new taxes" pledge. Office of Management and Budget director Richard Darman concocted the 1990 budget strategy with no input from the White House legislative affairs staff. Darman worked closely with the Democratic leadership, sounding them out repeatedly about the outlines of a budget deal, without consulting with the Republican leadership or the White House. The president and Congress reached a final agreement on the budget deal during a morning meeting in the White House that included Bush, Darman, White House chief of staff John Sununu, Speaker of the House Tom Foley, House Majority Leader Richard Gephardt, and Senate Majority Leader George Mitchell. The only two Republican congressional representatives attending were House Minority Leader Robert Michel and Senate Minority Leader Dole. According to their staffs' recollections, their involvement in the meeting was minimal. No one from the White House legislative affairs staff found out about the meeting and the agreement from lawmakers on Capitol Hill until later that morning as word began to leak out.

Building Trust

The president and his staff must work to build trust with legislators. Because of factors like political and institutional rivalries, trust between the branches may not be the natural state of affairs. Building effective relations with Congress means constantly assuring lawmakers that one will do what one says one will do. A promise to provide a legislator with a letter of support must be followed up. A promise for a presidential phone call must be delivered on.

Having the ability to "make things happen" is part of the building of trust from the standpoint of the White House staff. A White House staff that does not have the ability or stature to deliver on promises or commitments made will never glean the type of respect and trust from lawmakers to effectively lead or influence Congress.

Strategic Coordination

Coordinating with other executive branch agencies and building coalitions with outside groups are other keys to lobbying success. Both represent powerful tools that, if used in the right way, can strengthen a president's legislative muscle on Capitol Hill. How and when the White House chooses to coordinate with executive agencies is a key consideration. While the president and his staff want to utilize the agency resources at certain times and make sure that the executive branch departments do not get "off message," the White House also must guard against every agency initiative becoming a presidential priority.

During the first two years of the Clinton administration, cabinet officials and agency heads often wanted to make their agency priorities the same as the president's, hoping to give themselves more leverage on Capitol Hill.

White House staff studiously guarded the list of presidential priorities, pushing large pieces of the administration's agenda back to the agencies for implementation. After losing control of the Congress in 1994, the senior staff of the president reversed course with their agency counterparts and brought virtually the entire agenda of the administration inside the West Wing so that they could manage its execution on a daily basis. Coordinating the substance, message, and execution became a very nuanced and complex process in the highly charged political atmosphere of the Republican takeover. The White House wanted maximum control in all phases of its application under these conditions, whereas it allowed and even encouraged a liberal decentralization approach when operating under unified party control of the Congress and executive branch in the prior two years.

Coordination in the administration of George W. Bush has also been relatively strong. Many observers have noted that his White House and its political appointees have normally stayed "on message." And as Mr. Bush begins his second term, it appears the coordination will become even more tightly controlled as the president moves some of his key White House staff out to head cabinet-level agencies like the Defense, Education, and Justice departments.

Communications and Message Coordination

How an issue or policy is talked about is critical. But language matters in some nonobvious ways. The president has an enormous advantage in being able to frame an issue. His "bully pulpit" often gives him the first and last word on a matter, particularly if it is contentious. He can use the bully pulpit to frame a new initiative; for example, the need for normalizing trade relations with China or condemning congressional tardiness in completing business. His voice maximizes when it is coordinated with his political allies on Capitol Hill or sympathetic spokespeople around the country. Presidential communications in all these forms are formidable tools, particularly when used as part of a comprehensive strategy to advance or thwart an issue. However, this is not foolproof, as we saw in the repeated attempts by the Clinton administration to frame the problems and solutions implied in their proposal to solve the health care crisis in 1994.

Our experience suggests, however, that a strong message may do more to bolster the enthusiasm of core supporters rather than move public opinion. This conclusion is consistent with what Edwards found in his book *On Deaf Ears* (2003).

PRECEDING OUTCOMES II:
A COLLECTION OF CONTEXTS

Although building successful congressional relations depends on weaving a tapestry of activities like those outlined above, success also varies based on institutional and policy contexts. Below we consider how managing relations with Congress varies based on differing contexts such as mixed versus unified party government, interacting with the House versus the Senate, and the type of public policy Congress is considering.

Mixed versus Unified Party Governments

First, consider mixed versus unified party government. The Clinton administration had the unique opportunity to serve its first two years with its own party as the majority. But the balance of President Clinton's term was spent working with a Republican majority in Congress. President George W. Bush faced a similar fate when his new majority in the Senate was lost in June of 2001 when Senator James Jeffords changed parties. Mr. Bush regained a Senate majority eighteen months later.

In some respects, the president's political prowess in legislative affairs during periods of unified party government may be overrated. It is true that President Clinton and the Congress were able to enact a number of important pieces of legislation into law during 1993–1994, including motor voter, family medical leave, and a deficit-reduction budgetary measure. However, there were also glaring examples of failure by unified government, most notably in the form of President Clinton's health care reform package, which languished in a Democrat-controlled Congress and ultimately became fodder for a successful Republican campaign to take over Congress in the 1994 elections.

As Mayhew and others have pointed out,[4] unified control is not a sufficient criterion to predict significant differences in legislative accomplishment. Entire chapters or books could be written about different strategies to deal with unified party government. In the short space remaining, we make two points based on our experiences and those of others who have worked in the White House. First, we agree with Mayhew and others such as Binder that there are structural components to gridlock that make it difficult to enact major legislative accomplishments, even under conditions of unified party government. Given factors such as intrachamber member and committee rivalries, interchamber competition between the House and the Senate, Rule XXII in the Senate that requires sixty votes to break a filibuster, and the two-thirds majority required in both chambers to pass a bill over the president's objections, enacting any piece of legislation is difficult.

Second, given all the problems moving an agenda through Congress with the president's party in control, too little time is spent cultivating relationships and reaching out to members of the opposition party. Building strong relationships with the opposite party is one of the most challenging aspects of leadership in the legislative arena. From majority leaders in the Senate, to Speakers of the House, to presidents of the United States, finding a successful formula for working with the other party without alienating allies in one's own party eludes most modern-day political leaders in Washington. Yet presidents who can do it usually reap large benefits. If there is one common thread of underachievement running through all modern presidents, it is that the challenges of working with the opposition seem to have gotten the better of most of them.

BICAMERAL EFFECTS

Differences between the House and the Senate are another important variable in managing relations with Congress. Differing majority rules represent the most glaring difference, from the president's standpoint, in managing relations with Congress. In the Senate, some argue that the majority is not really "a majority" without sixty votes, since so much of Senate floor activity is dependent on unanimous consent or achieving a three-fifths supermajority. The minority often blocks majority initiatives without sixty votes in the Senate. This is not the case in the House. Even a slim majority, such as in the House in the 106th Congress, can process legislation efficiently and effectively using its Rules Committee, as long as it can keep its members unified.

Two implications for managing relations with Congress follow from this observation. First, the White House must incorporate this reality into its lobbying strategy, recognizing that each individual senator could potentially sabotage portions of the president's program. The White House should make personnel decisions and develop strategies based on this reality. The president's team should spend a good portion of its time working aggressively to develop relationships and gather input from a wide array of senators. Second, given the size of the House and its majority rules, working with the leadership in the House is relatively more important than working with Senate leaders (because power in the Senate is more diffuse). Although no White House should ignore rank-and-file House members, compared with those in the

Senate, the rules allow the White House team to focus relatively more attention on the House leadership.

Policy Contexts

The president's attempts to lead and manage relations with Congress also
depend on the type of policy under consideration. For example, President
Bush approached Congress a certain way in January 1991 when he attempted
to secure congressional authorization for the use of force in the Persian Gulf
War. Alternatively, President Clinton used a different set of tactics in 1993
when he successfully passed his economic-stimulus/deficit-reduction strategy.
Finally, both presidents used yet another set of strategies when responding
to more specific and particular requests from individual members, trying to
secure administration positions on narrower policy questions.

Some issues, by their very nature, in the current political environment are
highly partisan. In today's landscape, issues like health care and taxes are
difficult policies on which to reach bipartisan consensus. This suggests a
more partisan approach to managing these issues. Other policy areas, like
certain distributive policies such as transportation funding, military spending, or foreign policy issues legislation following major economic or foreign
policy shocks, like issues immediately following the 9/11 terrorist attacks, are
decidedly more bipartisan. In these areas, the president will find reaching
bipartisan consensus and gaining support from across the aisle much easier
tasks.

PRECEDING OUTCOMES III: STRATEGIC GOALS

Too often in the analysis of U.S. politics, Congress and the president are
simply viewed as the targets of outside societal influences. Outside forces, not
the president's or congressional purposive goals, almost exclusively shape
their actions, according to this view. This view is at odds with our experiences and observations in the real world. Individuals, their relationships, and
their goals make a difference.

David Mayhew, in his book *America's Congress*, recognizes this shortcoming in contemporary U.S. political analysis when he says,

> Public affairs [his word for significant public actions by individuals and legislators
> that come to be remembered], moreover, is a highly important realm in that much
> of what virtually anybody by any standard would consider to be politically impor-
> tant originates, is substantially caused, and happens within it—that is, endogenous

to it. This may be a commonsense view, but it is not all that common within the boundaries of modern social science, where politics tends to be seen as driven or determined by exogenous forces such as classes, interest groups, interests, or otherwise pre-politically caused preferences.

We agree with Mayhew and believe that recognizing the unique role that individuals and their strategic goals play helps illuminate many aspects of presidential-congressional relations. Evaluating these goals and how they change over time provides useful insights into the level of success or influence that presidents achieve in legislative outcomes. These strategic goals form part of the context, including the process and institutional variables outlined above, and help us better understand and interpret the meaning of outcome measures. Analyzing how the Clinton administration and congressional strategic goals interacted is a useful case study. Let us begin in 1993, during a period when Democrats controlled the House, the Senate, and the White House.

As is often the case in unified government, the Democrats worked to ensure that their proposals could pass without Republican support. As noted above, the cornerstone of the early agenda was a $500 billion tax increase and spending cut package to reduce the deficit. This measure was passed by one vote, and no Republicans supported it. While many Democrats wore this victory as a badge of honor, the Republicans gradually but successfully worked to characterize the Democrats' frenetic legislative agenda as extreme, excessive, and out of touch with most Americans. They successfully drove home this point in the health care reform debate. The administration and the Democratic congressional leadership's decision not to move their complex and controversial proposal until they were assured that it could pass without the support of Republicans, particularly in the House, was a strategic disaster. The Republicans capitalized on the Democrats' decision and crystallized this strategic message: Stop the Democrats by putting the Republicans in control of Congress. The Republicans successfully used this message to change the entire political context of the new presidency. They convinced the American public that the Democrats should lose their jobs, not because they had failed to do what they said, but precisely because they were doing what they had promised.

In January 1995, the new Republican majority in the Congress took the lead, attempting to shape the political and legislative agenda of the new Congress. The cornerstone of their strategy was the Contract with America, which included popular initiatives such as litigation reform, tax cuts, and cancellation of many traditional Democrat-sponsored programs. Democrats at both ends of Pennsylvania Avenue were unsure initially how to respond.

Congressional Democrats, particularly in the House, were not needed to pass any of these new proposals, leaving them in the comfortable position of being against everything. Because the House was going to take the lead legislative charge, the Senate Democrats were in a "wait and see" posture. The administration, desperately wanting to remain relevant, was anxious to see if there were policy issues on which staff could work together with the Republicans, knowing that there would be plenty of areas in which they could draw the bright lines of battle.

The House acted quickly and aggressively to implement its agenda. Like the Democrats in the previous Congress, Republicans relied on their own party to pass their proposals. Appearing to take a play out of the failed Democrat playbook, the House GOP advanced a partisan set of bills.

Soon the president and congressional Democrats realized that their best strategic position in response to these legislative proposals was to claim, as the GOP did in the previous Congress, that the Republican proposals were extreme, insensitive, and out of touch with the American people. Democrats pledged to do everything they could to prevent these draconian measures from becoming law. No legislation was passed into law that entire year except for a continuing resolution that was finally adopted in January 1996.

Victory in this case was not measured by traditional outcome measures. Instead, winning was defined by whose message was more believable to the American public. By most accounts the administration and congressional Democrats "won" for stopping the Republicans from going too far with the proposals. The boldness of the new Republican agenda fell on deaf ears. The Republicans now had ten months before the next election to decide whether to make a "halftime" correction in their strategy or stay the course.

It became apparent, especially after the departure of Majority Leader Dole, that the new GOP leadership team, Lott and Gingrich, wanted to play an entirely new card and, by doing so, set in place the third strategic dynamic between President Clinton and the Congress in three short years. The theme of this strategy was "cooperation." How and on what issues could the Republican majority work with a Democratic president? How could they quickly show they were not "extreme" and "insensitive" and were ready to do the people's business? The new majority in Congress and the new president both thought this was the ticket to their respective reelections in 1996. This was not a popular view among congressional Democrats, who felt that demonstrating that the Republicans could not handle governing the majority would surely be their ticket to regaining power. Congressional Democrats felt it would be far more preferable for the president not to cooperate with the Republican majority, showing the American people that the GOP could not govern.

Some conservative Republicans held the same position, though for different reasons. They believed that compromise was tantamount to capitulation and that working together with the Clinton administration would dilute the Republican cause and only help the president get reelected. Nevertheless the Republican leaders and the president forged a course of cooperation that resulted in small business tax cuts, minimum wage increases, welfare reform, and a framework for a bipartisan balanced budget package. The 1996 election returned President Clinton and the House and Senate Republican majorities.

Despite the success this strategy produced in the 1996 election, there was serious dissatisfaction among the Republican rank and file. After working with the president to enact a balanced budget and pass welfare reform, Republicans were not sure about the next act of this political play. Many had no desire to continue to work with the president after he won the 1996 election and in the wake of revelations about campaign financing irregularities and the continuation of the Whitewater investigation. The Republican leadership decided to disengage from a cooperative posture on policy and develop an aggressive strategy to use its oversight and subpoena authority to pursue the new campaign and personal financial investigations.

In addition to pursuing the truth, these investigations served at least two other strategic purposes for Republicans. They continued to fill the negative atmosphere surrounding the Clinton administration, with the GOP hoping to undo the administration's credibility in the eyes of the public and media. They also served to keep the administration at arm's length in the legislative arena.

"Scandal as diversion," as some would call it, appeared as a strategic approach through the hearing on Whitewater, through inquiry into the campaign financing of the 1996 election, and ultimately through the impeachment proceedings regarding the Lewinsky matter. It produced very little authorizing legislation of note, except by accident, and an appropriations process that generally served to the disadvantage of the Republicans and to the benefit of the president and Democrats. The 1998 elections were held in the height of this strategy, and the Republican majority in the Senate held its own while the GOP House majority lost a handful of seats, putting an already slim majority in serious jeopardy for 2000.

While the strategy of scandal as diversion was on the wane, the congressional leaders and the president contemplated an appropriate framework for the last dance of a lame-duck president. The nature of the final strategic relationship is still unclear. There is no doubt, however, that clarifying the strategic goals pursued by the actors in the legislative and executive branches is a critical precursor to understanding the legislative outcomes (or lack thereof) produced by the Clinton White House and the Republican Congress.

President George W. Bush has now begun his second term and expanded Republican majorities in the House and the Senate. It's clear, even early in 2005, that the Senate will be the pivotal battleground. The House will likely pass most of what Mr. Bush and the Republican leadership wants for the reasons outlined above—its numbers, partisan cohesiveness, and the rules. But with fifty-five votes, Republican leaders in the Senate will face a host of challenges, including Democratic filibusters and internal disagreements from the left and the right with the president's own party.

For example, many believe a major part of Mr. Bush's reelection success in 2004 was due to energizing Republican base voters. This "electoral" strategy had certain consequences and implications in the legislative arena in 2004. Mr. Bush could not achieve certain legislative accomplishments by negotiating with Senate Democrats because he was concerned about how such "deal making" might affect the Republican base.

Now, facing the need to garner Democrat support on several major initiatives like tax reform and Social Security, one of the bigger challenges for the White House may be keeping conservative Republicans in line who saw President Bush more as a "partisan" than a "deal maker." The challenge for the White House will be to persuade conservative Republicans to also adopt this new strategy embraced by a president who will never have to face reelection.

These variables will make presidential success and influence in the Senate for Mr. Bush's second term particularly challenging, despite an increase in the Republican numbers in that body.

CONCLUSION

Currently, most pundits', scholars', and reporters' views of presidential-congressional relations are too limited. Understanding the dance between presidents and lawmakers requires a broader perspective. Presidents do not sink or swim, succeed or fail, have influence or not, based solely on outcome-based measures like roll-call votes or sustaining vetoes. A broader perspective on presidential-congressional relations also requires the understanding that Congress tries to influence and lead the president as much as the president tries to lead Congress. Not only is too much of the research in this area "presidency centered," but there is also not enough emphasis on how Congress and the president try to influence each other through a dynamic process of give and take.

This chapter also highlights some of the secrets of success in managing presidential-congressional relations given these changing and differing contexts. Viewing presidential-congressional relations in this broader perspective sets the stage for a better and more realistic understanding of how these institutions can and should interact, including their potential and their limits.

Achieving success and influence with Congress as an American president is not easy. In fact, based on the variables discussed in this chapter, one might conclude that most presidents are destined to fail. Quadrennial discussions about "mandates" or what can be done in the "first hundred days" simply do not fit reality when it comes to presidential agendas with Congress.

We are not ready to throw in the towel and concede that all future presidents will underachieve. But we do think that someone needs to burst (or at least deflate) the public's overblown expectations about presidential influence in the legislative arena. If a president hopes to produce prodigious legislative accomplishments, many political and institutional stars will have to align. He will have to be blessed with large legislative majorities in both chambers of Congress, an activist agenda with wide public support, and a great deal of bargaining skill to overcome a host of potential institutionally based pitfalls in Congress that could thwart pieces of his agenda. Appreciating that these political and institutional stars rarely align will help lower public expectations for future presidents.

And even when they do "align," recent experiences suggest that unified party control does not always result in the expected outcome. As several scholars have noted recently, the theory of "responsible party government," whereby one party controls both the legislative and the executive branch and enacts an agenda, may be a sound normative theory. As a descriptive device, however, it is somewhat lacking.

We should also modify our criteria for success to include implementation of the process variables outlined in this chapter. Presidents set the "tone" of relations between the branches. Focusing on using many of the process suggestions outlined above will set a positive and civil tone, maximizing the possibility of successful influence.

Successful influence also varies across time. The dynamic nature of the relationship between the president and Congress deserves more attention. Presidents may find success at different periods of their administrations only to lose it during other periods. Understanding how and why presidential-congressional relations change over time may yield important clues about the keys to success.

And sometimes external shocks can dramatically change the tone, strategies, success, and influence of the White House. President Clinton learned this in his second term when impeachment proceedings made it difficult to focus, despite his best efforts, on most other issues. Impeachment—not by his own choice—became a consuming fire that shaped his final term. Moreover, President George W. Bush saw the entire focus of his presidency change and his tone of dealing with Congress altered (as well as the way Congress dealt with him) after the 9/11 terrorist attacks. External shocks seem to afflict every White House—no matter what degree of planning precedes them. Understanding that these events will occur, at one level or another, and learning how to adapt strategies and plans to fit these new realities is another key to successful influence.

Finally, we stress that successful influence depends on contexts. Success in the Senate does not guarantee success in the House. Winning on foreign policy does not translate into success in the domestic arena.

As President George W. Bush begins his second term, we hope pundits and analysts use the broader perspective we suggest to analyze his success and influence. Observers should consider contextual variables, like his party's majority support in the House and Senate, when comparing him to other presidents. Moreover, analysts should take note of our call for the dynamic nature of the relationship between the president and Congress (how it changes over time) as well as the conditional nature of the relationship (how it varies in different policy areas). Also, other variables such as his White House's consultation and presence on the Hill, addressing needs and wants of lawmakers, working with the leadership, and the other variables we raised earlier in this chapter that produce cordial relations between the branches should be used as criteria for success, rather than just whether he passes his legislative program. Whether or not George W. Bush is "successful" or "influential" in terms of his relations with Congress should be evaluated using the broader set of criteria we propose.

After reading this chapter one might conclude that we have raised more questions than we answered about the nature of White House–congressional relations. In some respects, that was our goal. The relationship between the branches is complex, dynamic, and fraught with misunderstanding. Yet, at another level, we hope that by outlining some of these complexities and raising these questions we have fostered a deeper and more critical understanding of the relationship that helps scholars, students, and pundits appreciate the possibilities and limitations of the president's relationship with Congress.

NOTES

1. George C. Edwards and B. Dan Woods, "Who Influences Whom? The President and the Public Agenda," *American Political Science Review* 93 (June 1999): 327–44.

2. Peterson, *Legislating Together*.

3. Charles O. Jones, *The Presidency in a Separated System* (Washington, DC: Brookings Institution, 1994), 19.

4. See David R. Mayhew, *Divided We Govern: Party Control, Lawmaking, and Investigations, 1946–1990* (New Haven: Yale University Press, 1991).

6

The Presidency and Congressional Time

Roger H. Davidson

The legislative workload, along with institutional arrangements for coping with it, is a major component of the structure and substance of legislative-executive relations. Given the Constitution and the political history of the United States, it could not be otherwise. Articles I and II, after all, lay out the interleaved lawmaking responsibilities of the two branches—from initiation ("He [the president] shall from time to time recommend to their [Congress's] consideration such measures as he shall judge necessary and expedient.") to implementation ("He shall take care that the laws be faithfully executed."). Beginning with George Washington, activist presidents have always inserted themselves into the legislative process. Franklin D. Roosevelt and his modern successors institutionalized "the legislative presidency." Today's chief executives are expected to present their legislative agendas to Congress and to provide their allies on Capitol Hill with policy leadership, bargaining parameters, and political cover.

As for Congress, one attribute sets it apart from virtually all of the world's other national assemblies: it is a working body that writes, processes, and refines laws that are typically its own handiworks, and it relies to a large degree on "in-house" resources. Until quite recently, scholars paid scant attention to legislative business as a research topic. Yet Congress's agenda and workload shape not only the behavior and operations of the Senate and House of Representatives but also the two chambers' relationships with the executive branch. What is more, the legislative workload reminds us of "what Congress actually does and how it does it, with all its duties and all its occupations, with all its devices of management and resources of power."[1]

Legislative activity is, of course, only one aspect of the interactions between presidents and Congresses. Executive communications to Congress, for example, have grown so rapidly over the past two generations that almost as many of them are referred to committees as are bills and resolutions. Making federal appointments is another joint enterprise that has become more burdensome at both ends of Pennsylvania Avenue. Implementation and oversight, not to mention administrative and judicial rule making, are other functions that repeatedly propel the president and Congress into joint action. Given the breadth and reach of modern government, these oversight duties remain burdensome even when few new statutes are produced. Yet oversight is closely linked to lawmaking: it flows from previously enacted statutes, and it influences how these statutes are carried out or revised.

THINKING ABOUT POLITICAL TIME

Thinking in terms of political time ought to come naturally to students of U.S. politics. After all, the Constitution separates the two policy-making branches, the presidency and Congress, chronologically as well as functionally. An interlocking system of terms of office—four years for the president, two years for representatives, and staggered six-year terms for senators—creates a perpetual timetable for electoral renewal or replacement of officials. If the constitutional scheme resembles an intricate machine of interlocked moving parts, that machine could very well be a timepiece.[2]

The two policy-making branches run on different but related time frames; rarely do they experience change at precisely the same moment or at exactly the same rate. Because presidents are limited to four or eight years, they are forced to focus on the most pressing policy issues and to seek quick results. By contrast, the houses of Congress display a durable continuity maintained by overlapping tenure and by the presence of experienced careerists. As a consequence, policies are typically incubated and nurtured by Capitol Hill policy entrepreneurs, oftentimes years or even decades before someone in the White House decides to elevate the item to a short list for urgent action.

These divergent time perspectives suggest why it is misleading to tell political time strictly according to electoral periodicity. Every new Congress is to some degree unique, but not every election makes substantial changes in the two chambers. As a continuing body the Senate is especially resistant to change; despite respectable turnover rates, the average senator these days has served more than two terms. The House of Representatives formally reconstitutes itself every two years, but only rarely is it as radically transformed as when the Republicans took control in 1995. Even then, the average representative had served nearly four terms; now the average exceeds six terms.[3]

Categorizing presidencies might seem a simpler matter, and indeed most historians and political scientists use particular presidencies as their unit of analysis. But even here things are not always what they seem. First, an administration may undergo substantial midcourse corrections caused by midterm elections, crises, or other events. Bill Clinton's first term was altered by the 1994 elections, which shifted party control on Capitol Hill. George W. Bush's first term was transformed by the events of 9/11. Such occurrences can alter a president's governing strategy and effectiveness.[4] Second, essential presidential governing strategies or styles may conceivably extend beyond a single administration, as, for example, in the Nixon-Ford or Reagan-Bush successions.

Political scientists tend to measure political time in terms of underlying and enduring political party coalitions. These "party systems" are initiated by realigning elections or periods: most notably the election of Andrew Jackson in 1828, the ascendancy of the Republican Party in 1860, the "system of 1896" that strengthened the GOP's dominance, and Franklin D. Roosevelt's election in 1932. To this list we must add the Republican resurgence of 1994, which gained momentum over the following decade.

Such a categorization assumes the existence of mass-based parties that can effectively mobilize the votes of loyal supporters in elections, unless and until these stable loyalties are disturbed by short-term forces or a more permanent reordering of party divisions.[5] The theory conforms to political development during the heyday of U.S. political parties, roughly from the 1830s through the 1960s; and it fits reasonably with events since that time—an era characterized by intense top-down partisan organization and elite mobilization, though with lower overall rates of participation. Despite its flaws, party alignment theory yields interesting insights into changes in presidential and congressional policy making.[6]

A related classification is offered by Stephen Skowronek, who links changing political apparatus to what he calls "emergent structures" of presidential policy making, depending on whether a given president challenges or adheres to the prevailing political order.[7] Skowronek plants himself right in the middle of the Oval Office: political time is "presidentially driven sequences of change encompassing the generation and degeneration of coalitional systems or partisan regimes."[8] He describes how presidents "make politics" by tirelessly building constituencies for change and striving to remove obstacles that stand in the way of their high-priority agendas. It is hard to square this presidentially centered model with, for example, the varied patterns of legislative-executive relations. Presidents are not always at the center of policy making, nor are they invariably agents of change. In our separated system, as the evidence shows, innovation and incubation of major policy departures can occur in many places, not the least of which is on Capitol Hill.

CONGRESSIONAL WORKLOAD AND OUTPUTS

Both the president and Congress today confront a number and variety of demands unmatched in all but the most turbulent years of the past. The history of Congress readily demonstrates that "the volume of output demands as well as the degree of their complexity, uniformity, and volatility, vary greatly over time."[9] Aggregate legislative statistics from the last six decades show how variable these workload measures can be.

One workload indicator is the number of bills and resolutions introduced by senators and representatives. In both chambers, bill introduction followed a long-term growth from the mid-1940s until the 1970s, followed by gradual and then precipitous decline. (Since the late 1990s, there has been a modest rise in the volume of bills.) In the House, a portion of the decline can be traced to changes in cosponsorship rules. Both chambers, however, have experienced parallel buildup, then a period of extraordinary legislative activity, followed by a sudden and striking contraction.

Bill introduction and sponsorship vary widely among individual senators and representatives. Some lawmakers are inveterate sponsors of bills and resolutions; others shy away from sponsoring measures. In the late 1940s, House members on average authored about eighteen bills or resolutions, compared to thirty-three for senators. Bill sponsorship peaked in the later 1960s, when the average member in both bodies authored almost fifty measures per Congress. Then in the late 1970s the figures plummeted, reaching a plateau that remains to this day. Today's lawmakers introduce fewer measures than those who served in Congress at the beginning of the post–World War II period— some thirty per senator and fewer than half that number per representative.

Legislators today are doubly disadvantaged: not only do they introduce fewer bills and resolutions, but their proposals are less likely to be approved by the full chamber. A Senate measure introduced in the 1940s had better than an even chance of passage in some form; the odds today are about one in four. A House measure used to have nearly one chance in four of passage; today the odds are about half that.[10] This situation stems from two trends: (1) the increased emphasis on broad-scale legislative vehicles—omnibus bills, usually shaped by party or committee leaders, that serve as catchalls for scores of specific provisions, and (2) the gradual elimination or contraction of large numbers of administrative or noncontroversial matters that were once the subject of separate bills.

Overall workload levels reverberate, to a greater or lesser degree, in the committee rooms of the two houses. To be sure, every committee is unique, as Richard F. Fenno Jr., has reminded us; one committee's business may soar while other panels are looking for work.[11] Yet most committees conform more or less to the overall boom-and-bust cycle, at least in terms of bills and resolutions referred to them. In the boom years of the 1970s, activity levels reached modern-day peaks. After about 1978, committee workload indicators declined markedly, to a plateau that has persisted to the present day.

Recorded votes on the House and Senate floors underscore these shifts in legislative activity. The numbers of recorded votes, traditionally quite low, accelerated in the 1960s and then exploded in the 1970s. The rise in floor activity was linked directly to changes in rules and procedures that made it easier for members to offer floor amendments and gain recorded votes. This shifted power perceptibly from the committee rooms to the chambers themselves. Party and committee leaders, especially in the House, soon fought back with procedural tactics aimed at limiting contentious floor votes. Accordingly, the number of recorded votes fell off markedly after 1978. In the Senate votes have stabilized to about 600 to 800 per Congress, compared to 1,000 or more in the 1970s. The House has 1,100 or more floor votes during each Congress, a resurgence that nearly matches the peak years of the 1970s.

Finally, consider the end product of lawmaking: bills and resolutions that survive the complex legislative process to become law. Working in tandem, Congress and the executive strictly regulate the flow of legislative outputs. Of the nearly ten thousand bills and resolutions introduced in the House and Senate in a given Congress, only about 5.5 percent find their way into the statute books. The size and shape of the legislative product are functions not only of political support or opposition but also of changing rules specifying which matters must be resolved by statute and which can be handled by other means.

Overall legislative output figures—measures passed by the two chambers, measures signed into law—look quite different from the input and activity figures described thus far. The number of enacted public bills (those dealing with general legislative issues) began at a high level after World War II, peaking at midcentury. Levels have descended gradually since then. Only a modest upsurge in the volume of public laws occurred during the activist era of the 1960s and 1970s; since then, there has been only a slight decline.

The number of enacted private bills (that is, bills granting benefits to named individuals, as in pension or land claims) has slowed to a trickle. In earlier times, private bills typically equaled or exceeded the number of public laws; today they are rare—one to two dozen in each two-year Congress.

The shrinkage in the volume of substantive bills is commonly attributed to the policy "gridlock" that has resulted from close party competition and heightened cohesion within the two parties. But it is equally a by-product of the increasingly common stratagem of packaging legislative proposals into massive measures—for example, continuing resolutions, reconciliation bills, tax reform packages, and broad-scale reauthorizations. This is attested to by the steady growth in the length of public statutes. Between 1947 and the present day, the average public law ballooned from two and a half pages to nearly thirteen pages. As recently as the 1960s, more than two-thirds of all public laws took up no more than a single page; nowadays very few are that brief. And the proportion of truly lengthy enactments—twenty-one pages or more—grew threefold in that same period. Legalistic verbosity is only partly to blame; legislative packaging is also at work.

These statistical trends, especially the activity and workload figures, lend strong support to the thesis that contemporary lawmaking has passed through a series of four distinct stages or eras (see table 6.1). Legislative-executive relations follow different paths during each of these periods. The first was a relatively static era dominated by a bipartisan conservative coalition (roughly 1937–1964); the second was an era of liberal activism and reform (1965–1978); the third was an era of contraction, of fiscal restraint and political stalemate (1979–1992). A fourth congressional era (1995–present), while still marked by elements of stalemate, is increasingly driven by a conservative partisan majority.

Like any artifacts of historical categorization, these eras are bound to arouse debate over their precise definitions and boundaries, and perhaps even over their validity or utility in illuminating legislative-executive relations. Historical developments, after all, are continuous and multifaceted, rarely yielding unambiguous boundaries. Although our primary data sets begin in 1947, we can extend the first era back to the second Roosevelt administration (1937–1941) by turning to fragmentary statistical indicators and a wealth of qualitative data. The boundaries of the second, liberal era are also problematic: reformist skirmishes broke out over a period of years starting in the late 1950s; by the time the climax occurred in 1974–1975, the era's energy was already waning. The third, postreform era was one of instability in which elements of the prior era coexisted uneasily with subsequent adjustments in economic and political trends. The years of the final era resist categorization, too, perhaps because of their very newness.

Despite these caveats, it is intriguing how closely these four eras coincide with changing journalistic and scholarly understandings of the legislative

Table 6.1. Four Eras in the Operation of the Modern Congress

Congressional Era	Approximate Dates*	Environmental Forces	Leadership Mode	Member goals	Activity and Workload
Bipartisan Conservative	1937–1964	Intraparty divisions	Chairmen of "corporate" committees	Public policy; internal influence sought by careerists; reelection stressed by marginal members	Stable (much of it routine in nature)
Liberal Activist	1965–1978	Liberal majorities	Democratic Caucus	Public policy now competes with reelection for most members; internal influence	Rising rapidly with legislative innovation; jurisdictional expansion by committees
Postreform	1979–1994	Divided government	Party leaders versus Committee majorities	Public policy sought by many, internal influence by a few; reelection important for most members	Declining rapidly (jurisdictional protectionism, oversight stressed)
Partisan Conservative	1995–	Interparty conflict	Republican leadership	Public policy predominant; careerism rebounds after initial decline; reelection stressed by marginal members	Short-term rise; party leaders drive committee productivity

*These dates are approximations, based on certain turning points that seem most clearly to herald a passage from one congressional regime to another—for example, the 1964 electoral surge that gave the Democrats two-to-one majorities in both houses, the 1978 revival of the Republicans that led to their wider victories in 1980, and the GOP takeover of both chambers in 1994. Of course, there is a certain arbitrariness in erecting these landmarks. These "regimes" are actually products of gradual and incremental changes in the institution's environment and operations. Democratic gains in 1958, for example, set the stage for an outpouring of liberal legislation following President Kennedy's assassination in 1963. More recently, the Republican regime was not fully operative until the aftermath of the terrorist attacks of September 11, 2001.

process. The "textbook Congress" that emerged from the first era was well researched and descriptively persuasive.[12] The same can be said for the liberal activist, or reform, era, which produced numerous journalistic and textbook analyses. There even emerged a measure of scholarly consensus on the nature and characteristics of the postreform era, with its emphasis on candidate-centered politics and cutback policy making.[13] The fourth era—marked by close competition between cohesive party cadres—is described by scholars as a state of "conditional party government."[14]

THE BIPARTISAN CONSERVATIVE ERA (1937–1964)

According to popular legend, Franklin D. Roosevelt overwhelmed Congress with his New Deal programs, dictating legislation that gained virtually automatic approval. The facts by no means support this legend. Aside from the emergency measures approved quickly in the spring of 1933, during the first months of his administration, Roosevelt's legislative record drew heavily on proposals already introduced and incubating on Capitol Hill. This inter-branch cooperation increased in the late 1930s. For the years 1931–1940, Lawrence H. Chamberlain found joint presidential-congressional influence at work in 52 percent of the major pieces of legislation; the president prevailed in 37 percent of the cases and Congress in 11 percent.[15] His finding affirmed "the joint character of the American legislative process," even in years of powerful presidential leadership.

The New Deal soon gave way to a long period of bipartisan conservative dominance, which lasted roughly from the second Roosevelt administration through the mid-1960s. Both parties were split internally between a progressive, internationalist wing and a reactionary wing. Although the progressives tended to dominate presidential selections, the conservatives held sway on Capitol Hill. An oligarchy of senior leaders, oftentimes called "the barons" or "the old bulls," wielded the gavels and commanded the votes in the committees and on the floor. Whichever party was in power, congressional leaders overrepresented safe one-party regions (the Democratic rural South, the Republican rural Northeast and Midwest) and reflected the limited legislative agenda of the bipartisan conservative majority that controlled so much domestic policy making.

This Capitol Hill regime proved a hostile environment for activist presidents and their ambitious legislative agendas. "For God's sake," a congressional spokesman telephoned the White House in April 1938, "don't send us any more controversial legislation!" Recounting this anecdote from Franklin

Roosevelt's second term, James MacGregor Burns summed up legislative-executive relations as "deadlock on the Potomac."[16]

Harry Truman's clashes with Congress began early and continued throughout his administration. "Except for the modified Employment Act of 1946," related Robert J. Donovan, "the [Democratic] Seventy-ninth Congress had squelched practically every piece of social and economic legislation Truman had requested."[17] Truman's other Congresses were equally frustrating, though in different ways. The Republican 80th Congress (1947–1949) "gave [Truman] his most enduring image. Facing an opposition-controlled legislative body almost certain to reject any domestic program he proposed, he adopted the role of an opportunist."[18]

Truman campaigned successfully in 1948 by attacking the "awful, do-nothing 80th Congress." Yet the Democratic 81st Congress (1949–1951) rejected virtually all his major Fair Deal initiatives, and the 82nd, marked by depleted Democratic majorities and the Korean War stalemate, was even more hostile to new domestic legislation.

The 1950s were years of outward quiescence accompanied by underlying, accelerating demands for action and innovation. Dwight Eisenhower, with far more modest legislative goals than Truman's, was increasingly placed in the position of offering scaled-down alternatives to programs launched on Capitol Hill by coalitions of activist Democrats and moderate Republicans.

The legislative workload throughout this era was, accordingly, relatively stable and manageable from year to year. A large proportion of the bills and resolutions were routine and dealt with matters not yet delegated to the executive branch for resolution—for example, immigration cases, land claims, and private legislation. Demands were building, however, for bolder legislation to address civil rights, housing, and other concerns of urban and suburban voters.

On Capitol Hill, the powerhouse committees (the taxing and spending panels plus House Rules) were cohesive groups—"corporate," to use Fenno's term—with firm leadership and rigorous internal norms of behavior.[19] They put a tight lid on new legislation, especially in fiscal affairs. The appropriations committees, in particular, stood as guardians of the U.S. Treasury, holding in check the more rapacious inclinations of the program-oriented authorizing panels.

In both houses of Congress power gravitated to a cadre of strong committee leaders. The best of them were able, vivid personalities whose safe constituencies enabled them to lavish their time and skills upon their committees' agendas. If they often behaved autocratically, they usually enjoyed the tolerance if not support of a majority within their committees. Southern Democrats, who chaired most of the key panels during those days, reached across the aisle to build their working majorities, often cultivating a close bond with their ranking minority-party colleagues. Younger and more liberal members, although initially shunned by the old bulls, slowly succeeded in restraining or replacing the committee barons. There survive from that era many colorful anecdotes and stories, some of them no doubt apocryphal, about the exploits and foibles of the old bulls—among them Rules Committee Chairman Howard W. Smith (D-VA); Ways and Means Chairman Wilbur Mills (D-AR); Senate Armed Services Chairman Richard Russell (D-GA); and, most of all, Senate Majority Leader Lyndon B. Johnson (D-TX).

Journalists and political scientists closely studied mid-twentieth-century Congresses, constructing a detailed and persuasive picture of their operations. Borrowing research concepts and techniques from sociology and anthropology, behaviorally trained political scientists illuminated Congress's workings through close personal observation, interviews, and statistical analyses. The Senate of that era was lovingly described by journalist William S. White and systematically analyzed by political scientist Donald R. Matthews.[20] Richard F. Fenno Jr. wrote powerful, detailed accounts of committee operations and the budgetary process.[21] To do justice to the many scholars who illuminated the workings of the midcentury Congress would require a lengthy list of names and citations.

The picture of the midcentury Congress that emerged from the behavioralists' assault upon Capitol Hill was so persuasive that one scholar labeled it "the textbook Congress."[22] According to the leading intellectual framework from that period, the institution was viewed as an interlocking pattern of personal relationships in which all the structural and functional parts worked in rough equilibrium. Ironically, by the time observers got around to completing this picture of a tight, closed, internally coherent congressional system, that world was already being turned upside down. Pressures for change and "reform" mounted, heralding a prolonged period of liberal reformist politics.

LIBERAL ACTIVIST PARTY GOVERNMENT
(1965–1978)

The cozy domains of the barons were eventually pulled apart by what journalist Hedrick Smith called a "power earthquake."[23] The metaphor is attractive but inexact. Although many observers associated the changes with the post-Watergate "class of 1974" and the subsequent overthrow of three House committee chairmen, these events signaled the high-water mark rather than the outset of the era of liberal legislative activism and procedural reform.

The boundaries of the liberal era, like those of the other eras, are some-what imprecise. The process of change began in earnest in the last two Eisen-hower years—after the 1958 elections, when the Democrats enlarged their ranks by sixteen senators and fifty-one representatives, many of them urban and suburban liberals. The elections had an immediate effect in both cham-bers. Senate Majority Leader Johnson's heavy-handed leadership style soft-ened perceptibly; in the House a small band of liberal activists formally orga-nized the Democratic Study Group (DSG), which set about launching a drive for procedural reforms. Two years later, Johnson bequeathed his Senate majority leader's post to the mild-mannered liberal Mike Mansfield (D-MT), while Speaker Sam Rayburn (D-TX), struggled to break the conservatives' control of the powerful Rules Committee. The reform era reached its high-water mark in the mid-1970s with successive waves of changes in committee and floor procedures and, in 1975, the ouster of three of the barons from their committee chairmanships.

One underlying cause of the upheaval was the policy demands of urban and suburban voting blocs as well as minority groups—demands already heeded by activist presidents.[24] The spirit of the era was reflected in the pop-ular movements that came to prominence: civil rights, feminism, environ-mentalism, consumerism, and rising opposition to the Vietnam War. These movements provided not only an extensive legislative agenda but also grass-roots activists who promoted that agenda—some of whom wound up serving in the House and Senate. Longer-range causes of the era's liberal activism included reapportionment and redistricting, demographic shifts, widened citizen participation, social upheaval, and technological changes in transpor-tation and communications.

The resulting changes left Congress more open and participant-friendly and encouraged legislative innovation and productivity. Individual lawmak-ers had greater leverage; influence was dispersed among and within the com-mittees. More leaders existed than ever before, and even nonleaders could exert more influence. More staff aides were on hand to extend the legislative reach of even the most junior members.

Individual senators and representatives, while enjoying their enhanced legislative involvement, were at the same time forced to devote increased attention to their constituents back home. No longer was frantic constitu-ency outreach confined to a few senators from large states and a few represen-tatives from swing districts; it was practiced by all members (or their staffs) in order to purchase electoral security in a time of dwindling grassroots party support. In their officeholding activities, members tended to exchange the role of workhorse, or legislative specialist, for that of the show horse, becom-ing legislative generalists, advertisers, and credit seekers.

The reforms were propelled by, and in turn helped to facilitate, an ambitious and expansionist policy agenda, as such themes as John F. Kennedy's New Frontier and Lyndon B. Johnson's Great Society suggest. This era witnessed a flood of landmark enactments in civil rights, education, medical insurance, employment and training, science and space, consumer protection, and the environment, not to mention five new cabinet departments and four constitutional amendments. Legislative activity soared by whatever measure one chooses to apply—bills introduced, hearings, reports, hours in session, floor amendments, recorded floor votes, or measures passed. The processing of freestanding bills and resolutions became the centerpiece of committee and subcommittee work.

This legislative outpouring formed a gigantic "bulge in the middle," which David R. Mayhew noticed in his study of lawmaking between 1946 and 1990.[25] Fifty-two percent of the 267 "major" enactments Mayhew identified over the fifty-four-year period were enacted between John F. Kennedy's inauguration in 1961 and the end of Gerald Ford's administration in 1976. Over this period 74 measures were produced under eight years of divided party control (Nixon, Ford), and 66 under eight years of unified control (Kennedy, Johnson). We will presently have more to say about this aspect of our analysis, which bears out Mayhew's thesis that party control made little difference in the output of major enactments or investigations.

The decentralization of the 1960s and 1970s was accompanied by a weakening of the appropriations committees' grip over spending and by a strengthening of the power of the authorizing committees (for example, Agriculture, Banking, Commerce). By ingenious use of "backdoor spending" provisions—such as contract authority, budget authority, direct Treasury borrowing, and especially entitlements—the ascendant authorizing committees stripped the appropriations panels of much of their former fiscal guardianship role.[26] Three-quarters of the domestic spending growth between 1970 and 1983 occurred in budget accounts lying outside annual appropriations—that is, beyond the appropriations committees' reach.[27]

The procedural autonomy of another prereform power center, the House Ways and Means Committee, was not breached until nearly the close of the liberal activist period. "During the congressional revolution of the 1970s," wrote Abner J. Mikva and Patti B. Sarris, "the Ways and Means Committee became a 'bastille' that symbolized the inequities of the old order."[28] The panel's independence was curtailed not only by chamberwide reforms (caucus ratification of committee chairmanships, modified or open rules for floor deliberation, open committee meetings), but also by provisions aimed explicitly at the committee (enlargement of the committee, transfer of Democratic committee assignments to the Steering and Policy Committee, jurisdictional encroachments, and, finally, mandated subcommittees). By this time Chairman Mills's remarkable House career was drawing to a close, and his successor was a less forceful leader.

Like the earlier period, this reform era was well documented by journalists and scholars.[29] The most popular scholarly paradigm of the era, drawn from economics, focused on Congress's decentralization and fragmentation.[30] Lawmakers were viewed not as role players enmeshed in a complex system of interactions in equilibrium but as individual entrepreneurs competing in a vast, open marketplace that rewarded self-interested competitiveness with little or no regard for the welfare of the whole institution.

THE POSTREFORM ERA (1979–1994)

During the 1980s Congress again faced an environment that departed in significant ways from what had gone before. Although the shift is popularly associated with the Reagan administration (1981–1989), it was already under way in the last two years of Jimmy Carter's presidency (the 96th Congress, 1979–1981).

The advent of what economist Lester Thurow called the "zero-sum society" no doubt lay at the root of the changed political atmosphere.[31] Between World War II and the early 1970s, the nation's productivity levels had soared along with real incomes for average citizens. These engines had enabled the nation to raise its standard of living while underwriting an expanding array of public services. After 1973 both the nation's productivity and the individual worker's real income stagnated, in comparison with both our economic rivals and our previous record. Indeed, the 1970s and 1980s were the century's poorest productivity decades.[32] The economy no longer seemed to support the federal government's vast array of services, many of them enacted or enlarged during the liberal activist period.

Lagging productivity affected not only government tax receipts but also citizens' attitudes toward their economic well-being. In the late 1970s the economy was buffeted by "stagflation," a coexistence of high inflation and high unemployment. Serious recessions occurred in the early 1980s and again in the early 1990s and 2000s. Meanwhile, the government's costly and relatively impervious system of entitlements, coupled with President Reagan's 1981 tax cuts and program reallocations, turned the midcentury's "fiscal dividends" into "structural deficits."

Intellectual fashions and political realities thus rejected the notion that government could solve all manner of economic and social ills. Disenchantment with the results of government programs, many of which had been shamelessly oversold to glean support for their enactment, led to widespread demands for a statutory cease-fire: disinvestment, deregulation, and privatization. At the same time, "bracket creep" raised the marginal and real tax rates of millions of citizens and spurred a series of tax revolts that swept through the states to Washington.

In the 1980s the president and Congress concentrated on resolving fiscal and revenue issues rather than on designing new programs or establishing new agencies in response to constituent preferences or national needs. In the domestic realm, the emphasis was on reviewing, adjusting, refining, or cutting back existing programs. "There's not a whole lot of money for any kind of new programs," remarked Senator Thad Cochran (R-MS), "so we're holding oversight hearings on old programs . . . which may not be all that bad an idea."[33] Accordingly, fewer individual members were tempted to put forward their ideas as freestanding bills or resolutions. Such new ideas as were salable were more likely to be contained in amendments to large-scale legislative vehicles: reauthorizations, continuing appropriations, and debt-limit or reconciliation bills.

Socioeconomic realities of the 1980s reversed the previous era's liberal activism. Government revenues were curtailed by lagging economic productivity, exaggerated after 1981 by tax cuts, program reallocations, and soaring deficits. Few new programs were launched, and few domestic programs were awarded additional funding. Although the public continued to expect Congress to take action to solve problems, there was equal sentiment for cutting back "big government" and reducing public sector deficits. Public faith in government's capacity to solve problems plummeted in the wake of criticisms of waste and ineffectiveness of government programs.

Elected officials at both ends of Pennsylvania Avenue sought profit from cutback politics. They engaged in creative bookkeeping to give the appearance of balancing revenues and outlays and trimming the deficit as required by a series of seemingly stringent budgetary process fixes, beginning in 1985. Conservatives seized upon revenue shortfalls as a way of snuffing demands for new programs and new spending. Liberals blamed the situation on the failures of the Reagan and Bush administrations and pledged to protect federal programs favored by middle-class voters. As for the voters, they naturally wanted to have it both ways. As Gary C. Jacobson put it, "They can vote for Republican presidential candidates committed to the diffuse collective goods of low taxes, economic efficiency, and a strong national defense, and for congressional Democrats who promise to minimize the price they have to pay for these goods in forgone benefits."[34]

The phenomenon of cutback politics influenced the postreform Congress in at least six ways. First, fewer bills were sponsored by individual senators and representatives. Second, key policy decisions were packaged into huge "megabills," enabling lawmakers to gain support for provisions that would be unlikely to pass as freestanding measures. Third, lawmakers employed techniques of "blame avoidance"—for example, in closing military bases—to protect themselves from the adverse effects of cutbacks. Fourth, more noncontroversial "commemorative" resolutions were passed—nearly half of all laws produced by Congresses in the 1980s. Fifth, party-line voting on Capitol Hill, driven mainly by changes in the parties' demography, soared to modern-day highs. Finally, leadership in the House and Senate was markedly stronger than at any time since 1910. Congressional leaders benefited not only from powers conferred by reform-era innovations of the 1960s and 1970s; they also responded to widespread expectations that they were the only people who could, and should, untangle jurisdictional overlaps and orchestrate the legislative schedule.[35]

The House Ways and Means Committee mirrored the shifts of the postreform era in Congress as a whole. Randall Strahan described the changed agenda that the committee faced after 1978. Following the reform-era assaults on the committee and a hiatus in leadership, Chairman Dan Rostenkowski (D-IL) set about systematically to strengthen the panel's position.[36] According to Allen Schick, the chairman's efforts succeeded in the main: "Ways and Means has regained its status and effectiveness by resorting to a simple formula that worked for it in the past: the committee is successful when it controls the House and when the chairman controls the committee."[37]

As the committee's exhaustive bicentennial history explained, the chairman "centralized control over staff and substantially diminished the autonomy of subcommittee chairs."[38] Rostenkowski's personal leverage was enhanced by his influence over Democratic assignments to the panel as well as his selective use of sanctions. To promote cohesiveness, he scheduled more closed meetings and arranged for weekend retreats and seminars to discuss policy questions.[39] The panel's internal politics settled somewhere between the extremes of bipartisan consensus of the prereform Mills and the reform period's divisive partisanship.[40]

Confronted by a lagging economy, a divided government, and the public's doubts about the efficacy of government programs, the president and Congress in the postreform era changed the way they approached the legislative workload. Presidents trimmed their agendas and hampered congressional initiatives through a combination of curtailed revenue and veto threats. Interbranch negotiations frequently took the form of high-level summitry. Divided control of the White House and Congress, along with rising party voting on the Hill, placed a premium on tough bargaining between the president, Senate leaders, and House leaders. Congress, for its part, moved away from the decentralized system established during the 1960s and 1970s to facilitate that era's frantic legislative activity. A knowledgeable British scholar put it this way: "There can be little doubt that the Congress of the mid-1980s differed from that of the late 1970s in terms of its emphasis on parliamentary reform, legislative activity, constituency attentiveness and distribution of power." In sum, "the reform orientation of the New [or reform-era] Congress [was] left far behind."[41]

Consider the kinds of institutional innovations made by the postreform Congress. Beginning in the late 1970s, Congress confronted an altered set of demands for legislative action. The political agenda shrank, narrowing the prospects for new programs or spending priorities. While many of the structural innovations of the earlier reform era remained intact, procedures were adjusted to cope with the altered environment. Committee and floor agendas contracted. Important decisions were more apt to be folded into lengthy omnibus vehicles, often processed by more than one committee and increasingly superintended by party leaders. Members and committees explored new categories of policy making, or rather they exploited existing categories—for example, oversight, commemorative, indexing, and symbolic measures—that were well suited to the uncertain policy environment.

CONSERVATIVE PARTY GOVERNMENT (1995–)

The early 1990s brought a new mix of challenges to governmental institutions—some continuations of long-term trends, others startlingly new. Prolonged economic uncertainty—manifested in sluggish growth, heightened foreign competition, and widely reported job layoffs—weakened citizens' self-confidence and optimism. Widening racial, ethnic, religious, and even sexual fissures, along with a seemingly permanent disadvantaged underclass, fueled growing suspicions that the nation had become uncontrollable and perhaps ungovernable. The public services that most people came in contact with—public schools, police, courts, welfare offices—seemed especially flawed. The end of the Cold War brought only fleeting satisfaction: losing the menace of the Soviet "evil empire" in fact also meant losing a certain sense of national purpose.

Public unrest deepened into what can only be called a crisis of governance. One member of Congress called it a massive "civic temper tantrum."[42] Few institutions escaped public censure. Scarcely more than a year after celebrating the Persian Gulf War in a burst of civic pride, citizens turned President George Bush out of office in 1992. With a plurality of only 43 percent, successor Bill Clinton's public-opinion "honeymoon" hardly survived the wedding night; his job ratings remained precarious. Although surveys uncovered public disgust with partisanship and "gridlock," the Democrats' victories that year ended divided government only in a formal sense; two years later, the Republicans captured the House and Senate, dissolving even that deceptive unity.

President Clinton's first two years, with a Democratic Congress, brought mixed results. Having run as a "new" centrist Democrat, Clinton tried to distinguish himself from both conservative and liberal party ranks on the Hill—a strategy that came to be known as "triangulation."[43] His greatest achievement, however, attracted not a single Republican vote and was enacted only when Vice President Al Gore cast the tie-breaking vote in the Senate. This was the Omnibus Budget Reconciliation Act of 1993, which raised taxes on upper-income citizens and—affixed to the booming economy of the later 1990s—helped wipe out the federal government's deficits by fiscal 1998. On other matters, the centrist strategy dictated cross-party alliances with Republicans. Their support ensured passage of 1993 legislation implementing the North American Free Trade Agreement (NAFTA); only 40 percent of House Democrats voted for it. Other cross-partisan efforts brought forth the Brady Handgun Violence Act, the Family and Medical Leave Act, the Motor Voter Act, a national service law (creating Americorps), and a crime law.

Of all public institutions, Congress bore the largest measure of public scorn. On top of the generalized public discontent, a series of scandals on Capitol Hill targeted five senators who had championed a failed savings and loan magnate, forced closure of the House "bank" (payroll office), and cast doubt on the personal ethics of numerous members. By the spring of 1992, only 17 percent of those questioned in a national survey approved of the way Congress was doing its job, whereas 54 percent approved of their own representative's performance. Both figures were all-time lows.[44] Such anger exceeded the usual level of Congress-bashing and recalled the public unrest that preceded the reforms adopted in the early 1970s.

Civic unrest caused a dramatic changing of the guard on Capitol Hill. The 1992 elections brought 110 new House members (87 of whom returned two years later) and fourteen new senators. The 1994 contests added 86 new representatives and eleven new senators. When the House convened in January 1995, nearly a majority of its members had arrived in the 1990s. Although the Senate changed more slowly, twenty-nine of its members were 1990s arrivals.

The 1994 elections had instant and visible effects. The party balance of nearly two generations was reversed. The public policy agenda was transformed. Issues that had long been simmering suddenly boiled over: downsizing the federal establishment, devolution of power to states and localities, welfare reform, budget stringency, and a regulatory cease-fire. Facing Clinton's struggling presidency, the resurgent Republicans seized command of policy initiatives, media attention, and public expectations.

Inside Congress, party leaders flexed their muscles, activity levels initially soared, and innovative procedures were explored, tested, and adopted. House Speaker Newt Gingrich (R-GA), backed by an unusually cohesive party numerically dominated by conservative newcomers, pushed wide-ranging changes in structures and procedures. Cuts were made in the number of committees, committee assignments, and committee staffs; committee and floor procedures were altered; administrative arrangements were streamlined; and most of all, the Speaker and other party leaders gained greater leverage over committee assignments, committee scheduling, floor scheduling, and administrative management. House leaders used all these tools to win committee approval and floor votes for all ten items of their campaign platform, the so-called Contract with America, within the first hundred days of the 104th Congress (1995). But political stalemate, manifested by the White House and a more contentious Senate, kept most of these proposals out of the statute books, with the exception of congressional accountability (1995) and welfare reform (1996); a line-item veto (1996) was subsequently invalidated by the Supreme Court.

Clinton's last six years, and arguably George W. Bush's first year in office, were clouded by persistent partisan competition and the absence of secure GOP majorities. Indeed, House Republicans lost ground in the three elections following their 1994 triumphs. Leadership miscalculations can be blamed for much of this erosion. The GOP was blamed for shutting down the federal government in the winter of 1995–1996, in the midst of fierce battles between budget slashers on the Hill and the veto-wielding president. Even more high profile was the 1998–1999 impeachment of President Clinton—a project launched by House Judiciary Committee Republicans and supported by party leaders. The whole affair played poorly with the public, who deplored the president's sexual dalliance but who approved of his second-term performance on the job.[45] Midterm election media ads highlighting the impeachment—a project of Speaker Gingrich—served only to remind voters that it was the GOP leadership that had targeted the president. After the midterm elections, the Senate quashed the impeachment fiasco by failing to muster the two-thirds majority needed to remove the president from office.

In reality, the Clinton-era events went far beyond clashes over the president's personal life or even federal spending levels. They reflected a bitter struggle between Capitol Hill Republicans and the White House over control of the policy agenda. Most key votes were along party lines: the various impeachment floor votes of both chambers found more than nine out of ten representatives and senators voting with their respective parties—Republicans opposing the president, Democrats supporting him.[46]

Republican leadership turned over during this period. Speaker Newt Gingrich, who had engineered the GOP takeover of the House in 1994, met increasing opposition, including an abortive coup from his own ranks, the 1998 midterm election fiasco, and, finally, reports of his own sexual dalliance. He and his heir apparent, Robert Livingston, both stepped aside in late 1998. The agreed-upon successor, J. Dennis Hastert of Illinois, inherited a fractured and disheartened GOP conference. Eventually he became a master of the House, first by ceding more powers to the committee chairmen and then by consulting widely and making binding decisions. Yet the partisan rule of the leadership cannot be denied: often minority Democrats were excluded from committee markups of bills, and sometimes even from House-Senate conference decisions on the bills' final provisions.

If the Republicans reigned but did not yet rule in 1995–2001, the terrorists' attacks of September 11, 2001, changed the environment of congressional decision making. First, it revitalized the presidency of George W. Bush as a wartime enterprise—a metaphor designed to enhance presidential leadership.[47] For another, it immediately consigned the Congress into a reactive, more compliant institution: initially, at least, it hastily approved the problematic USA Patriot Act and the use of force against 9/11 perpetrators (both 2001), and later a resolution authorizing use of force against Iraq (2002).

The congressional workload rebounded somewhat during the Republican years, in terms of bills and resolutions introduced, bills per member, and even enactments of public laws. The average page length of public laws continued to rise, reflecting the continuing popularity of large-scale omnibus measures. Although committee meetings tended to subside, hours of floor sessions continued to rise.[48]

Post-9/11 developments, including the 2004 elections, strengthened the Republicans as the dominant party—perhaps for the foreseeable future. Will this current congressional era endure? Future developments will determine the result. On the one hand, interbranch control could tempt the Republicans to embrace extreme and potentially disastrous policies that could lead to failure and a rejection by voters. On the other hand, majority-party divisions could open up—for example, between deficit hawks and big spenders, or between big-government conservatives and libertarian minimalists—that have the potential of destroying party consensus on key policy issues.

CONCLUSION

Shifting the viewpoint from the Oval Office to Capitol Hill radically changes one's perspective on congressional-executive relations. Rather than measuring political time in terms of successive presidencies, we have sought to identify congressional equivalents. By tracking one cluster of variables—legislative workload and productivity figures—we have identified four distinctive congressional eras or regimes. Examining legislative attributes within each era, and between succeeding eras, casts new light on interbranch policy-making since the New Deal and even helps resolve some puzzling historical anomalies (for example, Franklin Roosevelt's mixed legislative record and the unexpected productivity of the Nixon-Ford period).

Our foray into the thicket of legislative activity and productivity reveals two general truths about modern-day politics and policy making. First, legislative productivity does not necessarily coincide with the tenure of individual presidents. Second, legislative productivity is less determined by party control that one would think.

Presidencies and Legislative Regimes

The bipartisan conservative era outlasted several presidents of widely varying goals and skills. Roosevelt failed after 1936 to keep Capitol Hill safe for New Deal initiatives and, after 1940, was preoccupied with the war effort. Truman repeatedly broke his lance in efforts to push legislation through conservative Congresses—most memorably in housing, labor-management relations, civil rights, and medical care. Eisenhower's modest, moderately right-of-center legislative instincts were a better fit with the objectives of the conservative coalition that ruled Capitol Hill. More aggressive than Eisenhower, Kennedy enjoyed considerable success in a transitional period when the old order in Congress was crumbling.

The liberal activist era, with its huge Democratic majorities in both chambers of Congress, spanned the presidencies of Lyndon Johnson, Richard Nixon, Gerald Ford, and (in part) Jimmy Carter. Johnson's presidency was arguably the most productive in history, legislatively speaking. Yet the most telling point is that the flow of legislation continued unabated during the Republican presidencies of Nixon and Ford. A recitation of the legislative high points from the Nixon years suggests that the mutual hostility between the GOP president and Democratic Congresses did not stand in the way of significant legislative achievements. These laws included a comprehensive tax code revision, the National Environmental Policy Act of 1969, major air and water pollution control measures, endangered species protection, a comprehensive organized crime bill, postal reorganization, urban mass transit and reorganization plans, the Occupational Safety and Health Act of 1970, the Consumer Product Safety Act, the Comprehensive Employment and Training Act, the Federal Election Campaign Act, coastal zone management, the trans-Alaska pipeline, the War Powers Resolution, and the Congressional Budget and Impoundment Control Act of 1974—not to mention the Twenty-Sixth Amendment giving eighteen-year-olds the right to vote and an unratified amendment (the Equal Rights Amendment) on women's rights.

The liberal juggernaut continued during these conservative presidencies for at least two reasons. First, the Nixon and Ford presidencies were under relentless siege from Capitol Hill's liberal majorities, composed of Democrats and a scattering of moderate or liberal Republicans. Between 1973 and 1976, Ornstein and his colleagues write, these forces "attempted a much higher number of veto overrides than any of the other Congresses in the previous thirty years, and a large number of their attempts were successful."[49] Second, Nixon saw his primary mission to be in foreign affairs and diplomacy, which left his aides in the domestic departments relatively free to negotiate as best they could with Capitol Hill majorities. Nixon may have been a conservative president, but the legislative record compiled during his administration was expansive and liberal. This historical irony deserves more careful and dispassionate reassessment by historians and political scientists than it has yet received.

The next legislative regime, the postreform era, spanned part or all of the presidencies of Jimmy Carter, Ronald Reagan, and George H. W. Bush. The advent of zero-sum, stalemate politics was popularly associated with the Reagan administration, which took office in 1981 pledging to cut taxes, domestic aid, and welfare programs. To be sure, his election was interpreted at the time as a sea change in American politics; some of Reagan's initiatives—especially the 1981 revenue cuts and repeated threats to veto new domestic spending or taxes—helped to curtail the legislative agenda. However, deteriorating economic conditions and shifting attitudes had already caused President Carter to begin to curtail his legislative agenda.[50] By the 96th Congress (1979–1981) the altered environment led to a decline in the legislative workload.

Party Control and Legislative Regimes

Party control influences legislative outputs. No proposition is more widely accepted among scholars and other observers. Many would further contend that "things go better" when the same party controls both the executive and legislative branches and that divided government is a prescription for confusion, delay, and deadlock. Legislative productivity is, without a doubt, affected by party control. And certainly presidents are more apt to achieve their legislative goals if their partisans comfortably control both chambers.

Equally to the point, shifts in Capitol Hill partisan ratios can yield meaningful changes in policy outputs, quite apart from any questions of party control or alignment. The recession-driven Democrats in 1959–1961, the Johnson landslide class of 1964, the Watergate class of 1974, and the GOP shift in 1981 and again in 1995 were dramatic changes in partisan strength on Capitol Hill that led in turn to policy redirections and procedural innovations. Probably these changes far exceeded any underlying shifts in attitudes or voting habits within the electorate as a whole, not to mention the magnitude of long-term partisan realignments.

Yet party control is an incomplete guide to legislative activity and productivity. The administrations of Roosevelt, Truman, and Carter testify to the fact that party control of both branches is no guarantee of legislative productivity. By the same token, the Nixon-Ford period and the Reagan administration (in its first year and last two years) saw productivity far beyond what would be expected from divided government. The correlation between party control and legislative productivity seems even more tenuous when we consider Mayhew's most intriguing piece of evidence: during what we term the liberal activist era, annual productivity under split party control actually exceeded that under unified control.[51]

Legislative productivity and workload, in short, fit imperfectly with conventional political thinking that stresses presidential leadership or the locus of party control of the two branches. The record of the recent past, moreover, casts doubt on the assumption of many observers that unified party control always raises legislative productivity and that divided government necessarily leads to stalemate.

Nonetheless, recent events show that Congress's evolution has by no means run its full course, and that is influenced but not determined by the White House. Continuing changes in Congress's political environment will produce further alterations in the membership, organization, procedures, and policy-making capacities of the House and Senate. As in the past, these alterations will require leadership, ingenuity, and legislative professionalism if Congress is to make its way successfully through the twenty-first century. Will Congress be able to reassert its constitutional prerogatives in a time of party government and a quasi-wartime setting? Only history will judge the outcome.

NOTES

1. Woodrow Wilson, *Congressional Government* (1885; reprint, Baltimore: Johns Hopkins University Press, 1981), 56. See also Charles O. Jones, "A Way of Life and Law," *American Political Science Review* 89 (March 1995): 1–9.

2. See Michael G. Kammen, *A Machine That Would Go of Itself: The Constitution in American Culture* (New York: Alfred A. Knopf, 1986).

3. See Roger H. Davidson and Walter J. Oleszek, *Congress and Its Members*, 9th ed. (CQ Press, 2004), table 2.1.

4. For an account of the post-9/11 changes, see James P. Pfiffner, "The Transformation of the Bush Presidency," in *Understanding the Presidency*, ed. James P. Pfiffner and Roger H. Davidson, 3rd ed. (New York: Longman, 2003), 453–71.

5. The locus classicus of party alignment theory is V. O. Key Jr., "A Theory of Critical Elections," *Journal of Politics* 17 (February 1955): 3–18. More detailed analyses are found in William N. Chambers and Walter Dean Burnham, eds., *The American Party Systems: Stages of Political Development* (New York: Oxford University Press, 1967); Walter Dean Burnham, *Critical Elections and the Mainsprings of American Politics* (New York: W. W. Norton, 1970); and James L. Sundquist, *Dynamics of the Party System*, rev. ed. (Washington, DC: Brookings Institution, 1983), esp. chaps. 1–3.

6. See, e.g., David W. Brady, "Electoral Realignment in the U.S. House of Representatives," in *Congress and Policy Change*, ed. Gerald C. Wright Jr., Leroy N. Rieselbach, and Lawrence C. Dodd (New York: Agathon Press, 1986), 46–69.

7. Stephen Skowronek, *The Politics Presidents Make* (Cambridge, MA: Harvard University Press, 1993), 29–58.

8. Skowronek, *The Politics Presidents Make*, 50.

9. Joseph Cooper, "Organization and Innovation in the House of Representatives, in *The House at Work*, ed. Joseph Cooper and G. Calvin Mackenzie (Austin: University of Texas Press, 1980), 332. This essay draws upon statistical data originally compiled by the author, his former colleagues at the Congressional Research Service, and other investigators. The most relevant data are summarized in Norman J. Ornstein, Thomas E. Mann, and Michael J. Malbin, *Vital Statistics on Congress, 2001–2002* (Washington, DC: American Enterprise Institute Press, 2002), 145–54.

10. Ornstein, Mann, and Malbin, *Vital Statistics, 2001–2002*, 146–47.

11. Richard F. Fenno Jr., *Congressmen in Committees* (Boston: Little, Brown, 1973), 280.

12. Kenneth A. Shepsle, "The Changing Textbook Congress," in *Can the Government Govern?* ed. John E. Chubb and Paul E. Peterson (Washington, DC: Brookings Institution, 1989), 238–66.

13. See Roger H. Davidson, ed., *The Postreform Congress* (New York: St. Martin's Press, 1992).

14. The seminal work concerning this conceptualization is John H. Aldrich, *Why Parties? The Origin and Transformation of Party Politics in America* (Chicago: University of Chicago Press, 1995).

15. Lawrence H. Chamberlain, *The President, Congress, and Legislation* (New York: Columbia University Press, 1946), 450–53.

16. James MacGregor Burns, *Roosevelt: The Lion and the Fox* (New York: Harcourt, Brace, 1956), 337, 339.

17. Robert J. Donovan, *Conflict and Crisis: The Presidency of Harry S Truman* (New York: W. W. Norton, 1977), 260.

18. Alonzo L. Hamby, "The Mind and Character of Harry S Truman" in *The Truman Presidency*, ed. Michael J. Lacey (Cambridge: Woodrow Wilson International Center for Scholars and Cambridge University Press, 1989), 46.

19. Fenno, *Congressmen in Committees*, 279.

20. William S. White, *Citadel: The Story of the U.S. Senate* (New York: Harper & Brothers, 1956); and Donald R. Matthews, *U.S. Senators and Their World* (Chapel Hill: University of North Carolina Press, 1960).

21. Fenno, *Congressmen in Committees*; Richard F. Fenno Jr., *The Power of the Purse: The Appropriations Process in Congress* (Boston: Little, Brown, 1966).

22. Shepsle, "Changing Textbook Congress."

23. Hedrick Smith, *The Power Game: How Washington Works* (New York: Random House, 1988), chap. 2.

24. James L. Sundquist, *Politics and Policy: The Eisenhower, Kennedy, and Johnson Years* (Washington, DC: Brookings Institution, 1968), chap. 10.

25. David R. Mayhew, *Divided We Govern: Party Control, Lawmaking, and Investigations, 1946–1990* (New Haven: Yale University Press, 1991), 76.

26. Allen Schick, *Congress and Money: Budgeting, Spending, and Taxing* (Washington, DC: Urban Institute Press, 1980), 424–36.

27. John W. Ellwood, "The Great Exception: The Congressional Budget Process in an Age of Decentralization," in *Congress Reconsidered*, 3rd ed., ed. Lawrence C. Dodd and Bruce J. Oppenheimer (Washington, DC: CQ Press, 1985), 315–42.

28. Abner J. Mikva and Patti B. Sarris, *The American Congress: The First Branch* (New York: Franklin Watts, 1983), 292.

29. See, e.g., Roger H. Davidson and Walter J. Oleszek, *Congress against Itself* (Bloomington: Indiana University Press, 1977); James L. Sundquist, *The Decline and Resurgence of Congress* (Washington, DC: Brookings Institution, 1981); and Leroy N. Rieselbach, *Congressional Reform: The Changing Modern Congress* (Washington, DC: CQ Press, 1994), esp. chap. 3.

30. David R. Mayhew, *Congress: The Electoral Connection* (New Haven: Yale University Press, 1974).

31. Lester Thurow, *The Zero-Sum Society* (New York: Basic Books, 1980).

32. Paul Krugman, "We're No. 3—So What?" *Washington Post*, March 24, 1990, C1–2.

33. Quoted in Helen Dewar, "Congress Off to Slowest Start in Years," *Washington Post*, November 21, 1989, A18.

34. Gary C. Jacobson, *The Electoral Origins of Divided Government: Competition in U.S. House Elections, 1946–1988* (Boulder, CO: Westview, 1990), 112.

35. Barbara Sinclair, *Legislators, Leaders, and Lawmaking: The U.S. House of Representatives in the Postreform Era* (Baltimore: Johns Hopkins University Press, 1995), 48–57.

36. Randall Strahan, "Agenda Change and Committee Politics in the Postreform House," *Legislative Studies Quarterly* 13 (May 1988): 185–94.

37. Allen Schick, "The Ways and Means of Leading Ways and Means," *Brookings Review* 7 (Fall 1989): 17.

38. U.S. House of Representatives, *The Committee on Ways and Means: A Bicentennial History, 1789–1989* (Washington, DC: GPO, 1989), 369.

39. U.S. House, *Committee on Ways and Means*, 370–72.

40. Schick, "Ways and Means," 21.

41. Christopher J. Bailey, "Beyond the New Congress: Aspects of Congressional Development in the 1980s," *Parliamentary Affairs* 41 (April 1988): 246.

42. Quoted in Lawrence N. Hansen, "Our Turn: Politicians Talk about Themselves,

Politics, the Public, the Press, and Reform," Centel Public Accountability Project (March 1992), 5.

43. The term was invented by Dick Morris, at the time one of Clinton's chief advisers. See Paul J. Quirk and William Cunion, "Clinton's Domestic Policy: The Lessons of a 'New Democrat,'" in *The Clinton Legacy*, ed. Colin Campbell and Bert A. Rockman (New York: Chatham House, 2000), 200–225.

44. Richard Morin and Helen Dewar, "Approval of Congress Hits All-Time Low, Poll Finds," *Washington Post*, March 20, 1992, A16.

45. An analysis from the Capitol Hill perspective is Nicol C. Rae and Colton C. Campbell, *Impeaching Clinton: Partisan Strife on Capitol Hill* (Lawrence: University Press of Kansas, 2004).

46. Roger H. Davidson, "Congressional Parties, Leaders, and Committees: 1900, 2000, and Beyond," in *American Political Parties: Decline or Resurgence?* ed. Jeffrey E. Cohen, Richard Fleisher, and Paul Kantor (Washington, DC: Congressional Quarterly Books, 2001), 284–85.

47. See Kathleen Hall Jamieson and Paul Waldman, *The Press Effect: Politicians, Journalists, and the Stories That Shape the Political World* (New York: Oxford University Press, 2003), 150–52.

48. Norman J. Ornstein, Thomas E. Mann, and Michael J. Malbin, *Vital Statistics on Congress, 1999-2000* (Washington, DC: American Enterprise Institute Press, 2000), 146–50.

49. Norman J. Ornstein, Thomas E. Mann, and Michael J. Malbin, *Vital Statistics on Congress 1993–1994* (Washington, DC: CQ Press, 1994), 151.

50. Charles O. Jones, *The Trusteeship Presidency: Jimmy Carter and the U.S. Congress* (Baton Rouge: Louisiana State University Press, 1988), chap. 7.

51. Mayhew, *Divided We Govern*, 7.

7

The Legislative Presidency in Political Time: Party Control and Presidential-Congressional Relations

Richard S. Conley

On May 21, 2001, just four months into the presidency of George W. Bush, maverick senator Jim Jeffords of Vermont made a shocking announcement that rocked the Washington establishment: he was leaving the Republican Party. According to Jeffords the leadership of the Grand Old Party (GOP) had increasingly sidelined moderates, and negotiations over the president's budget pushed him over the edge.[1] With the Senate evenly split fifty-fifty after the 2000 elections, Jeffords's decision to become an independent and throw his support to the Democrats robbed Republicans of organizational control of the upper chamber. The consequences for George W. Bush's agenda were immediate and far-reaching. Changes in key committee chairmanships, including Finance, Education, and Judiciary, presaged turbulent relations between the White House and the Democratic Senate. Moreover, the new majority leader, Tom Daschle of South Dakota, was a veteran of prior battles with Republicans over the Contract with America and had few scruples about criticizing and blocking the president's agenda and judicial nominees. Indeed, George W. Bush made stalled court appointments and differences with Senate Democrats over the creation of the new Department of Homeland Security the centerpieces in his indefatigable, and ultimately successful, midterm campaign for Republicans to regain control of the Senate in 2002.[2]

Bush seemingly realized what some scholars have argued for decades: party control of Congress is indispensable for the legislative presidency. Other presidents' bouts with opposition Congresses were as, if not more, arduous than Bush's year-and-a-half-long skirmish with Senate Democrats. Bill Clinton waged protracted veto battles with Republican majorities for six of his eight years in office, endured a government shutdown, and faced the ultimate sanction, impeachment. In his second term Richard Nixon frequently found himself at odds with congressional spending, used impoundment in an attempt to halt profligacy, and was finally chased from office by Watergate and a resurgent Democratic majority. And Republicans Gerald Ford and George H. W. Bush, who faced opposition Congresses for the duration of their presidencies, made extensive use of the veto power to halt Democratic activism in Congress. From this vantage point, "divided government"— when an opposition majority controls one or both chambers on Capitol Hill—can place the president's agenda at a sharp disadvantage and is a recipe for gridlock and institutional combat.[3]

Such conclusions, however, are incongruous with select periods in the post–World War II political landscape. Divided government seemed to matter less to Dwight Eisenhower, who got along relatively well with Democrats during six years of split party control of the White House and Capitol Hill from 1955–1960. Richard Nixon had a surprisingly high "batting average" in Congress on his position votes during his first term (1969–1972). And in the contemporary period, Ronald Reagan was remarkably successful in convincing the Democratic House to approve his first-year agenda in 1981.

Many scholars also reject the thesis that single-party control of Congress and the presidency is paramount for American national institutions to function well. As David Mayhew has shown, party control of the presidency and Congress does not affect the production of "significant" laws with lasting impacts on public policy.[4] In addition, "unified government" is rare and has not necessarily been a boon to presidential legislative leadership. Between 1945 and 2004, single-party control of the White House and Congress has occurred only four out of every ten years. The legislative records of Presidents Carter (1977–1980) and Clinton (1993–1994), in particular, were less than illustrious to many—and suggest that unified government in the American context scarcely approximates "responsible party government" of the British parliamentary variety.

This chapter attempts to reconcile elements of this longstanding debate about party control of national institutions by focusing on the ways in which unified or divided government *does matter* for presidential legislative leadership.[5] Single-party control facilitates positive presidential engagement of Congress and furnishes more opportunities for credit claiming. Presidents prevail more often on congressional votes on which they express a position, and agenda synergy with Congress is consistently stronger. They are sometimes able to steer the congressional agenda. At other times, their role has been to cultivate support for continuing party objectives in Congress. Scholars focused solely on congressional lawmaking have overlooked these advantageous features of unified government for the legislative presidency.

Split-party control has had a much more variable impact on presidents' success in Congress, agenda leadership, and legislative strategy. In the early postwar period, divided government had less effect. Presidents were often able to reach across the aisle to the opposition majority and its leadership to cobble together winning coalitions on floor votes. It is in the last several decades that assertive opposition majorities have set more of the policy agenda and have forced presidents to preempt Congress or take a more reactive role in the legislative game. Heightened partisanship and organizational reforms in Congress have hampered presidents' efforts to construct cross-party coalitions. These factors have plummeted presidents' legislative success rates and complicated agenda control. But they have also provided contemporary presidents with a powerful, if different, form of leverage over Congress. In this era of party unity and narrow seat margins on Capitol Hill, presidents have turned increasingly to vetoes and veto threats to gain influence over lawmaking. Opposition majorities in Congress have little hope of finding two-thirds majorities capable of overriding chief executives' objections, enhancing the potency of even a mere veto threat by the president to win legislative compromise.

The chapter approaches the question of party control and presidential relations with Congress from a historical perspective. The first task is to outline a theory capable of explaining the conditions that subtend different forms of presidential leadership of Congress. The objective of the framework elaborated in the next section is to consider how the intersection of broad electoral dynamics and organizational features and voting patterns in Congress shapes types of leadership opportunities presidents have had under unified and divided government since 1953. Subdividing periods of unified and divided government within contextually appropriate "eras" in the post–World War II period places into sharper perspective individual presidents' contrasting bases for influence and success. The subsequent section examines longitudinal data on presidential success on floor votes in Congress as well as presidents' involvement in significant legislation—from agenda leadership to veto threats—to substantiate the central argument about the pivotal impact of shifting governing contexts and party control of Congress for the legislative presidency.

PRESIDENTIAL LEVERAGE AND THE "ERAS OF CONGRESS"

Presidential influence, or leverage, over Congress is best conceptualized by degree along a bounded scale. At one end of the spectrum is "positive leverage," ranging from assertive presidential direction of congressional lawmaking to cross-party coalition building when the president and Congress share agenda goals. On the other end of the spectrum is "veto leverage," a defensive strategy of partisan coalition building, vetoes, and veto threats to forestall congressional activism when the legislative agenda is sharply contested between the White House and the majority on Capitol Hill.

The broader electoral and institutional setting presidents have confronted has determined the type of leadership they are able to exercise along this continuum. The theoretical approach borrows from the "new institutionalism" perspective.[6] As "rational actors," presidents—whatever their partisan stripe—are likely to pursue similar strategies when faced with similar contextual circumstances vis-à-vis Congress. The notion of presidential influence in "political time"[7] hinges on the ways in which party control of Congress has merged with presidents' electoral resources and internal dynamics on Capitol Hill to mold presidential legislative strategy in predictable ways in the last fifty years. These criteria are critically important in understanding the historical patterns of presidential-congressional interactions as well as contemporary developments.

The Electoral Realm

One key factor in the president's influence in Congress is his electoral resources. Bringing more members of his own party into Congress upon his election legitimizes the president's agenda in the eyes of the press and the public. The president's electoral popularity in members' constituencies is also an important component of his "political capital."[8]

When members of Congress feel they owe their electoral victory to the president, "coattail" effects enhance the chief executive's potential for influence over members generally. A president's strong electoral linkage to copartisans may bolster his ability to set and lead the congressional agenda. "Candidates receiving coattail votes," James Campbell and Joe Sumners note, "may be a bit more positively disposed, out of gratitude, to side with a president who had helped in their election."[9] For their part, opposition members may fear electoral retaliation for failing to support a president who ran strong in their district. Many southern Democrats, for example, were concerned that a failure to support Ronald Reagan's early agenda in 1981 would lead to their ouster, given his widespread victories in their constituencies. In sum, legislators on both sides of the aisle must be concerned with their support of an electorally popular president because they believe that their constituents pay attention to their voting records.

The problem for presidents in the latter period of the postwar era is that coattails, however measured, have declined considerably. Gone are the days when presidents were able to realize significant seat gains in Congress and catapult members of their own party to victory. Greater electoral competition between the two parties in the electorate for the presidency and the growth of congressional members' incumbency advantage are complementary explanations for the phenomenon.

The House of Representatives is typically the reference point in analyses of coattails since all 435 seats are contested every two years. Figure 7.1 shows "seat-gain coattails" in the House from 1948–2004. The strong seat gains for Truman in 1948 and Eisenhower in 1952 reversed party control of Congress in the president's favor. Lyndon Johnson's landslide election brought thirty-eight new Democrats to Congress, and most were strong advocates of the president's Great Society agenda. Seat gains have tailed off significantly since the late 1960s. Ronald Reagan's victory is the exception to the rule, but even the gain of thirty-three Republican seats in 1980 was well short of the threshold to allow the GOP control of the House. Similarly, Nixon (1968, 1972) brought a handful of Republicans to Congress but not enough to overturn Democratic control.

Another dynamic is also visible in figure 7.1. The advent of "negative coattails," whereby the president's party *loses* seats in Congress upon his election, first occurred in 1960. John F. Kennedy's inability to solidify his partisan

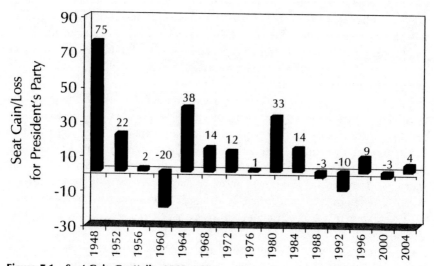

Figure 7.1   Seat Gain Coattails, 1948–2004

Source: Compiled by author from *Congressional Quarterly Almanacs.* 2004 coattail data as of 11/4/2004.

base on Capitol Hill certainly called into question his claim to a "mandate"—just as Democrats' loss of ten seats with Bill Clinton's election did little to legitimize his far-reaching agenda after the 1992 election. Both George H. W. Bush (1988) and George W. Bush (2000) witnessed seat losses for their party in Congress upon their election. For Bush *père* the lack of seat-gain coattails forced him to confront a large Democratic majority. For George W. Bush the loss of three seats was the third consecutive loss for the GOP since 1996, which left Republicans narrowly in charge of the House. In 2004, Bush was able to add slightly to the GOP's majority in the lower chamber following moderate seat gains in the midterm elections of 2002.

In tandem with the loss of seat-gain coattails, presidents' electoral popularity at the constituency level has also declined vis-à-vis members' own margin of victory. Members with district-level victory margins less than the president's should fall under greater pressure to back his legislative stands. Eisenhower's electoral popularity (1952, 1956) outpaced between half and nearly two-thirds of Republicans. Nixon ran ahead of over half of the GOP members elected in 1972. And Johnson's 1964 victory trumped that of over half the Republican members in their districts—in part due to the effect of Barry Goldwater's lackluster campaign.

Yet most other presidents have "run ahead" of fewer members of their own party or of the opposition party. Apart from Johnson, Democratic presidents have generally had few "marginal coattails" at the district level despite enjoying a majority of their copartisans in the House. John F. Kennedy (1960) and Jimmy Carter (1976) ran ahead of less than a tenth of Democrats, and hardly any Republicans. In the era of nearly consistent divided government in the last twenty years, Ronald Reagan (1980, 1984), George H. W. Bush (1988), Bill Clinton (1992, 1996), and George W. Bush (2000) ran ahead of no more than approximately a third of their copartisans and typically less than a sixth of opposition members.

The critical point is that presidents today frequently confront members on both sides of the aisle whose electoral victories owe little to the campaign for the White House. Members' incumbency advantage is a key factor in the disappearance of coattails. Incumbency advantage for members of Congress began to increase in the 1960s, and by the mid-1980s nearly nine in ten members garnered 60 percent or more of the two-party vote at the district level—a much greater percentage of the vote than most presidents are typically able to marshal in their copartisans' constituencies, let alone in opposition members' districts.[10]

The increasingly tenuous electoral linkage between presidents and congressional majorities has weakened presidential influence in the legislative sphere. As an aide to President Kennedy noted, "If the President runs behind in your district, he becomes a liability. If the President can't help you, why help him?"[11] Under unified conditions, recent presidents like Carter and Clinton have had a more fragile basis from which to set the legislative agenda and pursue their own independent policy goals compared to Johnson. They have frequently had to resolve themselves to lend support for congressional priorities, with much more narrow windows of opportunity opening for the pursuit of their own agenda objectives. Under divided party control, members of the opposition party have few incentives to follow the president's lead. Their constituents have rejected the president's electoral bid. The president's ability to construct cross-party coalitions erodes as coattails decline.

The Internal Configuration of Congress

Another critical factor in the president's influence in Congress is the internal configuration of Congress. The relative levels of centralization of the leadership structure on Capitol Hill and intraparty cohesion on floor votes operate together with presidents' electoral resources to condition the degree to which they can steer the congressional agenda and construct partisan or cross-partisan coalitions for their positions, whether under single- or split-party government.

Unified or divided government has occurred within distinguishable "eras" of Congress, as Roger Davidson calls them, marked by decisive turning points in leadership organization and voting alignments.[12] Grasping the essential features of Congress in the "bipartisan conservative" (1947–1964), "liberal activist" (1965–1978) and "postreform/party-unity" (1979–present) eras clarifies the nexus between party control, institutional dynamics in Congress, and presidential influence across time. Congressional "time" moves at its own rhythm, defying the regular cycle of presidential elections.

The Bipartisan Conservative Era

The policy-making context on Capitol Hill from 1947 through the mid-1960s enabled presidents—especially those with longer coattails—to lobby individual members and party leaders on both sides of the aisle. Presidents found that members often looked to them for issue leadership. Weaker leadership coordination and lower levels of party unity defined dynamics in Congress. The diffusion of power among senior committee members robbed the Speaker and majority leader of the tools for enforcing party cohesion in the House of Representatives. In the halcyon days of the "textbook Congress" of smoky, backroom bartering and "logrolling," fewer votes pitted a majority of one party against a majority of the other.

Cross-party coalitions were frequent because both Democrats and Republicans were internally divided. Moderate members often held the balance over legislative outcomes on the floor of the House. James MacGregor Burns' notion of "four-party" politics captured the essence of the period, as liberal Democrats and conservative Republicans in Congress faced a large contingent of their copartisans whose ideological stances were closer to the opposing party.[13] The influence of these cross-pressured legislators resulted in shifting voting alignments and de facto policy majorities that often changed according to the issue, no matter which party had the nominal majority in Congress.[14] Despite Democratic control of Congress for all but two years (1953–1954) from 1949–1964, the conservative coalition of southern Democrats and conservative Republicans often carried the day on economic, defense, and social issues. In other cases liberal Democrats and moderate Republicans could join together on select bills such as civil rights and prevail.

The conservative coalition did often frustrate the agendas of Democratic presidents Truman and Kennedy (not to mention Roosevelt)—despite the fact that each president had titular Democratic majorities in Congress. Southern Democrats, for example, bottled up Kennedy's Medicare proposal in committee. Yet cobbling together winning cross-party coalitions was not impossible. Kennedy was successful in brokering intra- and cross-party support for other important elements of his New Frontier domestic agenda, including housing, manpower training, and urban development, by highlighting constituency benefits to legislators on both sides of the aisle.[15] And through his perseverant leadership Lyndon Johnson was able to overcome staunch southern Democratic opposition to the 1964 Civil Rights Act by unifying liberal Democrats and moderate Republicans.[16]

Under divided government from 1955–1960, Republican president Dwight Eisenhower proved skilled at reading the congressional landscape and manipulating voting alignments on Capitol Hill to his advantage. Eisenhower successfully married southern Democratic and Republican support for his stands against domestic spending, including veto overrides occasionally attempted by the Democratic leadership. In other cases, such as civil rights and foreign affairs, he reached across the aisle and marshaled the support of moderates in both parties for his stands.[17]

It is little wonder that in this bipartisan conservative era from the 1940s through the 1960s party control of Congress seemingly mattered less to the legislative presidency. The conservative coalition was the dominant voting alignment, whatever the partisan configuration of the White House and Capitol Hill. Unified government for Democratic presidents was a tenuous arrangement marked by internal divisions between northern and southern Democrats that undermined any basis for "party government." The situation was compounded for Democratic presidents like Kennedy who had no coat-tails. By contrast, the ever-popular Eisenhower played those divisions in Congress like a fine-tuned instrument, often negotiating behind the scenes in what Fred Greenstein typecasts the "hidden-hand" presidency.[18] Given his relatively limited legislative agenda, Eisenhower was able to enjoy more than a modicum of success in the legislative arena.

The Liberal Activist Era

The lack of strong intraparty cohesion and a decentralized setting in Congress continued into the early 1970s. Lyndon Johnson's electoral landslide in 1964 momentarily broke the hold of the conservative coalition in Congress. Johnson's coattails provided a working legislative majority of liberal Democrats (at least before the midterm elections of 1966) that enabled him to direct the contours of lawmaking around his Great Society agenda. Much of the far-reaching legislation adopted from 1965–1972 passed by large bipartisan coalitions, which were a reflection of broad congressional agreement on public policies proposed or backed by the president.

Richard Nixon was caught up in the momentum of the consolidation of the Great Society agenda in Congress. During his first term he was generally unwilling to challenge the large Democratic majorities he confronted. Shifting policy coalitions sometimes permitted him to ally his administration with select policy endeavors and exercise some influence over the substance of legislation. But most of all Nixon sought opportunities for credit-sharing with Congress as he kept a keen eye on reelection. In light of the public mood for policy action, positive competition developed between the president and Congress to minimize protracted conflict.[19]

The continuing Democratic agenda on Capitol Hill was, nevertheless, anathema to Nixon's policy preferences. The proof came after his landslide reelection in 1972. Nixon's actions formed a critical turning point in executive-legislative relations. His extensive impoundment of funds for domestic programs and vetoes of congressional bills, followed by the Watergate scandal, set in motion an irreversible tide in Congress that brought about stronger party leadership and greater intraparty cohesion among Democrats. The post-Watergate environment on Capitol Hill presaged the twilight of the fluid legislative coalitions of yesteryear.

Democrats judged structural reforms essential to fend off Nixon's threat to the party's agenda. They revamped the committee system to loosen conservatives' grip.[20] The House speakership was strengthened to allow the Speaker greater control over committee appointments and the referral of legislation to committees.[21] The party whip system was also extended to co-opt members into the leadership structure and guarantee stronger party loyalty.[22] The objective was to reinforce Congress's autonomous policy-making capacity.

The sum total of these reforms produced an environment scarcely conducive to President Ford for building cross-party coalitions under divided government. The reforms also entailed ramifications for President Carter under unified conditions. The Republican Ford, who had been elected neither to the vice presidency nor the presidency, had no electoral leverage over Congress. He faced an uphill battle in attempting to marshal Democratic support among leaders, committee chairs, or rank-and-file members upon assuming the presidency after Nixon's resignation. He resorted frequently to the veto to halt domestic spending, casting a total of forty-eight vetoes in just over two years. Ford's biggest challenge was warding off Democrats' earnest attempts to override his vetoes. He strove to keep his small Republican minority unified and garner whatever Democratic votes he could to reach 33 percent in the House or the Senate—which was no easy task in light of Democrats' significant gains in Congress in the 1974 elections.[23]

The context of Carter's election, combined with stronger congressional organization, substantially weakened his influence over Congress, despite a Democratic majority in Congress from 1977 to 1980. Carter was the first president to come to office following the McGovern-Fraser reforms, which marginalized the role of party and congressional leaders in the presidential nomination process. His "outsider" and "anti-Washington" candidacy for the White House may have been in step with public sentiment following Watergate, but it compounded a breach in comity between him and the Democratic majority in Congress.[24]

As Charles O. Jones argues, "Democrats (and some Republicans) came to think of themselves as an alternative government during Nixon's second administration."[25] Though Nixon had departed, the mindset remained. Carter's travails were connected to changes in congressional policy-making ability, which curtailed members' need to look to him for policy leadership. In addition, Carter's own agenda—the "politics of the public good"[26] and an emphasis on deregulation—fit uncomfortably with his copartisans' aspirations. Congress often (and belatedly) passed scaled-down versions of his proposals, such as the energy plan. Finally, his vetoes "on principle" of Democratic constituency projects provoked a significant backlash and embarrassing overrides.

Carter was arguably most successful when he identified continuing legislative proposals or "promising issues"[27] in Congress that were aimed at calibrating government policy with the new and difficult economic context of the mid- to late 1970s, such as banking regulation, Social Security taxes, and minimum wage legislation. Unified government *did* matter, even if Carter's term hardly reflected the lionized FDR or LBJ models of strong presidential leadership of Congress. The electoral and institutional contexts surrounding Carter's term were simply not commensurate with these Democratic predecessors.

The Postreform/Party-Unity Era

More than any other single factor, Ronald Reagan's stunning legislative successes in 1981 marked another pivotal turning point in congressional organization and stability in voting alignments in Congress, with far-reaching consequences for the legislative presidency in the contemporary era. This defining moment in political time has continued to shape many of the contours of executive-legislative relations into the new millennium. The Democratic majority's reaction against Reagan foreshadowed trends that would dominate two decades of nearly constant divided government—and would outlive the Democratic majority itself as the 1994 elections dramatically ushered in the first Republican majority in the House in forty years. Republicans only bolstered the trend toward "conditional party government" in Congress that Democrats had begun a decade and a half earlier.[28]

Reagan's early agenda to cut domestic spending and taxes while increasing defense expenditures polarized Congress. His ephemeral legislative successes in 1981 owed to strong unity in the ranks of congressional Republicans and critical support from a waning contingent of cross-pressured southern Democrats whose ideological positions were closer to the median GOP member—and in whose districts Reagan had been particularly popular in 1980. Cross-party voting alliances in the early 97th Congress (1981–1982) represented a sort of "last hurrah" for the conservative coalition, which, in Reagan's first year, was instrumental in pushing his agenda across the threshold of victory.

Just as their leadership reforms in the early 1970s had been a reaction against Nixon, Democrats in the early 1980s embarked on an institutional reform program that was aimed at thwarting Reagan's ability to make the majority's preferred legislation vulnerable to the combination of Republican challenges and southern Democrats' defections from the party line. Progressive Democrats redoubled efforts to centralize power and authority in the leadership and reinvigorated the party whip organization. They bolstered the Speaker's ability to control the referral of legislation to committees and to implement restrictive rules on floor amendments to bills. The objective was to insure greater intraparty cohesion and enable a growing liberal core in the Democratic majority to control more fully policy outcomes.[29]

Electoral forces that coalesced during Reagan's term also fueled Democrats' reformist impulse. Congressional scholars Joseph Cooper and David

Brady argue that the institutional strength of parties in Congress is a reflection of polarized constituency configurations in the electorate.[30] Rank-and-file Democrats found the benefits of centralizing power and authority in a stronger leadership organization a necessary and desirable practice in order to enhance the party's agenda-setting capacity and safeguard constituents' interests.[31]

Reagan's early legislative successes provoked a sense of urgency for leadership reforms because the more steadfastly liberal Democratic membership in the 1980s resented the ability of a shrinking number of conservatives to thwart the majority's policy aspirations. Membership turnover and generational replacement of retiring senior Democrats with new Republicans in the South, as well as redistricting in the 1980s and 1990s, evaporated the traditional ideological rift between northern liberal and southern conservative Democrats. Indeed, by the 1990s, the few Democrats elected from the South were typically African-Americans whose ideological positions mirrored those of their colleagues across the nation. Thus, the "geographic realignment" of the southern electorate was a key factor in precipitating reforms as party competition increased with Republican gains in the Sunbelt.

By the end of 1982 the effects of Democrats' efforts were palpable for President Reagan's fortunes in the legislative sphere. The conservative coalition had all but disappeared as a structural force in the House. The more fluid voting alignments that Reagan had manipulated during his first year were replaced by growing interparty unity. The president's successive annual budgets were declared "dead on arrival" in Congress, and House leaders put forth their own alternatives. Reagan increasingly turned to the veto to halt Democratic legislation that threatened his early policy accomplishments.

Reagan's successor, George Herbert Walker Bush, inherited this highly structured policy-making environment on Capitol Hill after winning a bitter campaign in 1988 that left Democrats in charge of both chambers of Congress. Without much of a domestic agenda of his own, Bush focused instead on maintaining "veto strength" against the Democratic legislation he most vehemently opposed. Aided by party-unity voting in the House, Bush sought to ensure enough Republican votes (at least 33 percent) to sustain any override challenge to his vetoes. In this way he managed much legislative business through reactive veto threats aimed at forcing Democrats to drop objectionable provisions on bills ranging from the budget to social services. His threats were buttressed by a nearly perfect veto record.[32] Of the twenty-nine regular vetoes he cast, he suffered only a single override.

The importance of electoral and constituency factors as the driving force behind stronger party government in the House is accentuated by Republicans' organizational choices following the 1994 elections, which reversed forty years of Democratic control. All House GOP candidates signed the Contract with America, campaigned on the policy goals in the platform, and felt compelled to make good on their promises.[33] The principles of the Contract served as a basis for Republican unity in much the same way that Democratic rules of the 1980s and 1990s "bonded" members and conditioned their legislative support.[34] As Barbara Sinclair notes, Republicans were eager to give their leaders "many of the same tools that Democrats utilized when they were in the majority."[35] In the 104th Congress, party unity reached heights not seen for over a century.

The policy-making context on Capitol Hill following the 1994 elections redefined Bill Clinton's legislative presidency. In his first two years in office Clinton had struggled to mount a legislative *offensive* on health care reform, the federal budget, and crime. He confronted a hostile Republican minority and a frequently skeptical Democratic majority in Congress with which he shared few electoral connections. After 1994 the GOP contract supplanted Clinton's agenda as the focus of policy debate in Congress and relegated him to the sidelines. Clinton was forced to turn to a *defensive* strategy centering on veto leverage. His warning to the Republican majority that the president was still "relevant" to the legislative process because of his veto power was a harbinger of the intense policy battles that would follow.[36] Clinton maximized party unity to sustain his ability to threaten vetoes and force the GOP majority to compromise on policy specifics.[37] And like his predecessor, George H. W. Bush, Clinton had a nearly perfect veto record. Of the thirty-seven regular vetoes he cast from 1995 to 2000, he suffered only a single override.

From this brief narrative spanning the last fifty years, it is obvious that the postreform/party-unity era has been the most salient for executive-legislative relations during times of divided government. Stronger party cohesion in Congress has transformed presidential strategy. With few coattails vis-à-vis the opposition party and unable to build cross-party coalitions, presidents have had to turn to veto leverage to gain influence over lawmaking dynamics. It is not simply a question of presidents enduring low "batting averages" for their legislative positions in Congress. Rather, as the next section elucidates, divided party control in the postreform/party-unity era has complicated presidents' agenda-setting efforts and ability to claim credit for significant policy outcomes, which are more frequently driven by assertive opposition majorities. Stronger parties in Congress have also proved a mixed blessing to presidents under unified conditions. With few coattails and facing a more independent and better organized membership within their own congressional base, Presidents Carter and Clinton had a weaker basis for autonomous policy successes—and often their most considerable policy accomplishments were to further longstanding party objectives blocked by their predecessors.

PRESIDENTIAL SUCCESS AND SIGNIFICANT LEGISLATION ACROSS ERAS

Data on presidents' floor success in Congress and their involvement in significant domestic legislation substantiate the "eras" framework for grasping how executive-legislative relationships have changed with party control of national institutions over time. The much more variable impact of divided government on presidential success and legislative strategy contrasts significantly with the consistently higher presidential floor success rates and agenda synergy with Congress under unified conditions. Let us now examine several key empirical indicators in greater detail.

Presidential "Batting Averages" in Congress across the Eras

One benchmark for testing the effect of party control of Congress for the legislative presidency is the rate of presidential-congressional "concurrence,"[38] or the percentage of times floor outcomes correspond to presidents' positions. Figure 7.2 shows this measure of annual presidential success in the House of Representatives in times of unified and divided government.[39]

Consistently higher levels of presidential-congressional agreement during periods of unified control are unmistakable. Eisenhower (1953) and Johnson (1965) top the chart with success rates of over 90 percent. Similarly, Clinton (1993) and George W. Bush (2001–2003) enjoyed success rates of over 80 percent on their legislative stands. Carter's (1978) batting average is the lowest among presidents under unified government but never fell below 70 percent.

There is far more inconsistency in presidential success rates during divided government. In the bipartisan conservative era, Eisenhower's (1955–1960) success rate never dipped below 50 percent—and in 1956 and 1958 his legislative stands carried the day almost as frequently as under unified government in 1954. In the liberal activist era, Nixon's first-term success rate is stunning. Executive-legislative concurrence never dropped below 70 percent. The data allude to Nixon's strategic position-taking in favor of popular legislation during his first term as he eyed reelection. Following his successful 1972 campaign, Nixon's success rate fell by almost half as he began to oppose congressional action more much more frequently.

It is during the postreform/party-unity era, however, that the effects of

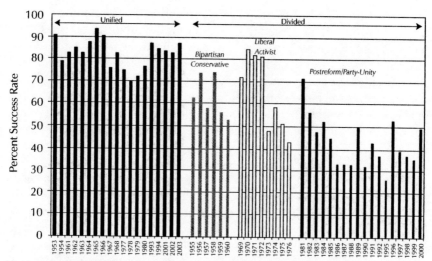

Figure 7.2   Presidential Success Rates in the U.S. House of Representatives

Source: Congressional Quarterly Almanacs. Data are yearly presidential position vote-success rates.

divided government on presidential-congressional concurrence have been most dramatic. Reagan's success rate of over 70 percent in 1981 marks a clear dividing line. Following Democrats' reorganization efforts his success rate fell steadily over time. In his last three years in office Reagan's positions carried the day no more than a third of the time. With few exceptions, divided government for Reagan's successors—Bush and Clinton—pushed presidential success rates below 50 percent.

Regression analysis enables a more systematic test of the net effects of party control on presidential success while controlling for the "natural" decay of presidents' influence over the course of their terms. Many scholars posit that as presidents make decisions and take policy positions, their "political capital" wanes, and members on both sides of the aisle may become disappointed or disaffected. Presidents' batting averages, therefore, should be the greatest at the beginning of their terms under both unified and divided conditions.

Time-series regression confirms how congressional eras in the postwar period have differentially affected presidential floor success rates. Details on the analysis are in endnote 40.[40] Time in office does take an inevitable toll for all presidents. Executive-legislative concurrence declines by about 2 percent for every year of a president's term, regardless of party control. But all things being equal, under unified government presidents can expect success rates of approximately 87 percent. Divided government causes a variable drop in the president's batting average. In the bipartisan conservative era the model does not predict dramatically lower presidential success rates compared to unified government. The equation estimates a success rate between 57 and 69 percent for Eisenhower, with the higher score coming in his first term. Even in the liberal activist era the model forecasts average presidential success rates to fall between 60 and 69 percent, controlling for time in office. It is in the postreform/party-unity era that divided government has the most damning effect on presidential success. The model forecasts success rates no higher than 51 percent—and as low as 36 percent for two-term presidents like Reagan and Clinton.

The greater impact of divided government on presidential success is intrinsically linked to more stable, partisan voting coalitions in Congress, ideological conflict between presidents and opposition majorities, and party leaders' authoritative control of the legislative agenda. In the postreform/party-unity era of divided government, presidents now oppose bills reaching the floor far more than they support them. And they lack essential electoral resources to persuade opposition majorities to take voting stances against their majority leadership. By the end of Reagan's second term he opposed nearly three-quarters of the congressional bills on which he took a position. Similarly, Clinton opposed approximately two-thirds of all bills that reached the floor. The current context stands in stark contrast to President Eisenhower, who had more opportunities to maneuver across party lines in Congress, or President Nixon, who chose to ally himself to elements of the congressional agenda.

Presidential "batting averages" in the Senate are similar to those in the House, despite important contrasts in structural features between the chambers. Leaders in the Senate cannot set rules governing floor debate in the same way that their House counterparts can. Other antimajoritarian features of the Senate—including the filibuster and nongermane amendments— render strong party leadership far more problematic in the upper chamber. Yet, while intraparty cohesion has been slower to coalesce in the Senate, "there is little question," as Burdett Loomis posits, "that the Senate has grown more partisan since the 1970s, under Democratic and Republican regimes alike."[41]

Time-series regression of presidential success rates in the Senate confirms that the "eras" approach also helps to explain executive-legislative concurrence in the upper chamber.[42] Under unified government presidents can expect success rates of 86 percent, with time eroding their batting average by 2 percent for each year in office. Divided government in the bipartisan conservative era yields an expected drop, per se, of only 7 percent in Eisenhower's annual success rate. But when presidents faced an opposition majority in either the liberal activist or postreform/party-unity era, their success rates drop dramatically—by 17 and 16 percent, respectively—holding time constant. In other words, presidents in these two eras can expect batting averages between 52 and 69 percent, depending on their year in term. Although these success rates are slightly higher than those in the House, the data validate that the Nixon and Reagan presidencies were pivot points in prompting internally cohesive parties and growing executive-legislative disagreement in the Senate.

Significant Domestic Legislation, Presidential and Congressional Agendas, and Veto Politics

The foregoing analysis of presidential success rates accentuates that in recent decades divided government has had a profoundly negative impact on one benchmark measure of presidential influence in Congress. But the story does not end there. To appreciate more fully the disproportionate impact of divided government on presidential legislative strategy in the contemporary era, and subtle differences in presidential leadership in periods of unified control, it is vital to examine presidential involvement in significant or "landmark" bills.

Mayhew's Landmark Bills

A reexamination of David Mayhew's "significant" legislation in the postwar period furnishes a more substantial focus on agenda-setting between the branches, presidential strategy, and legislative outcomes that further highlights differences in presidential legislative leadership across time and by party control.[43] Using historical "sweeps" of media and scholarly accounts of legislation that observers regard as having an enduring impact on American public policy, Mayhew assembled more than three hundred laws from 1947 to 2002. He is most interested in providing evidence that divided government does not produce legislative gridlock. The proportion of laws produced under unified and divided government, he shows, does not differ greatly. Yet Mayhew fails to answer a critical question for scholars of the presidency: are such laws the product of presidential or congressional agendas, and how does presidential strategy and engagement on such laws vary by party control across time?

Tables 7.1 and 7.2 recategorize Mayhew's significant laws by divided and unified government, respectively, for biennial congressional periods across the three eras. Landmark foreign policy laws were purged to leave a focus on the 260 domestic bills passed from 1953 to 2002. Detailed research of presi-

Table 7.1. Significant Legislation and Presidential-Congressional Agendas and Interaction, Divided Government, 1953–2002

Cong/# of Laws	Pres.	Agenda Connection & Presidential Position				Vetoes and Veto Threats			
		Pres. Priority	Cong. Agenda—Supported	Cong. Agenda—No Position	Cong. Agenda—Oppose	Pres. Priority—Veto Threat	Cong. Agenda—Veto Threat	Cong. Agenda—Prior Veto	Cong. Agenda—Vetoed/Overridden
Bipartisan Conservative Era									
84th [n = 4]	Eisenhower	3 (75%)	0	0	0	0	0	1 (25%)	0
85th [n = 9]	Eisenhower	6 (67%)	1 (11%)	1 (11%)	1 (11%)	0	0	0	0
86th [n = 5]	Eisenhower	2 (40%)	1 (20%)	1 (20%)	0	0	0	1[b] (20%)	0
Liberal Activist Era									
91st [n = 20]	Nixon	8 (40%)	2 (10%)	3 (15%)	3 (15%)	3 (15%)	1 (5%)	0	0
92nd [n = 15]	Nixon	3 (20%)	3 (20%)	5 (33%)	2 (13%)	1 (7%)	0	0	1 (7%)
93rd [n = 19]	Nixon/Ford	4 (21%)	6 (32%)	6 (32%)	0	0	2 (11%)	0	1 (5%)
94th [n = 14]	Ford	7 (50%)	0	6 (43%)	0	0	1 (7%)	0	0

Postreform/Party-Unity Era

97th [n = 9]	Reagan	3 (33%)	3 (33%)	1 (11%)	0	0	2 (22%)	0	0
98th [n = 6]	Reagan	2 (33%)	0	2 (33%)	0	2 (33%)	0	0	0
99th [n = 7]	Reagan	2 (29%)	0	2 (29%)	0	0	3 (43%)	0	0
100th [n = 10]	Reagan	3 (30%)	0	1 (10%)	1 (10%)	0	2 (20%)	0	3 (30%)
101st [n = 9]	Bush (41)	2 (22%)	2 (22%)	2 (22%)	0	1 (11%)	0	2 (22%)	0
102nd [n = 5]	Bush (41)	1 (20%)	0	1 (20%)	0	1 (20%)	0	1 (20%)	1 (20%)
104th [n = 14]	Clinton	5[c] (36%)	5 (36%)	3 (21%)	0	0	0	0	1 (7%)
105th [n = 7]	Clinton	1 (14%)	2 (29%)	3 (43%)	0	1 (14%)	0	0	0
106th [n = 5]	Clinton	0	0	4 (80%)	0	0	1 (20%)	0	0
107th [n = 13]	Bush (43)	3 (23%)	4 (31%)	3 (23%)	1 (8%)	2 (15%)	0	0	0

Note: Row percentages do not always equal 100% due to rounding.

[a] Congressional Quarterly did not begin recordkeeping of presidential positions until 1953; see text for discussion.

[b] Eisenhower vetoed the Housing Act of 1959 twice.

[c] Clinton vetoed welfare reform twice in the 104th Congress; he also issued prior vetoes on the budget.

Table 7.2.   Significant Legislation and Presidential-Congressional Agendas and Interaction, Unified Government, 1953–1994

Era	Congress/ # of laws	President	Presidential Priority	Congressional Agenda—Supported
Bipartisan Conservative	83rd [n = 8]	Eisenhower	7 (88%)	1 (13%)
	87th [n = 10]	Kennedy	10 (100%)	0
	88th [n = 11]	Kennedy/ Johnson	10 (91%)	1 (9%)
Liberal Activist	89th [n = 22]	Johnson	22 (100%)	0
	90th [n = 15]	Johnson	15 (100%)	0
	95th [n = 11]	Carter	8 (73%)	3 (27%)
Postreform/ Party-Unity	96th [n = 9]	Carter	8 (89%)	1 (11%)
	103rd [n = 11]	Clinton	10 (91%)	1 (9%)

Note: Row percentages do not always equal 100% due to rounding.

dents' State of the Union addresses, statements, and legislative histories was undertaken to test the degree to which significant legislation had at least some correspondence to the president's stated policy objectives—and if not, whether the president supported, opposed bills, or "stayed quiet" and took no position on bills inspired by Congress. Bill histories were also utilized to determine whether each bill was subject to "veto politics," including threats, prior vetoes, and veto overrides. This approach paints a vastly more intricate picture of presidential-congressional engagement in the legislative realm on legislative enactments with durable impacts on domestic public policy.

Analysis of presidents' involvement in "important" domestic lawmaking underscores the qualitative change in the way presidents have negotiated an increasingly contested agenda with opposition majorities through the veto power in the postreform/party-unity era. Presidents' recourse to veto leverage, and the higher proportion of significant laws with no connection to presidents' stated agendas, contrasts mightily not only with periods of unified government generally but also earlier periods of divided party control. The analysis also places into sharper perspective the subtleties involved in presidential management of shared agendas with Congress under unified government, depending on the strength of presidents' institutional position across eras.

Table 7.1 shows that during divided government in the bipartisan conservative era, the lion's share of significant legislation passed emanated from Eisenhower's priorities. Bills included the federal highway bill of 1956, the National Defense Education Act in 1958, and the civil rights bills of 1957 and 1960. No other period of divided government shows a similar linkage between significant legislation and the president's agenda, even if legislative "output" was rather modest overall. On bills that percolated up from Congress, the president generally took favorable positions.

Eisenhower utilized the veto as a last resort on congressional bills. He vetoed a farm bill and a housing bill but managed legislative coalitions in Congress to block override attempts by the Democratic majority. He won compromise on later renditions of the bills.[44] Eisenhower's electoral popularity, the fluidity of legislative alignments in Congress, and a weak leadership organization on Capitol Hill were key ingredients in his leadership on landmark bills. His amiable relations with Democratic leaders and the conservative policy-making environment of the 1950s enabled both the White House and Congress to share credit for policy accomplishments, with members on Capitol Hill often looking to him to take the lead.

The liberal activist era marks a qualitative change in presidential management of divided government. Examination of legislative data lends credence to the thesis that President Nixon was *not* the driving force behind many of the significant bills of the day.[45] The data convey a highly varied legislative strategy, particularly in the 91st Congress (1969–1970).

Nixon did garner a few clear policy victories. He successfully persuaded Congress to pass revenue sharing with the states, the extension of unemployment insurance coverage, and funds to improve the nation's air transit system. Yet in three cases *he threatened to veto his very own proposals* when the Democratic majority went further than he liked. Engaged in a tug-of-war with Congress to take credit for popular policies, Nixon proposed a 10 percent increase in Old Age, Survivor, and Disability Insurance benefits as part of the Social Security increase of 1969. In a move to upstage the president, House Democrats adopted a 15 percent increase. Nixon backed down from his veto threat over the costs given the program's widespread popularity.[46] Similarly, Nixon threatened to veto a bill on coal mine safety he had proposed after sparring with Democrats over workmen's compensation issues. He yielded when more than a thousand West Virginia miners walked off their jobs in protest of his veto threat.[47] Nixon was somewhat more successful in

exacting concessions from Democrats on his proposal for a 5 percent surcharge on higher incomes in the 1969 Tax Reform Act.[48]

The bulk of other legislation from 1969 to 1974 (91st, 92nd, and 93rd
Congresses) was the product of congressional action. Nixon took *no position*
on a third of the bills passed from 1971 to 1974, including Supplemental
Security Income (1972); the Higher Education Act of 1972, which established Pell Grants for college students; the Social Security increase of 1973;
or the Housing and Community Development Act of 1974. In other cases,
he publicly supported bills that originated in Congress in order to take a bit
of credit—as he did on so many roll-call votes. Nixon supported the Equal
Employment Opportunity Act of 1972, the Agricultural and Consumer Protection Act of 1973, and federal aid to health-maintenance organizations.

Nixon sought to avoid taking clear-cut opposition for many popular bills.
He was generally loath to veto significant legislation, and twice he was over-
ridden when he did—once in 1972 on water pollution and again in 1974 on
the Freedom of Information Act. Many of his veto threats on congressional
legislation were aimed at reducing the cost of bills, such as the Amtrak rail
passenger legislation of 1970. Still, in other cases, Nixon accepted legislation
he had neither asked for nor wanted. The best example is the passage of
price-control legislation in 1970. The legislation enabled the president to
control inflation by imposing wage and price freezes. Nixon signed the bill
reluctantly, contending that he would have rather vetoed it.[49]

On balance, the evidence shows that Nixon was co-opted to a large degree
by the continuing Democratic Great Society agenda in Congress that carried
over from Lyndon Johnson's term. On some policy issues the "public mood"
in Congress and in the nation prompted Nixon and Democrats to find common ground. But it is erroneous to argue that the majority of landmark bills
passed under Nixon's watch were linked to his preferred agenda. Nixon recognized his limited leverage over Congress. He tried to portray himself as a
conservative reformer while claiming credit for popular legislation as he pos-
tured for reelection. Thus, he "acted variously as initiator, acquiescer, foot-
dragger, and outright vetoer. But the bills kept getting passed."[50]

The effect of stronger parties on presidential leadership of significant lawmaking under divided government is unambiguous in the postreform/party-
unity era. The data accentuate three critical trends. First, few landmark bills
are consistently connected with presidents' stated policy objectives. No more
than approximately a third of the bills are linked to the president's stated
agenda. Second, presidents "stay quiet" and take no position on congressional legislation approximately a third of the time on average. They either
disagree with the legislation but choose not to challenge it, or they seek to
avoid calling attention to policy accomplishments spearheaded by the oppo-

sition. Bill Clinton is the exception. He frequently went out of his way to support congressional legislation in the 104th Congress. As Clinton eyed reelection in 1996, he sought to steal some of the thunder from popular elements in the Republicans' Contract with America, including congressional accountability, regulatory matters, and immigration reform. Finally, the veto power plays a considerably larger role in presidents' negotiation with opposition majorities in the current era. A little more than one-third of all landmark bills involved the presidential veto in some form—either implied or applied.

Presidents' increased use of veto threats underscores their adaptation to the highly partisan landscape on Capitol Hill. "Often the purpose of a veto threat is not to kill the legislation," Barbara Sinclair posits, "but to extract concessions from an opposition majority that has major policy differences with the president but lacks the strength to override his vetoes."[51] Reagan, for example, threatened to veto agricultural and job training bills in the 97th Congress in order to coax Democrats to reduce spending levels. Similarly, in the 106th Congress Bill Clinton threatened to veto the "Ed-flex" education bill in order to force Republicans to drop an amendment that would have shifted money to existing special needs students rather than to his objective of hiring new teachers.

In many other cases presidents use veto threats in the bid to reframe the policy debate and preempt congressional action with their own proposal. To gain an upper hand over policy making they threaten to veto any measure that does not correspond to their preferences or contain key provisions. In an era of narrow party margins and heightened party unity in Congress, their threats have been generally quite successful. George H. W. Bush threatened to veto his proposal for the savings and loan industry bailout in 1989 if Congress did not accord the Treasury Department greater latitude in the bill's implementation. In the 105th Congress Bill Clinton preempted congressional Republicans' longstanding calls for a balanced budget. He issued multiple veto threats to indicate which domestic program cuts were "off the table." Most recently, George W. Bush threatened to veto the USA Patriot Act if Congress refused to accord provisions for broader law enforcement leeway concerning suspected terrorists.

In a much more dramatic battle with Senate Democrats over homeland security, Bush saw momentum building in Congress to reorganize the federal government in the war on terrorism. After months of eschewing talk of reorganization, Bush launched his own proposal for reorganizing twenty-two existing agencies into a new Department of Homeland Security. When Senate Democrats refused to grant him the broad license he sought concerning hiring, firing, and appointments in the new entity, Bush threatened to veto the bill and it stalled. The president ultimately waged a successful electoral campaign on the issue, which brought about a Republican majority in the Senate and prompted the lame-duck Democratic majority in 2002 to pass the bill on the president's terms.[52]

In examining table 7.2, what distinguishes periods of unified government decisively from divided government in the postreform/party-unity era—and indeed, from split party control more generally—is the proportion of significant legislation that is steadily connected with the president's stated policy objectives and the absence of veto politics. Seventy-three to 100 percent of landmark bills are connected to presidents' agendas, whatever the congressional era, and presidents explicitly supported whatever proportion of significant legislation was spearheaded by their congressional majorities. The data are a testimony to the consistently stronger agenda synergy between the branches that is fostered by unified party control.

It would be a mistake, however, to conclude that each president had equivalent leverage over Congress and was able to *direct* significant lawmaking during the relatively brief interludes of unified government in the last sixty years. A more discriminating analysis underscores that in recent eras Presidents Carter and Clinton were better situated to *facilitate* continuing party objectives in Congress, some of which were blocked by their Republican predecessors under divided government.[53] The more electorally autonomous membership in Congress, in conjunction with stronger leadership organization, often hindered advances on their own independent policy agenda. By contrast, Lyndon Johnson's substantial leverage in the legislative realm translated into an unrivaled ability to manage and direct the congressional docket. Johnson's landslide election in 1964 legitimized his Great Society agenda in a way that neither Carter's narrow victory over Ford nor Clinton's plurality in 1992 did for their campaigns. Moreover, Johnson's coattails produced a largely deferential majority in Congress, which stood poised and willing to pass his policy priorities—a key ingredient missing for Carter and Clinton.

Much of the domestic legislation adopted from 1965 to 1968 was Johnson's initiative, from voting rights and bills connected to the War on Poverty to environmental and regulatory legislation. The pace of legislation was nothing less than extraordinary. More landmark domestic bills passed in Johnson's term than the Carter and Clinton single-party experiences combined. Many of the laws represented new programs targeted at urgent social issues, including the Elementary and Secondary Education Act (1965), the establishment of the Department of Housing and Urban Development (1965), and the Appalachian Regional Development Act (1965). Others represented continuing issues that carried over from Kennedy's presidency and had been blocked by southern conservatives in the Democratic majority, such as Medicare and the minimum wage.

Johnson's involvement in the legislative realm is unmistakable. Regulatory bills concerning environmental quality, food, and consumer rights often followed presidential blue-ribbon commissions he ordered. Johnson intervened in House organizational politics to force legislation, like Medicare, out of committee for a successful floor vote. He worked across party lines to co-opt Republican leaders Charlie Halleck and Everett Dirksen to build bipartisan consensus on social and civil rights legislation. He also had no qualms about giving legislators the "treatment," his highly effective technique of direct persuasion through personal confrontation. To be sure, congressional action was not always quick on the thirty-seven landmark bills. Congress delayed passage of Johnson's income tax surcharge proposal for nearly a year, and the National Scenic Trails system bill for three years. Sometimes Congress went beyond Johnson's proposed framework, as it did by adopting more stringent rules in the Clean Waters Restoration Act of 1966. Regardless, Johnson's policy objectives formed the core of the shared agenda with Congress. His strong leverage over Congress enabled him to direct the contours of lawmaking in the 89th and 90th Congresses, the results of which left an indelible imprint on American social policy.[54]

Jimmy Carter, like Bill Clinton, had much weaker leverage over Congress. Several landmark bills were linked to Carter's independent agenda, including trucking, airline, and railroad deregulation. Yet Carter lent his explicit support to several bills earlier blocked by President Ford that were clearly part of a continuing agenda on Capitol Hill. Carter reinforced support for surface-mining legislation in 1977, which Ford had vetoed twice. He also lent his support to rework Ford's stalled proposal on Social Security taxes and urged passage of the Clean Air Act amendments.[55] Alaska lands, minimum wage, and banking legislation also represented "unfinished business" in the Ford administration on which Carter spurred congressional action.

In a like manner, Bill Clinton also expended much effort lending support for the carryover agenda in Congress and making incremental adjustments to existing domestic programs. Clinton's potential to advance his independent agenda was more circumscribed. The Omnibus Deficit Reduction Act of 1993 (though it gained not a single Republican vote), national service (Americorps), education goals (Goals 2000), and reforming college loan financing policies were among his greatest agenda victories. But as many priority bills were linked to the continuing agenda in Congress. Clinton's predecessor, George H. W. Bush, had vetoed Democrats' efforts to pass gun control, family leave, and "motor voter" bills. Clinton unequivocally supported the Family and Medical Leave Act, Motor Voter Act, and the Brady Bill and

Omnibus Crime Act as a means of advancing the party agenda and sharing credit with Democrats in Congress for the passage of long-standing party objectives.

CONCLUSION

Critics who contend that party control of Congress and the presidency does not matter often make several broad arguments. First, they tend to focus on the disappointments of presidential legislative leadership under Carter and Clinton—what did *not* pass in Congress versus what did. The failure of Clinton's health care reform without a vote and the laborious passage of Carter's energy plan are routinely cited as examples. Second, critics point out that unified government has not, even under the best circumstances, yielded "responsible party government" in the United States. Finally, scholars focused on legislative productivity posit, quite correctly, that the pace of landmark legislation is not stifled by split party government.

This chapter has provided evidence to show precisely why party control of national institutions *does matter* to the legislative presidency, notwithstanding critics' objections. Recent presidents have not profited from the type of leverage over Congress that a single president—Lyndon Johnson—did in an earlier era. Carter and Clinton struggled with a more autonomous membership and because of their lack of coattails. But they were able to facilitate the passage of many bills that had been blocked under former presidents, and such successes were often made possible by the president's ability to marshal partisan unity. Higher levels of executive-legislative concurrence on floor outcomes testify to the greater agenda synergy between the branches. All told, even if presidents under unified government have differed significantly in their autonomous influence over Congress, single-party control extended opportunities for joint credit-claiming and the attainment of shared partisan policy goals across time.

Divided government has erected a much greater challenge to the legislative presidency in the postreform/party-unity era. Split party control today bears little resemblance to the 1950s. The old adage that "the president proposes and the Congress disposes" has frequently been inverted. Assertive, policy-focused opposition majorities look less to the president for policy leadership and have steered the lawmaking agenda away from the president's preferred direction. Organizational change and party cohesion have rendered presidents' influence over individual legislators in the opposition much more difficult. Executive-legislative concurrence has fallen to historical lows for the postwar period. Presidents spend more time fending off the majority's agenda and attempting to recast the national policy debate through vetoes and veto threats. Preemptive politics place a premium on presidents' rhetorical skills and the manipulation of the public presidency to reframe policy choices in order to claim a modicum of credit. George H. W. Bush was less adept at the new politics of this partisan era, at least in making a solid public case for his frequent use of the veto. Bill Clinton was arguably more adroit in this regard, insofar as his successful reelection in 1996 hinged on convincing the electorate that he could, through the veto power, act as a "buffer" against the alleged excesses of the GOP majority.

The institutional and electoral politics surrounding George W. Bush's legislative presidency accent the importance of party control of national institutions in the contemporary era. Unified government aided his early agenda and the passage of sweeping tax cuts. With his agenda stifled after losing Republican control of the Senate just a year into his term, Bush used veto threats and "strategic disagreement" with Democrats over the establishment of the Department of Homeland Security to campaign for a GOP Senate in the 2002 midterm elections.[56] As he stands poised for his second term, Bush's moderate coattails in the House (and Senate)—and most importantly, a popular vote margin exceeding 3 million votes in the 2004 election—bode well for potential leverage over Congress. The question is how Bush will capitalize on the institutional context of his second term and which issues or combination of issues he will focus on, from the war on terror to pressing and thorny domestic problems.

Viewed through the lens of political time, the modern legislative presidency has shown remarkable resilience. George W. Bush, like his predecessors, has demonstrated a keen capacity to adapt to changing policy-making contexts and shifts in the balance of power and influence between the branches of our national institutions. Grasping the particular limits and opportunities presidents face in the legislative arena is key to appreciating the varied impact of party control of the White House and Capitol Hill.

NOTES

1. Douglas Waller, "Why Jeffords Bolted from the GOP," *Time*, May 27, 2001. http://www.time.com/time/columnist/waller/article/0,9565,128099,00.h tml, accessed September 7, 2004.

2. Andrew E. Busch, "National Security and the Midterm Elections," in *Transforming the American Polity: The Presidency of George W. Bush and the War on Terrorism*, ed. Richard S. Conley, Real Politics in America series (Upper Saddle River, NJ: Prentice Hall, 2005).

3. James L. Sundquist, *Constitutional Reform and Effective Government* (Washington, DC: Brookings Institution, 1986); and James L. Sundquist, "Needed: A Political Theory

for the New Era of Coalition Government in the United States," *Political Science Quarterly* 10 (1988): 613–35; Lloyd N. Cutler, "To Form a Government," *Foreign Affairs* 59 (1988): 126–43; Benjamin Ginsberg and Martin Shefter, *Politics by Other Means: Politicians, Prosecutors, and the Press from Watergate to Whitewater* (New York: W. W. Norton, 1999); James P. Pfiffner, "Divided Government and the Problem of Governance," in *Cooperation and Conflict between the President and Congress*, ed. James A. Thurber (Washington, DC: Congressional Quarterly, 1991).

4. David R. Mayhew, *Divided We Govern: Party Control, Lawmaking, and Investigations, 1946–1990* (New Haven: Yale University Press, 1991); and David R. Mayhew, "The Return to Unified Party Control under Clinton: How Much of a Difference in Lawmaking?" in *The New American Politics: Reflections on Political Change and the Clinton Administration*, ed. Bryan D. Jones (Boulder, CO: Westview, 1995).

5. The more detailed argument and analysis is in Richard S. Conley, *The Presidency, Congress, and Divided Government: A Postwar Assessment* (College Station: Texas A&M University Press, 2002).

6. James G. March and Johan P. Olsen, "The New Institutionalism: Organizational Factors in Political Life," *American Political Science Review* 78 (1984): 734–49.

7. The concept is borrowed from Stephen Skowronek, *The Politics Presidents Make: Leadership from John Adams to George Bush* (Cambridge, MA: Harvard University Press, 1993).

8. Paul C. Light, *The President's Agenda: Domestic Policy Choice from Kennedy to Carter* (Baltimore: Johns Hopkins University Press, 1982).

9. James E. Campbell and Joe A. Sumners, "Presidential Coattails in Senate Elections," *American Political Science Review* 84 (1990): 521.

10. John R. Alford and John R. Hibbing, "Increased Incumbency Advantage in the House," *Journal of Politics* 43 (1981): 1042–61; Alan I. Abramowitz, "Incumbency, Campaign Spending, and the Decline of Competition in U.S. House Elections," *Journal of Politics* 53 (1991): 34–56; Richard Born, "Reassessing the Decline of Presidential Coattails: U.S. House Elections from 1952–80," *Journal of Politics* 46 (1984): 60–79.

11. Quoted in Light, *The President's Agenda*, 28.

12. Roger H. Davidson, "The Presidency in Congressional Time," in *Rivals for Power: Presidential-Congressional Relations*, ed. James A. Thurber (Washington, DC: Congressional Quarterly, 1996).

13. James MacGregor Burns, *The Deadlock of Democracy: Four-Party Politics in America* (Englewood Cliffs, NJ: Prentice Hall, 1963).

14. The term "cross-pressured" is borrowed from Jon R. Bond and Richard Fleisher, *The President in the Legislative Arena* (Chicago: University of Chicago Press, 1990).

15. Conley, *The Presidency, Congress, and Divided Government*, 170–73.

16. Robert D. Loevy, "The Presidency and Domestic Policy: The Civil Rights Act of 1964," in *Understanding the Presidency*, ed. James P. Pfiffner and Roger H. Davidson (New York: Longman, 1997).

17. Loevy, "The Presidency and Domestic Policy," 96–102.

18. Fred I. Greenstein, *The Hidden-Hand Presidency: Eisenhower as Leader* (Baltimore: Johns Hopkins University Press, 1982).

19. On this point, see Paul J. Quirk, "Domestic Policy: Divided Government and Cooperative Presidential Leadership," in *The Bush Presidency: First Appraisals*, ed. Colin

Campbell and Bert A. Rockman (Chatham, NJ: Chatham House, 1991); see also John C. Whitaker, "Nixon's Domestic Policy: Both Liberal and Bold in Retrospect," *Presidential Studies Quarterly* 26 (1996): 131–53.

20. Fiona M. Wright, "The Caucus Reelection Requirement and the Transformation of House Committee Chairs, 1959–94," *Legislative Studies Quarterly* 15 (2000): 469–80.

21. David W. Rohde, *Parties and Leaders in the Postreform House* (Chicago: University of Chicago Press, 1991), 20–23.

22. Lawrence C. Dodd, "The Expanded Roles of the House Democratic Whip System: The 93rd and 94th Congresses," *Congressional Studies* 7 (1979): 27–56.

23. Richard S. Conley, "Presidential Influence and Minority Party Liaison on Veto Overrides: New Evidence from the Ford Presidency," *American Politics Research* 30 (January 2002): 34–65.

24. Tinsley E. Yarbrough, "Carter and the Congress," in *The Carter Years: The President and Policy Making*, ed. M. Glenn Abernathy, Dilys M. Hill, and Phil Williams (New York: St. Martin's Press, 1984).

25. Charles O. Jones, *The Trusteeship Presidency: Jimmy Carter and the United States Congress* (Baton Rouge: Louisiana State University Press, 1988), 59.

26. Erwin C. Hargrove, *Jimmy Carter as President: Leadership and the Politics of the Public Good* (Baton Rouge: Louisiana State University Press, 1988).

27. William W. Lammers and Michael A. Genovese, *The Presidency and Domestic Policy: Comparing Leadership Styles, FDR to Clinton* (Washington, DC: Congressional Quarterly, 2000).

28. John H. Aldrich and David W. Rohde, "The Logic of Conditional Party Government," in *Congress Reconsidered*, ed. Lawrence C. Dodd (Washington, DC: Congressional Quarterly, 2001).

29. Rohde, *Parties and Leaders*, 83–118; Roger H. Davidson, Walter J. Oleszek, and Thomas Kephart, "One Bill, Many Committees: Multiple Referrals in the U.S. House of Representatives," *Legislative Studies Quarterly* 13 (1988): 3–28; Paul S. Herrnson and Kelly D. Patterson, "Toward a More Programmatic Democratic Party? Agenda Setting and Coalition Building in the House of Representatives," *Polity* 27 (1995): 607–28.

30. Joseph Cooper and David W. Brady, "Institutional Context and Leadership Style: The House from Cannon to Rayburn," *American Political Science Review* 75 (1981): 411–25.

31. On this latter point, see also Bruce I. Oppenheimer, "The Importance of Elections in a Strong Congressional Party Era: The Effect of Unified vs. Divided Government," in *Do Elections Matter?* ed. Benjamin Ginsburg and Alan Stone, 3rd ed. (Armonk, NY: M. E. Sharpe, 1996).

32. Richard S. Conley, "A Revisionist View of George Bush and Congress, 1989: Congressional Support, 'Veto Strength,' and Legislative Strategy," *White House Studies* 2 (Winter 2002): 359–74.

33. James G. Gimpel, *Legislating the Revolution: The Contract with America in Its First 100 Days* (Boston: Allyn & Bacon, 1996).

34. Gary W. Cox and Matthew D. McCubbins, "Bonding, Structure, and the Stability of Political Parties: Party Government in the House," *Legislative Studies Quarterly* 19 (1994): 215–31.

35. Barbara Sinclair, "Trying to Govern Positively in a Negative Era: Clinton and the

103rd Congress," in *The Clinton Presidency: First Appraisals*, ed. Colin Campbell and Bert A. Rockman (Chatham, NJ: Chatham House, 1996), 113.

36. In an April 13, 1995, interview with CNN's Wolf Blitzer and Judy Woodruff, President Clinton commented on the Republicans' "100 days": "Well, they had an exciting 100 days, and they dealt with a lot of issues that were in their contract. But let's look at what happens now. The bills all go to the United States Senate, where they have to pass, and then I have to decide whether to sign or veto them. So now you will see the process unfolding. And I will have my opportunity to say where I stand on these bills and what I intend to do with the rest of our agenda. I have enjoyed watching this last 100 days, and have enjoyed giving them the chance to do what they were elected to do. And also I made it clear what I would not go along with." *Public Papers of the President, 1995* (Washington, DC: GPO, 1995), 527–28.

37. Richard S. Conley, "President Clinton and the Republican Congress, 1995–2000: Political and Policy Dimensions of Veto Politics in Divided Government," *Congress and the Presidency* 33 (2004): 133–60.

38. Lyn Ragsdale, *Vital Statistics on the Presidency: Washington to Clinton* (Washington, DC: Congressional Quarterly, 1996). Ragsdale prefers the term "concurrence" to better reflect that presidents take positions on votes concerning not only their agenda but also legislation generated in Congress.

39. Data are from yearly *Congressional Quarterly Almanacs* of all presidential position votes.

40. To correct for serial correlation, estimates for the House model were generated using the Prais-Winsten (AR 1) technique in STATA 6.0. The dependent variable is the president's annual success rate. The variable for time in office ranged from one to eight years. The variables for each "era" are dummy variables for the respective period and as such, provide a "stylized" account of the effect of divided government across time. The equation yields the following coefficients, all of which are significant at $p < .01$ or better: Presidential support $= 86.97 - 1.88$ (time in office) $- 13.89$ (bipartisan conservative era) $- 18.40$ (liberal activist era) $- 35.52$ (postreform/party-unity era); N $= 51$; adjusted $R^2 = .69$; rho $= .285$; Durbin $h = 2.05$.

41. Burdett A. Loomis, *The Contemporary Congress* (Boston: Bedford/St. Martin's, 2000), 147.

42. Coefficients for the Senate support model were generated using ordinary least squares (OLS) regression. The equation yields the following coefficients, all of which are significant at $p < .05$ or better: Presidential support $= 86.52 - 2.05$ (time in office) $- 7.0$ (bipartisan conservative era) $- 16.90$ (liberal activist era) $- 15.85$ (postreform/party-unity era) $+ 21.90$ (George W. Bush, 2001–2002); N $= 50$; adjusted $R^2 = .61$; Durbin-Watson $= 2.11$ (indicating no serial correlation).

George W. Bush's high Senate success rates in 2001 (88 percent) and 2002 (91 percent) are "outliers," which may be explained by two factors. First, Bush's batting average was artificially inflated by his strategic position-taking. He took very few positions on Senate votes in either year and steered clear of more controversial domestic policy issues. Second, judicial appointments were not included in success-rate calculations for the Senate to keep the data comparable to the House.

43. Mayhew, *Divided We Govern*.

44. *Congressional Quarterly Almanac, 1956*, 375–92; *Congressional Quarterly Almanac 1959*, 245–56.

45. For an opposite perspective that credits Nixon with many of the policy accomplishments of the 91st–93rd Congresses, see Joan Hoff, *Nixon Reconsidered* (New York: Basic Books, 1994).

46. *Congressional Quarterly Almanac, 1969,* 833–40.

47. *Congressional Quarterly Almanac, 1969,* 735–46.

48. *Congressional Quarterly Almanac, 1971,* 430.

49. *Congressional Quarterly Almanac, 1970,* 433.

50. Mayhew, *Divided We Govern,* 82.

51. Barbara Sinclair, "Hostile Partners: The President, Congress, and Lawmaking in the Partisan 1990s," in *Polarized Politics: Congress and the President in a Partisan Era,* ed. Jon R. Bond and Richard Fleisher (Washington, DC: Congressional Quarterly, 2000), 145.

52. For details, see Richard S. Conley, "Presidential and Congressional Struggles over the Formation of the Department of Homeland Security," in *Transforming the American Polity: The Presidency of George W. Bush and the War on Terrorism,* Real Politics in America Series, ed. Richard S. Conley (Upper Saddle River, NJ: Prentice Hall, 2005).

53. The distinction between direction and facilitation is owed to George C. Edwards III, *At the Margins: Presidential Leadership of Congress* (New Haven: Yale University Press, 1989).

54. For details, see Conley, *The Presidency, Congress, and Divided Government,* chap. 6.

55. *Congressional Quarterly Almanac, 1977,* 161–72 and 627–46.

56. John B. Gilmour, *Strategic Disagreement: Stalemate in American Politics* (Pittsburgh, PA: University of Pittsburgh Press, 1995).

8

The Institutional Context of Veto Bargaining

C. Lawrence Evans and Stephen Ng

By all accounts, the presidential veto is a central feature of the American constitutional system of separate institutions sharing power. Not surprisingly, we have accumulated a substantial body of empirical knowledge about the veto. We now know a lot about the incidence of vetoes across administrations, the relationship between veto usage and the electoral cycle, the role of the veto in the early American Republic, the prevalence of threatened vetoes, and the implications of the veto for policy gridlock.[1] In recent years, theories of the lawmaking process also have been extended to more fully incorporate the veto prerogative. Still, the burgeoning scholarly literature has not settled key conceptual questions about the role of the veto in American national government. For example, are veto threats crafted to take advantage of congressional uncertainty about White House preferences, or are veto threats and vetoes better conceptualized as position-taking before a broader audience of interest groups and the general public? More generally, very little is known about the process through which veto threats are formulated within the executive branch, the different forms that such threats can take, and the linkages that exist between presidential legislative signals and the message agendas of the congressional parties. What factors explain the significant variance that can exist in the intensity and ambiguity of veto threats? What impact does the threat of a veto have on legislative strategies? How do the answers to these questions vary across issues, different threat levels, and over time?

The purpose of this chapter is to shed light on these questions. Our focus is on the institutional context within which congressional-presidential bargaining is nested. Over time, the White House and Congress have both developed institutionalized mechanisms for confronting the internal coordination and collective action problems that (to varying extents) characterize all complex political organizations. These mechanisms also condition how the branches bargain with one another. Of particular importance are the central legislative clearance process within the Executive Office of the President and party institutions within the House and Senate, especially the party message operations. In section 1 of this chapter, we review the leading theories of the veto. In section 2, we consider the executive branch side of the institutional context of veto bargaining—the clearance process through which most veto threats are formulated. In section 3, we focus on the internal partisan characteristics of Congress. Section 4 is an exploration of the consequences of presidential signaling for several aspects of legislative strategy on a sample of major bills from 1997 to 2000. We conclude by considering the likely role of veto bargaining during the second term of President George W. Bush.

FOUNDATIONAL THEORIES

Although there long has been a rich empirical literature about congressional-presidential relations, theoretically informed research about the veto took a major step forward in 2000 with the publication of Charles Cameron's landmark book, *Veto Bargaining*.[2] Cameron presents several competing conceptualizations of the veto and its place in legislative-executive relations. First, congressional-presidential interactions can be conceptualized as a *sequential game with complete information*. This scheme is the simplest model of veto bargaining. Here, the interaction is assumed to begin with Congress passing legislation. If the administration's preferred policy is closer to the measure passed by Congress than to existing law, the president responds by signing the measure. However, if the administration prefers existing law to the bill, members of Congress will anticipate—correctly—that the measure will be vetoed unless changes are made. As a result, they will respond by either (1) anticipating the president's response and making the adjustments necessary to garner administration support, or (2) not bothering to pass legislation. Although the veto prerogative is central to this model, Cameron points out that no actual vetoes will occur in equilibrium. The model falls short, he concludes, as a tool for understanding key elements of the veto bargaining process.

Second, legislative-executive bargaining can be conceptualized as a *commitment game*. Here, the interaction begins with the administration making a strong statement of its position prior to congressional action, promising to veto any legislation that does not reflect the president's program. Such a pledge, if viewed as credible on Capitol Hill, will effectively reduce the president's negotiating discretion, and thus strengthen the administration's hand by limiting its ability to make concessions. If the president miscalculates and draws the line in the wrong place, or if the threat is not perceived as credible, Congress may not pass legislation that the president can sign, leading to a veto. How does the commitment game comport with evidence? The commitment game implies that presidents will seldom capitulate to congressional demands on measures with veto threats—to do so would undermine the administration's credibility. Cameron demonstrates, however, that presidents often do sign threatened bills that have not been fundamentally modified by Congress. Thus, although intuitively plausible, the commitment game is of limited value for understanding when vetoes occur and bargaining between the branches.

A third approach is to portray congressional-presidential bargaining as a *coordination game*. In this model, the administration knows more about presidential preferences than does the Congress. Based on expectations about presidential preferences (which are based in part on past behavior by the White House), members of Congress will make strategic calculations about the likelihood of a veto for the different policy alternatives under consideration. By issuing carefully calibrated veto threats, the administration may be able to use its informational advantage to pull legislative outcomes toward the president's preferred outcome. The underlying intuition is similar to brinksmanship interactions in international relations. And just as brinksmanship can result in war, the strategic posturing of presidents and lawmakers can lead to vetoes.

Cameron concludes that the coordination game best fits the available evidence about veto politics. For instance, vetoes are much more common during periods of divided government, and the coordination game predicts an increase in vetoes precisely when preferences are configured in a manner that we associate with divided party control. Major bills are significantly more likely to draw vetoes during periods of divided government, but not when the same party controls both the White House and Congress—another finding consistent with the coordination game. Moreover, vetoed bills are often repassed by Congress (occasionally multiple times), which suggests that lawmakers may be updating their expectations about what the president will sign (phenomena that Cameron labels "veto chains").

In contrast to Cameron's emphasis on strategic posturing between the president and Congress, Tim Groseclose and Nolan McCarty have advanced a qualitatively different treatment of veto bargaining, called the *blame game* model.[3] According to this view, the strategic interactions between the president and Congress are best conceptualized as bargaining before an audience, which might include the general public, party activists, interest groups, and so on. In the blame game, Congress is fully informed about presidential preferences on legislation. But the public (or some subset of the public to which politicians must respond) is only partially informed. In the blame-game model, members of Congress pass legislation that is popular with the relevant audience but contrary to presidential preferences and likely to draw a veto. The goal is to induce the administration to cast unpopular vetoes, reducing support among audience members for the president. Groseclose and McCarty offer preliminary evidence that popular support for the president does drop following a veto. Moreover, it is well known that vetoes are more common during election years, which may imply the existence of audience effects *à la* the blame game.

Which approach—Cameron's coordination game or the blame-game model of Groseclose and McCarty—is most helpful for understanding the bargaining that occurs between Congress and the president? The existing evidence is mixed. The coordination game does imply the increase that we observe in vetoes during divided government. But this pattern resonates equally well with the blame game: we would not expect a congressional majority to repeatedly send veto bait to a president of the same party. The interesting relationship that Cameron finds between divided government, major bill status, and the incidence of vetoes is also consistent with the Groseclose-McCarty model. An opposition party seeking to embarrass a president during times of divided government would probably target major measures as veto bait because of the increased public visibility. No such pattern would be expected under unified control. Cameron's analysis of veto chains is also consistent with blame-game dynamics. Forcing a president to repeatedly veto popular measures might further undermine public support for the administration.[4] On the other hand, the evidence for the blame-game model is preliminary at best. For instance, the linkage that Groseclose and McCarty find between vetoes and presidential popularity is intriguing, but how closely do voters actually follow congressional-presidential bargaining, even on major issues?

Our view is that the Cameron and Groseclose-McCarty models should be treated as *foundational* theories. There is a degree of empirical support for both models. But useful new light can be shed on the essential features of veto bargaining by carefully examining the *processes* through which presidential veto threats are formulated and congressional bargaining stances are devised—that is, by examining the broader institutional context. We begin by examining the internal politics of the executive branch.

CENTRAL LEGISLATIVE CLEARANCE

In contemporary American government, presidential positions on pending bills are formulated through an elaborate clearance mechanism, centered in the Office of Management and Budget (OMB). The signals that presidents transmit to Congress often take the form of complex documents running eight to ten pages in length. The phrases included in these documents are carefully calibrated, with an eye toward influencing legislative deliberations on Capitol Hill. How does the central clearance process function?

Five decades ago, Richard Neustadt published a classic article in the *American Political Science Review* about the evolving process of policy coordination within the White House. He described how the Bureau of the Budget (renamed in 1970 the Office of Management and Budget, or OMB) was allocated over time increased responsibilities for ensuring that agency legislation reflected the president's agenda—the process of central legislative clearance.[5] It is well known that coalition building in Congress is complicated by internal problems of coordination and collective action.[6] Members represent diverse constituencies and seek to promote divergent interests, hindering efforts by congressional leaders to forge coalitions. As the leader of a hierarchy, the president has more organizational leverage (relative to congressional party leaders) for overcoming problems of coordination and collective action. The executive branch is better able to speak with one voice and thus tends to have certain bargaining advantages relative to Congress.[7]

Still, the modern executive branch is a large and fragmented hierarchy, and there is at least the potential for coordination and collective action problems *absent certain key institutional arrangements*. On tobacco issues, for instance, agency heads within the Agriculture Department will have different policy priorities than leaders in the Department of Health and Human Services or the Department of Commerce. Even when jurisdiction over an issue is concentrated in a single department or agency, bureaucratic leaders may disagree with the president on pressing policy matters. Moreover, the vast array of issues in play every year on Capitol Hill creates the potential for coordination problems within the executive branch. The White House is asked to take positions on countless policy matters. Without an effective clearance mechanism, the president would not be able to adequately monitor the policy positions that bubble up from the bureaucracy.

The potential for coordination and collective action problems should increase with the scope of the national policy agenda. In American national government, such increases occurred gradually throughout the twentieth century, but also via rapid bursts of change during the New Deal era and the Johnson-Nixon years. Interestingly, as the scope of the policy agenda expanded, the Bureau of the Budget was repeatedly charged with new responsibilities for coordinating policy proposals and positions within the executive branch. It was natural that the Budget Bureau, rather than some other organizational entity, would take on this role. As Neustadt observed, the federal budget traditionally has been the primary mechanism for policy coordination across agency and departmental lines. Moreover, the Budget Bureau (and now OMB) is formally located within the Executive Office of the President and is thus directly under the supervision of top White House staff and the president. In 1934, President Roosevelt mandated that the Budget Bureau clear all agency proposals for new legislation. Five years later, the bureau was given responsibility for evaluating the contents of all enrolled bills, and thus for advising the president on vetoes. During the Johnson-Nixon years, the central clearance process was further institutionalized through increased staff and more regularized patterns of operation.[8] By the early 1980s, the central clearance process also included responsibility for the signaling of White House views about pending legislation in Congress. Such signals are now transmitted through a number of mechanisms, ranging from cleared correspondence to agency reports and formal statements of administration policy.

Statements of administration policy (called SAPs, for short) have become perhaps the central *formal* mechanism through which presidential views about pending legislation are communicated to Capitol Hill. A few days or weeks before chamber action on a measure, OMB will send a formal document to the House Rules Committee, the full House, or the Senate (depending on which chamber is acting) summarizing the president's views about the legislation. In the 106th Congress (1999–2000), for instance, the Clinton administration sent 368 SAPs to Congress; 62 to the House Rules Committee, 236 to the full House, and 70 to the Senate. SAPs can range from a few sentences to ten or more pages, but the modal length is around one page. Typically included are a sentence about the president's overall position on the bill, criticisms of certain provisions, perhaps requests for specific modifications, and often veto threats of varying ambiguity. The SAPs provide the richest and most systematic evidence available about presidential positions on pending legislation.[9]

Almost all bills of any significance are the subject of one or more SAPs. They are less often sent to the Senate, however, because of the relative unpredictability of the Senate floor agenda. Executive branch officials often cannot predict when a Senate SAP will be needed or the precise contents of the underlying legislation. That said, even when no SAP is sent to the Senate for a measure, one typically is forwarded to the House if and when the bill surfaces in that chamber. As a result, SAPs can provide a highly useful window for analyzing presidential legislative rhetoric in a systematic fashion on a broad cross-section of bills.

On June 8, 2000, for instance, OMB sent to the House a SAP for HR 8, a bill to repeal the federal estate tax. The measure was a central element of the Republican message agenda that year, and it created significant partisan conflict on Capitol Hill. "The President strongly opposes H.R. 8," the SAP began, and "the President would veto this legislation . . . if it were presented to him." The SAP outlined the Clinton administration's basic approach to estate tax reform and endorsed a substitute measure proposed by the House Democratic leadership.

Based on a systematic review of recent SAPs, as well as interviews with current and former White House aides, OMB staff, and congressional staff, we have learned that standard phrases and code words are routinely included in the SAPs as part of efforts to carefully calibrate the information sent to Congress about presidential preferences. For the White House, the goal is to craft these signals in a manner that enhances the president's strategic leverage in the lawmaking process. Top leadership and committee staff— especially aides to the House and Senate Appropriations Committees—are fully aware of the rhetorical nuances included in the SAPs and other cleared communications.

The formal SAP process grew out of the correspondence, reports, and other communications that OMB has been transmitting to Congress for decades. It became significantly more institutionalized, however, during the period when Richard Darman served as OMB director (1989–1993). Top OMB staff remarked that the Darman changes have been maintained through successive administrations because they facilitate effective bargaining between the branches. "There are lots of pending bills on Capitol Hill that the administration might take a position on," observed a former OMB deputy director. "There are significant time constraints. The SAPs help people deal with the time pressures. People know where to go to get information about the administration position. The right people know how to interpret that information."[10]

Along what dimensions can we usefully compare the signals and messages included in SAPs? First, the direction and intensity of the president's overall position on a bill typically is communicated via one of five phrases, phrases that surface repeatedly in SAP after SAP. Either the president "strongly supports passage;" "supports passage;" "does not object to passage;" "opposes passage;" or "strongly opposes passage." (On a subset of the SAPs, no explicit position on final passage is referenced.) In addition, SAPs often include veto threats, which are calibrated to capture different levels of ambiguity or commitment to the veto strategy. Again, these phrases surface repeatedly across different SAPs and over time in almost identical language. The least ambiguous form of threatened veto is the *presidential veto threat*: "If the legislation were presented to the President in its current form, he would veto the bill." The *senior advisers threat*, in contrast, is generally viewed as more ambiguous: "If sent to the President in its current form, the President's senior advisors would recommend that he veto the bill." Carrying still more ambiguity are threats that reference the relevant departmental secretary or agency head, but not White House staff or the president. "If sent to the President in its current form, the Secretary of _____ would recommend a veto." Participants remark that Congress will take a secretary's threat referencing multiple agencies more seriously than a threat from a single entity within the executive branch.

This ordering of veto threats is directly related to the proximity of the "threatener" to the Oval Office. Secretary's threats typically originate within the relevant department or agency, or from the staff level inside OMB. The OMB director, and perhaps personnel from the White House Office of Domestic Policy or the National Security Council, depending on the subject matter, formally clears the threats. Staff from the White House Office of Legislative Liaison also are often included in deliberations about SAP contents. The goal is to gauge the likelihood of a successful override if a veto actually occurs. For the past three administrations (Bush 41, Clinton, and Bush 43), the White House chief of staff has made the final decision about whether to issue a senior advisers threat on a measure. Presidential threats are personally cleared with the president. As the threat level shifts from the secretary to the senior advisers to the presidential level, participants in the process perceive that the administration retains less "wiggle room" regarding the veto decision. As a result, presidential veto threats are taken very seriously; secretary's threats, less so. If a SAP references presidential opposition but does not contain an explicit veto threat, legislators do not necessarily perceive that a veto is completely off the table—just less likely to occur.

There are, of course, additional sources of ambiguity in SAPs and other forms of cleared presidential communications. Veto threats can reference a number of problematic provisions without delineating the precise changes necessary to secure the president's signature. The language in which concerns are phrased is strategically calculated. SAPs for appropriations bills, for instance, tend to be long, usually referencing dozens of individual programs. For certain provisions, the administration is said to be "concerned," while on others it is "strongly concerned." For certain programs, the administration "urges that funding be reinstated;" but for others, it "strongly urges" such modifications. Occasionally, certain issues are omitted entirely from a SAP for strategic reasons. And on some major bills (not many), the administration does not send a SAP to Congress, perhaps enhancing the president's bargaining flexibility.

For the purposes of analysis, we have collapsed references in the SAPs to vetoes and the administration's overall views into a single signaling scale that ranges from a presidential veto threat (an unambiguous pledge to veto the bill) to strong support for a measure (almost no chance of a veto). The levels of the signaling scale are as follows.[11]

- presidential veto threat
- senior advisers veto threat
- secretary's veto threat (single and multiple agency)
- strongly oppose passage
- oppose passage
- no position on passage
- do not object to passage
- support passage
- strongly support passage

Table 8.1 summarizes the frequency of the different levels in the signaling scale for the 105th, 106th, and 107th Congresses—that is, for the two Congresses in Clinton's second term and the first Congress of the George W. Bush administration. In all three Congresses less than 25 percent of the SAPs included *explicit* veto threats for the underlying measure. However, if the focus is on major bills, the prevalence of veto threats is much higher.[12]

Table 8.1. Variation in Presidential Signals on Pending Legislation, 105th–107th Congresses

Position	105th Congress	106th Congress	107th Congress
Presidential Veto Threat	18 (5.5%)	21 (6.8%)	4 (2.9%)
Senior Advisers Veto Threat	33 (10.0%)	50 (16.1%)	4 (2.9%)
Secretary's Veto Threat	22 (6.7%)	8 (2.6%)	0
Strongly Oppose Passage	23 (7.0%)	21 (6.8%)	6 (4.3%)
Oppose Passage	40 (12.2%)	33 (10.6%)	6 (4.3%)
No Position on Passage	55 (16.7%)	65 (20.9%)	25 (18.1%)
No Objection to Passage	43 (13.1%)	22 (7.1%)	3 (2.2%)
Support Passage	66 (20.1%)	63 (20.3%)	59 (42.8%)
Strongly Support Passage	29 (8.8%)	28 (9.0%)	31 (22.5%)
Total	329	311	138

Note: The unit of observation is the signal, or position, as articulated in a Statement of Administration Policy (SAP). For some bills, there are multiple SAPs (sent to the House Rules Committee, full House, or full Senate). To avoid double counting, when SAPs are sent to both the House Rules Committee and the full House for a measure, only the signal in the latter document is included in the analysis.

Moreover, a number of SAPs that did not include explicit threats on the underlying measure did include *contingent veto threats*—that is, the threat of a veto if certain provisions were removed from or added to the measure. As expected, the distribution of observations across the scale shifts downward in the 107th Congress. The 105th and 106th Congresses were periods of divided government—Bill Clinton was president and Republicans organized both chambers of Congress. During the 107th Congress, Republicans controlled the White House, the House, and, before June 2001, the Senate as well. As a result, only 8 of the 138 SAPs (5.8 percent) for the 107th Congress included threatened vetoes of the underlying measure, reinforcing Cameron's observation that veto bargaining is closely associated with divided government.

What does our description of the central clearance process (especially SAP formulation and structure) imply about the nature of interbranch bargaining? In our view, the contents of the SAPs are best conceptualized as strategies in a signaling game of the sort modeled by Cameron. The SAPs vary in content based on strategic calculations about presidential preferences and the decision-making context on Capitol Hill. There are nuanced patterns in these communications that have been maintained across (at least) three different administrations, covering periods of divided and unified party control. There is a shared understanding among key participants in the bargaining game about the meaning of different phrases. And administrations clearly craft their signals on pending legislation to communicate different levels of ambiguity.

It is possible, of course, that some of this ambiguity helps the White House minimize public opposition to administration positions à la the blame game. But the observations of top White House and congressional aides, the rich complexity of the SAPs, and the highly calibrated nature of the veto threats call to mind the types of strategic signaling that have been modeled by Cameron. The SAPs, in short, provide compelling prima facie evidence that presidents systematically use signaling strategies in attempts to shape congressional expectations about administration preferences. Still, we need to consider more detailed evidence about the bargaining context and legislative strategy to gauge with confidence the explanatory power of the competing models of congressional-presidential bargaining.

It is instructive, for instance, to consider the legislation that drew presidential veto threats—the highest level on the signaling scale. For these items, the administration transmitted an unambiguous signal that a veto was forthcoming unless significant modifications were made in the underlying bill. A list of the measures is provided in table 8.2. Notice that these items disproportionately are major bills that touch on issues prominent on the mes-

Table 8.2. Issues Subject to Presidential Veto Threats, 105th–107th Congress

105th Congress	106th Congress	107th Congress
Compensatory Time (2)*	Banking Overhaul	Foreign Relations
Education Testing	China	Authorization
Foreign Operations	Defense Authorization	Foreign Operations
Appropriations	Education (ESEA)	Appropriations
Labor/HHS Appropriations	Ergonomics	Homeland Security
Labor Rights (2)	Estate Tax (2)	Managed Care Reform
Military Construction (2)	Labor/HHS Appropriations (3)	
Nuclear Waste (2)	Medicare Prescriptions	
Partial-Birth Abortion (3)	Minimum Wage (4)	
Private Property Rights	Nuclear Waste	
Social Security	Partial-Birth Abortion (2)	
Supplemental Appropriations	Tax Cuts (2)	
Taxes/Social Security	Teacher Empowerment	

* If multiple measures, the number is in parentheses.

sage agendas of one or both parties. Included are important initiatives pertaining to education, health care, tax reduction, Social Security, labor rights, and national defense. Such items typically divide the political parties and are associated with preference distributions that in Cameron's models are particularly likely to predict vetoes and veto threats. But the lack of ambiguity in these veto threats, combined with their high relevance to the party campaign agendas, suggests that congressional-presidential interactions (on these items, at least) are best conceptualized as bargaining before an audience. The conceptual approach that is most appropriate for understanding presidential signals may vary by issue area, depending in part on the relevance of a measure to the message agendas of one or both political parties. Our attention now turns to the consequences of message politics for veto bargaining and legislative strategy.

MESSAGE POLITICS AND LEGISLATIVE STRATEGY

As mentioned earlier in this chapter, internal deliberations within the House and Senate are also characterized by problems of coordination and collective action. Indeed, these problems typically are much more severe in a legislature than in a hierarchy such as the federal executive branch. Legislators are often cross-pressured on major issues by parochial constituency concerns on the one hand, and by broader concerns relating to party goals or the collective interests of the chamber on the other. The internal structural arrangements of Congress can help overcome problems of coordination and collective action, and party leaders play a particularly important role here.[13] Under the right conditions, party leaders in Congress can use their procedural and political prerogatives to advance the party agenda and help their fellow partisans promote a favorable partisan "name brand" with voters, which is an important collective goal for the party.

The concept of a party "name brand" resonates with a significant, but understudied, process through which mass attitudes and congressional decision making are linked—a process called *message politics*. In the contemporary Congress, members of the two political parties develop organized message agendas, "which are comprised of the issues, themes, and policy symbols that legislators believe will generate a positive response toward their party among voters." Message politics, in turn, refers to the "interconnected set of electoral, communications, and legislative strategies that congressional parties employ to advance their respective messages."[14]

Party leaders tend to focus their message agendas on policies and proposals that unify their rank and file, differentiate their party from the opposition, evoke public interest, and reflect public attitudes about their party's issue strengths.[15] Unity matters because internal divisions on a matter will blur the party's message, and thus complicate leadership efforts to develop a coherent name brand in the area. Similarly, if members of the public do not perceive substantial differences between the parties on an issue, the matter will not help voters make decisions at the polls. Salient issues—or issues that are potentially salient—are more likely to be factored into the voters' decision calculus and thus have more message value than is the case with less salient matters. Finally, the public perceives the two parties as having comparative advantages at handling different issues. Republicans, for instance, are generally viewed as the party best able to handle tax reduction and defense, while voters traditionally have perceived the Democrats as the stronger party on Medicare, Social Security, and the environment. Other factors held constant, people will respond most favorably to a party's message when it features issues upon which the party is viewed as most competent.

The congressional parties and their message operations are a critical feature of the institutional context of veto bargaining, calling to mind the basic structure of the blame-game model. Under the blame game, Congress passes popular legislation that the White House will veto, with the aim of undermining public support for the president and the president's party. Such dynamics are most likely during periods of divided government and in issue areas that are central to the party message agendas. These items, after all, are designed to distinguish between Republicans and Democrats, reflect core public attitudes about the strengths and weaknesses of each party, and touch on the issue priorities of the American people. It is on message issues that we would particularly expect to see blame-game dynamics.

What are the likely linkages between a bill's message status and bargaining? Here, it is useful to engage in a simple thought experiment. Since veto bargaining and the blame game are largely characteristics of divided government, assume for the purposes of argument that different parties control the White House and Congress—that is, take as given the partisan configuration of the 105th and 106th Congresses. The strategic calculations of message politics imply several hypotheses about presidential signaling and legislative bargaining. It is critical to distinguish between different kinds of message items. There are four main categories.

Shared Message Priorities. Some policy areas (education is an example) are prominent on the message agendas of both political parties. For the two parties, the goal on these items is to distinguish themselves from the opposition, galvanize their own activist base, and convince citizens that they will govern in the public interest. There will be strong disincentives for either party to completely acquiesce on substance during the lawmaking process. Most likely, the congressional majority will advance legislation reflecting its core values and the president will respond with strong opposition and a veto threat. If the public is demanding governmental action in the area and there exists a degree of middle ground, after successive rounds of position-taking, the president and congressional majority may split the difference and both claim victory. Absent a pressing need to pass legislation, however, neither party will offer major concessions and gridlock will ensue. Thus, on shared message priorities, there should be strong and relatively unambiguous initial opposition from the White House and then a symmetric bargaining response leading to either mutual intransigence or middle ground. We would not expect to see ambiguous presidential signals or patterns of asymmetric bargaining, where one side concedes significantly more ground than does the other.

Majority Message Priorities. Other issues are prominent on the message agenda of the majority party in Congress, but not that of the minority party (which by assumption is also the party of the president). For the Clinton years, defense issues are an example. As we know from our description of message formulation, majority message priorities typically unite the majority party and reflect public views about the party's strengths. In addition, these issues usually divide the minority party or raise significant public concerns about the party's governing abilities. On such items, we would expect the congressional majority to move strong legislation that reflects the party program. The president likely will respond with signals that are somewhat ambiguous or with relatively low levels of opposition. We expect to observe presidential positions that are clustered near the middle of the signaling scale. Of course, the president might dig in tactically, leading to gridlock. But in this message category, we expect to see a relatively high incidence of major concessions from the White House, perhaps even acquiescence. The congressional majority, though, will probably not offer major concessions unless the president is intransigent and there are major pressures to enact something.

Minority Message Priorities. Now consider a third category of message issue—items that are prominent on the message agenda of the minority party on Capitol Hill (again, by assumption the party of the president), but not on the message agenda of the majority party. For the 105th and 106th Congress, prominent examples of minority-party message priorities would include campaign finance reform and the Patients' Bill of Rights. The majority leadership generally will attempt to keep these items off the floor. By their nature, however, minority message priorities tend to unite the minority party and divide the majority party. As a result, the president and his fellow partisans likely will "go public," attempting to move the issue onto the active decision-making agenda. Minority-party senators may exploit the free-flowing floor procedures of their chamber to force action via nongermane amendments. And a cross-partisan coalition of sufficient size may emerge in the House to secure access to the floor, perhaps via the discharge petition.

The character of the bargaining that results will depend on the strategic posture adopted by the majority party. The majority leadership may opt for a "strategy of inoculation" and make major concessions. In response, the administration will probably dig in, transmitting signals of unambiguous opposition, including veto threats. Alternatively, the opposition to the initiative within the activist base of the majority party may be so strong that the leadership will refuse to compromise. Under such conditions, given the underlying distribution of preferences, the minority party in Congress (with help from the White House and majority-party moderates) may gain the upper hand, advancing to the floor a measure that the president can support. Thus, for minority message priorities, we expect to observe strongly negative signals from the White House and either major concessions from the congressional majority or intransigence on their part and the emergence of a strong cross-partisan coalition that includes the president.

Other Bills. The remaining issues are not directly tied to the message agendas of either party. Here, the strategic calculations of message politics will be much less relevant. Presidential signals and congressional-presidential bargaining will be driven by idiosyncratic features of the bargaining context—for instance, whether or not cleavages are mostly partisan or cross-partisan, the personal policy agendas of the president and key legislators, issue salience, whether or not a measure is a "must pass" item such as an appropriations bill, and so on. And here, the essential characteristics of the blame game should be less apparent.

Our thought experiment generates a number of predictions about legislative bargaining. But to gauge how well the hypothesized linkages between message status and congressional-presidential bargaining are supported by evidence, we need to consider information about message relevance and interbranch bargaining on a sample of measures, ideally major bills under conditions of divided government. We adopt a three-pronged approach to gathering this evidence.

First, using the listings of "major legislation" routinely compiled by *CQ Weekly Report*, we constructed a sample of major bills from the 105th and 106th Congresses (1997–2000) that also were the subject of SAPs from one or both chambers.[16] Although a few of the CQ major measures did not receive SAPs, the vast majority of them did make the cut. The total number of measures included in our major bill sample is sixty-three. Because our interest is in interbranch bargaining, companion House and Senate bills are treated as a single piece of legislation.[17] And because veto bargaining is especially important under conditions of divided government, we focus on a period when the Democratic president Bill Clinton confronted a GOP-controlled Congress.

Second, we used the "one-minute" speeches delivered on the House floor at the beginning of most legislative days as an indicator of the two parties' message priorities. For over a decade, House Republicans and Democrats have employed the one-minute speeches as a forum for articulating their party messages. If a bill or issue area surfaced repeatedly in the one-minute speeches delivered by members of a party, then the measure is treated as a message priority for that party. Some major bills are not referenced explicitly by name in the one-minutes but clearly touch on policy areas that are mentioned regularly. These bills also are treated as message items for the purposes of analysis.

The message status of the sixty-three major bills is summarized in table 8.3. Notice that the allocation of issues across message quadrants is largely consistent with public attitudes about party competence as revealed in mass opinion surveys. Defense issues, targeted tax reductions, and crime are all message items for the Republicans but not for Democrats (and thus are considered majority message priorities). Campaign finance reform, managed care reform, and the minimum wage are prominent on the Democratic Party message, but not on that of the Republicans (they are minority message priorities). The shared message priorities include several education bills but also across-the-board tax cuts. During this period, Democrats generally responded

Table 8.3 Message Relevance of Major Bills with SAPs, 105th–106th Congress

	Democrats High	Democrats Low
GOP High	*Shared Message Priorities*	*Majority Message Priorities*
	105th Congress Education Savings Accounts Private School Vouchers *106th Congress* Education Block Grants Education Impact Aid Student Literacy Teacher Training Title 1 (ESEA) Medicare Prescriptions Tax Reduction	*105th Congress* Defense Authorization 97 Defense Authorization 98 Juvenile Justice IRS Overhaul *106th Congress* Debt Reduction (90-10 Plan) Defense Authorization 99 Defense Authorization 00 Education Flexibility Estate Tax Juvenile Justice Marriage Penalty Military Pay Missile Defense
GOP Low	*Minority Message Priorities*	*Other Major Bills*
	105th Congress Campaign Finance Managed Care Reform *106th Congress* Campaign Finance Gun Control Managed Care Reform Minimum Wage	*105th Congress* Banking Overhaul Bankruptcy Reform Caribbean Trade Chemical Weapons Treaty Cloning Ban Compensatory Time Endangered Species Act FDA Revisions Higher Education Housing Overhaul Internet Taxes Nuclear Waste Disposal Partial Birth Abortions Private Property Rights State Department Authorization Transportation Reauthorization Workers Visas	*106th Congress* Aviation Reauthorization Census Banking Overhaul Bankruptcy Reform Community Renewal/New Markets Electronic Signatures Federal Land Acquisition Fetal Protection Internet Taxes Nuclear Waste Disposal Partial Birth Abortions Pension/IRA Tax Breaks Product Liability Satellite TV State Department Authorization Steel Imports Tax Extenders Y2K Liability

to GOP omnibus tax-cut proposals by linking them to the long-term viability of Medicare and Social Security, which are core Democratic priorities.[18]

The third prong of our measurement strategy was to use the extensive legislative coverage provided in CQ *Weekly Report* for the sixty-three major bills to code a range of variables relating to the bargaining process within Congress and between the branches. Included are the nature of the conflict (partisan, regional, and so forth), the identities of the key bargainers (committee leaders, party leaders, administration officials), the concessions offered by the main competing coalitions, the relative significance of such concessions, the point when the concessions were offered (House or Senate committee, floor, conference), and the outcome of the bargaining process.[19]

BARGAINING BETWEEN THE BRANCHES

What does the evidence suggest about legislative-executive bargaining? In tables 8.4–8.6, several of the bargaining indicators are summarized by message category. Table 8.4 presents the distribution of presidential signals across the four message categories. Evidence about bargaining concessions is provided in table 8.5. For each issue, we focused our attention on two main coalitions: (1) the president and his supporters on Capitol Hill, and (2) the primary coalition of opponents. For the vast majority of the measures, conflict divided along party lines and the opposing coalition was largely comprised of congressional Republicans (with perhaps some conservative Democrats as allies). On a number of the bills, there were significant policy differences between the House and Senate, with one chamber (usually the Senate) embracing a position that was substantially closer to the president's position. In such instances, we identified as the opposing coalition the main group (of opponents) from within the chamber that was furthest from the position of the White House. For two of the measures in our sample, there was minimal conflict, and in table 8.5 these items are placed in the "none needed" category for concessions. Table 8.6 provides summary information about how far in the legislative process each measure progressed, distinguishing between message categories. Interestingly, none of the major bills in our sample passed the Senate and failed in the House, reflecting in part the high legislative hurdle created by the Senate filibuster.

For the most part, the evidence summarized in these tables is consistent with our expectations about the linkages between message status and interbranch bargaining. Once again, consider each message category in turn. Recall that we expect high scores on the presidential signaling scale for the shared message priorities, and then either mutual intransigence or mutual

Table 8.4 Presidential Signals by Message Category, Major Bills with SAPS, 105th–106th Congresses

Position	Shared Message Priority	Majority Message Priority	Minority Message Priority	Other Major Bills	Total
Presidential Veto Threat	3	2	1	6	12
Senior Advisers Veto Threat	2	3	2	8	15
Secretary's Veto Threat	1	0	0	7	8
Strongly Oppose Passage	0	0	0	3	3
Oppose Passage	0	3	1	3	7
No Position on Passage	0	4	0	2	6
No Objection to Passage	1	0	0	1	2
Support Passage	2	1	0	4	7
Strongly Support Passage	0	0	2	1	3
Total	9	13	6	35	63

Note: Entries denote the number of bills falling in a particular category.

accommodation. Acquiescence by either side should be rare. Of the nine measures in this category, six drew an explicit veto threat (three of them presidential threats). In the 106th Congress, Republican leaders divided the reauthorization of the Elementary and Secondary Education Act into five separate bills as part of an effort to maximize media attention on their education agenda. Certain of the education items, particularly the student literacy and education impact aid bills, were not controversial and largely account for the supportive signals among the shared message priorities in table 8.4. As expected, neither the White House nor congressional Republicans capitulated on any of the shared message priorities. Most of the concessions were minor. And the major concessions that were made were insufficient for enactment. Only two of the nine measures in this category were signed by the president (both minor education bills). And two bills were vetoed (education savings accounts in the 105th Congress and the omnibus tax-reduc-

Table 8.5 Bargaining Stances by Message Category, Major Legislation with SAPs, 105th–106th Congresses

Concessions	Shared Message Priorities	Majority Message Priorities	Minority Message Priorities	Other Major Bills	Total
None/Minor					
Pres*	6	4	3	18	31
Opp**	5	7	3	12	27
Major					
Pres	2	7	3	15	27
Opp	3	6	3	21	33
Capitulation					
Pres	0	2	0	1	3
Opp	0	0	0	1	1
None Needed	1	0	0	1	2

Note: Entries denote the number of bills falling in a particular category.
"Pres" = Presidential Coalition; "Opp" = Opposition Coalition.

tion measure in the 106th). The remaining items failed to clear both the House and the Senate.

We predicted somewhat different bargaining patterns for the majority message priorities. Here, we expect presidential signaling that tends toward the middle range of the scale in table 8.4. Compared to the shared message priorities, there should be a lower percentage of presidential and senior advisers

Table 8.6 Legislative Fate of Major Bills with SAPs by Message Category, 105th–106th Congresses

Outcome	Shared Message Priorities	Majority Message Priorities	Minority Message Priorities	Other Major Bills	Total
Passed Neither Chamber	1	0	0	3	4
Passed House, Not Senate	4	2	3	8	17
Passed Both Chambers	0	1	3	4	8
Vetoed by the President	2	2	0	4	8
Enacted	2	8	0	16	26
Total	9	13	6	35	63

Note: Entries denote the number of bills falling in a particular category.

threats. We also hypothesized an asymmetric bargaining pattern: the White House should concede more than the opposing coalition (primarily congressional Republicans). Indeed, of the thirteen observations in this category, seven (53.8 percent) do fall toward the middle range of the scale. Five observations, however, are in the highest levels, including two presidential veto threats. One of the presidential threats was on the fiscal year 2000 Defense authorization Bill. The veto threat focused on a single provision that would have prohibited the use of fiscal year 2000 funds to pay for the ongoing Kosovo mission. Clearly, the provision touched on war powers, a core presidential prerogative. The other presidential threat was on a bill to repeal the federal estate tax.

As expected, though, the evidence in table 8.5 does indicate an asymmetric bargaining process for the majority message priorities. On over half of the measures in the category, the opposing GOP coalition offered minor or no concessions, while on nine of the thirteen the White House made major concessions or capitulated. Interestingly, the two examples of presidential capitulation were on a military pay hike and a bill to overhaul the Internal Revenue Service. The Clinton administration initially opposed the IRS overhaul but flipped positions after the Senate Finance Committee conducted a series of highly emotional, nationally televised hearings about IRS investigatory abuses. As mentioned, majority message priorities tend to unify the majority party and divide the minority: during divided government, this preference configuration also weakens the president's negotiating leverage. As a result, over 60 percent of these initiatives were eventually enacted—the highest success rate across the four message quadrants.

Now consider the minority message priorities. We predicted a cluster of observations at the top and/or at the bottom of the presidential signaling scale, with very few in the middle range. We also predicted that the president would seldom offer major concessions on these bills. Moreover, we expected that the opposing Republican coalition would either make major concessions or be rolled on the floor. The prospects for gridlock on these issues are high because of majority-party control over the legislative agenda.

In fact, five of the six measures do fall near the top or at the very bottom of the signaling scale. However, the presidential coalition also offered major concessions on half of the measures—not the pattern that we expected. Two of the three cases dealt with the McCain-Feingold campaign finance reform proposal. In both the 105th and 106th Congresses, Senator John McCain (R-AZ) chose to dramatically scale back his proposal as part of an effort to pick up the GOP support necessary to cut off a filibuster by Mitch McConnell (R-KS). Clinton supported McCain's tactics but also expressed his preference for the stronger bill. The third example was a proposed minimum-wage hike in the 106th Congress. Here, the president conceded very little on the underlying measure but was willing to accept the addition of a small business tax package endorsed by GOP leaders. Interestingly, none of the six minority message priorities reached the president's desk.

As expected, there are no clear patterns within the "other major bills" category. Roughly half of the measures drew explicit veto threats, indicating the general importance of veto bargaining on major legislation during divided government. Still, there was considerable variance across the different levels of the signaling scale for this quadrant. Bargaining concessions were about equally divided between minor and major modifications. A little less than half of the measures were eventually enacted, with the rest fairly equally distributed across the remaining outcome categories. Most of the cleavages in this quadrant also were partisan, reflecting the overarching party polarization of contemporary American politics. Based on our review of the legislative histories, though, party position-taking and other audience effects were relatively muted in this issue quadrant.

For the most part, then, our analysis of bargaining dynamics is consistent with the hypotheses rooted in message politics. Audience effects do appear to significantly influence the process of interbranch bargaining. These effects, however, are *conditional* on the relevance of a measure to the message agendas of the majority and minority parties. The blame-game model appears to be most applicable to shared message priorities. During 1999, for instance, the Republican Congress sent to President Clinton a reconciliation package that would have reduced federal taxes by $792 billion. Prior to House and Senate passage, the White House repeatedly issued a presidential veto threat. No significant policy concessions were offered by either side, the measure cleared both chambers on near party-line votes, and the president vetoed the bill to great fanfare. The Republicans clearly were playing the blame game.

Notice, though, that over half of the shared message priorities did not pass the Senate in 1997–2000, suggesting that the president's fellow partisans may sometimes circumvent the blame game by filibustering potential veto bait into oblivion. Blame-game calculations also can characterize issues that are majority message priorities. But the president is also more likely to make major concessions in this message quadrant and may be able to duck public blame by simply signing the relevant legislation. In contrast, the blame game does not really fit the minority message category. Here, the majority leadership uses its agenda prerogatives and other resources to keep the targeted legislation away from the president's desk. If anything, it is the president's party that will attempt to assign blame to the congressional majority.

The bottom line? We find compelling evidence that veto bargaining has certain essential features of a signaling game. However, during divided government, the more relevant an issue becomes to the message agenda of the majority party in Congress, the more unambiguously negative will be the legislative signals emanating from the executive branch. Relatively clear-cut veto threats will become more common. And congressional-presidential bargaining will resonate more with the blame-game approach.

CONCLUSION

The coordination and blame-game models can help clarify our understanding of congressional-presidential bargaining. These theories isolate many of the essential features of veto bargaining and make explicit certain strategic calculations that drive the bargaining process. Still, the American Congress, by its very nature, is a mechanism for collective choice, and the federal executive branch is one of the most internally complex political hierarchies in existence. The internal characteristics of both branches condition how they bargain with one another. And we need to consider the processes through which bargaining strategies are developed within Congress and the White House to fully understand the rivalry for power that exists between the branches.

The ideas of Cameron and Groseclose and McCarty provide a critical foundation for understanding elite bargaining in American national politics. Cameron's approach focuses almost exclusively on the elite bargainers themselves. Although he marshals extensive evidence that key features of veto bargaining are consistent with the implications of an elite-driven coordination game, much of that evidence is also consistent with alternative conceptualizations. In this chapter, our examination of the institutional context within the executive branch generates strong prima facie evidence for exactly the kinds of strategic dynamics that characterize the coordination model.

The blame-game model of Groseclose and McCarty also captures important aspects of elite-level bargaining in politics. From David Mayhew's classic description of position-taking to contemporary accounts of party campaigning, there is ample evidence that bargaining stances may also serve as public appeals to a wider audience.[20] The offering of such appeals, however, should vary with a range of issue-specific factors. In the contemporary era, the two political parties play a central role in selecting the issues upon which organized position-taking will occur. As a result, to understand the position-taking aspects of interbranch bargaining, we need to consider the party message operations within Congress—as well as the role that presidents themselves play in message formulation. In American national government, the essential features of the blame game—and, we believe, of audience-conditioned bargaining in general—are most prevalent for policy areas prominent on the message agendas of one or both political parties.

To some extent, then, the strategic manipulation of information and the tactic of position-taking are always present in bargaining over legislation. The real issue here is one of extent. As a result, the important question to ask is not, "Does the coordination model or the blame game better explain congressional-presidential bargaining?" Rather, we should ask, "Under what conditions does bargaining more closely approximate the coordination model and under what conditions does it most resemble public posturing before an audience?" We can help identify these conditions by considering the institutional context within which congressional-presidential bargaining occurs.

What are the implications for the second term of President George W. Bush? As table 8.1 indicates, the incidence of veto threats declines sharply when both branches are controlled by the same political party, which is the political configuration of the 109th Congress. Veto bargaining is simply less useful as a political strategy under unified party control, and even when the president's party controls one chamber (but not the other). With unified government, the degree of policy conflict between the administration and the congressional majority will be less pronounced, and powerful incentives will exist for both sides not to publicly embarrass their fellow partisans at the opposite end of Pennsylvania Avenue. As a result, veto threats have been— and should remain—a less integral component of congressional-presidential relations during the Bush administration than was the case during the Clinton presidency.

Still, presidents do engage in strategic signaling when both branches are controlled by the same party, and we can expect to witness such posturing throughout Bush's second term. During the fall 2004 consideration of the 9/11 Recommendations Implementation Act, the Bush White House released a SAP stating the president's overall support for the measure but also expressing strong opposition to the section dealing with the detention and extradition of suspected terrorists. There was no explicit veto threat, in part because the legislation was highly popular with the public. Following the November elections, conservative elements within the House Republican Conference threatened to block the 9/11 Commission bill because of concerns about the proposed national intelligence directorate and related immigration issues. But throughout the legislative endgame on the measure, there were strong incentives for the administration and Republicans on Capitol Hill to hold intraparty conflict in check. The antiterrorism fight was critical to the public's assessment of the Bush White House and to the message agenda of congressional Republicans. The legislation was enacted in the closing days of 2004.

Highly confrontational posturing between the branches—including the issuance of veto threats—can also occur under conditions of unified party control if a measure cuts across party lines or does not directly relate to the name brand of the majority party. Congressional action on the highway reauthorization bill during 2003–2004 is a case in point. The federal highway program allocates distributive benefits to every congressional district in the country, and Republicans on Capitol Hill face the same parochial pressures as do their Democratic counterparts. For legislators from both political parties, more spending on highways is usually preferred to less. The Bush administration, in contrast, was primarily concerned about holding transportation pork to a minimum. And the bill was not central to the message agendas of either political party. The SAP sent to the House for the measure in 2004 included a senior advisers veto threat, largely because of the proposed funding level. The SAP for the Senate version of the bill also featured two distinct veto threats, as well as statements of strong presidential opposition to several sections of the legislation. As a consequence of this strategic infighting between the branches, as well as dilatory tactics by Senate Democrats, the highway bill died during the 108th Congress.

Most important, the 2004 elections produced Republican majorities in both chambers of Congress that are fairly slim. There is a real chance that the Democrats will regain majority status in one or both chambers following the 2006 midterm elections. The American electorate remains sharply divided along partisan lines, further raising prospects of a return to divided partisan control in the foreseeable future. If and when divided government does reoccur in political Washington, we can expect an increased emphasis on veto bargaining between the branches, conditioned, of course, by the importance of an issue area to the message agendas of the two political parties.

NOTES

1. Empirical studies that touch on veto bargaining include David W. Rohde and Dennis M. Simon, "Presidential Vetoes and Congressional Response: A Study of Institutional Conflict," *American Journal of Political Science* 29 (1985): 397–427 (on trends in veto usage across administrations and the electoral cycle); Nolan McCarty, "Presidential Vetoes in the Early Republic," unpublished manuscript, Princeton University, 2003 (on nineteenth-century use of the veto); Stephen J. Wayne, Richard L. Cole, and James F. C. Hyde Jr., "Advising the President on Enrolled Legislation," *Political Science Quarterly* 94 (1979): 303–18 (on the process of internal White House deliberations about vetoes); and

Barbara D. Sinclair, "The President in the Legislative Process: Preferences, Strategy, and Outcomes," presented at the Annual Meeting of the American Political Science Association, Boston, 2002 (on the strategic implications of threatened vetoes).

2. Charles M. Cameron, *Veto Bargaining: The Politics of Negative Power* (New York: Cambridge University Press, 2000).

3. Tim Groseclose and Nolan McCarty, "The Politics of Blame: Bargaining before an Audience," *American Journal of Political Science* 45 (2001): 100–119.

4. Gilmour uses media accounts to show that most vetoes are fully expected at the time of initial congressional passage, raising some questions about Cameron's informational assumptions. See John B. Gilmour, "Sequential Veto Bargaining and Blame Game Politics as Explanations of Presidential Vetoes," presented at the Annual Meeting of the Midwest Political Science Association, Chicago, 2001.

5. Richard E. Neustadt, "Presidency and Legislation: The Growth of Central Clearance," *American Political Science Review* 48 (1954): 641–70.

6. Gary Cox and Mathew McCubbins, *Legislative Leviathan: Party Government in the House* (Berkeley and Los Angeles: University of California Press, 1993); and Barbara D. Sinclair, *Legislators, Leaders, and Lawmaking: The U.S. House of Representatives in the Postreform Era* (Baltimore: Johns Hopkins University Press, 1995).

7. Terry Moe, "The Politicized Presidency," in *The New Direction in American Politics*, ed. J. Chubb and P. Peterson (Washington, DC: Brookings Institution, 1985); and Terry Moe, "The Presidency and the Bureaucracy: The Presidential Advantage," in *The Presidency and the Political System*, 4th ed., ed. Michael Nelson (Washington, DC: CQ Press, 1995).

8. See Wayne, Cole, and Hyde, "Advising the President."

9. See C. Lawrence Evans and Walter J. Oleszek, "Herding Cats: Presidential Coalition Building in the Senate," in *Rivals for Power: Presidential-Congressional Relations*, ed. James Thurber (New York: Rowman & Littlefield, 2002).

10. Personal interview conducted in Washington, DC, February 2003.

11. This composite scale is a combination and elaboration of the measures introduced in Evans and Oleszek, "Herding Cats." In the real world of legislative politics, the perceived likelihood of a veto is closely tied to perceptions about the direction and intensity of the administration's policy views. Thus, the scale comports well with the concrete markers that participants in the process use to gauge the probability of a presidential veto. For instance, it closely resembles the hierarchy of veto threats presented in an insightful media analysis of the topic, "Assessing the Spectrum of Veto Threats," *Congressional Quarterly Weekly Report*, September 4, 1999, 2026. OMB staff occasionally make even finer distinctions in presidential signals to Capitol Hill. Some cleared documents describe the president's stance as "oppose unless amended," "oppose as currently drafted," "cite concerns," or "support if amended." For the purposes of this chapter, though, the nine-point scale captures the essential features of presidential signaling.

12. For evidence, see C. Lawrence Evans and Stephen Ng, "The Institutional Context of Veto Bargaining," paper presented at the annual meeting of the Midwest Political Science Association, Chicago, Illinois. 2003.

13. See Cox and McCubbins, *Legislative Leviathan*; and Sinclair, *Legislators, Leaders, and Lawmaking*.

14. C. Lawrence Evans, "Committees, Leaders, and Message Politics," in *Congress*

C. Lawrence Evans and Stephen Ng

Reconsidered, 7th ed., ed. Lawrence C. Dodd and Bruce I. Oppenheimer (Washington, DC: CQ Press, 2001), 219.

15. Patrick J. Sellers, "Winning Media Coverage in the U.S. Congress," in *U.S. Senate Exceptionalism*, ed. Bruce I. Oppenheimer (Columbus: Ohio State University Press, 2002).

16. *CQ Weekly Report* is generally viewed as the most complete and authoritative media coverage of the congressional legislative process. Sinclair, *Legislators, Leaders, and Lawmaking*, for instance, uses CQ as a source for developing indicators of leadership involvement on major bills.

17. For this chapter, we chose not to add (to the major bills sample) appropriations measures, which typically have long, detailed SAPs and distinct patterns of bargaining.

18. In coding message status, we adopted a conservative strategy. A number of the bills in the "other major bills" category did relate to party issues. Trent Lott, for instance, described the compensatory time measure as a major GOP priority for the 105th Congress, and the bill also touched on labor issues that are central to the Democratic agenda. But the legislation was only referenced during five one-minute speeches on a single day. As a result, we placed it in the "other bills" category. Similarly, Republicans often use the partial-birth abortion issue to force pro-choice Democrats to cast politically difficult floor votes. The item was not a major feature of the one-minutes, however, and thus was not coded as a message issue.

19. Both authors coded these variables and talked through all judgment calls.

20. David Mayhew, *Congress: The Electoral Connection* (New Haven: Yale University Press, 1973).

9

Politics of the Federal Budget Process

Leon E. Panetta

"EVEN A GREAT BUDGET ISN'T WORTH A DAMN IF IT CAN'T PASS!"

As chairman of the House Budget Committee, I had the responsibility not only to develop the congressional budget but also to sell it to the key House committee chairmen and my colleagues. In 1992, on presenting the key elements of our proposed budget to a senior chairman, he looked at me, smiled, and said: "It's a great budget, Leon, but you know, even a great budget isn't worth a damn if it can't pass!"

The point was clear: budgets are not just about numbers and priorities; they're about politics. The real test of an executive branch budget is whether a president can convince a majority of the American people that his priorities are right for them and the nation. The real test of a legislative budget is whether the leadership can convince a majority of the members of the House and Senate that the budget is in the best interest of them and their constituents. Either way, success or failure is dependent on politics.

In putting together a federal budget, the process involves a careful analysis and balancing of policy, priorities, and politics. Obviously, it should begin with good policy.

In the executive branch, the professional staff of the Office of Management and Budget (OMB) make their recommendations for increases or reductions in programs based on their expertise and experience with those areas of the budget. The departments and agencies can and often do challenge those recommendations on the basis of substantive policy arguments.

209

But inevitably in every policy debate, there comes a point where the question is asked: what are the politics on this issue? Whether the answer to that question is accurate often determines the fate of a president's priorities.

As an example, during the development of President Clinton's first economic plan, it was determined on a policy basis that significant savings could be achieved by striking all funding for highway projects that were not authorized in the law. Under the normal legislative process, a particular highway has to be approved in a transportation authorization bill before it can be funded in a transportation appropriations bill. Powerful members, however, recognized that they could bypass that process by simply placing a favorite new highway project directly into the transportation appropriations bill. This was viewed by the administration's budget staff as both bad policy and bad budgeting. They, of course, were right . . . on the process. They turned out to be wrong on the politics.

It turned out the then chairman of the Senate Appropriations Committee, Senator Robert Byrd of West Virginia, had funded a number of projects in his home state that had not been authorized. They were among those projects targeted for elimination. Of course, once that simple reality became clear, the conclusion followed that it would not be smart to antagonize the chairman of the Senate Appropriations Committee if the president was interested in getting his other budget priorities funded. These well-intentioned savings never saw the light of day!

The congressional budget process involves the same political analysis because every member is a vote for or against the budget. In close votes, the budget can be held hostage by the demands of one member. Oftentimes, those demands may not even relate to national budget policy but to projects or funding issues within that member's district or state. The ability to balance the enactment of important budget policy with the political demands of individual members is the chemistry that defines victory or defeat.

That is the nature of the budget process. It also happens to be the nature of our democratic process.

To fully understand how process and politics work, it is essential to consider the following: the budget process itself; the history of politics and deficits; the present challenge of politics and the deficit; and the role of leadership in balancing the tension between good policy and good politics.

THE FEDERAL BUDGET PROCESS: "BUDGETS, LIKE SOUP, NEED ONE CHEF, NOT 535!"

The fundamental difference between the branches when it comes to the budget is simple—the executive branch is an intensive and predictable "top to bottom" process, while the legislative is a more freewheeling and unpredictable "bottom to top" process. As one frustrated OMB career official once remarked to me, "Budgets, like soup, need one chef, not 535!" That, in a sentence, summarizes how one president has the consummate power to determine what an administration's budget will look like, whereas 535 members of both the House and Senate can have a multitude of conflicting views as to the numbers and priorities. The fundamental differences in each process explain the genius of our forefathers in establishing a system of checks and balances between the president and the Congress.

Executive Budget Process

The president throughout our early history was responsible for presenting to the nation a comprehensive and detailed budget. President Washington detailed his budget requests as part of his annual messages, as did many of his successors. In 1921, the Budget and Accounting Act specifically required presidents to submit budgets, stating priorities to Congress, no later than the first Monday in February. The Congress, on the other hand, only recently came to the task with the passage of the Budget and Impoundment Control Act of 1974.

OMB Spending Targets

In the administration, the process of preparing a budget begins with the Office of Management and Budget (see figure 9.1). With its professional staff, this executive branch office, once known as the Bureau of the Budget, issues a proposed general target for spending to each agency and department. That number is arrived at by an analysis of the next fiscal year's total budget and what is likely to be required for both discretionary and mandatory spending. It begins with economic projections on growth, inflation, unemployment, interest rates, etc., which are translated into income and spending estimations. Since budgets are prepared with five- to ten-year projections in most areas, these past numbers are a good place to start the analysis to determine if they are still relevant to the current state of the economy.

In providing these targets to the various departments and agencies, the director of OMB will normally use the most conservative estimates of how much funding will be available. This forces the budget officers outside the White House to operate within tight constraints and allows OMB to make *future* adjustments if needed to protect the president's priorities and deal with *future* contingencies.

These targets are usually sent out in the late summer of the year before

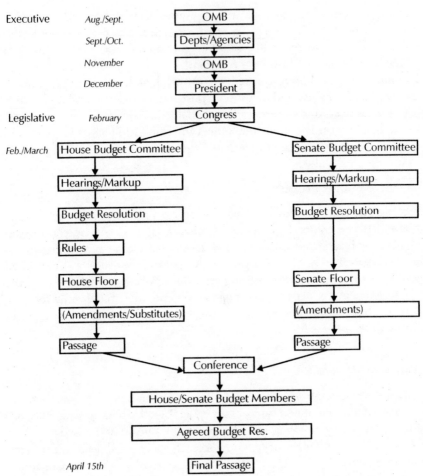

Figure 9.1 Phase One of the Budget Process: Development of Budget

the formal budget is presented to the nation in February. Often complicating this timetable is the fact that the prior fiscal year budget is being held up in the Congress. If few appropriations bills have been passed, then the administration is attempting to project future needs without really knowing what Congress will provide for current programs. Nevertheless, the process must go forward if budget deadlines are to be met.

As figure 9.1 indicates, the responses to OMB's directive are returned in late September or early October. OMB then recommends a "pass back" number to the departments and agencies. That begins a negotiating process between the budget and policy staffs of the departments and agencies and OMB to resolve and clarify differences. The principal goal is to arrive at as much consensus as possible on the final recommendations to the president in order to limit the number of conflicts and appeals.

Appeals to the President

At this point, cabinet secretaries and agency heads have to make a basic decision: is it in their interest to accept the recommendations of the OMB director to gain his support on future budget battles or to challenge the OMB position by going directly to the president and risk the possibility of both denial and future antagonism at the highest levels?

Because of the obvious risks, the issues are generally resolved with most departments and agencies. However, whether the reason is based on legitimate policy differences as to what should be spent on certain programs or on political tactics that involve the departments, the president, or the press, there will always be a few who will want to appeal their position. Their reasoning often reflects the delicate balancing of politics between the secretary and his or her department and the nature of their relationship with the president. It is the view of some that, win or lose, the good fight must be made, and possibly, just possibly, a few more dollars will be provided. Others base the appeal on testing the depth of support they have with the president.

To deal with these appeals to the president and last-minute revisions, most OMB directors set aside a reserve amount for these kinds of contingencies. My approach as director was to set aside at the very beginning of the budget process a reserve fund that would be available to resolve all of the final issues. Additional funds could also be provided with an adjustment here or there to economic estimates. The president was aware of the reserve and was urged to listen to all of the appeals but not to specifically commit or agree to any increased funding. At the end of the appeals, as director, I would recommend to the president an approach to dividing up the reserve account among some of the priority programs advocated by the department and agency heads. The president often would make additional changes on the final formula but always within the bounds of the reserve.

The consequence of this process served the interests of all those involved: the president gave the impression he was willing to listen without giving away the store; the department and agency heads felt that while they did not receive all they were asking for, they had put up the good fight and had something to show for their efforts; and the OMB director had protected the core budget with the reserve fund, and the small increases that were provided did not encourage others to challenge the process in the future.

This decision-making process by the president usually concludes in late December. With the final decisions made, the OMB staff and the budget staffs of the departments and agencies begin the task of ensuring that the final numbers in the budget add up. The month of January is spent refining details, preparing all of the appropriate tables, double-checking the line items in the budget, and preparing the text of the final budget document—a foot-high pile of four to five volumes along with a summary text.

Building Support for the Budget

January is also used for another purpose—to build political support for the budget. On a carefully targeted basis, selective leaks to the press are made on the president's priority programs and the funding levels contained in the budget. For example, if the president was doubling funds for the Head Start program, that fact, along with additional background, would be provided to a national newspaper. Headlined stories in the *New York Times*, *Washington Post*, and *USA Today* would gradually make clear to the public and the Congress the parameters of the president's budget. At the same time, the agencies and departments, particularly the Defense Department, would often provide their own off-the-record details of the budget decisions, both those they supported and those they opposed. The purpose of all of this is to begin a drumbeat of interest in the final details of the budget.

The most significant policy decisions are protected for the president to reveal as part of his State of the Union address. By the time the budget itself is formally unveiled in February, the nation has a pretty good sense of the priorities of the president and how they are addressed in the context of the final document. If done right, all of these strategies present a clear summary of the president's agenda to the nation.

The basic lesson of the entire executive branch budget process is that the president controls both the policy and politics—from the first numbers provided by OMB to the departments and agencies, to the president's final decisions, to the State of the Union address, to the presentation of the budget itself. In that sense, it is very much a "one-chef" operation—a top-to-bottom process—with the power, focus, and final decisions reserved to the president of the United States.

Legislative Budget Process

In the Congress, however, it is a "multi-chef" process. The budget cannot be dictated by the Speaker, the leadership, or a few key chairmen. It has to be negotiated chairman by chairman, committee by committee, member by member until a consensus is developed that commands a majority vote. It is the product of the democratic process, and as such, it is very much a bottom-to-top formula that can be every bit as chaotic as the executive branch process is efficient and orderly.

The president's budget, as outlined in figure 9.1, is referred to both the House and Senate budget committees for their consideration. If Congress is controlled by the opposing party to the White House, the president's budget is often proclaimed by the congressional leadership as "dead on arrival." During the 1980s, when President Reagan presented his budget to the Congress, Democrats immediately would denounce it as "DOA." On the other hand, if the White House and Capitol Hill are controlled by the same party, the president's budget can become a foundation on which to build the congressional budget. In either scenario, it is a sure bet that the House and Senate will want to have their impact on the final numbers and priorities.

In addition to the lack of a central authority controlling the process, the budgets themselves are very different between the executive and legislative branches. As mentioned before, the president's budget is very detailed and voluminous, with each department and agency budget carefully presented on a line-by-line basis. The congressional budget, on the other hand, is contained in a brief resolution that lists some twenty functional areas that set broad targets for spending in categories ranging from national defense, international affairs, general science, energy, space, and technology to natural resources and environment, agriculture, education, health, Medicare, income security, and others. The House Budget Committee recently added a functional area for homeland security, but neither the Senate nor the Congressional Budget Office has recognized that approach. For a complete list of the accepted functional categories, see table 9.1.

Although specific program funding is discussed in each area by the budget committees in order to arrive at a final functional number, these decisions are not binding on the appropriations process. For example, the budget committee may believe that Title I funding in education should be at a certain level in order to arrive at an overall function 500 education number, but that recommendation is not binding on the appropriations committee. The congressional budget, therefore, is more of a guideline to areas of the budget than a specific line-by-line mandate.

Hearings and Negotiations

The legislative process itself begins with hearings in the budget committees. These hearings are held in each body to allow the White House and cabinet secretaries the opportunity to defend the president's budget. They

Table 9.1   Functional Tables Contained in Congressional Budget Resolutions

Natural Defense
International affairs
250   General science, space and technology
270   Energy
300   Natural resources and environment
350   Agriculture
Commerce and housing credit
Transportation
Community and regional development
Education, training, employment, and social services
Health
Medicare
Income security
Social security
Veterans benefits and services
Administration of justice
General government
Net interest
Allowances
950   Undistributed offsetting receipts

normally begin with the director of OMB and the secretary of the treasury rotating between the House and Senate budget committees the first two days. From there, the various cabinet secretaries are scheduled for their testimony along with various public interest groups and congressional members, who generally appear near the end of the hearing process. These hearings normally take place in the February to mid-March period of the congressional session.

During this period, the chairmen of the budget committees and their respective leaderships are trying to determine a likely course of action. What are the changes or revisions that have to be implemented in the president's budget in order to gain the majority support of their parties?

While efforts have been made to develop bipartisan budgets, particularly in years when budget summits or negotiations took place between the White House and the Congress, the general pattern in recent years is that the minority deliberately stands back and forces the majority to pass the budget with their votes only. The first budget resolutions enjoyed bipartisan support because of the cooperation of such leaders as Democratic senator Ed Muskie of Maine and Republican senator Harry Belmon of Oklahoma. The 1990 budget agreement is another example of both parties and the White House working together for months to develop an agreed-upon budget. But in most years, the budget resolution must be developed, passed, and implemented by a partisan majority.

That means that the chairman of the budget committee has no alternative but to work within his party, negotiating with key chairmen and members. As chairman of the House Budget Committee, I began with an analysis of the major areas of contention in any budget—defense, education, Social Security, Medicare, and taxes. Other areas—veterans, health, agriculture, transportation, housing, and space—were also important to certain constituencies within the House. If a chairman can develop consensus on the big issues, the others fall more easily into place. In the days of large deficits and split government between a Democratic Congress and a Republican president, the key was to achieve a lower deficit figure than the president. The basic formula was: (1) show a lower deficit than the president; (2) raise domestic spending; (3) lower defense spending; (4) protect Social Security and Medicare; and (5) add more fees and revenues if possible. If you could balance all of these issues, the chances were you could get a Democratic majority to support the budget resolution.

For a Republican majority, again facing large annual deficits but with a Republican president, the key is to largely reflect the president's budget priorities. That formula usually involves: (1) a deficit projection similar to the president's; (2) additional or permanent tax cuts; (3) increased defense spending; (4) lower domestic spending; and (5) no significant benefit reductions in Social Security and Medicare. All of this, combined with some optimistic economic assumptions, can usually produce a Republican majority for the budget resolution.

To arrive at party consensus, the process begins with the key chairmen. To lose the chairman of the Ways and Means Committee or the appropriations committee could spell doom for the budget resolution. For me, it meant taking time to sit down and meet with each and every chairman and the staff of their committees to talk numbers and priorities. It resembles the executive process of discussions between the OMB director and the cabinet secretaries, except that the chairman of the budget committee has less leverage because every other chairman and their committees represent valuable votes for or against the budget itself.

This process gives the chairman a good idea of where the key problem areas are and what each chairman will or will not tolerate. Following this probing period and the hearings, the chairman then begins a negotiating process with the members of his party on the budget committee. I was fortunate enough as chairman to have a broad cross section of members represented on the committee, from representatives Barney Frank of Massachusetts and Barbara Boxer of California on the left to Charlie Stenholm and

Marvin Leath of Texas on the right. If I could get their concurrence on the budget, chances were pretty good I could get broad support on the floor of the House.

Each of these members had his or her special issue of concern—from agriculture to AIDS research programs, from cancer studies to defense, from education to highways, from the FBI to legal aid, from foreign aid to elderly housing. Since the minority members will provide no help in passage of the budget, every vote on the majority side is crucial to success. A chairman is left with little alternative but to provide as much as he can to meet the priorities of each key majority member.

If necessary, the chairman of the budget committee may have to engage the leadership of the party, particularly if a caucus of majority party members is threatening to oppose the budget resolution. It may be necessary for the Speaker or majority leader to negotiate or plead for party loyalty to achieve the necessary majority. The argument is that since the budget resolution only sets broad targets, changes can be made in the implementation of the budget to pacify dissidents within the party.

The Chairman's Mark

The end result of these negotiations and consultations is a chairman's mark—a draft of a proposed budget resolution for consideration of the full committee. The goal is to hold enough of the majority members to defeat any amendments and provide final passage to move the resolution to the floor of the House.

Since the minority knows it does not have the votes to defeat the resolution, its members will offer amendments largely directed at embarrassing the majority. For example, if defense spending is less than the president's, the minority might offer an amendment to restore that funding, forcing the more defense-oriented members of the majority to go on public record for or against such an amendment. Some members have standard amendments that they offer because of their constituencies or ideology, ranging from increased funds for Head Start or AIDS research to cuts in funds for rural legal assistance or a questionable weapons system. Assuming the chairman and the leadership have done their work, the majority can generally hold firm against these amendments on the argument that it is time to move the resolution to the floor for action.

The Floor

The challenge on the floor, of course, is how to hold that same majority together to adopt the resolution. In the House, the resolution must go to the

Rules Committee to determine the type of rule that will control the debate on the floor. The first budget resolutions in the House during the mid- to late 1970s enjoyed totally "open rules," which permitted any member to offer any amendment. When resolutions were taking more than two legislative weeks to complete because of the large number of amendments, the leadership decided that a tighter rule was required that only permitted total budget substitutes to be offered.

These large substitutes in the past have been pretty predictable. First of all, few members have the individual or staff capability to put together entire budget resolutions on their own. Second, once those members and caucuses have developed a substantive budget, they tend to repeat their efforts from year to year. In general, substitutes could be expected from the liberal side—usually the black caucus; and the conservative side—usually from members who were experienced with budgets, like John Rousellot of California in the 1970s or John Kasich of Ohio in the 1990s; the minority may or may not have a substitute; and usually the president's budget is offered, particularly if the party that doesn't control the White House thinks the president will be embarrassed by receiving few votes. The goal of the majority is to allow members the opportunity to vote for a liberal, conservative, or other alternative, depending on their district constituencies, with the hope that those members will then vote for final passage of the budget resolution. The logic is simple: "I tried to get my kind of budget adopted but it failed, so I voted for the committee resolution to meet our responsibilities under the Budget Act."

To accomplish this, the House rule permits votes on all of the alternative budgets first, on the assumption that none of them will pass. The final vote comes on the committee resolution. On the Senate floor, which is not controlled by a rules committee as in the House, the debate is limited by the Budget Act, and that tends to reduce the number of amendments.

On both sides of the Hill, the ultimate driving force behind passage is the responsibility of the majority to run the business of the nation and the Congress, meet the Budget Act deadlines, and allow the appropriations process to move forward. Whether members agree or disagree with every element of the budget, the rationale of completing the budget process is the most compelling argument to getting it passed.

Although the budget resolution is not signed by the president, it does require a final conference report to be passed resolving the differences in the numbers between the House and Senate versions. Again, because this is usually the total responsibility of the majority party, the conference on a budget resolution generally splits the difference between the two Houses. For example, if the Senate number on defense is $410 billion and the House number is $400 billion, there's always a good chance the final number will be $405 billion. The chairmen of the House and Senate budget committees usually sit down with their respective staffs and decide unilaterally where the most logical consensus can be found. That consensus must be tested with key members to ensure a majority vote.

If the differences involve matters of policy rather than numbers, this could prove more difficult to resolve. Recently, the Senate voted for a budget resolution that required the so-called pay-go discipline to apply to paying for both tax cuts and new spending. The House budget resolution applied pay-go only to spending and not to tax cuts. The conference was not able to resolve the differences, and no budget resolution was adopted for only the second time in the history of the budget process.

In the Senate, passage of a conference is viewed as more pro forma and accomplished by a voice vote. In the House, recorded votes are almost always requested, forcing the majority to again make sure they have every vote needed for passage.

Reconciliation

Final passage of the budget resolution allows the Congress to begin the process of implementing the budget. Referring to figure 9.2, there are two principal tools of implementation. One is reconciliation, which requires the Congress to achieve, through changes in the law, savings in entitlements or mandatory programs as well as additional taxes or fees. Directions are provided by the budget committees to each of the authorizing committees requiring them to come up with the savings or revenues mandated by the budget resolution. In this process, the individual chairmen and committees have great discretion in deciding exactly how they will achieve the specific targets under the budget resolution.

In general, the Ways and Means Committee portion of reconciliation is the engine that drives reconciliation, because taxes and health care savings are both the most controversial and the most substantive parts of the package. When Dan Rostenkowski was chairman of the Ways and Means Committee, it was advisable to allow him to complete his portion of the reconciliation package before putting the other committee sections in place. The ability of a committee chair to get reconciliation savings adopted by his committee, particularly Ways and Means, was a good indication of whether a final reconciliation package could be adopted.

On the Senate side, it should be noted, the principal procedural advantage of reconciliation is that the bill itself cannot be filibustered by the minority. This may be the single most important procedural tool available to the majority under the Budget Act if they want to pass their priority legislation.

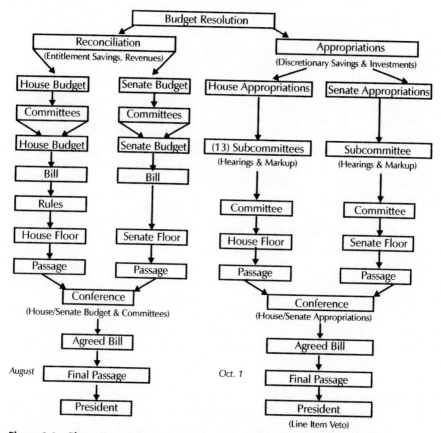

Figure 9.2 Phase Two of the Budget Process: Implementation of the Budget

Instead of having to put together sixty votes to break a filibuster, they can pass a reconciliation bill with a simple majority. This has led to what many consider an abuse of the reconciliation process.

In fighting deficits, reconciliation was a common implementation weapon, because any serious budget resolution required either significant savings from mandatory programs or revenue increases, and usually both. While the majority might use the reconciliation process to expand some program areas in order to sweeten an otherwise difficult vote on cuts and taxes, the overall purpose of reconciliation was to achieve deficit reduction.

In the period of budget surpluses, however, reconciliation was used to pass tax cuts that could otherwise be blocked by a filibuster. Although the Senate parliamentarian has determined that such use of reconciliation is acceptable the rules, Senator Byrd of West Virginia and budget enforcement ities strongly believe that it should only be used to achieve budget savings. Nevertheless, it remains a tempting legislative tool for the majority party in order to avoid a filibuster.

Appropriations

The second tool of implementation is the appropriations process. While the budget resolution sets an overall cap on discretionary spending, the House and Senate appropriations committees divide up that amount between their respective thirteen subcommittees. Each of the subcommittees reports out an appropriations bill, but the total of these bills cannot exceed the amount in the budget resolution or a point of order can be made on the floor of the House or Senate. Emergencies are not subject to these limitations, and, of course, the House and Senate can waive the points of order subject to a majority vote. These appropriations bills, because they provide spending on a bipartisan basis, are often supported by both Republicans and Democrats.

It is in these appropriations bills that the rubber meets the road in the legislative process, because this is not just language, this is real money that counts when it comes to bringing home the bacon to a member's home state or district. Here, the principal force for agreement is within each appropriations subcommittee, where the chairman and the members ensure that they each get a fair share of the action. If done right, that process of "give and take" among members can guarantee passage. The one barrier is if the president vetoes the bill because it does not sufficiently fund his priorities or contains provisions he opposes.

Traditionally, most of the operations of federal departments and agencies are funded each year through the separate enactment of the thirteen regular appropriations acts. Since these measures expire at the end of the fiscal year, the regular appropriations bills for the subsequent fiscal year must be enacted by October 1. However, one or more regular appropriations bills are typically delayed beyond the deadline. When this occurs, the affected departments and agencies are generally funded under temporary continuing appropriations acts until the final funding decisions are enacted.

Over the last thirty years, the nature, scope, and duration of continuing resolutions has gradually expanded. From the early 1970s through the present, continuing resolutions have gradually expanded from interim funding measures of comparatively brief duration and length to measures providing funding through the end of the fiscal year. The chances of the appropriations process meeting its funding deadlines usually improve if there is agreement on budget disciplines and targets. In the years of broad budget agreement between the president and the Congress, the appropriations process tends to proceed more efficiently with regard to its deadlines. In the absence of agreement or budget discipline, the appropriations process is prolonged, controversial, and usually dependent on continuing resolutions.

In the end, the differences in the budget process are defined by the powers outlined in the Constitution. The executive, as commander in chief, controls the development, policy decisions, and implementation of the executive budget. The legislative branch, by virtue of the "power of the purse," controls the actual spending. But because there are more than 535 members of Congress as opposed to one president, the development, policy decisions, and implementation of any congressional budget are often more chaotic and unpredictable. Final action is a roll of the dice that may often depend on politics, threats, crisis, and the need for a Congress to adjourn.

Ultimately, although budgets are developed differently in the two branches, the fate of each budget depends on whether the president and the Congress can work together to resolve their differences. The often reluctant cooperation of both branches is the engine that can more effectively drive the budget process forward. And that only happens when both the executive and legislative branches are convinced that the politics of resolving their budget differences is on their side.

THE BATTLE OVER DEFICITS:—"IT HAS TAKEN US OVER TWENTY YEARS TO GET OUT OF THIS HOLE!"

Although it is clear that there are distinct differences between the executive and legislative branches as to the development of a budget, over the last twenty or more years of deficits, both have faced similar challenges in trying to discipline their spending.

To designate federal dollars to certain federal programs is a power that the president, the Congress, and both parties thoroughly appreciate. Cutting spending or raising taxes, on the other hand, is a nasty and unrewarding responsibility that no one enjoys. When you spend money, you generally make people happy, and happy people are more likely to vote for you. When you reduce or cut funding or raise taxes, you generally anger people, and angry people will most likely vote against you. All of this is basic politics, and that is why deficit reduction is never easily embraced absent strong and courageous political leadership.

When the Congressional Budget and Impoundment Control Act of 1974 was adopted, the goal was not so much to impose budget discipline as to limit President Nixon's ability to impound expenditures approved by a then Democratic Congress. The Congress reluctantly adopted a budget process because they understood that politically they could not limit the president's ability to impose spending restraint without appearing to adopt some restraint on their own.

Few, in fact, expected that the new process would work or change business as usual. The original drafters—members like Representative Dick Bolling of Missouri, Senator Ed Muskie of Maine, and Representative John Rhodes of Arizona—believed it was important for Congress to have its own budget in order to put the entire budget's legislative priorities into one context. But they also knew how difficult it would be to change the addiction to the historical open-ended appropriations process. Indeed, both the tenure and membership of the new budget committees—particularly on the House side—were structured to limit their power. Members rotate off after three terms. The chairman would have to leave as well when his term on the committee was up. The key committees, like Appropriations and Ways and Means, were given a set number of members on the budget committee. The early provision requiring two budget resolutions in each congressional session was designed to accommodate additional spending. In a word, the intent was to limit the power of the budget committee to interfere with business as usual in the Congress.

The Early Years

In the early years, the challenge of budget chairmen was not so much to force action to control deficits but to cajole and accommodate other key chairmen and the leadership to go along with the targets set by the budget resolution. An example of this was the reconciliation process. As discussed before, reconciliation is the one enforcement tool in the Budget Act with teeth. It controls and expedites the process of achieving savings and deficit reduction. But for over six years, it was a tool that was never used. As a freshman member of the House Budget Committee in the late 1970s, then chairman Bob Giaimo asked me to head up the Reconciliation Task Force. But my role was not to require but to encourage budget savings. These savings were defined in the budget resolution. I had the responsibility of going to such committee chairmen as Jamie Whitten of Mississippi (Appropriations), Dan Rostenkowski of Illinois (Ways and Means), Bill Ford of Michigan (Post Office and Civil Service), and Carl Perkins of Kentucky (Education and Labor) to urge that they voluntarily achieve these savings. Needless to say, it was not very persuasive to simply encourage such savings because it was good policy for the nation. Most of these chairmen had earned their reputations because of domestic programs they had established or funded, many of them named in their honor.

It was not until the first Reagan budget passed in the early 1980s and Democrats lost control of the legislative process that the full force of a mandatory reconciliation enforcement tool was realized. The then director of OMB, David Stockman, drafted the reconciliation bill off the floor of the House, and, with scribbles and notes in the margins, it was passed. The Republican Senate was able to clean up a great deal of the haphazard drafting that mistakenly eliminated some popular programs, but it was clear to all of the members that reconciliation was a powerful tool that could change the very structure of government itself. But the Reagan budget also called for large tax cuts and defense increases. As a result, instead of reducing the deficit, it exploded, and the national debt went from less than $1 trillion to close to $4 trillion.

Gramm-Rudman-Hollings

The growing deficit forced additional action by the president and the Congress. In 1985, the so-called Gramm-Rudman-Hollings Act was passed—the Balanced Budget and Emergency Deficit Control Act. The bill introduced the concept of the mandatory trigger to force savings in the absence of congressional leadership. It set mandatory deficit reduction targets that, if not met, required "sequestration" or cuts across the board that automatically met those targets. The problem was that despite the fact that certain sensitive programs like Social Security were spared some of the deep across-the-board cuts, Congress prevented Gramm-Rudman-Hollings from taking full effect because of the arbitrary damage that would be done to programs and constituencies.

Although some form of sequestration has remained as part of the budget enforcement process when the Congress exceeds caps on discretionary spending, the reality is that it is much more limited than the large across-the-board cuts first envisioned by the original Gramm-Rudman-Hollings proposal. The experience with this legislation confirms that any enforcement tool is only as good as the politics that support it. No automatic trigger works unless there is a majority of votes willing to back it up in the Congress. As Congress continued to change the targets established by the Gramm-Rudman-Hollings law, it gradually eroded its impact and enforceability.

Budget Summits

Following the Gramm-Rudman-Hollings experience came a series of "budget summits" that provided a forum for both the president and the Congress to try to find consensus on deficit reduction. The challenge always came down to several key but difficult issues: Should additional revenues be raised, how much, and who should carry the burden of additional taxes? Should entitlements be reduced to achieve long-term savings, and what would these reforms mean for programs like Medicare, Medicaid, and farm programs? How much should be spent on defense? And what limits should be placed on domestic discretionary spending? The ability to balance these issues often determined whether or not an agreement could be achieved.

The most fundamental political change was that both the president and the Congress were willing to have a select group of negotiators determine broad policy for the nation. The president's agenda was placed in the hands of his secretary of the treasury, the director of OMB, and his chief of staff, and legislative decisions were no longer being made by chairmen and committees but by the select members of the leadership and key chairmen and members sitting at the negotiating table. While this process was effective at expediting agreements, it became more unpredictable when the legislation was brought to the floor. Most members did not feel they were part of the process. At the same time, because a number of controversial issues were combined into one large omnibus bill, members also recognized that there was some political protection in voting for a large deficit reduction package supported by the president, even though they did not always agree with every element.

The 1990 budget summit was probably the most significant bipartisan effort made at achieving consensus, in terms of both the deficit reduction achieved and the length of the negotiations between the president and the Congress. Negotiations began in early June and continued throughout the summer, with final negotiations taking place at Andrews Air Force Base. Although differences were narrowed on a final package, it took a group of six—the key leadership of the House and Senate, the OMB director, and the secretary of the treasury—to make the final decisions. Even then, when the package was brought to the floor of the House, it was defeated because of opposition by some Republicans led by Newt Gingrich of Georgia. That required further negotiations to pick up the additional Democratic votes needed for passage. The final package included not only a budget resolution and reconciliation savings but all of the appropriations bills as well. It is by far the largest single piece of legislation to be enacted at one time. It took a wheelbarrow to bring it to the floor.

Within that package, however, were some very important budget enforcement tools that would have been politically impossible to implement outside of a large agreement. The most important tool was a so-called pay-go requirement that provided that no entitlement spending or tax cuts could be enacted unless they were fully paid for either by other spending reductions or by revenue increases. The second tool was to place caps on discretionary spending that established fixed targets for reducing discretionary spending over a five-year period. A limited sequestration tool was added to ensure that those targets would be met. The passage of this agreement was perhaps the most significant bipartisan deficit reduction package to be enacted by the Congress.

Toward a Balanced Budget

In 1993, the Clinton economic plan providing for $500 billion in deficit reduction was passed by Democratic votes only. In the House, the plan passed by one vote—a vote that came by the intervention of then Speaker Tom Foley of Washington at the last minute on the floor. In the Senate, the vice president cast the deciding vote.

The closeness of this vote, combined with the loss of the Democratic Congress and the government shutdown in late 1995, increased the tensions between the two branches on budget issues. In the Congress, while Republicans attempted to advance the agenda contained in their Contract with America, President Clinton vetoed these efforts. Although the parties did agree to the 1997 Balanced Budget Act, the tense relationship between the president and the Congress—exacerbated by the impeachment process—continued to force political confrontation on budget and appropriations issues. Both sides became increasingly dependent on crisis in order to resolve budget issues. The parties realized that little could be achieved absent the threat of government shutdown. The budget cycle became a predictable exercise in gridlock politics. Each party played to their individual constituencies during a good part of the legislative year, relying on the last-minute threat of chaos to provide the excuse needed to conclude final budget negotiations. The one good result of this gridlock was that the failure to agree on large budget spending or tax cut proposals often left more of the surplus available for debt reduction.

By the late 1980s and 1990s—some twenty years after passage of the Budget Act—the hard-fought deficit battles were beginning to produce reduced deficits and eventually a balanced federal budget. As one veteran member of Congress admitted to me, "It has taken us over twenty years to get out of this hole!" And he was right!

The budget process, as a result of bipartisan support between the president and the Congress, developed some strong enforcement tools and discipline. Indeed, during the 1980s there was pressure to go even further, with proposals to have a constitutional amendment to require a balanced budget and bills to give the president the additional power of a line-item veto to strike specific spending added by the Congress. This later proposal did pass the Congress in the 1990s, only to be struck down by the Supreme Court as a violation of the separation of powers clause of the Constitution. Crucial to deficit reduction was the fact that political campaigns made deficit control a national political issue. Presidential candidate Ross Perot made it the center-piece of his campaign and forced both the Democrats and the Republicans to acknowledge that something had to be done about the growing national debt.

During these last twenty years, the budget process played an important role. While it was by no means perfect or immune from the pressures to spend more on priorities from defense to domestic needs, and while it failed to develop effective tools to control the mandatory side of the budget, it has been a powerful incentive for both the executive and legislative branches to discipline spending and eventually achieve a balanced federal budget. Unfortunately, neither the discipline of the budget process nor a balanced budget lasted very long. The nation has again returned to deficit spending.

WHY DEFICITS HAVE RETURNED: "THE IMPORTANT LESSONS THAT SHOULD HAVE BEEN LEARNED."

It was generally assumed that once the nation achieved a balanced budget and surpluses, the politics of the budget process would become less contentious as both sides found additional resources to spend on their priorities. But rather than pursuing their objectives in the context of established budget disciplines, both parties repeated the mistakes of the 1980s. The Republicans enacted large tax cuts and increased defense spending; Democrats supported increases in domestic and entitlement spending; and neither was prepared to enact necessary fiscal reforms in Social Security or Medicare.

When this runaway spending was combined with the economic impact of a recession and a war, the result was a record federal deficit. One frustrated budget staffer commented to me that all of the difficult work of the past twenty years had been lost because neither the president nor the Congress was willing to recognize "the important lessons that should have been learned" on budget discipline.

The Congressional Budget Office now projects budget deficits for the entire ten-year window of its estimate. The federal deficit for 2004 will be a record $413 billion, and over the next ten years the deficit will total $2.3 trillion.

Collapsed Budget Discipline

The reality is that there is little or no discipline left in the congressional budget process. The purpose of the budget resolutions under the 1975 Congressional Budget Act was to define clear priorities and to set enforcement spending limits. Budgets are now cast aside each year with limits easily broken by appropriations bills and supplemental funding requests. In two of the last four years, the Congress has failed to enact a budget resolution at all.

Important budget enforcement tools like caps on discretionary spending and the so-called pay-go rule, which required any new spending program or tax cut be paid for, have been allowed to expire.

While the administration and the Congress are now proposing to restore these enforcement tools, the president and the House of Representatives have taken the position that the pay-go discipline should not apply to tax cuts. The key lesson to controlling deficits, however, is uniform enforcement with regard to both tax cuts and spending so that neither results in greater borrowing and debt.

Exploding Costs

While both the executive and legislative branches are making the effort to reduce the deficit by half over five years, that will not be easy. Excluded from the baseline calculations are increases in spending above current law levels, additional tax cuts, extending the individual tax cuts enacted in 2001 and 2003, revision of the alternative minimum tax to avoid tax increases, reform of the tax code, emergency funding, costs above the baseline levels for Iraq and Afghanistan, the possible costs of Social Security reforms, and downward adjustments in economic performance or technical assumptions.

Adding pressure to the deficit situation are the exploding costs related to the major demographic shift occurring in our society. Over 70 million baby boomers will start retiring over the next twenty to thirty years. Life expectancy rates are increasing by as much as 22 percent while fertility rates are going down. As a result, federal expenditures for Social Security, Medicare, Medicaid, and veterans' health-care benefits are expected to dramatically increase.

All of this occurs at the same time that we are looking at a decreasing revenue base. Federal revenues are now at their lowest level since 1950 as a share of the economy. If tax cuts are made permanent, federal revenue will further decline. This crisis is aggravated by a serious slowdown in the growth of the American workforce, which in the first half of the twenty-first century is expected to grow by 0.4 percent. That means fewer workers supporting the programs that will be serving their parents and grandparents.

This combination of "borrow and spend" fiscal policies combined with the clear projection of higher expenses in the future presents an unprecedented fiscal challenge to the leadership of both the executive and the legislative branches.

Partisanship

This challenge comes at a time of increasing partisanship. The politics of the budget have become more partisan, confrontational, and divisive. Crisis is the primary driving force to resolve disputes. In many ways, the same issues that divided the parties in the past continue to haunt the present: should the nation provide for tax cuts and increased defense spending, or increased funds for education, health care, and other domestic needs, or should both parties be willing to discipline all sectors of the budget for the sake of debt reduction?

Both parties view the budget as a reflection of their national priorities. To that extent, budgets are political documents that tell you where the president stands, where the Congress stands, and where the political parties stand as they relate to their voting constituencies.

But the most effective budgets are not only those that set out clear priorities but those that are credible, realistic, and ultimately enforceable. In a closely divided government, enforceable means that there must be consensus and compromise, or else there will be crisis. In a unified government where the executive and legislative branches are controlled by the same party, enforcement means strict party loyalty sufficient to pass the House, but it also means a willingness to compromise in order to avoid a filibuster in the Senate. If not, the result will also be crisis.

Today, rather than bipartisan compromise, the budget process is driven to the edge of a cliff late in the congressional session. There is the threat of a potential shutdown or failure to pass an extension of the debt limit or the pressure of an election or holiday adjournment. Ultimately, it is crisis that forces a final deal. The only hope for change is if the public provides one of the parties with an overwhelming majority that can avoid a filibuster, or if both parties decide it is in their interest to govern rather than to fight.

Important Lessons

The important lessons from twenty years of experience need to be learned: (1) budget discipline will not happen without presidential leadership that forces compromise; (2) bipartisanship is a more effective way to develop credible budgets, enforce them, and avoid the political backlash of dealing with controversial issues; (3) credible budgets reduce the deficit through both spending restraints and increased revenues; (4) there are no magic answers, no silver bullets, rosy scenarios, accounting gimmicks, economic growth or waste, fraud or abuse to effectively control deficits; while process reforms are important, they will only work if there is leadership; and (5) nothing will happen unless there is a broad consensus on the part of the president, the Congress, and both parties that deficits do matter to the economic health of the nation. If the basic message is that deficits are not that harmful to the economy, neither party will have the incentive to take the necessary action.

THE ROLE OF LEADERSHIP: "THINGS ARE DONE EITHER THROUGH LEADERSHIP OR CRISIS."

In the end, the key to the budget process is not procedural or resorting to legislative mandates of one kind or another. You cannot resolve conflicting priorities and the budget process without those who are willing to exercise leadership and take risks. I have often said, "In a democracy, things are done either through leadership or crisis." It was the tough leadership of presidents, members, and others that produced a strong economy: the tough leadership of business CEOs who had to decide on downsizing and implementing productivity through technology; the tough leadership of the Federal Reserve in fighting inflation and implementing interest rate hikes when necessary; the tough leadership of presidents and Congress on trade issues to expand a global market; and the tough leadership of presidents and Congress in reducing the deficit and in taking the risks necessary to achieve these goals.

In 1990, President Bush agreed to the budget compromise, and it achieved the most significant debt reduction to date and established caps on spending and pay-go disciplines. It took political courage, and he paid a price in political support in the 1992 election, but he did the right thing.

In 1993, President Clinton pushed through his economic plan and it passed by a single vote. The president pushed it hard and members voted for it, and many paid a price in the 1994 election, losing their seats and control of the Congress. But they did the right thing.

In the end, the budget process—presidential and congressional—is only effective if there are those willing to take risks necessary to make it work. Clearly, the Constitution provides a legal framework within which both the president and the Congress can exercise their defined powers. And throughout the history of the budget, both the president and the Congress have sought agreements and procedural tools to strengthen their ability to discipline spending and establish priorities. All of this has been fashioned and beaten into shape in the hot cauldron of politics. But history has also shown us that politics alone cannot work unless leaders are willing to lead.

That is the essence of the budget process. It is the essence of our democracy.

10

Ending a Transatlantic Trade War: The Art of Coalition Building on Capitol Hill

Mark J. Oleszek and Walter J. Oleszek

"**D**isgraceful," declaimed Senator John McCain (R-AZ), "a classic example of the special interests prevailing over the people's interest." This tax bill is "a cookie jar of tax cuts for corporate interests," stated Representative Jim McDermott (D-WA). "On issue after issue, page after page, [the bill] puts the interest of the big corporations above the public interests," exclaimed Senator Edward Kennedy (D-MA). Responding to critics who charged that the tax bill was filled with special-interest provisions, Senate Finance Chairman Charles Grassley (R-IA) replied, "Well, that's true. But that's how the Senate [and House] work." "Veto This Bill," declared an editorial in the *Washington Post*.[1] Instead, President George W. Bush signed the legislation into law (PL 108-357). Advocates of the corporate tax cut contended that, among other things, it promoted job creation, provided needed tax relief to corporations, and ended a transatlantic trade war.

Despite the criticism, the House (280–141) and Senate (66–14) agreed to the tax conference report by comfortable margins. A superficial assumption might be that it is relatively easy to forge winning coalitions if congressional leaders distribute enough special provisions, or "particularistic benefits," to enough colleagues. As House Ways and Means Chairman William Thomas (R-CA), a key leader in winning enactment of the corporate tax measure, said, "The way you get the votes to pass anything is to ask whoever would possibly vote for something, what do they want. It is an additive process."[2] The additive process can be anything but easy, even when legislation is larded with special benefits sought and won by many lawmakers. The process is filled with uncertainty, conflict, and complexity. Opponents of bills may simply refuse to "buy" with their votes what proponents are trying to sell, no matter the attractiveness of their offers. Distributing particularistic benefits to build winning coalitions is least effective on those issues that evoke strong and negative feelings among lawmakers and their constituents.[3]

Lawmakers and presidents know that one of the main ways to promote policy-passing action by the House and Senate is to employ the lubricant of "pork"—the so-called special benefits, projects, or perks that individual lawmakers want for their states or districts. (Of course, there are many "pork" projects that serve the national interest.) Pork is often a necessary but not sufficient ingredient for forging winning coalitions. A host of other considerations also shape the lawmaking enterprise. Persuasion, procedure, and modification are among the strategies used by legislators to mobilize majority or even supermajority coalitions.[4] All three were in play on the corporate tax bill, which was considered in an institutional context replete with electoral politics, time constraints, maverick lawmakers, White House concerns, dilatory threats, lobbying by special interests, bicameral conflicts, and much more.

Significantly, a transnational event unique to this bill triggered congressional action. The World Trade Organization (WTO)—a global organization representing 147 governments—ruled that certain export subsidies provided to American businesses via the U.S. tax code were illegal. It was this ruling by an international body that forced the issue onto Congress's agenda. The WTO's ruling underscored that in today's world the globalization of nearly every aspect of the American economy shapes decision making by our nationally elective branches. If economic internationalization and political localism are sometimes difficult to reconcile, as suggested by Speaker Thomas P. O'Neill's (D-MA) (1977–1987) adage that "all politics is local," then the corporate tax bill demonstrates how an array of forces and factors came together to accommodate these dual phenomena.

This chapter focuses on the diverse strategies used to move the Foreign Sales Corporation/Extraterritorial Income Act (FSC/ETI) through the House, Senate, and conference committee stages to enactment into law. Also known as the American Jobs Creation Act, FSC/ETI demonstrates the importance of the artful use of political and procedural choices to achieve legislative success. The point is that there is more to lawmaking than simply handing out special projects to members to win their support. Lawmaking requires hard "pick-and-shovel" work by determined and talented members—sometimes over several years—if even "must pass" measures are to be enacted in a timely manner. As Speaker J. Dennis Hastert (R-IL) noted, "The art of what is possible is what you can get passed in the House, what you can get passed in the Senate and signed by the president. It is a three-sided game."[5] Before examining the "game" in the House, the Senate, and the conference committee, it is first necessary to provide some background on the origins of the FSC/ETI legislation.

GLOBAL ECONOMIC-LEGISLATIVE BACKGROUND

Origins of the Transatlantic Trade Conflict

In 1995, the World Trade Organization came into being as a forum to facilitate free trade and to settle trade disputes among the nations that compose the organization. Because the tax practices of WTO members differ considerably from those of the United States, many U.S. corporations operate at a competitive disadvantage in the international marketplace. For example, many European nations raise revenue through a value-added tax (VAT) system—taxes are imposed at each stage of the production and distribution of goods—and provide tax rebates under that system to their home-based businesses. The result: foreign goods and supplies can be sold for less than their U.S. equivalents.[6] Further, unlike many foreign governments that tax income earned only within their borders, the United States taxes the income of American companies or individuals whether that income is earned at home or abroad. As a result, this subjects American businesses operating overseas to a double tax: by the United States and by the country where the companies' profits are made. Or, as Senate Finance Chairman Grassley put it, American companies "are often taxed twice. They are taxed by the foreign country in which they are doing business and also, as they properly should be, by the U.S. Government."[7]

To level the international economic playing field, Congress enacted legislation in the 1980s that provided tax benefits to the foreign subsidiaries of U.S. corporations that export U.S.-made goods to other nations. Collectively, these various revenue laws made up the foreign sales corporation (FSC) tax regime.[8] Some "6,000 American companies, among them Microsoft, [General Electric], and Boeing," organized FSCs offshore to take advantage of the export subsidy.[9] In 1997, the European Union (EU)—an organization of twenty-five nations formed to foster European integration and economic prosperity—filed a complaint with the WTO arguing that the FSC regime constituted an illegal export subsidy under WTO rules. After several unsuccessful attempts by trade representatives of the United States and EU officials to resolve their differences through negotiations, a WTO disputes panel in October 1999 ruled against the United States. In February 2000, an appeal body of the WTO "upheld the disputes panel's October 1999 report condemning the U.S. foreign sales corporation tax regime as an illegal export subsidy, marking the largest defeat of the United States in an international trade dispute."[10]

To protect domestic industries and avoid a harmful transatlantic trade war with punitive tariffs imposed by European nations on hundreds of U.S.-imported goods—such as textiles, agricultural products, electrical equipment, paper, and glass—Congress enacted legislation both repealing and replacing the FSC tax system. The bill was titled the FSC Repeal and Extraterritorial Exclusion Act of 2000. When President Bill Clinton signed the bipartisan must-pass bill (H.R. 4986) into law on November 15, 2000, he said: "Never before has the United States had to enact legislation—and particularly legislation in the sensitive field of taxation policy—in order to implement the findings of a dispute settlement panel of the World Trade Organization."[11] The new law replaced the FSC tax rules with an extraterritorial income (ETI) exclusion, which meant that the gross foreign trade income of American companies operating overseas would not be considered taxable income under the United States tax code. In effect, the ETI exclusion ended the double taxation faced by U.S. multinational firms.[12]

The EU Lodges Another Complaint

Hardly before the ink was dry on H.R. 4986 the EU, on November 17, 2000, petitioned the WTO to declare the new U.S. law a failure in meeting the WTO's free trading rules. The EU also asked that trade sanctions of more than $4 billion be imposed on the United States.[13] After a series of unsuccessful appeals by the United States, the WTO declared in January 2002 that the ETI Act, like its FSC predecessor, constituted an illegal and unfair export subsidy. Seven months later the WTO approved the EU's request to impose sanctions of more than $4 billion on imports from the United States. Once more Congress and the White House—now occupied by President George W. Bush—had to act to avoid trade sanctions against U.S.-made goods.

Understandably, the chairman of the tax-writing Ways and Means Committee, Republican William Thomas of California, assumed a lead role in resolving the transatlantic trade controversy.[14] (The Constitution requires that revenue-raising measures must originate in the House.) Chairman Thomas wanted to do more than simply pass a narrowly crafted measure to address the EU's concerns. He argued that America's "corporate tax structure is in need of major restructuring, not another attempt at a short-term fix."[15]

Thomas's idea quickly aroused opposition and set the stage for the controversies that would erupt in the next Congress. Ways and Means ranking Democrat Charles Rangel (NY) exclaimed that there was little bipartisan support for overhauling the corporate tax code to comply with the WTO's decision. Rangel urged the Bush administration to "come to this committee with a strong recommendation as to how we could maintain the integrity of our tax system and at the same time fulfill our international obligations."[16] Several weeks later President Bush declared, "I will work with our Congress to fully comply with the WTO decision," but he specified no timetable to achieve WTO compliance.[17]

Time Runs Out on the 107th Congress But Not the 108th

Lawmakers from both chambers worked with White House and Treasury Department officials during 2002 to determine how to revise the United States' international tax system so as to make it WTO-compliant. Chairman Thomas did introduce legislation (H.R. 5095) in July as the Senate waited on the House to move the bill. In the end, the legislative clock ran out on the 107th Congress (2001–2003) as members and the president focused their time and energies on other priority matters, such as the November 2002 elections and creation of a new cabinet-level Department of Homeland Security. For its part, the EU was willing to wait on Congress to enact corrective legislation before starting a trade war with the United States.

The 108th Congress did enact WTO-compliant legislation, but not without sharp intra- and interparty disagreements as well as bicameral conflict and some administration opposition. Much of the dissension involved successful efforts by lawmakers and lobbyists to add provisions to the law that went far beyond the goal of complying with the WTO's decision. Critics complained, for example, that a bill designed to meet a $4.5 billion international trading problem mushroomed to around $143 billion in unnecessary tax concessions to corporations.[18] Passage of a repeal and replacement measure was predicted for 2003, but things did not work out quite that fast, as other issues took precedence. Sharp disagreements over the form of the replacement bill further slowed action on the measure.

When 2004 began, some lawmakers, such as Senator Richard Lugar (R-IN), observed that it would be "nearly impossible in an election year to make changes in tax laws needed to lift European sanctions," which could soon accumulate into the hundreds of millions of dollars.[19] Nonetheless, Congress did pass the first major overhaul of the corporate tax code in almost two decades, which included over $140 billion in business tax cuts and repeal and replacement of the FSC/ETI tax regime. A combination of factors produced these results, including the drive, determination, and strategic talent of key lawmakers, the clout of various lobbyists, the electoral timetable, and the global trade context in which all this took place. It is to an analysis of the sometimes convoluted FSC/ETI lawmaking process of 2003 and 2004 that we turn to next.

THE HOUSE INITIATES BUT
DISCORD STALLS ACTION

When the 108th Congress began, Republicans had won back the Senate as a result of the November 2002 elections, and their numbers were increased in the House. Although President Bush and Congress recognized the need to act on FSC/ETI repeal, other issues took priority in 2003, particularly enactment of a $350 billion tax cut, an $87 billion supplemental appropriations bill for Iraq, and a new Medicare prescription drug benefit for senior citizens. Still, the key players understood that the export-subsidy issue required resolution. Leaders of the House and Senate tax-writing committees worked closely with Treasury and trade officials to try to reach a consensus on an export-subsidy repeal plan that could move through Congress with some dispatch. An early agreement was impossible to achieve because of contentious policy and political differences within the House majority party and in the business community.

What began as a transatlantic trade dispute soon "evolved into a battle between the two leading House GOP tax writers for the hearts and minds of the business community."[20] The two were Ways and Means Chairman Thomas and the second-ranking Republican on the panel, as well as its Trade Subcommittee chairman, Philip Crane of Illinois. (Worth noting is that the more senior Crane—and the most senior House Republican—lost the Ways and Means chairmanship in 2001 to Thomas after a yearlong intraparty struggle over who would succeed William Archer, the incumbent term-limited chair. House GOP leaders opted for Thomas, and their decision was ratified by the GOP Conference. Crane lost his reelection bid in the November 2004 elections.) Crane joined with Ways and Means Democrat Rangel to introduce legislation (H.R. 1769) in April 2003 repealing the FSC/ETI Act. Their bill proposed using the $50 billion saved over ten years by terminating the illegal tax subsidy to provide corporate tax breaks to domestic manufacturers on their U.S.-derived revenues. Crane and Rangel also declared their measure "revenue neutral" (it produced the same tax revenue as it was expected to lose), an important consideration in a period of escalating fiscal deficits triggered by the costs associated with Iraq and homeland security, tax cuts, and a sluggish economy.

Crane-Rangel versus Thomas

The Crane-Rangel bill, introduced during a time of public anxiety over the outsourcing of American jobs and the workforce's sense of economic vulnerability, attracted over one hundred cosponsors in the House and the support of important Senate Finance Committee members, such as Max Baucus (D-MT), the ranking minority member, as well as Republicans Orrin Hatch (UT) and Trent Lott (MS). A few Republicans on Ways and Means (Mac Collins [R-GA] was a cosponsor) leaned toward the Crane-Rangel legislation. On a panel with twenty-four Republicans and nineteen Democrats, Thomas faced the prospect that he might not have sufficient GOP votes to report out his soon-to-be-introduced approach to resolving the trade dispute and updating the United States' international tax system.

Chairman Thomas saw in the trade dispute an opportunity to undertake a major overhaul of the tax code and "to use the revenue saved from ETI repeal to pay for tax relief for *foreign* operations of U.S. multinational corporations."[21] The Crane-Rangel proposal, by contrast, proposed to use that revenue for tax cuts for *domestic* manufacturers. Thus, not only did the two approaches reflect different tax policies, they also sowed divisions within the GOP's usually solid corporate backers. Domestic manufacturers like Microsoft, Boeing, and Caterpillar tilted toward Crane-Rangel, while multinational corporations such as Coca-Cola, IBM, and ExxonMobil favored Thomas's general plan. The conflict between the two sides underscored the broad challenge Congress faced in devising federal tax policy for our internationalized economy. One observer asked, "Should federal tax policy support the activities of U.S.-based businesses in foreign countries? Or should it support business operations only on U.S. soil?"[22]

In July 2003 Thomas introduced his competing legislation (H.R. 2896) to Crane and Rangel's. The Thomas bill, in broad outline, proposed "to repeal ETI, implement tax cuts for overseas investment, enact new tax benefits for domestic investment, and offset part of the revenue cost by means of several revenue raisers."[23] However, the political and policy infighting between the two camps stymied House action on either the Thomas or Crane-Rangel bill for months. To break the stalemate and get his bill reported favorably from his committee, Chairman Thomas made various revisions to it as a way to attract additional Republican support.

In mid-October 2003, for example, Chairman Thomas convened a Republican-members-only briefing to try to satisfy "a handful of GOP fence-sitters who insist on more parity between domestic and multinational manufacturing relief and who want to extend the 'soft landing' [easing the transition from the illegal ETI regime to the proposed new system] for current U.S.

exporters."[24] Thomas's various concessions to his GOP committee colleagues were successful. Ways and Means Republicans who previously opposed or expressed concern with Thomas's bill, such as the aforementioned Collins, Nancy Johnson (CT), Jennifer Dunn (WA), and Jerry Weller (IL), indicated their support for the revisions, which moved Thomas's bill closer to features contained in the Crane-Rangel measure. "It's a lot better than what [Thomas] started with," said Representative Collins.[25]

Speaker Dennis Hastert (IL), whose district is next to Crane's, also had a keen interest in Thomas's legislation. He wanted to ensure that domestic manufacturers, such as Illinois-based Caterpillar Inc., received the "lion's share of the $50 billion raised by repealing the export tax break."[26] (Caterpillar had joined with Boeing and Microsoft to oppose the original Thomas bill.) Once Thomas incorporated the Crane-Rangel domestic production benefit into his bill, Speaker Hastert gave the Ways and Means chairman the signal to mark up the corporate tax package. On October 28, 2003, the Ways and Means Committee, on a party-line vote, reported Thomas's American Jobs Creation Act of 2003. Even Crane abandoned his alliance with Rangel and voted to report the Thomas bill. Ranking member Rangel declared, "This bill is not going to become law."[27]

A Shortage of Votes

The House did not take up the legislation before the first session of the 108th Congress ended. The lack of time was a factor, but, more importantly, the votes were not there to win House passage of Thomas's bill. Democrats under Minority Leader Nancy Pelosi (CA) opposed Thomas's bill, but they could not defeat it without Republican votes. To Thomas's chagrin there was a group of about twenty-five Republicans, led by House Small Business Chairman Donald Manzullo (IL), who wanted more tax benefits for domestic rather than multinational manufacturers. Hundreds of jobs in Manzullo's district had been lost because of plant closings. "Members of Congress see the world through the people they represent," he said, echoing Tip O'Neill's adage. "Thomas does not represent a heavy, heavy manufacturing base. We are creatures of our constituents."[28]

The day after Ways and Means reported Thomas's bill, a GOP conference was convened of all House Republicans to discuss the tax measure and other matters. Manzullo railed against the bill, as did allies of the Small Business chairman, arguing that the measure created tax incentives for businesses to move American jobs overseas. Manzullo's strong and relentless opposition so strained the relationship between the two chairmen that they "stopped talking to each other and rely on an intermediary [Ways and Means member

Jim McCrery (R-LA)] to negotiate over corporate tax-reform legislation."[29] Adding to Thomas's concerns was word from the EU that a tariff of 5 percent would be imposed on hundreds of U.S. goods starting March 1, 2004, which would increase by 1 percent each month thereafter until it reached a top of 17 percent, unless Congress acted to repeal the illegal export subsidy.

Speaker Hastert stated that he would "delay floor action until it is clear there are the votes to pass the House bill."[30] Despite efforts to mobilize a winning coalition by Majority Whip Roy Blunt (R-MO), Chairman Thomas, House supporters, and outside lobbyists, it became evident that the bill lacked the votes to pass. "There are between 20 and 60 potential 'no' votes, including members who are either against or leaning against the bill," said Representative Michael Castle (R-DE), who was among the undecided.[31] The year 2003 ended without House action on Thomas's bill.

As for the Senate, it had its own corporate tax reform bill (S. 1637), which the Finance Committee had reported in November 2003, but Senate Majority Leader Bill Frist (R-TN) stated, "We're going to wait and see what the House does."[32] His position changed soon after the new year began. Although Thomas worked to attract more support for his bill, he was making little headway during the early months of 2004. Treasury officials tried to assist the tax writers, but their options did little to advance repeal of the ETI Act. With trade sanctions imminent (March 1), Senate Finance Chairman Grassley wanted faster action so tariffs would not be imposed on agricultural goods produced in his home state of Iowa. The Bush administration issued a statement of administration policy (SAP) urging the Senate to act quickly on S. 1637. And House GOP leaders came around to the view that they would wait for the Senate to pass S. 1637 "before negotiating further with House Republican factions that oppose the House ETI Act repeal bill, H.R. 2896."[33]

THE SENATE TAKES THE LEAD

Compliance with the Constitution

There are occasions, as in this instance, when the customary pattern of the House initiating revenue bills is reversed and the Senate takes the lead. For example, in 1982, when the House was controlled by Democrats, the Senate by Republicans, and Ronald Reagan was in the White House, House Democrats wanted no part of a tax increase in an election year. President Reagan was proposing the hike to compensate for part of the deep tax cut enacted the previous year. House Democrats preferred to let the GOP Senate initiate the tax legislation. Compliance with the Constitution occurs when the Senate calls up a House revenue measure, strikes everything after the enacting clause (the opening phrase of every House and Senate bill), and then substitutes its own tax plan into a bill carrying the "H.R." logo. Typically, this is a routine and noncontroversial procedure in the Senate, but in 2004 it proved to be otherwise, as noted below.

Floor Action amidst Partisan Battles

On March 3, 2004, the Senate began consideration of its bipartisan bill (S. 1637) repealing the ETI Act, reported by the Finance Committee on a 19–2 vote. The legislation was called the Jumpstart Our Business Strength (JOBS) Act. As is customary, the majority floor manager, Finance Chairman Grassley, led off the debate with an opening statement. He said, among other things, that the JOBS bill balanced domestic tax relief with international tax reform; that S. 1637, unlike the Thomas bill, provided tax cuts to all American manufacturers (farmers and family businesses, for example), while the House focused its tax cuts on multinational corporations or large American manufacturers; and, significantly, that the Senate bill was revenue neutral. With deficits estimated to be around $450 billion and President Bush urging that the measure not add to the deficit, Grassley pointed out that the Finance legislation "provides $112 billion in business tax relief" to stimulate job creation, which is "paid for [by revenue-raising offsets] shutting down tax shelters and by closing abusive [tax] loopholes."[34]

Minority floor manager Baucus followed Grassley and made comparable points, but stressed the loss of 3 million manufacturing jobs since July 2000. Cutting "taxes for domestic manufacturers will help prevent layoffs," he stated.[35] Both senators also noted that party leaders were working to put together both a list of amendments and the sequence of their consideration. Things seemed to be running smoothly, and expectations were high that it might be possible to complete the bill in a relatively few days.

Despite predictions for smooth Senate passage of the ETI, events proved otherwise. By the end of the first day, over one hundred amendments had been filed for possible floor consideration, signaling that senators wanted to change or challenge the substance of the legislation. Further, fearing "it may be their last opportunity to enact new tax cuts in the 108th Congress," numerous members were anxious in an election year to win benefits for their constituents.[36] Because the corporate tax bill enjoyed bipartisan support and seemed headed to the White House, it proved to be a magnet for credit claiming and politically motivated amendments.

Useful to note at this juncture is that the Senate is well known for granting members two big parliamentary freedoms: unlimited debate (the so-called filibuster) and the right to offer nonrelevant amendments to pending matters. There are ways to restrict both freedoms, but they are not always easy to invoke. A common way to achieve both is to encourage all senators to enter into a "unanimous consent agreement." This is a binding contract that typically limits opportunities to debate and structures the amendment process.

A broad unanimous consent agreement establishing detailed ground rules for floor consideration of S. 1637 was not possible to obtain. Thus, it did not take long for the debate on the bill to take a sharp partisan turn. To the dismay of Republicans, Democrats began to offer nonrelevant amendments designed to raise issues (sending U.S. jobs overseas and providing additional weeks of unemployment compensation to the jobless, for instance) important to their electoral constituencies. Most Democrats supported S. 1637, but they also wanted to offer amendments heading into the high-stakes November elections that contrasted their position with that of the Republicans. For example, Senate Democrats offered amendments blaming President Bush for the lack of significant domestic employment growth and having the worst record of job losses since the Hoover administration. Seeking to capitalize on voter anxiety about the loss of factory and white-collar jobs overseas and with 8.2 million Americans officially jobless, the Democratic jobs strategy gained added momentum after the chairman of Bush's Council of Economic Advisers said in February 2004 that the outsourcing of American jobs to places such as India or China is "probably a good plus for the economy in the long run."[37]

The partisan stalemate over the FSC/ETI bill went on for over two months (March 3 until May 11). The measure was brought to the floor several times and then yanked by Majority Leader Frist, largely because Republicans did not want to consider election-year Democratic amendments. Democrats argued that since the majority party controls the agenda of the Senate, offering amendments to pending legislation is the only way to get their priorities debated by the membership. These legislative skirmishes triggered Republican complaints at Democratic obstructionism; Democrats responded by castigating Republicans for blocking their policy priorities.

In the end, a variety of elements came together to gain Senate passage of the Grassley-Baucus bill. Two merit some discussion because they illuminate the arduous political, policy, and procedural efforts required to move even must-pass legislation in an intensely partisan environment. The two intertwined elements are amendment limitations and procedural maneuvers.

Amendment Limitations and Procedural Maneuvers

On March 4, 2004, the second day of S. 1637's consideration, Senator Tom Harkin (D-IA) urged the Senate to take up his amendment blocking the

Department of Labor from issuing new regulations on overtime pay. Democrats contended that 8 million workers would no longer be entitled to overtime pay under new Labor Department rules. Republicans argued that the updated Labor Department rules affected far fewer workers and permitted more low-income workers to be eligible for overtime. They also complained that Harkin's amendment was nonrelevant to the corporate tax bill. In 2003 both the House and Senate had endorsed Harkin's proposal, but it was dropped in a House-Senate conference at the insistence of the White House. Angry Democrats protested the decision. Recognizing that the Senate could again adopt the Harkin amendment and politically embarrass the president, Majority Leader Frist pulled the bill from the floor until both sides agreed to impose limits on the offering of amendments.

The two sides privately negotiated without success to reach an accord restricting the number of permissible amendments. Democrats insisted that the Senate be allowed an up-or-down vote on Harkin's proposal and other nonrelevant amendments. When the Senate resumed consideration of S. 1637 on March 22, Senator Grassley asked and received unanimous consent that Harkin be allowed to offer his amendment with no second-degrees (an amendment to Harkin's amendment that might dilute or "gut" its intent) allowed to it. Harkin offered his overtime pay amendment, but Majority Whip Mitch McConnell (R-KY)—whose wife (Elaine Chao) headed the Department of Labor—made back-to-back procedural moves to foil Senate action on it. First, McConnell offered a motion to recommit S. 1637 to the Finance Committee with instructions that it report the measure back forthwith with a new amendment sponsored by the majority leader. (Under Senate rules, a motion to recommit a bill takes precedence over a motion to amend a measure.) Second, McConnell immediately filed cloture on his motion to recommit. If invoked with sixty or more votes, cloture ends extended debate and imposes a germaneness requirement on all amendments. After McConnell filed cloture, the Senate moved to other business. (Under Senate rules, the vote to invoke cloture occurs two days after the motion is filed.)

What purposes did McConnell's procedural maneuvers intend to serve? The motion to recommit, if adopted, would immediately change the bill by proposing "tax sweeteners" (Frist's amendment) of keen parochial interest to specific lawmakers, thus bolstering GOP leaders' efforts to win the support of more Democrats. And if sixty senators voted for cloture, Harkin's amendment would automatically fall because it would be ruled nongermane by the presiding officer. As Senator Grassley noted, "The bill before us is a tax relief bill. . . . The amendment of my friend from Iowa is a labor law matter."[38] Invoking cloture also prevents senators from filibustering a bill to death.

In a related procedural move, Senator Grassley submitted amendments to "fill the tree" on the motion to recommit (the "tree" is a Senate chart that identifies the number and order of amendments that may be proposed to a pending measure). His objective was to block Harkin from offering his overtime pay amendment to McConnell's motion to recommit and thus have his proposal strategically positioned to be voted on first. Until the cloture vote occurred, floor proceedings on S. 1637 were at a standstill.

On March 24, the Senate failed to invoke cloture by a 51–47 vote. Majority Leader Frist expressed dismay at the outcome. "Our Democratic colleagues have voted in effect in support of the Euro tax on manufacturing," he said, referring to the EU sanctions. Senator Harkin responded by noting that Republicans were "more willing to pay tariffs to Europe than overtime to American workers."[39] Minority Whip Harry Reid (D-NV) (the new Democratic leader in the 109th Congress with the November 2004 electoral defeat of Tom Daschle [SD]) pointed out that all Harkin wanted was "to take 15 minutes" to debate and vote on his overtime amendment. Senator Grassley replied, it is "one thing to deal with an overtime amendment; it is quite another thing to deal with an environment in which the minority may be expecting us to deal with vast numbers of nongermane amendments. [I]t is that sort of environment which brings about a cloture vote" to minimize message amendments designed to score political points.[40]

For weeks thereafter the Senate was again in a state of stalemate on S. 1637. Private negotiations continued between the majority and minority parties with the objective of reaching an agreement on a finite number of amendments. "I'll bring it up as soon as we can get a reasonable number of germane amendments," Frist told reporters. "Right now, I can't get them down to even single-digits on nongermane amendments."[41] Harkin warned Republicans, "The FSC bill will not proceed without a vote on my amendment."[42] Both sides continued to support enactment of the legislation, but each was unwilling to jettison their position on amendments. As March faded into April and with businesses urging Senate action to stop the European-imposed tariffs on their goods, Majority Leader Frist and Minority Leader Daschle continued their efforts to break the stalemate.

Frist returned to the FSC/ETI bill on April 5. As a way to woo more votes for cloture, he planned to add $13 billion in energy tax subsidies to the bill, including an ethanol tax break wanted by Democratic leader Daschle for his South Dakotan corn farmers. Frist used the same procedural tactics as McConnell. First, he received unanimous consent to withdraw the pending McConnell motion to recommit. Then he offered his own motion to recommit S. 1637 to the Finance Committee with instructions that it report back forthwith with an amendment that included the aforementioned $13 billion in energy tax breaks plus other policy sweeteners. Frist then filled the tree on his motion to recommit and filed a second cloture motion on the FSC/ETI bill. On April 7, the Senate failed to invoke cloture by a 50–47 vote, one vote fewer than on the first cloture attempt.

Frist knew beforehand that his bid to win more votes for cloture by adding energy tax breaks to the bill would not work. "The energy tax package is too big," said Senator John Sununu (NH), one of the four Republicans who voted with the Democrats to oppose cloture. "And I don't think it should be added to this bill," he stated.[43] Majority Leader Frist forced the vote on cloture to spotlight a few things. "We want to govern and we want to get on the record that we want to govern," he declared. "These cloture votes are signals [to the Democrats]: Stop obstructing the bill."[44] Interesting, the ostensible purpose of cloture is to end a talkathon. But given how hard it is to attract the required sixty votes, the trend today is to use cloture for other purposes, as in this case. These purposes include trying to impose a germaneness requirement on amendments, restart bipartisan negotiations, or cast the minority party in an unfavorable public light. Procedural tactics, even if unsuccessful, are commonly employed with multiple goals in mind.

The next day, after further closed-door negotiations among senators, the standoff between the two sides gave way to a unanimous consent agreement. It permitted upwards of eighty germane and nongermane amendments to be offered to the measure, including Harkin's overtime pay proposal. "We have defined a universe of amendments," said Frist. "It's not going to be growing. We ultimately expect a smaller number to be considered."[45] Frist also won unanimous consent to retain in the bill tax sweeteners (including the energy tax provisions) worth $27 billion. The addition of the $13 billion in energy tax breaks so displeased Senator John McCain (R-AZ) that he threatened to stall action on the measure by offering the twenty amendments that the April 8 agreement allocated to him personally.

The Debate Drags On

Before the FSC/ETI bill was returned to the floor, both parties wanted to negotiate a reduction in the number of amendments made in order for possible floor consideration. Other political and procedural considerations suffused the legislative environment. For instance, Daschle was in a difficult reelection race and wary of being portrayed as an obstructionist by his GOP challenger, former representative John Thune. Republicans were also busily crafting a more palatable alternative to Harkin's overtime amendment. Some Republicans worried that Daschle might block the convening of a conference committee even if the Senate passed S. 1637. Meanwhile, the EU-imposed tariffs on U.S. exports continued to climb month after month.

The Senate returned to the bill on May 4 and handed the administration a second defeat (recall the first was in 2003) on the overtime pay regulation. By a vote of 52–47, the Senate adopted the Harkin amendment blocking implementation of the Labor Department's overtime regulations. Republican leaders did offer a competing stand-alone overtime alternative. Their goals were to provide lawmakers who opposed Harkin with something to vote for and to stave off GOP defections. The Republican alternative was adopted 99–0, but five GOP senators then voted for Harkin's amendment. Almost immediately after adoption of the Harkin amendment, the two parties clashed over what many Republicans viewed as another Democratic "message" amendment. Senator Maria Cantwell (D-WA) proposed an amendment to provide up to thirteen weeks of additional unemployment compensation for workers who had exhausted their eligibility for further benefits.

Democrats insisted on a vote on Cantwell's amendment. Troubled that they might suffer a second defeat on an amendment they viewed as politically inspired, Republicans blasted Democrats for practicing the politics of obstruction. "Gridlock, uncertainty, inaction, backlog, and delay is all that is on the menu in the Senate these days," said Majority Whip McConnell. "Do you know what is holding up the FSC bill?" replied Minority Whip Reid. He answered his own rhetorical question: Republicans, "as they do all the time, will not let us finish the bill."[46]

Despite the partisan dispute, both sides strived to negotiate a way out of the impasse. Party leaders agreed on the importance of ending the punitive tariffs and revamping the corporate tax system to assist both domestic manufacturers and multinational corporations. "This is 'must do' legislation," said Senator Reid. "It has to pass before we leave here this year."[47] And with scores of special tax provisions added to the legislation, many senators on both sides of the aisle had a political stake in supporting passage of the bill.

The Impasse Ends

A creative procedural approach permitted a "win-win" for both sides on the Cantwell amendment. It also ensured Senate enactment of the FSC measure. On May 7, Majority Leader Frist filed cloture on the bill. If invoked by the required sixty votes, the bill would certainly pass, but the Cantwell amendment would be ruled out of order as nongermane. At issue was how to win enough Democratic support to invoke cloture yet permit a vote on the Cantwell amendment in a postcloture situation.

After intense negotiations by party leaders, the Senate agreed by unanimous consent to the following procedure. The Senate would first vote to determine if cloture could be invoked on the bill. If that should occur, then notwithstanding the requirement that only germane amendments are in order postcloture, the Senate would "then proceed immediately to a vote in relation to the pending Cantwell amendment."[48] The unanimous consent agreement stipulated that if a point of order was raised against the Cantwell amendment on budgetary grounds—a parliamentary objection which requires sixty votes to waive under the 1974 Budget Act—a successful vote to waive also meant automatic adoption of Cantwell's unemployment extension amendment. In short, only by voting for cloture could the Senate then vote on Cantwell. This rather unusual procedure reflected the high level of distrust that existed between the majority and minority parties. "Our members demanded that the price for voting on Cantwell was that Democrats would support cloture as they claimed," remarked a senior GOP leadership aide.[49]

On May 11, by a 90–8 vote, the Senate overwhelmingly agreed to the cloture motion. Cantwell's amendment now became the pending business. After a brief period of debate, Senator Don Nickles (R-OK), the chair of the Budget Committee, observed that Cantwell's amendment, if adopted, would increase the deficit in excess of what was agreed to in the most recently passed budget resolution. "Therefore, I raise a point of order against the amendment." Senator Cantwell immediately moved to waive Nickles's point of order, but her motion failed on a 59–40 vote. Absent sixty votes, intoned the presiding officer, the "point of order is sustained, and the amendment falls."[50] Senator John Kerry (D-MA), the presumptive Democratic presidential nominee, was on the campaign trail and missed the vote.[51]

After the Senate considered a few more amendments, such as rejecting Senator McCain's bid to strike the energy tax breaks from the bill, S. 1637 passed the Senate by a 92–5 vote. Over to the House went the Senate-passed FSC/ETI measure with an estimated $170 billion in corporate tax cuts over ten years—entirely offset by closing tax loopholes and other revenue raisers. The revenue raisers assuaged senators concerned about the escalating deficits. Because of press criticism that the business tax breaks amounted to corporate pork, proponents reframed the discussion to emphasize that the tax provisions strengthened a core objective of the bill: JOBS (Jumpstart Our Business Strength).

THE HOUSE PASSES A REVISED BILL

During Senate consideration of its FSC/ETI bill, Ways and Means Chairman Thomas continued trying to muster support for his stalled measure. He proposed adding more tax benefits for domestic manufacturers. Speaker Hastert met with Manzullo to determine what actions might be taken to win his support and that of his other twenty-four GOP supporters. Their opposition continued to prevent Thomas's bill from reaching the floor. None of these efforts ended the stalemate in the House until the Senate passed S. 1637. The Senate's action added the momentum Thomas needed to end the gridlock in the House. As Chairman Thomas remarked the day after Senate passage of the FSC measure: "I would have to say that institution, the Senate, has shown remarkable maturity in assisting the House in coming to a conclusion on this important bill."[52]

Thomas soon circulated ideas on what to accept or reject from the Senate's bill. He met repeatedly behind closed doors with Ways and Means Republicans and consulted many others to fashion a revised bill that would attract majority support in the House and also pass the Senate. A strategic thinker, Thomas already was looking ahead to probable conference negotiations with the Senate. "How often has the Senate moved on a major tax bill so the House has an opportunity to examine the Senate bill?" he said.[53] The examination aimed to ensure that the House was not disadvantaged during bicameral negotiations because its bill did not include important provisions contained in the Senate-passed version. His chamber might then be stuck bargaining between the Senate's "something" and the House's "nothing."

Beyond the continued opposition of the Manzullo-led group, Thomas also faced the reality that other Republicans would use their personal vote as leverage to obtain tax breaks for industries in their districts. "It's the one last major vehicle coming out of the Ways and Means Committee this year. All kinds of people will be holding onto their votes," remarked a GOP House member.[54] Still, Thomas managed to assemble a winning coalition by making revisions that attracted lawmakers' votes. He incorporated the various changes in a new bill (H.R. 4520), which he introduced on June 3. Eleven days later the measure was reported from the Ways and Means Committee by a 27–9 vote. The House passed the bill on June 17 by the comfortable margin of 251–178. At least three major factors contributed to Thomas's success: capitalizing on the reelection concerns of lawmakers by wooing them with various sweeteners; mobilizing outside group support; and receiving a "closed rule" (a resolution reported from the Rules Committee prohibiting amendments to legislation) for his bill.

Wooing Votes with Sweeteners

Thomas made a number of key decisions to attract votes for his revised new bill. One of the most important was to add a completely unrelated provision to H.R. 4520: a $9.6 billion payment to tobacco growers. Thomas took a tobacco buyout bill introduced by Representative Ron Lewis (R-KY) and folded it into his legislation. Lewis suggested this approach to Thomas, who was reluctant at first to accept the recommendation. Thomas told Lewis that he would include the tobacco buyout provision if he could find ten Democrats who would then vote for the tax package.[55] Lewis found the ten Democrats. The buyout provision would end a Depression-era government program of tobacco subsidies and quotas. With tobacco farmers struggling because of antismoking campaigns and more foreign tobacco imports, the buyout provides tobacco farmers with "billions to help them survive in a new world of unbridled competition—or, if they choose, to make their way in another profession."[56]

The tobacco provision sparked controversy. For example, liberal Representative Henry Waxman (D-CA) and conservative Representative Jeff Flake (R-AZ) joined to oppose the buyout "as a bad deal for taxpayers."[57] Democrats and Republicans from tobacco-growing districts disputed the charge and urged their colleagues to support Thomas's bill. After the House passed H.R. 4520, forty lawmakers, mainly from tobacco-producing areas, wrote to Thomas and said that "their votes for his corporate tax bill depended, to a large extent, on his decision to add a buyout for tobacco farmers to the bill."[58]

Another attractive sweetener to certain lawmakers was a provision allowing residents of the nine states without state income taxes to deduct state and local sales taxes from their federal income tax. This provision had a strong advocate in Majority Leader Tom DeLay (R-TX), who was a representative from one of the states with no state income tax. Six Texas Democrats, two Florida Democrats, and the Democrat from South Dakota—all states without a state income tax—voted for Thomas's bill. For example, Texan Max Sandlin—a chief deputy whip for Democrats and a lawmaker who faced a difficult reelection because his district had been redrawn at the instigation of Majority Leader DeLay to include more Republican voters—crossed party lines to vote with Thomas. Noting that the state sales tax provision would save Texans $926 million annually, Sandlin said: "Each member represents his district. I understand there is a tension that sometimes flies in the face of our [Democratic] caucus and our [Democratic] message."[59] (Sandlin lost his seat in the November 2004 elections.)

These two provisions, along with a number of other targeted tax breaks, were particularly important in winning passage of the House FSC bill.[60] Some lawmakers and commentators lamented how the winning coalition was forged, calling the process an outrage, but in Thomas's view, "There is room for purists, but none of them are chairmen of committees."[61] Only four of the twenty-four Republicans who supported Manzullo voted against Thomas's bill.

Outside Assistance

Thomas and others met with lobbyists to encourage them to whip support for the FSC bill. Of course, many lobbyists had special provisions in the bill that they wanted to protect. Numerous trade associations mobilized to prod lawmakers to vote for the tax package. In an election year, lawmakers are particularly sensitive to the requests of businesses and industries in their districts. Chairman Thomas also requested assistance from the General Electric Co., which formed a twenty-six-member coalition to lobby for the legislation. Other industry groups, such as aerospace and high technology, supported the measure in large part because the bill extended a research and development (R&D) tax credit. This provision will "inevitably broaden the base of support among Democrats and Republicans from high-tech-intensive and high-skilled manufacturing areas such as California, Texas, Massachusetts, Florida and Virginia," said a spokesperson for the Aerospace Industry Association.[62] Thomas won the support of large domestic manufacturing enterprises such as Caterpillar, Boeing, and Microsoft by including in the bill significant tax cuts for domestic manufacturing.

As for the Bush administration, it advocated swift passage of H.R. 4520. The administration issued a statement of administration policy, which Thomas cited during floor debate. The SAP urged the House "to pass H.R. 4520 promptly. . . . The Administration looks forward to working with the conferees on this legislation to move it toward budget neutrality, and to enacting legislation that removes the threat of escalating EU sanctions and encourages economic growth and job creation at home."[63] Other than these types of exhortations, President Bush and Treasury Secretary John Snow mainly left it to House and Senate leaders to work out the details of the FSC measure. The administration, like the Senate, wanted any tax cuts in the House bill to be offset by revenue raisers. Not all the provisions in Thomas's bill were offset; this issue was left to the conference committee to resolve.

A "Closed" Rule

Traditionally, tax bills reported from the Ways and Means Committee are considered under a closed rule prohibiting lawmakers from offering discrete amendments to the measure. The Rules Committee does permit complete substitutes (the functional equivalent of another bill) to be offered to Ways and Means–reported legislation. "We have always as a tradition discouraged amendments, but we have encouraged substitutes," noted Majority Leader DeLay.[64] As expected, the Rules Committee on June 17 issued a closed rule on H.R. 4520, which angered Democrats because their substitute was not made in order, even though Rules Chairman David Dreier (R-CA) had indicated to Rangel that Democrats would have the opportunity to propose one. The Democratic alternative included some tax sweeteners similar to those contained in Thomas's bill, plus new provisions, such as extending unemployment benefits to jobless workers.

Rangel was upset that the Democratic substitute was not made in order and wondered why Republicans were afraid to have the members debate his alternative. Rules Chairman Dreier replied that what Rangel proposed before the panel was "an amendment, not a substitute, which is what we stated was necessary for us to even consider it. . . . [W]e did not make a substitute in order because it was not even an option for the Committee on Rules."[65] In brief, the Rangel proposal did not meet the technical definition of a complete substitute because it failed to rewrite the underlying bill in its entirety. Rangel's substitute failed to include any reference to the tobacco buyout. Democrats were outraged because they had no opportunity to determine if their alternative could have won in a matchup with Thomas's measure.

The Rules Committee did permit Thomas to make several changes to H.R. 4520 via a so-called self-executing provision in the closed rule. In this case, Thomas proposed various changes to H.R. 4520 during his testimony before the Rules Committee. They were automatically incorporated, or self-executed, into the text of his bill upon adoption of the rule by the House. Thomas's changes to H.R. 4520 addressed concerns that various lawmakers had raised since the bill was reported from the Ways and Means Committee. A self-executing feature folds provisions into a bill without separate consideration by the House. A goal of this device is to solidify or win the support of wavering lawmakers by locking their policy preferences into the text of the bill.

With House passage of H.R. 4520, the bill was sent to the Senate, where it was amended and agreed to on July 15 by voice vote. Although the Senate had acted first on the FSC bill, the origination clause of the Constitution, as noted before, obligates the Senate to act on House-passed revenue bills, which senators can further amend. The usual procedure would be for the Senate to call up H.R. 4520, amend it by replacing its FSC version (S. 1637) for the House-passed bill (retaining the House bill number), and then request a conference with the House. This general procedure was followed, but not without contention in getting the bill to conference.

THE SENATE AGAIN CONSIDERS THE FSC/ETI BILL

Leaders in both chambers predicted a difficult conference because of the significant differences between the two bills. Among the key differences were these: the Senate bill included energy tax breaks but the House's bill did not; the Senate's bill was revenue-neutral, but not the House's; the House measure, but not the Senate's, contained a sales tax deduction from federal income taxes for the taxpayers of certain states; the Senate's bill contained an overtime pay provision for workers which was not in the House's bill; and the House bill, unlike the Senate's, had a $9.6 billion tobacco buyout provision. Before getting to conference, the Senate had to grapple with two large issues: the tobacco buyout and the procedural steps necessary to formally convene a conference committee.

Tobacco Buyout Joined with FDA Regulation of Tobacco

The House's tobacco buyout provision ignited strong bipartisan opposition in the Senate. Many senators had long advocated that any buyout should only occur if tobacco products are regulated by the Food and Drug Administration (FDA). Absent FDA regulation of tobacco, these senators would filibuster the House-passed bill, oppose going to conference, or try to strike the tobacco provision from the House's bill. After weeks of intense negotiations, an unusual Senate alliance was formed. Senators from tobacco-growing states who long had opposed FDA regulation of tobacco joined with public-health-minded senators to craft an amendment combining both features. Each side recognized that neither provision could pass on its own, so they decided to join forces. Among the chief sponsors of the combined amendment were pro-FDA senators Edward Kennedy (D-MA), Michael DeWine (R-OH), and Richard Durbin (D-IL).

Allied with the FDA senators were senators from tobacco-growing states, such as the two Kentucky members, McConnell and Republican Jim Bunning. "FDA regulation is a steep price to pay for a buyout," remarked Senator Bunning. "But if it's the only way to get my growers relief, this senator will vote for it."[66] On July 15, the Senate adopted the "shotgun marriage" amendment by a 78–15 vote. Several senators who wanted the FDA to regulate tobacco products had even canvassed "40 House members from tobacco-growing districts to determine whether they would support federal regulation of tobacco in exchange for a buyout of tobacco farmers."[67] The senators wanted some sense that the House would accept FDA regulation in any negotiated conference report. They received an affirmative response from the

House members. Top House party leaders, such as Majority Leader DeLay, strongly opposed FDA regulation of tobacco.

Obstacles in Getting to Conference

With Senate passage of an amended version of H.R. 4520, several procedural steps are required to convene a conference with the House. A party or committee leader on the majority side would propose a motion that contains three discrete parts: the Senate *insists* on its amendment (the text of S. 1637 recast as an amendment and including the FDA provision), *requests* a conference with the House, and *authorizes* the chair to appoint conferees. Significantly, this motion, which is quickly adopted in most cases, can be divided, and each of the three parts is subject to a filibuster requiring sixty votes to stop. Before Democratic leader Daschle would allow H.R. 4520, as amended, to clear the necessary procedural requirements to proceed to conference, he wanted assurances from the majority leader that Democratic conferees would be full participants in any negotiations with the House. Daschle had raised his concern about the Democratic role in any conference committee since the legislation first passed the Senate in May 2004.

Daschle was miffed that on several previous occasions Democratic conferees were excluded by Republicans from participating in bicameral negotiations on major tax, health, highway, and appropriations measures. In protest, Daschle stymied the appointment of Senate conferees on H.R. 4520 until Frist agreed that Democratic conferees would be full participants in the bargaining sessions with the other body. Further, before H.R. 4520 would be allowed to proceed to conference, Daschle required the Senate to vote on combining the FDA provision with the tobacco buyout to ensure that the FDA provision would be considered during the House-Senate negotiations.

On July 14, Frist and Daschle agreed that not only would the Senate vote on the combined amendment but also that Democratic conferees would be full participants in conference negotiations. Frist stated that Senator Grassley had agreed not to sign any conference report "that would alter the text of S. 1637 in a way that undermines the broad bipartisan consensus S. 1637 achieved on final passage." Daschle added that changes in conference "will be the result of mutual agreement of the lead Senate conferees [Grassley and Baucus], as well as the Majority Leader and the Democratic Leader, acting in good faith."[68] Senator Grassley also personally assured Ways and Means ranking member Rangel that House Democratic conferees "would be able to participate fully in the FSC/ETI conference."[69] (House Democratic conferees were also sometimes excluded from conference negotiations.) The next day, following adoption of the tobacco-buyout–FDA amendment and the subsequent passage of H.R. 4520, as amended, the Senate easily advanced the bill to the conference stage, naming twelve Republicans, ten Democrats, and one independent (James Jeffords of Vermont) as conferees. Among the conferees were Democratic leader Daschle and GOP whip McConnell.

House GOP leaders such as Thomas and DeLay, who criticized Daschle for obstructing the appointment of conferees and delaying the start of the conference, postponed appointing House conferees until after the traditional August recess. They wanted to prevent Democrats from repeatedly offering nonbinding motions to instruct House conferees and force Republicans to vote on issues that could embarrass them in the upcoming November elections. Under House rules, if a conference committee fails to report an agreement within twenty days, then repetitive motions to instruct are in order. To be sure, there were numerous informal bicameral discussions prior to the formal convening of the conference committee.

On September 29, just eight days before Congress's scheduled adjournment for the November 2004 elections, Speaker Hastert named seventeen conferees: eleven Republicans, including DeLay (House majority leaders often serve on major tax conferences to protect institutional and leadership interests), and six Democrats. Electoral politics ensured that the Speaker named Representative Richard Burr (R-NC) a conferee. Burr was locked in a close senatorial contest for the seat held by John Edwards, the retiring incumbent and Democratic vice presidential nominee. Republicans wanted to give Burr a prominent role in delivering the tobacco buyout to the farmers of North Carolina. "It's quite possible our majority [in the Senate] depends on this," remarked a senior GOP aide.[70]

A SPRINT TO THE FINISH LINE

Deadline lawmaking is common on Capitol Hill. Party and committee leaders use time pressures associated with impending recesses, adjournments, or elections to achieve legislative breakthroughs. The clock and calendar were instrumental factors in forcing the FSC/ETI bill through conference and enactment into law. Most of the conferees and numerous outside business interests were insistent on finishing the bill to halt the escalating tariffs on products made in their home states and to gain the tax benefits contained in the legislation for home-state corporations.

A Brief but Strategic Conference

Thomas chaired the overall conference and employed innovative procedures that contributed to its success. Senator Grassley, the leader of the Senate's conferees, concurred in these procedures. Conferences on major tax legislation typically take weeks or months as conferees work through all the bicameral disagreements. In this case, the conference started on the day the House named its conferees, on September 29, and concluded on October 6. Thomas, with Grassley's backing, made several key decisions that expedited conference negotiations.

First, Thomas consulted extensively with key House and Senate conferees prior to the formal convening of the conference to determine their priorities and preferences. Mindful of the targeted adjournment date of October 8, Thomas laid out an ambitious schedule to meet the deadline. The shortage of time not only served as action-forcing pressure, but it limited opportunities for both conferees and lobbyists to mobilize support for major adjustments to the legislation.

Second, based on their informal discussions, Thomas and Grassley developed a bipartisan "discussion draft," which they presented to the conferees at their first meeting. The draft included provisions contained in both bills and incorporated several specific items wanted by each chamber. Thomas agreed, for example, to produce a revenue-neutral bill and accepted another Senate priority: "that all manufacturers receive the benefit of the [tax] deduction."[71] Grassley went along with the House's broader definition of "manufacturing," which attracted support from a wider range of lawmakers. ("Manufacturers" eligible for tax deductions included, for example, architects, roofers, software producers, newspapers, movie makers and renters, and coffee roasters.) On the other hand, the discussion draft did not include such controversial issues as the tobacco buyout and FDA regulation of tobacco. Thomas and Grassley also required the conferees to present them in advance with any of their planned amendments to the discussion draft.

Third, after reviewing the suggestions of the conferees, Thomas on October 4 presented his "mark"—the revised discussion draft—to the conference committee. (A mark is a document provided to lawmakers for amendment purposes.) Thomas, certain of majority support in the House and among his chamber's conferees, carefully designed the mark to attract broad support among Senate conferees and the general Senate membership, which would aid Frist in invoking cloture should a filibuster occur on the conference report. Thomas included ethanol tax breaks for Daschle and state sales tax deductions for senators from the nine states with no state income tax.

Thomas's mark contained the tobacco buyout but not the FDA regulation of tobacco products. Deleting the FDA provision from the mark meant that it would have to be added by amendment. As one account noted, "It would have taken agreement of both House and Senate negotiating teams to add the FDA language, which turned out to be impossible."[72] House conferees rejected several attempts by Senate conferees to add the FDA provision to the conference report (the compromise bill). House conferees also turned down Senator Harkin's overtime pay provision.

The FDA outcome was disappointing to several Senate conferees. As a result, they threatened to filibuster the conference report when it was taken up in the Senate. Majority Whip McConnell disputed the potency of the threat. "There are a lot of things in this bill that are very popular with senators of both parties," he said. "And I think killing the conference report over the fact that something isn't in it is highly unlikely." Senator Kennedy conceded McConnell's point, saying: "I wouldn't be surprised [if the Senate votes to invoke cloture on the conference report], with the amount of tax goodies in there."[73] Indicative of overall Senate support for the conference report, six of the eleven Senate Democratic conferees, all from farm or energy-producing states, "supported the compromise tax measure without the FDA provision."[74]

Finally, the conference markup was conducted in public. On tax conferences, noted Senator Grassley, nearly "all of the toughest decisions come down to private negotiations between the two chairmen. . . . In this conference, however, all discussions were aired publicly."[75] Thomas added that this was the first tax conference in his memory that was held "entirely with the public permitted complete access, televised over the internal television [network] for the entire time of the conference. There were no separate conference meetings. All of the conference meetings were public."[76] Thomas told reporters that the rationale for openness was to blunt any allegations from opponents that untoward deals were being made in secret. "The last thing you want to do is not have it completely open, in public, and then have somebody walk out of a closed room and make statements . . . that aren't true."[77]

The Bush administration monitored conference proceedings but left the negotiations to Thomas and Grassley to guide and direct. President Bush "took an arms-length approach to the legislation in an effort to ward off attacks from Democratic rival John Kerry over the many corporate tax breaks in the bill."[78] The Bush administration was successful in urging conferees to drop a provision establishing a commission to simplify provisions in the internal revenue code which were made more complex by the FSC/ETI legislation. Bush was highlighting tax reform in his presidential campaign and planned to create a tax reform commission should he win reelection to a second term. Treasury Secretary Snow did send a letter on October 4 to Thomas criticizing all the special interest provisions in the bill, but Grassley contended that Snow's letter did not reflect the White House's position. "Snow's letter is a cover your rear end, particularly to conservatives" worried that the bill benefits relatively few taxpayers. The senator predicted that President Bush would sign the legislation before the election because "he can't ignore the fact that we're not in compliance with our international obligations."[79] Before the president could sign the bill into law, the conference report first had to pass the House and then the Senate.

Partisan Flare-up in the House

The day after House-Senate negotiators agreed to the conference report, the House on October 7 approved it by a vote of 280–141. To get to final passage required some procedural ingenuity. Traditionally, conference reports, as in this case, are made in order for House consideration via a "waiver" rule reported by the Rules Committee. A waiver rule sets aside all points of order that might be raised against a conference report and cause its rejection. The rules of the House, for example, state that before conference reports can be taken up, lawmakers must have at least three days to read and examine their contents. With Congress slated to adjourn the next day, there was no time to provide for a three-day layover period. There was still another procedural hurdle that had to be cleared before the House voted on the waiver rule.

The House rulebook states that a rule from the Rules Committee cannot be brought up for consideration on the same day that it is reported unless the House, by a two-thirds vote, agrees to waive that requirement. So the Rules Committee first sent to the floor a rule (dubbed a "martial law" rule by opponents) waiving the so-called same-day requirement. A simple majority vote is sufficient to waive, or set aside, the supermajority requirement. Democratic opponents of the conference report were outraged by this procedure. "We are considering a rule for a [conference report] that has been available a few minutes," declared Rules Democrat Jim McGovern (MA). "The American people do not know what is in the [conference report], but we are here rushing it through at the eleventh hour."[80]

Time was so short that a GOP congressional aide "bypassed the Government Printing Office and used a Kinkos print shop late October 7 to copy the 1,200 page conference report [and joint explanatory statement], putting the $5,000 bill on his personal credit card."[81] A computer printout of the conference report in a loose-leaf binder was available to House members to examine during the debate. Republicans pointed out that the entire conference report and joint explanatory statement were available for lawmakers to read on the Ways and Means website.

The House adopted the same-day rule and then agreed to the rule waiving all points of order against the FSC/ETI conference report. Democrats continued to lament the lack of time to examine the conference report and criticized the report for providing corporations with tax incentives to send jobs overseas. Republicans lauded the work of the conference committee. With House passage secured, it was now the Senate's turn to take up the conference report.

Brakes Are Applied in the Senate

"Tomorrow morning" [October 8], said Majority Whip McConnell, "the Senate will begin consideration of the FSC/ETI JOBS conference report. We will be unable to reach a limited time for debate; therefore, cloture will be filed on the conference report."[82] Senators Kennedy, Harkin, DeWine, and others were still livid that conferees had dropped the FDA provision but retained the tobacco buyout. They were threatening to filibuster the conference report. Senator Mary Landrieu (D-LA) was also furious that the conferees deleted a provision she authored providing tax credits to employers who continue to pay members of the National Guard or armed forces reservists activated to fight in Iraq or Afghanistan. Multiple filibuster threats precipitated the filing of cloture on the conference report. The GOP leadership was confident they had more than the required sixty votes to invoke cloture and shut down any talkathon.

In a rare Sunday session, the Senate voted on October 10 to impose cloture by a 66–14 vote. Some of the furor over the FDA provision was reduced when Senator Grassley pointed out that during a presidential campaign trip to North Carolina, John Kerry stated he would support the tobacco buyout without the FDA regulation of tobacco. Grassley added, "And, he even had his candidate for the North Carolina Senate seat up here lobbying right over in the conference committee room to get his buyout through, with or without FDA."[83] Senate Democrats realized the electoral fate of their challengers for the five open southern Senate seats hinged on the fate of the tobacco buyout. Most backed away from an all-out fight on the FDA issue.

Senators Landrieu and Harkin vowed to continue their opposition. Even with cloture invoked, Senate rules provide thirty more hours of postcloture debate. They promised to consume all thirty hours until the Senate was able to vote on the conference report, which is nonamendable. The majority leader prepared for an around-the-clock session to run out the thirty hours. Instead, Frist and Daschle brokered a compromise that satisfied the two senators. On October 10, by unanimous consent, the Senate passed two bills favored by Harkin: one required FDA regulation of tobacco and the other clarified overtime pay regulations. The next day, Columbus Day, Senator Landrieu added her tax credit provision to a House-passed measure pending in the Senate. With all three bills agreed to by the Senate, they were sent to the House. Both Senators could claim victory knowing full well that the House would not take up the three bills.[84]

On October 22, President Bush—on Air Force One—signed the revenue-neutral $143 billion corporate tax cut and FSC/ETI replacement bill into law. Some Republicans wanted a high-profile public signing ceremony, but White House officials preferred that the bill be signed in private. They were concerned that the measure could be portrayed "as a special-interest give-away—and the impact of any negative press this close to the election" could hurt the president's reelection chances. With the bill signed into law, the EU lifted trade sanctions against 1,600 U.S.-made products, but requested the WTO to determine if the new law actually complies with WTO trading rules.[85]

CONCLUSION

Lawmaking is a process filled with complexities and uncertainties. Scores of participants play diverse roles and operate in a legislative context replete with electoral, policy, political, institutional, procedural, and even global dimensions. Our objectives in this chapter were to look closely at one measure, delving into some of the significant features associated with the enactment of a major tax bill and discussing the most relevant factors and tradeoffs that contributed to its passage. Among an array of important and overlapping elements, we highlight five because they capture best the features that often produce successful lawmaking, regardless of the policy area.

Critical to the passage of legislation is the hard work, legislative skill, and perseverance of key lawmakers. There is little question that the two tax-writing chairmen—Representative Thomas and Senator Grassley—were key to the passage of the FSC bill. They artfully modified the bill to win votes and overcome procedural and political obstacles to achieve success after several years of determined effort. Although their bill was criticized as pork-laden, this lubricant facilitated enactment of a measure to meet the nation's international trading obligations.

Second, constituency and electoral interests encourage the construction of winning coalitions. This was certainly the case with the FSC/ETI measure. There was widespread support in both chambers because numerous members won special-interest provisions that benefited the "folks back home." Speaker Hastert, for example, successfully pressed for an $11 million reduction in excise taxes on fishing tackle boxes. His "district includes a big producer of tackle boxes."[86] The tobacco buyout not only attracted votes for the bill but was a huge electoral issue in the closely contested Senate race in

North Carolina, which Burr won. In short, winning particularized benefits for constituents gave many lawmakers a large stake in voting for the tax measure. Whether these benefits collectively represent good tax policy is an issue that sparks considerable debate.

Third, successful lawmaking is shaped by a strong sense of pragmatism on the part of committee and party leaders. A shorthand definition of the pragmatic approach is that lawmakers charged with shepherding legislation to passage make adjustments, or compromises, to accommodate changing legislative and political reality in order to achieve a practical result: majority support for their bill. Recall Chairman Thomas's earlier observation that lawmaking is not for "purists." A statement by Senator Pat Roberts (R-KS) makes the same point, albeit in a different legislative context: "While this is not the best possible bill, it is the best bill possible."[87] Or as Representative Barney Frank (D-MA) said on one occasion about coalition building: "Our goal is to find something that's 60 percent acceptable to 52 percent of the members and I think we have a 75 percent chance of doing that."[88]

Fourth, the role of lobbyists and presidents is often critical to the shape and success of national policies. In this case, lobbyists for various businesses and corporations won significant benefits for their clients. General Electric was among the most successful in winning tax benefits, in part because it employs numerous contract lobbyists who are highly regarded and experienced tax specialists, such as former Treasury officials and chief counsels to Congress's tax-writing committees. In 2004, GE's political action committee was in the top ten among corporations in campaign contributions to congressional candidates.[89]

President Bush, in his dealings with Congress on the FSC bill, followed the same general pattern he observed during his first term on most administration-backed measures: outline broad goals, objectives, or principles and then allow congressional leaders to fill in the details of the legislation. Treasury Secretary Snow did have some concerns with various parts of the bill, but the president did not disapprove of the legislation, because it was revenue-neutral and reflected his tax-cutting philosophy for strengthening the national economy.

Fifth, deadlines are often vital components in enacting major and controversial legislation. They promote successful legislative action by heightening the sense that time is growing short to resolve differences and reach majority consensus. With both the end of the 108th Congress approaching and the November elections close at hand—plus the monthly tariff increases on U.S. goods—lawmakers recognized that failure to act on the FSC legislation would mean the new 109th Congress would have to restart the whole bill-enacting process anew. The twin deadlines galvanized the Congress to clear the FSC bill before time ran out.

In sum, this case example suggests how Congress makes certain decisions. The strategies employed by coalition leaders on the FSC bill provide empirical support for two theories of congressional policy making. To Professor Douglas Arnold, successful lawmaking often depends on the skillful use of congressional procedures by coalition leaders to cement winning coalitions on the House and Senate floor. Several key procedures were utilized prior to and during consideration of the FSC measure. In the Senate, Majority Leader Frist, with input from Democratic leader Daschle, crafted a novel unanimous consent agreement to invoke cloture on the measure. From the point of view of Frist, however, the unanimous consent agreement came at the expense of guaranteeing a vote on the unwanted Democratic-backed Cantwell amendment extending unemployment benefits to jobless workers.

House floor consideration of the FSC bill was governed by a closed rule. Importantly, that rule included a self-executing provision that would, with passage of the special rule reported by the Rules Committee, automatically incorporate controversial but coalition-expanding changes proposed by Thomas into the legislation. Coalition leaders, argues Arnold, often "break the traceability chain" in Congress to shield their rank-and-file from electoral retribution at the polls.[90] If voters cannot figure out who is responsible for specific policy outcomes on account of procedural complexities, then they might have difficulty in pinning blame on particular lawmakers.

Another key ingredient for passage of the FSC measure was the strategic allocation of specific benefits, or pork, to key swing groups of lawmakers. Professor Diana Evans demonstrates that, in certain situations, coalition leaders use the lubricant of pork-barrel benefits to "grease the wheels" of lawmaking and solidify passage of legislation. For example, to attract the support of lawmakers from tobacco-growing areas, Chairman Thomas added to the bill a $9.6 billion payment to tobacco growers. In the Senate, Majority Leader Frist tacked $13 billion in energy tax breaks to the bill in order to gain support among senators who represent energy-producing states.

Considered separately, the theories of congressional policy making developed by Professors Arnold and Evans provide useful insights into the strategic calculations of the members who succeeded in constructing winning coalitions for the FSC legislation. Taken together, their analyses promote understanding of the wide range of strategies and tactics available to resourceful lawmakers. As an institution filled with "elaborate and obtrusive details" and "complicated forms," as Woodrow Wilson noted, a detailed look at how a bill became law may clarify "the vision, and [reveal] the system which underlies [Congress's] composition."[91]

NOTES

1. The quotes from Senators McCain and Kennedy are from Jonathan Weisman, "Senate Passes Corporate Tax Bill," *Washington Post*, October 12, 2004, A4; the remark of Representative McDermott is from the *Congressional Record*, October 7, 2004, H8654; Senator Grassley's comment is from National Journal's *CongressDailyPM*, October 12, 2004, 11; and the editorial is from the *Washington Post*, October 7, 2004, A38.

2. *Congressional Record*, April 2, 2004, H2120.

3. Diana Evans, *Greasing the Wheels: Using Pork Barrel Projects to Build Majority Coalitions in Congress* (Cambridge: Cambridge University Press, 2004).

4. R. Douglas Arnold, *The Logic of Congressional Action* (New Haven: Yale University Press, 1990), chap. 5.

5. Mark Wegner, "Hastert: GOP to Take Political Offensive," National Journal's *CongressDailyAM*, March 15, 2004, 5.

6. Economists, unlike businessmen, reject the view that the VAT is an unfair subsidy provided to foreign companies by their own governments. They state that the European practice of rebating the value-added tax to their producers is necessary to ensure that exported goods are in relative alignment with the price structure of the country importing the goods. CRS economist David L. Brumbaugh kindly shared this observation with the authors.

7. *Congressional Record*, October 10, 2004, S11037.

8. *American Jobs Creation Act of 2004*, Report of the House Committee on Ways and Means, House Rept. 108-548, Part 1, 108th Congress, 2nd Session, 113–14.

9. Lee Sheppard, "An Export Subsidy Is an Export Subsidy," *Tax Notes*, February 28, 2000, 1196.

10. Robert Goulder, "WTO Rejects U.S. Appeal Regarding FSC Regime," *Tax Notes*, February 28, 2000, 1196.

11. Warren Rojas, "FSC Repeal Slides under the Wire; Congress Skips Town Yet Again," *Tax Notes*, November 20, 2000, 983.

12. Rojas, "FSC Repeal," 983.

13. The $4 billion penalty was based on the estimated value of the illegal FSC subsidy in February 2000 when the WTO ruled it in violation of international trade agreements. Heather Bennett, Robert Goulder, and Charles Gnaedinger, "European Union Requests Sanctions against U.S. in FSC Dispute," *Tax Notes*, November 20, 2000, 986.

14. When Republicans won control of the House following the November 1994 elections, they imposed a six-year term limit on committee and subcommittee chairmen. Thomas became the new chairman of Ways and Means in 2001, replacing term-limited William Archer (R-TX), who retired from the House.

15. Charles Gnaedinger, "Thomas: Fundamental Tax Reform Is the Way to Resolve FSC Dispute," *Tax Notes*, March 4, 2002, 1096.

16. Gnaedinger, "Thomas," 1096–97.

17. Charles Gnaedinger and Natalia Radziejewska, "Bush Promises Compliance with WTO FSC Ruling," *Tax Notes*, May 6, 2002, 835.

18. *Congressional Record*, October 8, 2004, S10795.

19. Jill Barshay, "Tax Writers' Winning Formula: Billions in Targeted Provisions," *CQ Weekly*, October 9, 2004, 2364.

20. Martin A. Sullivan, "Thomas vs. Crane: At Odds on How to Keep Jobs in U.S.," *Tax Notes*, April 28, 2003, 462.

21. Sullivan, "Thomas vs. Crane," 462.

22. Sullivan, "Thomas vs. Crane," 462.

23. David L. Brumbaugh, "The 2004 Corporate Tax and FSC/ETI Bill: The American Jobs Creation Act," CRS Report for Congress, October 22, 2004, 4.

24. Warren Rojas, "Thomas Floats Dual-Pronged Plan for Final ETI Resolution," *Tax Notes*, October 20, 2003, 303.

25. Jill Barshay and Stephen J. Norton, "House GOP Tax Writers Ending Mutiny against Thomas," *CQ Today*, October 22, 2003, 5.

26. Barshay and Norton, "House GOP Tax Writers," 5.

27. Warren Rojas, "ETI Repeal Bill Reveals Caucuswide Manufacturing Split," *Tax Notes*, November 3, 2003, 559.

28. Jonathan Kaplan, "Not on Speaking Terms," *The Hill*, June 3, 2004, 8.

29. Kaplan, "Not on Speaking Terms," 1.

30. Alan Ota and Stephen Norton, "Grassley Wants Senate to Act Now on Corporate Tax Bill, Not Wait for the House," *CQ Today*, November 12, 2003, 5.

31. Alan Ota and Stephen Norton, "Thomas Says He Is Winning Support for His Version of Corporate Tax Bill," *CQ Today*, November 6, 2003, 17.

32. Ota and Norton, "Thomas Winning Support," 17.

33. Heidi Glenn, "Senate Deal Paves Way for Action on ETI Act Repeal," *Tax Notes*, April 12, 2004, 145.

34. *Congressional Record*, March 3, 2004, S2066.

35. *Congressional Record*, March 3, 2004, S2068.

36. Alan Ota and Jill Barshay, "Corporate Tax Bill Attracting Wave of Add-Ons," *CQ Today*, March 5, 2004, 3.

37. Jonathan Weisman, "Democrats Seize on Offshoring as Campaign Issue," *Washington Post*, March 6, 2004, E2. See Stephen Norton, "For Democrats Blasting Bush on Jobs, Outsourcing Is In," *CQ Weekly*, March 13, 2004, 620–25. There are benefits associated with outsourcing, as many economists point out. See Bob Davis, "Some Democratic Economists Echo Mankiw on Outsourcing," *Wall Street Journal*, February 12, 2004, A4. As a way to highlight the benefits of free trade, Senate Republicans introduced the term "insourcing" as a way to spotlight the movement of foreign jobs and investment into the United States. See Josephine Hearn, "Outsourcing Is Bad, Insourcing Is Better," *The Hill*, March 9, 2004, 1.

38. *Congressional Record*, March 24, 2004, S3066.

39. Alan Ota and Jill Barshay, "House May Trim a Trimmed-Down Corporate Tax Bill," *CQ Today*, March 25, 2004, 4.

40. *Congressional Record*, March 24, 2004, S3067.

41. Martin Vaughan and Susan Davis, "Tax Bill Stalls in Senate after Cloture Fails by 51-47 Vote," National Journal's *CongressDailyPM*, March 24, 2004, 1.

42. Vaughan and Davis, "Tax Bill Stalls in Senate," 1.

43. Jill Barshay and Alan Ota, "Senate Leaders Closer to Agreement on Amendments to Corporate Tax Bill," *CQ Today*, April 8, 2004, 3.

44. Barshay and Ota, "Senate Leaders Closer to Agreement," 3.

45. Jill Barshaw, "Senate Sets Debate on Terms for Corporate Tax Bill," *CQ Today*, April 9, 2004, 1.

46. *Congressional Record*, May 6, 2004, S4941.

47. *Congressional Record*, May 7, 2004, S5045.

48. *Congressional Record*, May 10, 2004, S5167.

49. Jill Barshay, "Agreement Clears Way for Senate Vote on Tax Bill," *CQ Today*, May 11, 2004, 6.

50. *Congressional Record*, May 11, 2004, S5184–S5186.

51. Whether Kerry's vote would have been decisive is a matter of some dispute. Democrats believe that GOP whips would have successfully persuaded one or more party colleagues to switch their vote if that was necessary to defeat Cantwell's amendment. Nonetheless, the Bush-Cheney presidential campaign argued that missing the vote demonstrated Kerry's commitment to politics rather than policy. "Today [Kerry] had the chance to actually vote on [the extension of unemployment benefits] but he was too busy playing politics when he would have made the difference in the Senate," declared a spokesman for the Bush-Cheney campaign. See Bill Swindell, "With Kerry Absent, Senate Turns Aside Jobless Aid," *CQ Today*, May 12, 2004, 6.

52. Jill Barshay and Alan Ota, "Thomas Says Senate OK of Corporate Tax Bill Gives His Approach Momentum," *CQ Today*, May 13, 2004, 6.

53. Heidi Glenn, "House ETI Repeal Undergoes Another Face-Lift," *Tax Notes*, May 24, 2004, 936.

54. Emily Pierce, "Road Map," *Roll Call*, May 18, 2004, 17.

55. Josephine Hearn, "Forty Members Say Buyout Key to Their Votes on Tax Bill," *The Hill*, June 30, 2004, 7.

56. Patrik Jonsson, "Along Tobacco Row, a Changed Culture," *Christian Science Monitor*, October 21, 2004, 1, 10.

57. Josephine Hearn and Klaus Marre, "Waxman, Flake Decry Tobacco Buyout," *The Hill*, June 15, 2004, 18. The bill started out as a government-financed tobacco buyout program, but that was changed in conference to require tobacco companies to fund the buyout.

58. Hearn, "Forty Members Say Buyout Key," 7.

59. Jill Barshay, "Cracks Appear in Thomas's Corporate Tax Coalition," *CQ Today*, June 17, 2004, 3.

60. During floor debate, Democratic representative Jim McGovern (MA) pointed out many of what he characterized as "sweetheart deals, special fixes, and big giveaways to special interests." He cited as examples: "The list of provisions that favor particular companies or industries include cruise-ship operators, whale hunters, Chinese ceiling fans, foreign gamblers, NASCAR track owners, timber companies, cattle ranchers, bourbon distillers, movie theater owners, small plane manufacturers, bow and arrow sets, fishing tackle boxes, and corporate jet owners." *Congressional Record*, June 17, 2004, H4296.

61. Jill Barshay and Alan Ota, "Thomas Trades Pure for Practical to Move Much-Altered Tax Bill," *CQ Weekly*, June 12, 2004, 1409.

62. Josephine Hearn, "FSC Bill Brings Corporate Heavyweights on Board," *The Hill*, June 9, 2004, 10.

63. *Congressional Record*, June 17, 2004, H4403.

64. *Congressional Record*, March 4, 2004, H843.

65. *Congressional Record*, June 17, 2004, H4298.

66. Emily Hall, National Journal's *CongressDailyAM*, July 16, 2004, 10.

67. Jill Barshay and Mary Clare Jalonick, "Tobacco Buyout Backers Tempted to Accept Regulation," *CQ Today*, July 13, 2004, 1.

68. *Congressional Record*, July 14, 2004, S8104.

69. National Journal's *CongressDailyPM*, September 15, 2004, 3.

70. Shailagh Murray, "Congress Seeks to Pass Tax Bill Loaded with Perks," *Wall Street Journal*, October 5, 2004, A15.

71. *Congressional Record*, October 9, 2004, S10929.

72. Dan Morgan and Helen Dewar, "House Blocks FDA Oversight of Tobacco," *Washington Post*, October 12, 2004, A4.

73. Heidi Glenn, "Congress Poised to Send ETI Bill to President Bush," *Tax Notes*, October 11, 2004, 136.

74. Morgan and Dewar, "House Blocks FDA Oversight of Tobacco," A4. Of the twenty-three Senate conferees, seventeen signed the conference report. For the House, twelve Republicans and one Democrat signed the report; five Democrats and one Republican refused to sign the conference report.

75. *Congressional Record*, October 9, 2004, S10929.

76. *Congressional Record*, October 7, 2004, H8656.

77. Martin Vaughan and Paul Singer, "When Loyalty Adds Up to Big Tax Breaks," *National Journal*, October 16, 2004, 3150.

78. Martin Cutsinger, "Deal Made on Corporate Law Change," *USA Today*, October 7, 2004, 19A.

79. Jill Barshay and Alan Ota, "Tax Bill Nears Completion, but Time Running Short," *CQ Today*, October 6, 2004, 7.

80. *Congressional Record*, October 7, 2004, H8652.

81. Jill Barshay, "Tax Writers' Winning Formula: Billions in Targeted Provisions," *CQ Weekly*, October 9, 2004, 2368.

82. *Congressional Record*, October 7, 2004, S10759.

83. *Congressional Record*, October 10, 2004, S11025.

84. Jill Barshay, "Two Senators Who Held Up the Bill—and What They Got in Return," *CQ Weekly*, October 16, 2004, 2438.

85. Scott Miller, "EU Moves to Lift Trade Sanctions on U.S. Exporters," *Wall Street Journal*, October 26, 2004, A2.

86. Edmund Andrews, "How Tax Bill Gave Businesses More and More," *New York Times*, October 13, 2004, C15.

87. Quoted in "Midday Update," *CQ Today*, December 8, 2004, 1. Senator Roberts was referring to the 2004 intelligence reform bill.

88. Quoted in the *Washington Post*, February 24, 1988, A22.

89. Jeffrey Birnbaum and Jonathan Weisman, "GE Lobbyists Mold Tax Bill," *Washington Post*, July 13, 2004, A4.

90. Arnold, *The Logic of Congressional Action*, 144.

91. Woodrow Wilson, *Congressional Government* (Boston: Houghton Mifflin, 1885), 57.

11

The Making of U.S. Foreign Policy: The Roles of the President and Congress over Four Decades

Lee H. Hamilton

The relationship between Congress and the president in foreign policy has evolved over the past four decades in response to changes in the world and in U.S. society and politics. Prior to 1965, when I entered the Congress, the president's authority in foreign policy was rarely challenged by a largely deferential legislature. Harry Truman's claim that the president alone made foreign policy had substantial merit. Vietnam, Watergate, the end of the Cold War, the proliferation of special interest groups, the intensification of the political environment, and the explosion of twenty-four-hour news and information then led Congress, for various reasons, to assert its power in foreign policy more often and in new and complex ways, with members of Congress speaking out on foreign policy issues in a cacophony of voices. The onset of the war on terror and the war in Iraq has once again tilted the pendulum back toward an empowered presidency and executive branch.

Despite this evolution, the fundamental foreign policy roles of the president and Congress remain essentially the same. The president is the chief foreign policy maker, crafting policy with a handful of top advisers. Most major initiatives in foreign policy originate with him. Congress serves as both a partner and a critic of the president, though in recent years it has shown a reluctance to be openly critical of major foreign policy initiatives.

As has been the case since the beginning of the Republic, sustained consultation between the president and Congress remains the most important mechanism for fostering an effective foreign policy with broad support at home and respect and punch overseas; that consultation works best when

Congress is willing to serve as both a partner and an independent critic to the president in the development and implementation of foreign policy.

HISTORICAL TRENDS

The relative influence of the president and Congress has fluctuated throughout U.S. history. During the nineteenth century, as the United States was consumed with domestic developments and westward expansion, Congress sometimes exerted greater power than the president. Teddy Roosevelt and Woodrow Wilson asserted greater presidential authority in the early twentieth century as they expanded the U.S. role in the world and brought America into World War I. Congress then regained influence following its rejection of U.S. entrance into the League of Nations, which began a twenty-year period of scaled back U.S. involvement in international affairs. The U.S. entry into World War II fostered a renewed presidential dominance of foreign policy, which lasted until the domestic upheaval and eventual congressional outcry caused by the Vietnam War. After Vietnam, presidents maintained great authority in foreign affairs but found themselves challenged on many fronts by a more assertive Congress. Following the terrorist attacks of September 11, 2001, George W. Bush reasserted a level of presidential control that had not been seen in decades.

These ebbs and flows have been linked to broader changes in the world environment. The president tends to have the greatest power in foreign policy during times of national crisis, war, or heightened public interest in foreign affairs. The twentieth-century presidents who enjoyed the greatest control over foreign policy—Woodrow Wilson until 1918, Franklin Roosevelt after 1941, Harry Truman, Dwight Eisenhower, John Kennedy, Lyndon Johnson—governed during major wars or at the height of the Cold War. Congress has tended to assert more authority when the United States has been at peace and the American people have been disengaged from world events, such as in the aftermath of World War I and following the end of the Cold War.

U.S. domestic politics have also had a major impact on the relative power of the president and Congress. This has been illustrated vividly over the past four decades. The national trauma over Vietnam, and a growing perception of abuses by the so-called imperial presidency, prodded Congress to assert greater influence over foreign affairs. The national trauma over 9/11 and a domestic consensus for a vigorous response abroad empowered George W. Bush to take aggressive international action and dissuaded members of Congress from vigorously challenging the initiation of the war on terror or the war in Iraq.

The historical fluctuation in the relationship between Congress and the president ultimately stems from the division of foreign policy powers stipulated by the Constitution. Because the Constitution assigns some of these powers to the president and others to Congress, it invites them to struggle, as the great constitutional scholar Edwin Corwin has noted, for the privilege of directing U.S. foreign policy. The president is the commander in chief and head of the executive branch. Congress has the power to declare war and the power of the purse. The president can negotiate treaties, but the Senate must ratify them. This shared responsibility leaves the door open to both branches to assert their authority. Historical circumstances and the will and capability of each branch at any given time, then, determine their relative influence.

The ideal established by the Founders is neither for one branch to dominate the other nor for there to be a uniformity of views between them. Rather, the Founders wisely sought to encourage a creative tension between the president and Congress that would produce policies that best advance U.S. national interests and reflect the views of the American people.

CHANGES SINCE THE 1960s

The fluctuations in the influence of Congress and the president since the 1960s are striking and complex. Members of Congress have become far more engaged in foreign policy. Yet while Congress as a whole has at times challenged the president's authority, it has not exercised consistent power and influence, because its foreign policy capacity is diffuse and its stances are often varied. The president has generally retained more power but has occasionally struggled to command and sustain the nation's attention and Congress's support, particularly at times when the nation is not involved in a crisis or war.

The changes of recent decades began with the Vietnam War. Most members of Congress, and much of the American people, became concerned during the war that the United States had moved too far and too fast in concentrating war-making and other powers in the hands of the president. Believing that such a concentration of power was neither necessary, nor desirable, nor tolerable in a democratic society, these members gradually sought to restrict presidential power and enhance the foreign policy influence of Congress.

Congress was slow to take dramatic action on Vietnam—in part because many members who had reservations about the war did not want to use the blunt tool of rejecting appropriations for defense—but by 1973 Congress

passed legislation that helped to end the war and established a new framework for executive and legislative war-making authority. The War Powers
Act of that year, passed over President Nixon's veto, imposed groundbreak-
ing procedural restraints on the capacity of the president to unilaterally commit U.S. armed forces abroad. The act stipulates that the president must consult with Congress before introducing U.S. forces into hostilities or
imminent hostilities, must report to Congress when such forces are introduced, and must terminate the use of forces within sixty to ninety days unless
Congress authorizes their use or extends this time period. The act's guiding
principle is that a democracy should go to war only with the consent of the
people, as expressed by their elected representatives. Although the act has
often been ignored in the decades since by both the president and Congress,
its advocates at the time argued that it would provide Congress with the
means to fulfill the war-making responsibility assigned to the legislature by
the Constitution.

    Congress continued to flex its muscle in subsequent years. The Watergate
scandal of 1973–1974 weakened the personal position of President Nixon
and the institutional power of the presidency, while revelations of secret CIA
operations abroad, particularly in Chile, further emboldened Congress to
take the offensive in ways it would not have considered a decade before. In
1974 Congress challenged administration policy in southeastern Europe by
prohibiting military aid to Turkey and stymied commercial agreements that
President Nixon had reached with the Soviet Union by enacting the Jack-
son-Vanik amendment, which tied increased trade with the Soviet Union to
its freedom of emigration. A year later, Congress enacted an amendment to
the Arms Export Control Act that required any U.S. sale of military equipment worth more than $7 million to be submitted to Congress for approval.
This new congressional assertiveness did not mean that Congress had gained
the upper hand in foreign policy, but it did indicate that Congress was playing an increasingly important role. President Carter recognized Congress's
growing independence when he devoted an enormous amount of time and
energy to winning congressional approval of the Panama Canal Treaty and
arms sales to Saudi Arabia. He realized that Congress could no longer be
expected to rubber-stamp the president's policies.

    President Reagan regained some of the president's authority because he
was viewed by the American people as a strong leader with a clear vision of
the world. But he faced serious congressional challenges as well, particularly
on U.S. policy toward South Africa and Central America. Congress overrode
President Reagan's opposition to tough economic sanctions on South Africa,
effectively initiating a harder stance against the apartheid government. And
Congress refused on multiple occasions to support President Reagan's

requests for funding of the contras in Nicaragua—resistance that led his administration to subvert the law in order to provide the aid anyway.

After the end of the Cold War, foreign policy relations between Congress and the president were frequently rocky. President George H. W. Bush managed to win congressional support for the Gulf War after an intensive lobbying campaign on Capitol Hill, but President Clinton struggled to gain congressional approval for a slew of foreign policy initiatives, including an inability to pass the Comprehensive Test Ban Treaty and fast-track authority for trade agreements, and difficulty in getting funding for the United Nations, the International Monetary Fund, international peacekeeping, and foreign aid. Executive-legislative relations reached a new low point with President Clinton's impeachment, which exacerbated the mutual mistrust between Congress and the president and made foreign policy cooperation between the branches increasingly rare during Clinton's second term.

Under President George W. Bush, the combination of an aggressive presidential foreign policy after 9/11 and a deferential Congress has reasserted the dominance of the president in international affairs. Like any war, the war on terror has focused an extraordinary amount of power in the president's hands—on issues ranging from the use of military force and covert operations to the treatment of prisoners of war and detainees at home and abroad and the use of intelligence, law enforcement, and financial resources. This trend was heightened by the congressional resolution authorizing the use of force in Iraq in 2002, which granted President Bush sweeping authorities to go to war in Iraq with virtually no restrictions, after limited congressional debate. Congress has remained generally supportive of the president through the conduct of the two wars, providing little in the way of vigorous oversight, though criticism from individual members has emerged as the United States has run into difficulties in Iraq.

Changed International Environment

These changes in Congress's approach to foreign policy mirror changes in the international environment. During the Cold War, particularly until Vietnam but again to a lesser degree during the Reagan years, the president commanded greater authority in large part because Americans felt a strong collective threat to their national security. Members of Congress who challenged the president could be charged with lacking patriotism, not supporting American troops, and subverting the national interest. That political environment encouraged members to fall in line behind the president, except during periods of presidential weakness, such as the 1970s, or when public opposition to the president's policies was especially strong.

In the 1990s, a more complicated set of international challenges emerged. Technological evolutions in finance, trade, travel, and communications changed relations among nations and helped usher in new security threats like terrorism, proliferation, environmental degradation, and drug trafficking. Instead of clashes between nations, the United States was often confronted by brutal wars within nations, which spawned massive human rights violations. The Cold War doctrine of containment was easy to articulate and understand, but there was no overarching framework that easily described the emerging challenges presented by globalization in the 1990s. Without a single, strong rationale for foreign policy, Congress and the president got involved in issues in a more ad hoc and uncoordinated way, focusing on China and Russia one day, the Balkans and Colombia the next, while placing more prominence on economic issues.

September 11, 2001, brought with it a new rationale for American foreign policy. Terrorism now dominates the agenda. Americans feel personally threatened by events abroad in a manner that was only reached at the hottest points of the Cold War. As in the Cold War, this has generated popular support for a strong presidency and has reinitiated the likelihood that members who are openly critical of the president can be charged with lacking patriotism or subverting the national interest. President Bush's embrace of a strong military posture, new executive powers at home and abroad, and a willingness to focus on terrorism in his bilateral and multilateral relations despite the priorities and concerns of other nations, has further centralized foreign policy making in the hands of the executive branch, recalibrating the balance between the branches.

More Actors

Another fluctuation in recent years involves the number of actors involved in U.S. foreign policy and their relative influence. During the 1960s, foreign policy was largely the domain of a small group of people—the president, the secretaries of state and defense, the national security adviser, the chairs of the House and Senate foreign relations committees, and other members of the elite foreign policy establishment. To consult with Congress, the president and his advisers simply needed to call up the key congressional leaders.

In the years following Vietnam, more members of Congress became interested in international affairs, and power within Congress became more diffuse. As more members took an interest, more members wanted to be heard on international issues, and the executive branch needed to consult with as many members as possible to advance an agenda. In recent years, power within the Congress has again consolidated with the congressional leadership, and the post-9/11 powers of the Bush administration have given the executive branch a freer hand in foreign policy making. Yet congressional interest in foreign affairs remains high, and the executive branch is still served by extensive consultation to retain support for major foreign policy initiatives.

The last four decades have also seen a proliferation of groups outside of government seeking to influence foreign policy: the business community, labor unions, ethnic constituencies, nonprofit organizations, foreign countries, former officials, international organizations, think tanks, universities—and the list goes on. All of these groups and individuals seek to advance their views on Capitol Hill and in the White House, adding another dimension to relations between the branches.

For instance, ethnic groups have emerged as a set of powerful actors in U.S. foreign policy. Their influence is certainly not new; it dates back to the earliest days of the republic. But the number of politically active ethnic groups has grown tremendously, and their lobbying techniques have become much more sophisticated. The ethnic groups with the most influence are those that are well funded and have large numbers nationally, heavy concentrations in particular areas of the country, or positions of power in society. Ethnic groups have an especially large influence on Congress because members with large concentrations of particular ethnic groups in their districts have great incentives to promote the foreign policies advocated by those constituencies. Ethnic congressional caucuses now abound. In the House, there is an Indian caucus, an Armenian caucus, and many more. These caucuses often act as fundraising mechanisms for members who support their objectives. For the executive branch, ethnic constituencies can also play an important role in electoral politics. Cuban Americans have long had a great impact on U.S. policy toward Cuba because of their concentration in a few areas, particularly in Florida, which has been a key swing state in recent presidential elections. Thus ethnic constituencies provide an example of how the influence of outside sources can affect both branches.

In the period after the end of the Cold War and preceding 9/11, the absence of an overarching framework for U.S. foreign policy allowed outside special interest groups to bring many once peripheral issues to the forefront of the foreign policy debate. For instance, as more Americans became tied to the global economy, businesses—even small companies and small farmers—found themselves with a greater stake in foreign policy. Business lobbyists played a major role in building congressional support for the North American Free Trade Agreement and trade with China. Conversely, labor and environmental groups often lobbied against free trade, fearing that it would export jobs out of the United States and lower environmental standards abroad. The result was that trade policy became one of the most important and contested foreign policy issues of the 1990s and was determined not only by the relationship between the branches but also by the relative influence of various special interests, particularly business and labor.

A similar pattern holds true for nongovernmental organizations (NGOs), including think tanks, public interest groups, and private volunteer associations. These groups—ranging from the Christian Coalition to Human Rights Watch—advocate positions, and exert power, on every imaginable issue in international affairs. The more powerful NGOs sometimes draft legislation themselves that members subsequently introduce in Congress. They also shape the public debate through congressional testimony, television commentary, grassroots activities, and op-ed writing. In the 1990s, as U.S. foreign policy dealt with a diffuse set of issues, these groups could proactively push issues to the front of the foreign policy debate. Since 9/11, those groups that deal with issues related to the war on terror have been forced to be more reactive to an assertive executive branch, and those groups dealing with other issues have had to compete with the war on terrorism and the war in Iraq for the attention of the public and members of Congress.

The period from the Vietnam era through the 1990s also saw a rise in the influence of international organizations. Forty years ago, few members of Congress could even name the top officials of major international institutions. Increasingly, the leadership of the United Nations, the International Monetary Fund, the World Bank, and the World Trade Organization established almost constant contact with U.S. officials and members of Congress. The Gulf War and the 1990s marked a particular zenith for these groups, as U.S. foreign policy was often designed in tandem with the policies of these institutions. This influence began to recede under President George W. Bush, as the United States moved toward a foreign policy that stressed U.S. freedom of action and an unwillingness to get tied down in international treaties and agreements. Yet the practical contribution of these various institutions to U.S. foreign policy goals ensures their continued seat at the table in many foreign policy making and implementation decisions.

And then there is the media—a powerful foreign policy actor in its own right. In the 1990s, television asserted its ability to set our foreign policy agenda through the impact of images. In 1992, television images of starving children in Somalia provoked American outrage and led former President Bush to send U.S. troops to Somalia to help combat its famine. Yet, some months later, television images of dead American soldiers being dragged through the streets of Mogadishu led President Clinton to withdraw soldiers.

The information revolution also exponentially increased the amount of information available to ordinary Americans and policy makers. Specialized publications, cable outlets, satellite television, and the Internet enable people to access almost unlimited data on foreign policy issues, while enabling people to communicate with one another instantaneously. The challenge for the citizen and policy maker alike is sifting through all of the information to carefully weed out the important and accurate from the inconsequential or misleading. For instance, few Americans inside or outside of government noticed Osama bin Laden's voice declaring war on America in the 1990s among the constant stream of voices and images from abroad.

Changes in Congress

Changes in the institution and practices of Congress have altered the influence of each branch in foreign affairs. Since 1965, the foreign policy capacity of Congress has grown both more expert and more diffuse. Congress has become more representative of widely varying American viewpoints. Like most Americans, members of Congress hold strong opinions on foreign policy issues, which they relate with more and more frequency—speaking out on issues, writing articles and opinion pieces, appearing on television and radio, and responding to constituent interest in global affairs. Yet while Congress has developed its own expertise and interest in international affairs, this expertise and interest does not always lead to strong influence or oversight over foreign policy.

After Pearl Harbor, a whole generation of members tended to defer to the president and congressional leadership on foreign affairs. After Vietnam, many new members felt that they could formulate foreign policy just as well themselves. Members began to accumulate larger and highly professional staffs—both in their own offices and in committees. The staff of the House International Relations Committee, for instance, tripled between 1971 and 1978. Congress also gained access to more executive branch documents and sources and made greater use of its own independent research bodies, such as the Congressional Research Service, the General Accounting Office, and the Congressional Budget Office. This increased expertise enabled Congress to get involved in far more aspects of foreign policy than ever before.

Many members also became less tied to their parties or the institution of Congress and more willing to speak out on issues of particular concern to them or their constituents. In 2000, for example, an individual senator used his power as chairman of a Senate appropriations subcommittee to block hundreds of millions of dollars that had been approved by Congress for UN peacekeeping missions because he opposed the Clinton administration's policy on Sierra Leone. This fragmentation could also be seen in the trade blocs that emerged across party lines in the 1990s. Pro-trade Republicans and

Democrats have often been allied against members of both parties who want the United States to take stronger stances on labor standards, human rights, religious freedom, national security, or the environment.

The greater ethnic diversity of Congress also added to its independence and wide-ranging interests. Over the last four decades, Congress welcomed far more women, African Americans, Latinos, and members of other ethnic groups than it once did. These members brought new concerns to the foreign policy debate. For example, the sanctions placed by Congress on South Africa in the 1980s and the increased national focus on women's rights overseas reflected the growing power of black and female members.

Yet the diversity of individuals, views, and expertise within the Congress has not always led to influence vis-à-vis the executive branch, particularly as Congress has grown more timid in recent years. To begin with, members of Congress are usually reactive in foreign policy making, rather than being proactive in developing policy. In the 1980s and 1990s, even when Congress did assert itself, it was often in opposition to a foreign policy initiative of the executive branch. Through the 1990s, Congress—like the executive branch—did not adjust to the emerging threat of terrorism, holding few hearings and initiating little in the way of counterterrorism legislation. After 9/11, Congress basically ceded the formation of a new national security strategy to the president.

Congressional responsibility has been further weakened by the growing influence of domestic political concerns on the foreign policy process. Many members of Congress view foreign policy as nothing more than an extension of U.S. politics. They use it to curry favor with supporters or constituents, or to score political points. The rise of the perpetual political campaign has rendered the congressional foreign policy capacity even thinner because members spend so much time campaigning and fundraising that less time is left for careful policy deliberation. Foreign policy just becomes a means by which a member of Congress chooses to align his or herself with the president, or opposes the president.

Perhaps the most urgent weakening of congressional responsibility can be attributed to declining oversight of foreign policy, which extends over a period of years. Oversight of foreign policy in the Congress has been increasingly shifted away from the main foreign policy authorizing committees, which have the greatest foreign policy expertise. This, along with a turnover of members with historical memory in international issues, has made it all the more difficult for Congress to develop a coherent foreign policy approach. In fact, the greatest concentration of foreign policy power is now in the congressional leadership, which often works to implement the policies of the executive branch; in the appropriations committees, in which foreign policy concerns are usually secondary to domestic political and fiscal concerns; and—since the onset of the war on terror and the war in Iraq—in the armed services committees, whose expertise lies primarily in setting defense budgets and supporting the military rather than setting and overseeing the implementation of foreign policy.

As power has been shifted away from the authorizing committees whose responsibility it is to delve into the activities of specific executive branch agencies, these committees have met less frequently and exercised far less influence. As Congress has chosen to fund the federal government through so-called "continuing resolutions," massive appropriations bills, and emergency supplementals, the routine reauthorization hearings that probed an agency's or policy's effectiveness have largely disappeared. As foreign policy has become more politicized, many members in both parties have avoided taking stands based upon the national interest and have instead deferred to political expediency. The cost in all this is more than a loss in congressional power. For instance, congressional failure to ask tough questions leading up to the war in Iraq about the case for war, the plans for the postwar occupation, and the methods of detention for Iraqi prisoners helped lead to policy shortcomings. Failing to ask tough questions and demand answers allows the executive branch to sidestep a careful examination of its positions and policies. This hurts the nation, and it ultimately weakens the president's policies.

Changes in the Executive Branch

Some of these changes in the way Congress approaches and handles foreign policy have been mirrored in the executive branch. Today, as in years past, U.S. foreign policy is ultimately made by the president along with a handful of top advisers. Yet the responsibility for carrying out foreign policy in the executive has become more diffuse, as the number of federal agencies involved in foreign policy has proliferated. The State Department, the Defense Department, and the CIA remain the central bodies for much of U.S. foreign policy, but they are no longer the exclusive authorities. Counterterrorism, for instance, cuts across the entire government, with important roles for the Treasury Department, the Justice Department, and the Departments of Transportation, Health and Human Services, and Agriculture, just to name a few. Each of these agencies and departments must in turn work with international partners because of the transnational nature of the terrorist threat.

Counterterrorism has also brought on two of the most significant national security reorganizations of the executive branch in the post–World War II period: the creation of the Department of Homeland Security in 2002, which unified twenty-two federal agencies in one cabinet department; and the intelligence reform act of 2004, which, among many changes, created a new director of national intelligence to oversee the U.S. intelligence community and a national counterterrorism center designed to pull together and coordinate these dispersed counterterrorism responsibilities.

Along with the diffusion of foreign policy authority has come greater responsibility for the National Security Council (NSC). The NSC must act as the primary manager and coordinator of the various foreign policy activities being conducted by the different departments of government. As more actors have become involved in executive branch foreign policy making over the last three decades, it has become more difficult for an administration to manage dissent and speak with one voice. It is the job of the national security adviser to see that it does.

The policy-making process has also become more politicized in the executive branch. Every issue—from trade to energy policy to the conduct of the war in Iraq—is now subject to intense scrutiny based on political, and sometimes partisan, concerns. The 2004 presidential election saw a level of interest in foreign policy and national security issues that was unique since the height of the Cold War. As foreign policy has become more political, much attention has been focused upon how foreign policy events are being portrayed rather than on the important work of crafting and carrying out a foreign policy rooted in the national interest.

Perhaps the most important change in executive branch foreign policy making is the open-ended nature of the war on terror. Presidents always assume more power during wartime—this was true of Woodrow Wilson, Franklin Roosevelt, Harry Truman, and Lyndon Johnson in the twentieth century. Yet our twentieth-century wars were conflicts between or among nations, with an enemy that was at least somewhat clear and a definitive endpoint. The war on terror is unique. Like other wars, it harnesses the full resources of the U.S. government in defense of the American people and enhances the power of the president who, as commander in chief, commands those resources. Yet because it is being waged against a shadowy global network and a murderous ideology, there is no clearly defined enemy or endpoint to the conflict, so there is no clearly defined endpoint to these expanded powers of the presidency. There is no foreign capital to conquer or standing army to destroy. President Bush has assumed the power and standing in foreign policy making relative to Congress of a wartime president. No one can say for sure when that enhanced power and standing will end.

WHAT HAS NOT CHANGED

There has also been much that has remained the same in U.S. foreign policy since the mid-1960s. The essential ingredients for a successful foreign policy are unchanged: presidential leadership and congressional partnership, facilitated by sustained presidential consultation with Congress, and independent congressional examination of the president's proposals, policies, and implementation.

Role of the President

The president is still, by far, the most important foreign policy maker. He must lead in order for the United States to advance its interests and values around the world. Only the president is accountable to, and speaks for, all Americans, and only he can rally public support to a foreign policy cause. The American people generally support the president on major foreign policy issues, especially when they believe the security of the nation is at stake. When he vigorously takes his case to Congress and the American people, he usually wins their support.

U.S. presidents have played the central role in nearly every major foreign policy achievement of the past thirty years. Nixon overcame years of distrust to renew U.S. relations with China; Carter negotiated the Panama Canal Treaties and the Camp David accords establishing peace between Israel and Egypt; Reagan intensified the U.S. challenge to the Soviet Union and began deep cuts in nuclear weapons; George H. W. Bush skillfully managed the end of the Cold War and built the coalition that forced Iraq out of Kuwait; Clinton led U.S. efforts to strengthen and expand NATO, protect peace in the Balkans, and advance international trade; George W. Bush has launched a war on terrorism, overthrown the Taliban and installed a new government in Afghanistan, and toppled Saddam Hussein and occupied Iraq. Congress often provided needed support and helpful refinements of these policies, but their achievement would have been impossible without presidential leadership.

What must the president do to be an effective leader in foreign policy? Most importantly, he must make foreign policy a priority. Success demands substantial time, energy, and a sustained focus on critical foreign policy issues. Too frequently—although often for compelling reasons given by the many demands of the job—the president's attention (as well as the attention of the American people) moves away from a foreign policy problem once the initial guns go silent or before a full solution has been achieved. Because of the constant press of many world crises demanding American leadership, sustaining U.S. policy over time can be extremely difficult. Only a president can do it.

The president must also decide which issues to focus on. Faced with a long list of international challenges, he must determine which are the critical issues that deserve his attention and leadership and where he can make a difference. He must know where he wants to go and how he intends to get there; he must explain what his goals are, articulate his policy proposals clearly, and specify what kinds of resources he is prepared to expend.

One of the greatest challenges for the president is explaining the international environment and U.S. national interests to members of Congress and the American people. Public and congressional support will come only if Americans understand the fundamentals of the challenges we confront and are committed to meeting them. This task of educating the American people and sustaining congressional and public determination will prove especially difficult as we face the evolving threat of catastrophic terrorism, which will likely threaten Americans and U.S. interests for decades to come. The president must make himself heard above a clamor of competing voices and sustain a process of public education that begins the first day of his term and ends the last.

Finally, the president must work in partnership with Congress and with friendly leaders around the world. U.S. foreign policy is far more effective when it has strong bipartisan support in the Congress and support from other nations. When the U.S. acts with limited domestic or international support, the costs and risks of action are much greater. Good personal relations between the president and foreign heads of state help build international backing for U.S. policy. These relationships are especially important in the struggle against terrorism, which demands international cooperation to root out an enemy that operates in some eighty nations around the globe. Similarly, good relations between the president and members of Congress are essential to build and maintain support at home. Members of Congress will tend to back a president more strongly and over a longer period of time if they are involved in the policy process from the beginning rather than simply being informed of decisions after the fact.

Role of the Congress as Partner

Congress, too, has important foreign policy responsibilities that have remained constant. A strong foreign policy requires that Congress live up to its constitutional mandate to be the president's partner in the development and implementation of foreign policy. To succeed, Congress must serve as both a partner and an independent critic of the president.

Congress can bring many strengths to the foreign policy process. It best represents the diverse views of the American people, is far more accessible than the president, contains a wide range of opinion and knowledge, and can at times supply a streak of independence that makes for vigorous and healthy debate. Congress can also help to refine and improve the proposals of the president through oversight and the legislative process.

Historically, Congress has a better record than many of its critics maintain. It has generally supported the major themes of U.S. foreign policy over the past several decades: containment of the Soviet Union; close relations with key allies in Europe, Asia, and elsewhere; a strong defense; free international trade; support for democracy and human rights abroad; and counterterrorism. Congress has supplied necessary funding for aid to Israel and other Middle East peace partners, endorsed enlarging NATO, supported some debt relief for the world's poorest nations, and restructured the homeland security and intelligence functions of the federal government in response to the terrorist threat.

Yet there are serious flaws with the way Congress approaches foreign policy. Congress often does not take foreign policy seriously enough, viewing challenges from a narrow or limited perspective rather than taking the time to understand the total national interest involved in an issue. For example, some members look at China only in terms of its human rights performance or its export of military technology—ignoring our other security, economic, political, and humanitarian interests in China.

Congress can be disruptive if it micromanages. Sometimes Congress fits bills with overly detailed performance and reporting requirements that can hamstring the president's flexibility in implementing foreign policy. The president's job is also complicated when Congress links unrelated issues together rather than considering them on their individual merits. During the 1990s, for instance, Congress linked UN funding to abortion and linked nonproliferation legislation on Russia and Iran to its ratification of the Chemical Weapons Convention. When Congress links tough foreign policy issues to other controversial measures, it makes it all the more difficult to move forward on them.

Congress has a very poor record of considering international treaties that have been signed by U.S. presidents and await Senate ratification. In some cases when the Senate votes to reject a treaty, it is asserting its independent judgment, which is its proper constitutional role. But dozens of treaties signed by U.S. presidents and submitted to the Senate over the past fifty years simply collected dust without being taken up for debate—on issues ranging from human rights, to the environment, to maritime regulations.

Treaties are not the only areas where Congress often shirks its responsibilities. Take the authorization of military force. In the thirty years since the War Powers Act, Congress often stood on the sidelines and failed to authorize the deployment of U.S. troops—including in Grenada, Panama, Somalia, Haiti, Bosnia, and Kosovo. Most recently, when Congress did authorize military force in Iraq, a passive Congress gave the president sweeping powers without a vigorous examination of the case for war or an insistence on sustained consultation.

Role of the Congress as Critic

While Congress must be an effective partner to the president in foreign policy making, it should also be an independent critic, though that criticism must always be in the interest of improving and strengthening U.S. policy.

This leads to the most disturbing defect with Congress's recent foreign policy performance: the lack of robust oversight. Good congressional oversight is fundamental to our democracy and the conduct of an effective foreign policy. At its best, oversight helps Congress—and the American people—evaluate the merits of a president's proposal and how well our government is performing. Oversight is necessary to compel executive branch officials to explain their policies and substantiate the reasoning that underlies them and to ensure that our foreign policy is acting in the best interests of the nation.

When the Congress puts itself on the sidelines during the run-up to a massive military invasion of Iraq and the ensuing occupation, hard questions are not asked, progress is not measured, potential problems are not ferreted out, and the American people lose a source of education and expertise. Congress—the people's branch of government—has not just the right, but the duty, to be at the table through these monumental decisions and the implementation of far-reaching foreign policies.

Congress must also serve as an independent overseer and critic if it is to fulfill its role in educating the public. Members of Congress have the advantage of being close to their constituents. Yet Congress rarely leads on educating the public about foreign policy. It is generally reactive instead of proactive—dealing with foreign policy issues only when forced to by the president or the media. Occasionally members give good foreign policy speeches or hold effective hearings, but they rarely feel any real burden to explain our foreign policy challenges to the American people. The members who do so are a distinctive minority.

To play a more constructive role, Congress needs to rethink the way it approaches foreign policy as both a partner and an independent critic to the president—providing rigorous oversight, asking tough questions, taking a more proactive stance to policy challenges, and doing its part to educate the American people. A thorough and fair congressional probing of presidential proposals and directives will ultimately help the president by refining his policies and ensuring their effective implementation. By fulfilling its dual role as a partner and critic, Congress will best serve the nation and fulfill the Founders' vision of a government of coequal branches.

Consultation

The best way to foster effective foreign policy cooperation between the president and Congress throughout the ebbs and flows in their relative influence is through sustained consultation. Consultation is the process of policy discussion and mutual exchange between the president and Congress. It can take many forms, including executive branch testimony at congressional hearings, briefings by foreign policy officials, and informal conversations. More important than its form is the attitude of the parties involved. Consultation is most effective when each branch makes a sincere effort to involve the other branch in its decision-making process. Consultation fosters mutual trust between the president and Congress, and it encourages them to develop our foreign policy together. It does not—and should not—ensure agreement between the branches. But even on the toughest issues, it helps smooth some of the hard edges of disagreement, and it almost always refines and strengthens our policy.

It is very hard to get consultation right on a sustained basis. Different presidents have consulted well on specific issues, but both the president and Congress often give short shrift to consultation. On the executive branch side, presidents tend to inform Congress of their decisions after the fact rather than consulting it during policy development. Presidents begin talking to Congress only when a congressional vote is upcoming, a media story is breaking, or a crisis is at hand. They tend to treat Congress as an obstacle to be overcome instead of as a partner in the policy-making process. And they often consult with only a limited number of members, excluding others who are heavily interested in particular foreign policy issues.

The most prominent examples of poor consultation in recent decades include the Vietnam War and aid to the contras in Nicaragua. The failure of Presidents Johnson, Nixon, and Reagan to consult Congress sufficiently over those issues led to major political controversies and serious congressional backlashes. These examples stand out because consultation was not simply poor; it was intentionally poor because the administrations wanted to conceal information from Congress and the public. Policy was controlled by a small group of high-level officials, and few others either inside or outside the administration knew the full extent of our government's activities. Other examples of poor consultation abound. The Clinton administration, for instance, consulted poorly on our interventions in Somalia, Bosnia, and Kosovo and during its efforts to obtain funding for the United Nations and the ratification of the Comprehensive Test Ban Treaty. The George W. Bush administration consulted poorly about the treatment of prisoners in Afghanistan and Iraq, revealing horrifying abuses in places like the Abu Ghraib prison in Iraq only when those stories started to leak out in the press.

Congress, too, regularly displays several consultation shortcomings. Members often are simply not receptive to consultation. They are either uninterested in foreign policy or want only to be briefed by the president, the secretary of defense, or the secretary of state. After the 1994 so-called Agreed Framework with North Korea was negotiated, for instance, I organized two briefings for members on Capitol Hill with the administration official who negotiated the agreement. A total of one member showed up.

Partisanship in Congress can also weaken consultation further. Congressional leaders have sometimes refused to be consulted by an administration while members of the other party were present. That kind of attitude makes it extremely difficult to develop a bipartisan foreign policy with broad support.

Despite these deficiencies, there have been a number of times in recent decades when consultation has worked well. President Carter consulted very effectively to achieve congressional approval of the Panama Canal Treaty and arms sales to Saudi Arabia. The George H. W. Bush and Clinton administrations consulted well to gain congressional support for aid to former Soviet bloc countries after the fall of communism and for preserving normal trade relations with China. The George W. Bush administration consulted well to forge a national consensus for immediate action in the days and weeks after 9/11.

What, then, must the president and Congress do to overcome, or at least to mitigate, the common deficiencies in the consultative process? First, each side must understand its proper role, powers, and limitations in foreign policy. The president must recognize that Congress plays an important role in policy formulation and refinement and can provide our foreign policy with stronger public support. Congress must recognize that its role is to help develop policy, while balancing the need to give the president flexibility in implementation while providing robust and effective oversight.

Second, the president and Congress must build a relationship based on mutual respect, trust, and partnership. Administration officials must take the perspectives of Congress seriously and respond to congressional concerns. Members of Congress must be sensitive to the complexity of foreign affairs and the difficulty of crafting and implementing policy. The branches must engage in a genuine dialogue on the problems that concern them most.

Third, consultation must take place, to the extent feasible, prior to decisions, not after they have already been made. The administration should inform Congress of the range of policy alternatives and seek Congress's advice. If the administration does intend simply to inform Congress of a decision, it should make this clear and not pretend to be seeking congressional input.

Fourth, support for consultation must come from our leadership. Consultation is most effective when the president himself is personally involved. For their part, leaders of Congress must set the example for other members by their constructive approach to the making of foreign policy. They can also help the administration understand the many perspectives of members.

Fifth, consultation must be bipartisan. Too often administration calls for bipartisanship are simply appeals for the opposing party in Congress to approve the administration's agenda. Real bipartisanship means engaging the other party in policy formulation. Congress must also strive for bipartisanship. It is most effective in advancing a foreign policy position, and avoiding politicization of foreign policy, when that position has strong support in both parties.

Sixth, the president must devote more resources to consultation—535 independent members of Congress cannot be reached by a handful of administration lobbyists. The administration should increase the number of people working to consult with Congress and assign high-quality people to that task. It should frequently send mid-level, as well as high-level, officials to Capitol Hill; keep closer track of the foreign policy views and concerns of every member; and hire more members to work in the executive branch as a means of strengthening ties between the branches.

Seventh, the administration must have sustained focus on consultation. It should not consult only during crises or when it needs immediate congressional support. On critical issues like terrorism, Iraq, Afghanistan, the Middle East, China, Russia, and international financial institutions, the administration should begin educating members as soon as they enter office.

Eighth, the administration must consult in many different ways and have a flexible approach. The kind of consultation required varies from issue to issue, from situation to situation, and from member to member. One-on-one discussion between officials and members can be especially effective. President Johnson was a master at these because he knew where each member was coming from and what was most important to him or her.

Ninth, Congress must make consultation a higher priority. Members should encourage consultation by attending briefings and displaying interest in foreign policy. Congress should be receptive to consultation from mid-level as well as high-level officials and should hire more former executive branch officials in order to improve its understanding of the workings and perspective of an administration.

Finally, Congress should create a permanent consultative group of congressional leaders. In 1993, I joined several other members of the House in introducing a bill to establish such a group made up of the congressional leadership and the chairs and ranking members of the main foreign policy committees. Other members with special interest or expertise could join the group's work on certain issues. The group would meet regularly—perhaps as often as once a month—with the top foreign policy officials in the administration, including the secretary of state, secretary of defense, and director of central intelligence. The agenda for these meetings would not be strictly limited, allowing members to raise issues of concern to them. The group would also meet on an emergency basis whenever the president was considering military action abroad. Such a group would enable the administration to consult with a wide range of congressional leaders in a single setting, mitigating the difficulty of consulting with the many centers of congressional power. The group would encourage the congressional and administration leadership to work through important policy questions together and would provide a centralized forum for foreign policy discussion and for dissemination of appropriate information to other members.

Improved consultation will not foster a perfect relationship between the president and Congress in foreign policy making. But more often than not, good consultation will help an administration gain greater backing in Congress while helping members better understand issues and policy choices. It will almost always foster a stronger, more refined, and more unified U.S. foreign policy.

CONCLUSION

The changes in the foreign policy relationship between Congress and the president since 1965 have had both positive and negative consequences. There have been ebbs and flows in congressional assertiveness and influence. When Congress has been more assertive, it has helped make foreign policy more representative of the American people, and the greater scrutiny of robust oversight has helped keep the president from amassing too much unchecked power; however, that assertiveness has also led to a diffusion of foreign policy authority that has made it easier for domestic politics and special interests to take priority over national interests, and it has made the task of achieving consensus around tough issues more difficult. When Congress has been more passive, presidents have found it easier to take assertive action; however, that passivity has come at the expense of the sustained and serious oversight that is necessary to aid and refine policy making and implementation.

These changes underscore the continuing importance of the basic principles that have been the source of a strong foreign policy throughout U.S. history. In an era of globalization and the threat of catastrophic terrorism, as in the early days of the republic, U.S. foreign policy works best when marked by strong presidential leadership, responsible congressional partnership, independent congressional oversight, and sustained dialogue and consultation. These are the fundamental and timeless building blocks for effective U.S. foreign policy.

Together, the president and Congress have achieved a lot in foreign policy in the past four decades. They have led us to victory in the Cold War and a position of unmatched international preeminence. To maintain that position, face down the threat of Islamist terrorism, and remain secure, prosperous, and free, the United States must continue to lead. That leadership requires a committed president and a responsible Congress working together to advance and oversee a foreign policy that reflects the views of the American people and serves our national interests in a time of extraordinary change and challenge.

12

Justifying War against Iraq

Louis Fisher

On October 7, 2002, President George W. Bush spoke to the nation from Cincinnati, explaining why military force might be necessary against Iraq to prevent it from using weapons of mass destruction (WMD) against the United States. That speech prompted Congress, days later, to pass the Iraq resolution authorizing military force. Congressional support helped the administration gain from the UN Security Council a resolution threatening military action unless Iraq rid itself of WMDs. Although UN inspectors spent several months in Iraq and found no prohibited weapons, military operations began on March 19, 2003. Despite concerted efforts by U.S. inspectors over the next two years, no weapons of mass destruction were discovered in Iraq.

In the Cincinnati speech, President Bush said that Iraq "possesses and produces chemical and biological weapons" and had a "growing fleet of manned and unmanned aerial vehicles" to disperse those weapons.[1] Moreover, he stated that Iraq was reconstituting its nuclear weapons program by purchasing aluminum tubes to enrich uranium for nuclear weapons. It might also, he warned, try to produce, buy, or steal highly enriched uranium.[2] Those statements and others were sharply contested at the time within the government and by the press. Both before and after the war, inspections failed to find any corroborating evidence to support the claims that Iraq had WMDs. Going to war on the basis of unsubstantiated claims damaged American credibility around the world, created distrust over subsequent statements from the administration, and cast doubt on the capacity or willingness of Congress to function as a separate branch to provide constitutional checks on presidential wars.

AN IRAQ–AL QAEDA LINK?

Immediately following the terrorist attacks of September 11, 2001, Congress passed legislation to authorize President Bush to use "all necessary and appropriate force against those nations, organizations, or persons he determines planned, authorized, committed, or aided" the 9/11 attacks.[3] It was understood that the statute, at a minimum, authorized military action against the Taliban regime and al Qaeda camps in Afghanistan. Repeatedly, the Bush administration tried to establish a connection between Iraq and al Qaeda. By demonstrating a link, it could justify war against Iraq on both moral and statutory grounds.

On September 25, 2002, President Bush claimed that Saddam Hussein and al Qaeda "work in concert."[4] A day later he stated that the Iraqi regime "has longstanding and continuing ties to terrorist organizations, and there are [al Qaeda] terrorists inside Iraq."[5] Yet members of Congress who attended classified briefings said that credible evidence of the link between Iraq and al Qaeda had not been presented.[6] There was some evidence of possible al Qaeda activity in the northeastern part of Iraq—the community of Ansar al-Islam—but that was Kurdish territory made semiautonomous by American and British flights over the no-fly zones. Saddam Hussein was not in a position to do anything about Ansar. Moreover, members of al Qaeda were present in some sixty countries. Presence alone could not justify military force.

Allies in Europe had been actively investigating al Qaeda and radical Islamic cells. Interviews with top investigative magistrates, prosecutors, police, and intelligence officials could reveal no evidence of a link between Iraq and al Qaeda. Investigative officials in Spain, France, and Germany dismissed the claim of a connection between them.[7] At a news conference on September 27, 2002, Defense Secretary Donald Rumsfeld announced that the administration had "bulletproof" evidence of Iraq's links to al Qaeda. Declassified intelligence reports, he said, showed the presence of senior members of al Qaeda in Baghdad in "recent periods." He described his claim as "factual" and "exactly accurate." When reporters sought to substantiate his statements, officials offered no details to back up the assertions. Rumsfeld, under questioning, backed off, conceding that the information was "not beyond a reasonable doubt."[8]

Bush's Cincinnati speech claimed that Iraq "has trained Al Qaeda members in bomb-making and poisons and deadly gases." Intelligence officials, however, played down the reliability of those reports.[9] After Congress voted to support the Iraq resolution a few days later, the administration promoted a story about Mohamed Atta, the principal hijacker of the 9/11 attacks, meeting with an Iraqi intelligence officer in Prague in April 2001. Czech president Vaclav Havel and the Czech intelligence service denied that there was any evidence of such a meeting. CIA director George Tenet told Congress that his agency had no information that could confirm the meeting.[10] Additional research disclosed that at the time Atta was supposedly in Prague, the FBI had evidence he was in Florida.[11]

On February 11, 2003, the month before war began, Secretary of State Colin Powell described an audiotape, believed to be by Osama bin Laden, as evidence that he was "in partnership with Iraq."[12] The tape does not reveal a partnership. Bin Laden specifically criticized "pagan regimes" and the "apostasy" practiced by socialist governments in the Middle East such as Iraq. In a military confrontation between the United States and Iraq, the tape certainly supported Iraq, but that was not evidence of a partnership. It merely meant that as much as al Qaeda detests Iraq, it detests the United States even more.

The administration began to emphasize the connection between a Jordanian terrorist, Abu Musab Zarqawi, and Iraq, but there was no direct evidence that he was a member of al Qaeda, that he functioned as part of its organization, or that he pledged allegiance to bin Laden.[13] CIA Director Tenet told Congress that Zarqawi was not under the control of Saddam Hussein and that Zarqawi and his network were "independent."[14] Reporters with access to a still-classified national intelligence report concluded that it offered a less clear link between Iraq and al Qaeda than the one claimed by President Bush and top administration officials.[15]

Throughout this period of controversy, and well after the war, Vice President Dick Cheney remained convinced of the connection between Iraq and al Qaeda. In an appearance on NBC's *Meet the Press* on September 14, 2003, he suggested that Iraq was tied to the 9/11 attacks. Previously he had told NBC that Mohamed Atta "had, in fact, met with Iraqi intelligence in Prague," but when asked whether the CIA found the claim credible, he replied, "It's credible. But, you know, I think the way to put it would be it's unconfirmed at this point."[16] If unconfirmed, why present the matter as a "fact"?

On September 17, 2003, President Bush seemed to undercut Cheney by saying he had seen no evidence that Saddam Hussein was involved in the 9/11 terrorist attacks, even if reports put Zarqawi in Baghdad.[17] Secretary Rumsfeld also said he had no reason to believe that Saddam Hussein had a hand in 9/11.[18] The dispute broke open two months later when a secret memo, put together by Undersecretary of Defense for Policy Douglas J. Feith, was leaked to the press. Prepared for the Senate Intelligence Committee, it was printed in the *Weekly Standard*, a conservative journal that strongly supported military action against Iraq. The magazine claimed that the memo demonstrated that Osama bin Laden and Saddam Hussein had an "operational relationship" from the early 1990s to 2003, including training in explosives and weapons of mass destruction.[19] The leak was controversial on several grounds: (1) it released secret information to the public, (2) Feith's small group of analysts was attempting to counter CIA evaluations, and (3) they relied on raw, unconfirmed reports by Iraqi exiles without the ability or training to judge their reliability.[20]

The staff of the 9/11 Commission dismissed the claim that there was a "collaborative relationship" between Saddam Hussein and al Qaeda. Their investigation found that Hussein had rebuffed or ignored requests from al Qaeda leaders in the 1990s for assistance and that there was "no credible evidence that Iraq and al Qaeda cooperated on attacks against the United States." The staff report concluded that the meeting between Atta and an Iraqi intelligence official in Prague never occurred. On the date of the supposed meeting, Atta was in Florida.[21] The 9/11 Commission reviewed the available evidence on Atta and concluded that it did not support the original Czech report that he met an Iraqi official in Prague in April 2001.[22] Although the commission staff found no operational ties between Iraq and al Qaeda, it did find long-running contacts between Osama bin Laden and Iran.[23]

At about the same time that the commission staff released its study, the Senate Select Committee on Intelligence issued a report on prewar intelligence assessments on Iraq. In a section on Iraq's links to terrorism, it examined five CIA reports and an alternative analysis prepared by Feith's office. The committee analyzed the information known to the intelligence community (which consists of the CIA, the National Security Agency, and thirteen other agencies) and reported that there was "no credible information that Baghdad had foreknowledge of the 11 September attacks or any other al-Qaida strike, but continues to pursue all leads."[24] The CIA "refrained from asserting the Iraqi regime and al-Qaida were cooperating on terrorist operations."[25] The committee found that the CIA reasonably concluded that "there were likely several instances of contacts between Iraq and al-Qaida throughout the 1990s, but that these contacts did not add up to an established formal relationship."[26]

In October 2004, Defense Secretary Rumsfeld said that even though there had been interactions between the Iraqi government and al Qaeda operatives, he had not seen "strong, hard evidence" linking Saddam Hussein and al Qaeda. Moreover, he doubted that Zarqawi had a formal allegiance to bin

Laden.[27] A new CIA report also raised doubts that Iraq had harbored members of Zarqawi's group.[28] As to Zarqawi's record in Iraq after the United States intervened militarily, the relationship between Zarqawi and al Qaeda appeared to be closer, but this activity occurred after the war, not before.[29]

ALUMINUM TUBES

In his Cincinnati speech, President Bush told the nation that Iraq had attempted to purchase aluminum tubes to enrich uranium as part of the process for making nuclear weapons. Appearing on CNN the previous month, on September 8, National Security Adviser Condoleezza Rice expressed no uncertainty about the relationship between the tubes and Iraq's program for making nuclear weapons: "We do know that there have been shipments . . . into Iraq, for instance, of aluminum tubes that are only suited . . . for nuclear weapons programs, centrifuge programs."[30]

However, almost a year earlier her staff had been told that the government's foremost nuclear experts doubted that the tubes were part of a nuclear weapons program. They believed that the tubes were most likely intended for small artillery rockets.[31] In October 2002, when the CIA issued its National Intelligence Estimate (NIE) on Iraq's weapons of mass destruction, the CIA and the Defense Intelligence Agency (DIA) supported the assessment that the aluminum tubes were intended for Iraq's nuclear weapons program. On the other hand, the Department of Energy's Office of Intelligence and the State Department's Bureau of Intelligence and Research (INR) believed that the tubes were intended for a conventional rocket program.[32]

In the months prior to the war, administration officials studying the issue knew that the tubes had two possible uses: to enrich uranium to produce nuclear weapons or as shells for rockets. Specialists from UN inspection teams concluded that the specifications of the tubes were consistent with tubes used for rockets. The tubes could have been modified to serve as centrifuges for enriching uranium, but the modifications would have had to be substantial. Moreover, there was no evidence that Iraq had purchased materials needed for centrifuges, including motors, metal caps, and special magnets.[33]

On January 9, 2003, Dr. Mohamed ElBaradei briefed the UN Security Council on inspections in Iraq by the International Atomic Energy Agency (IAEA). Indicating that the investigation was continuing, he said that the agency's analysis "to date indicates that the specifications of the aluminum tubes sought by Iraq in 2001 and 2002 appear to be consistent with reverse engineering of rockets. While it would be possible to modify such tubes for the manufacture of centrifuges, they are not directly suitable for it."[34] ElBaradei returned to the Security Council on January 27, explaining that IAEA inspectors had inspected "the relevant rocket production and storage sites, taken tube samples, interviewed relevant Iraqi personnel and reviewed procurement contracts and related documents." From the agency's analysis, he said "it appears that the aluminum tubes would be consistent with the purpose stated by Iraq and, unless modified, would not be suitable for manufacturing centrifuges."[35]

A day later President Bush appeared before Congress to deliver the State of the Union message. He announced that U.S. intelligence sources "tell us that [Saddam Hussein] has attempted to purchase high-strength aluminum tubes suitable for nuclear weapons production."[36] Bush did not explain, in this brief reference to the tubes, that the U.S. intelligence community was divided on the issue, that the tubes could have a legitimate use as ordinary artillery shells, and that IAEA inspectors had reached that conclusion.

On February 5, 2003, with little more than a month to go before the war, Secretary of State Colin Powell challenged ElBaradei's findings and laid out the case for military operations. In his presentation to the Security Council, he offered a number of arguments to explain why Saddam Hussein was intent on reconstituting his nuclear program:

> Saddam Hussein is determined to get his hands on a nuclear bomb. He is so determined that he has made repeated covert attempts to acquire high-specification aluminum tubes from 11 different countries, even after inspections resumed.
>
> These tubes are controlled by the Nuclear Suppliers Group precisely because they can be used as centrifuges for enriching uranium. By now, just about everyone has heard of these tubes, and we all know that there are differences of opinion; there is controversy about what these tubes are for. Most U.S. experts think they are intended to serve as rotors in centrifuges used to enrich uranium. Other experts and the Iraqis themselves argue that they are really to produce the rocket bodies for a conventional weapon, a multiple rocket launcher.
>
> Let me tell you what is not controversial about these tubes. First, all the experts who have analyzed the tubes in our possession agree that they can be adapted for centrifuge use. Second, Iraq had no business buying them for any purpose; they are banned for Iraq.[37]

Powell's case depended heavily on work done by a CIA analyst who argued that the aluminum tubes were so "overspecified" that Iraq would not waste money by using a costly alloy on a conventional rocket. The evidence for that position was strongly challenged by experts within the Department of Energy before the war.[38] When ElBaradei appeared before the UN Security Council on March 7, 2003, less than two weeks before military operations, he underscored his conclusion that the aluminum tubes did not represent evidence that Iraq was attempting to reconstitute a nuclear weapons program:

> With regard to the aluminum tubes, the I.A.E.A. has conducted a thorough investigation of Iraq's attempt to purchase large quantities of high-strength aluminum tubes. . . . Extensive field investigation and document analysis have failed to uncover any evidence that Iraq intended to use these 81-millimeter tubes for any project other than the reverse engineering of rockets. The Iraqi decisionmaking process with regard to the design of these rockets was well documented. . . .
>
> Based on available evidence, the I.A.E.A. team has concluded that Iraq's efforts to import these aluminum tubes were not likely to have been related to the manufacture of centrifuge; and moreover, that it was highly unlikely that Iraq could have achieved the considerable redesign needed to use them in a revived centrifuge program.[39]

Additional evidence to support the use of aluminum tubes for conventional rockets appeared after the war.[40] When the Senate Intelligence Committee issued its report on July 9, 2004, it analyzed the debate within the administration on whether Iraq intended to reconstitute its nuclear weapons program. It reviewed numerous intelligence reports on Iraq's effort to procure high-strength aluminum tubes and concluded that "the information available to the Intelligence Community indicated that these tubes were intended to be used for an Iraqi conventional rocket program and not a nuclear program."[41]

Appearing on an ABC news program on October 3, 2004, Condoleezza Rice was asked about her comment two years earlier that the tubes were "only suited" for nuclear weapons programs. She said at the time she was aware of the debate within the administration about the tubes: "I knew that there was a dispute. I actually didn't really know the nature of the dispute."[42] If she knew only of the debate in general and not the specific details, why go on record on September 8, 2002—a month before Congress voted on the Iraq resolution—and pretend to speak with such assurance and finality on one side of a contested, unsettled issue?[43]

YELLOWCAKE

The question of whether Iraq was trying to reconstitute its nuclear weapons raised other issues. There were reports in the press in October 2002 that Saddam Hussein had tried to buy uranium oxide (yellowcake) from a country in Africa.[44] In response to a UN Security Council resolution, Iraq produced a lengthy "declaration" on December 7 on its WMDs. On December 19, the

State Department released a "Fact Sheet" (prepared jointly with the CIA) that cited examples of "omissions in the Declaration." According to the department, the declaration "ignores efforts to procure uranium from Niger. *Why is the Iraqi regime hiding their uranium procurement?*"[45] In an op-ed piece for the *New York Times* on January 23, 2003, Condoleezza Rice called the Iraqi document a "12,200-page lie." As support for that condemnation, she said that the declaration "fails to account for or explain Iraq's efforts to get uranium from abroad."[46]

The State Department fact sheet was peculiar in many respects. The department's own intelligence agency, INR, had substantial doubts that Iraq had tried to buy uranium ore from Niger, and so did many CIA analysts. To place disputed material in a "fact sheet" and release it to the public seemed more like partisan propaganda than professional analysis. When the department issued the fact sheet, one executive official recalled, "people winced and thought, 'Why are you repeating this trash?'"[47]

In his State of the Union address in January 2003, President Bush told Congress that the "British Government has learned that Saddam Hussein recently sought significant quantities of uranium from Africa."[48] Why was Bush relying on *British* intelligence instead of American intelligence? What did the CIA think about this claim? The previous October, when President Bush prepared to give his address in Cincinnati, CIA Director George Tenet personally intervened to ask that the reference to the uranium ore be removed from the speech. The White House took it out.[49] Why did the claim reappear in the State of the Union address, and why didn't Tenet insist once again that it be stricken? In a letter to a member of Congress on April 29, 2003, the State Department disclosed that its December 19 fact sheet had been developed jointly with the CIA.[50] Had the CIA uncovered new evidence between October and December to justify this entry on the fact sheet? Apparently not. Tenet would later publicly apologize for allowing the Niger claim to appear in the State of the Union address.

The assertions by Rice and Bush were discredited on March 7, 2003, when ElBaradei told the Security Council that the key piece of evidence on Iraq seeking uranium ore from Africa was a fake. Someone had fabricated the documents. ElBaradei explained why the evidence was unreliable:

> The I.A.E.A. was able to review correspondence coming from various bodies of the government of Niger and to compare the form, format, contents and signature of that correspondence with those of the alleged procurement-related documentations. Based on thorough analysis, the I.A.E.A. has concluded, with the concurrence of outside experts, that these documents, which formed the basis for the reports of recent uranium transaction between Iraq and Niger, are in fact not

authentic. We have therefore concluded that these specific allegations were unfounded. However, we will continue to follow up any additional evidence, if it emerges, relevant to efforts by Iraq to illicitly import nuclear material.[51]

Reporters explained that whoever forged the documents "made relatively crude errors that eventually gave them away—including names and titles that did not match up with the individuals who held office at the time the letters were purportedly written."[52] A U.S. official, after reviewing the documents, remarked, "We fell for it."[53] However, the mistake was not merely an unfortunate error that occurs in any human activity. Instead, it reflected the willingness and eagerness of the administration to go public with information that was tenuous and suspect, had been flagged by the CIA director as unreliable, and depended on British rather than American intelligence.

During an appearance on NBC's *Meet the Press* on Sunday, June 8, 2003, Condoleezza Rice said she was unaware that there were doubts about Iraq's attempt to buy uranium from Niger: "Maybe somebody knew down in the bowels of the agency, but no one in our circles knew that there were doubts and suspicions that this might be a forgery."[54] Her explanation did not put the matter to rest. On July 7, the administration conceded that Bush should not have included in the State of the Union address the claim that Iraq tried to buy uranium in Africa.[55]

The role of the CIA continued to be explored. In July 2003, it was reported that the CIA in the previous September tried to persuade the British government to drop from an official intelligence paper a claim that Iraq attempted to buy uranium in Africa.[56] That would help explain why Tenet urged Bush to remove that material from the Cincinnati speech but would not account for its appearance in the State of the Union address. On July 11, 2003, Tenet took personal responsibility for the assertion being included in the State of the Union address. Without saying that he had personally read and cleared the draft speech, he said, "I am responsible for the approval process in my agency."[57] He explained that agency officials, in approving the President's address, "concurred that the text in the speech was factually correct—i.e., that the British government report said that Iraq sought uranium from Africa." Tenet went on to say that it was a mistake to clear a presidential address on that ground: "This did not rise to the level of certainty which should be required for presidential speeches, and C.I.A. should have ensured that it was removed."[58]

His explanation helped clarify part of the dispute, but it is inconceivable that Tenet would delegate to someone else in the CIA the responsibility to review and approve sixteen words in a State of the Union address. Tenet received a hard-copy draft of the speech but testified that he never read it.[59]

Senator Pat Roberts (R-KS), chairman of the Senate Intelligence Committee, said it was Tenet's job to tell Bush directly about questionable intelligence assertions and not leave it to his subordinates.[60] Especially is that so because Tenet had earlier flagged the issue and insisted that language be removed from the Cincinnati speech. Why did he step aside when the State of the Union draft circulated for comment?

The controversy deepened when Tenet explained that the White House had taken the initiative in including the uranium material in the president's address: "Portions of the State of the Union speech draft came to the C.I.A. for comment shortly before the speech was given."[61] The question was now, who in the administration drafted the speech? It was only a matter of time before the finger pointed in the direction of the National Security Council. The press learned that Tenet had personally spoken to Stephen J. Hadley, the deputy national security adviser, in early October 2002 and warned against Bush making reference in his Cincinnati speech to Iraq trying to buy uranium ore from Niger.[62]

Rumsfeld and Rice added new life to the story. They claimed on national television that Bush's State of the Union address was accurate: the British had indeed referred to Iraqi interest in acquiring uranium from Africa. On *Fox News Sunday*, Rice said that Bush's statement "was indeed accurate. The British government did say that." Rumsfeld, on *Meet the Press*, remarked that "it turns out that it's technically correct what the president said, that the U.K. does—did say that—and still says that. They haven't changed their mind, the United Kingdom intelligence people."[63] If the statement was correct, why did the White House find it necessary to apologize for including the material in the State of the Union speech, and why did Tenet decide to take the blame?

Hoping to finally quell the controversy, the White House held several briefings for reporters. On July 18, a "senior administration official" discussed the ninety-page National Intelligence Estimate entitled "Iraq's Continuing Programs for Weapons of Mass Destruction." The reporters received a declassified version. The official referred to a section that described how Iraq had been trying to procure uranium ore and yellowcake. A reporter asked how Rice and other members of the National Security Council could be unaware that some agencies in the U.S. intelligence community objected to the yellowcake claim. The official explained that they "did not read footnotes in a 90-page document," adding that the "President of the United States is not a fact-checker."[64] The reporters found it disquieting to learn that Rice and her NSC staff did not read footnotes in a crucial intelligence report. Moreover, looking at the declassified report on their laps, they could see that the disagreement within the Intelligence Community was not buried in footnotes.

The reservations by the State Department were flagged in the very first paragraph of the opening section on key judgments.[65]

Additional apologies were soon on their way. On July 22, Stephen Hadley announced that the CIA had sent two memos to the White House on October 5 and 6, 2002, voicing doubts about Iraq trying to buy nuclear material in Africa. The memos went to Hadley and Bush's chief speechwriter, Michael Gerson. Hadley now took the blame for allowing the material to be placed in the State of the Union address.[66] His statement threw a shadow over Rice's earlier explanation that questions about the Niger story might have been raised "down in the bowels of the agency," but "no one in our circles" knew about it. The information reached at least to the level of her deputy. A week after Hadley's statement, Bush said he took "personal responsibility for everything I say."[67] Rice added that she felt "personal responsibility."[68] The initial effort to pin the blame on the CIA had obviously backfired.

On July 9, 2004, the Senate Intelligence Committee released its analysis of intelligence assessments about Iraq's WMDs. In the report's section on Niger, the committee concluded that up to October 2002, "it was reasonable for analysts to assess that Iraq may have been seeking uranium from Africa" based on CIA reporting "and other available intelligence."[69] However, the language in the October 2002 NIE that "Iraq also began vigorously trying to procure uranium ore and yellowcake" was inappropriate because it "overstated what the Intelligence Community knew about Iraq's possible procurement attempts."[70] Moreover, even after obtaining the documents and being alerted by the State Department about problems, CIA and DIA analysts "did not examine them carefully enough to see the obvious problems with the documents."[71] Finally, Tenet "should have taken the time to read the State of the Union [draft] speech and fact check it himself."[72]

CHEMICAL AND BIOLOGICAL WEAPONS

In his Cincinnati speech, President Bush claimed that Iraq "possesses and produces chemical and biological weapons." His address relied on a CIA report of October 2002. On the first page, under "Key Judgments," the second sentence rang out: "Baghdad has chemical and biological weapons as well as missiles with ranges in excess of UN restrictions."[73] Note the dramatic language. Baghdad *has*, not Baghdad "had" or "might have." Baghdad possesses chemical and biological *weapons*, not merely programs.

The CIA released the report at a critical time, when members of Congress were about to consider legislation to authorize military operations against Iraq. Placing the claim that Baghdad has chemical and biological weapons in the opening paragraph, under key judgments, maximized the impact on President Bush and Congress. Policy makers were likely to read the opening paragraph of a report, not necessarily the rest. Yet the detailed analytical section in the body of the report contradicted the flat and sweeping assertion in the key-judgments section. The statements in the analytical section were much more cautious and qualified:

- "Iraq has the ability to produce chemical warfare (CW) agents within its chemical industry."
- "Iraq probably has concealed precursors, production equipment, documentation, and other items necessary for continuing its CW effort."
- "Baghdad continues to rebuild and expand dual-use infrastructure that it could divert quickly to CW production."
- "Iraq has the capability to convert quickly legitimate vaccine and biopesticide plants to biological warfare (BW) production and already may have done so."[74]

None of the statements in the analytical section supported the striking claim in the first paragraph of the CIA report or in Bush's statement to the nation. The Senate Intelligence Committee later reviewed the process used by the intelligence community to prepare the October 2002 NIE. Analysts told the committee that the compressed time period available to write the report led to problems with the key-judgments section, so that it did not accurately reflect what was in the body of the report.[75] The committee agreed that more time would have given analysts an opportunity to correct some minor inaccuracies, but it did not believe "that any of the fundamental analytical flaws contained in the NIE were the result of the limited time available to the Intelligence Community to complete the Estimate."[76] That observation is quite extraordinary. Even with additional time the NIE would have contained basic analytical errors. The flaws revealed deeper problems within the intelligence community.

Three days after publication of the classified NIE, the CIA produced an unclassified version that was released as a "white paper" on Iraqi WMDs. The committee noted that the key judgments were "almost identical in layout and substance in both papers," although the key judgments in the unclassified papers were "missing many of the caveats and some references to alternative agency views that were used in the classified NIE."[77] Caveats such as "we judge" or "we assess" were changed in the unclassified paper to present statements of fact rather than assessment.[78] By eliminating caveats from the unclassified white paper, the intelligence community "misrepresented their judgments to the public which did not have access to the classified National

Intelligence Estimate containing the more carefully worded assessments."[79] What the committee report underscores is that a "key judgment" is just that: a *judgment* and not necessarily a fact.

After evaluating the October 2002 NIE, the committee concluded that the statement in the key-judgment section that Iraq "has" chemical weapons "overstated both what was known about Iraq's chemical weapons holdings and what intelligence analysts judged about Iraq's chemical weapons holdings."[80] The committee also said that the key judgment that "Baghdad has biological weapons" overstated what was known about Iraq's biological weapons holdings.[81] Statements about Iraq's biological weapons came from a source called "Curve Ball," who, in addition to having a drinking problem, was an Iraqi design engineer but not a biological weapons expert or a life science expert.[82] Information about the biological weapons program also came from an Iraqi exile whom some intelligence analysts regarded as unreliable and a fabricator.[83]

When Secretary Powell appeared before the UN Security Council on February 5, 2003, to build support for war against Iraq, he said that "every statement I make today is backed up by sources, solid sources. These are not assertions. What we're giving you are facts and conclusions based on solid intelligence."[84] He noted that a teaspoon of dry anthrax shut down the Senate in the fall of 2001, forcing several hundred people to undergo emergency medical treatment. Two postal workers died. He reported that although Iraq had declared 8,500 liters of anthrax, UN inspectors estimated that it could have produced 25,000 liters. He referred to the existence of mobile production facilities used to make biological agents (discussed in the next section) capable of producing anthrax and botulinum toxin. Other potential agents, he said, included aflatoxin and ricin. He pointed out that Iraq had produced and stockpiled such chemical weapons as mustard and nerve gas.

Initially, Powell's presentation received a favorable review in many American newspapers.[85] France and key allies were less impressed.[86] A year after his presentation, following the efforts of U.S. inspection teams to scour Iraq and find WMDs, the assessments of Powell's performance were uniformly critical. Careful and methodical inspections, supervised by David Kay and Charles A. Duelfer, uncovered no weapons of mass destruction. What Powell presented were not facts but assertions, and the assertions were not grounded on solid intelligence. Frequently he depended on sources who turned out to be Iraqi exiles who offered inaccurate information. He relied heavily on the NIE of October 2002, which suffered from the same problem.[87] The Senate Intelligence Committee concluded that much of the information provided or cleared by the CIA to be included in Powell's speech to the UN "was overstated, misleading, or incorrect."[88] Some of the information that the CIA gave to Powell, which he decided not to use, was also "incorrect" and "should never have been provided for use in a public speech."[89] The committee faulted the CIA for failing to alert Powell to problems about Iraq's "alleged mobile biological weapons program."[90]

MOBILE LABS

The State Department "Fact Sheet" of December 19, 2002, challenged Iraq's declaration to the UN Security Council on several grounds, including what the department called "Mobile Biological Weapon Agent Facilities." The declaration contained no information about these mobile labs. The department asked: *"What is the Iraqi regime trying to hide about their mobile biological weapon facilities?"* President Bush, in his State of the Union address of January 28, 2003, stated, "From three Iraqi defectors we know that Iraq, in the late 1990s, had several mobile biological weapons labs. They are designed to produce germ warfare agents and can be moved from place to place to evade inspectors. Saddam Hussein has not disclosed these facilities. He's given no evidence that he has destroyed them."

Powell spent considerable time in discussing these mobile labs in his speech to the UN Security Council on February 5, 2003. "One of the most worrisome things," he said, "that emerges from the thick intelligence file we have on Iraq's biological weapons is the existence of mobile production facilities used to make biological agents. Let me take you inside that intelligence file and share with you what we know from eyewitness accounts. We have firsthand descriptions of biological weapons factories on wheels and on rails. The trucks and train cars are easily moved and are designed to evade detection by inspectors."

According to Powell, the mobile lab program began in the mid-1990s and UN inspectors at that time "only had vague hints" of the program. "Confirmation," he said, came from "an eyewitness, an Iraqi chemical engineer who supervised one of these facilities" and was present during biological agent production runs. Powell said this engineer was at the site when an accident occurred in 1998, killing twelve technicians from exposure to biological agents. Powell identified a second source, an Iraqi civil engineer "in a position to know the details of the program." A third source, "also in a position to know," reported that Iraq in the summer of 2002 had manufactured mobile production systems mounted on road trailer units and on railcars. A fourth source "confirmed that Iraq has mobile biological research laboratories."[91] Powell showed the Security Council drawings of these "Factories on Wheels and on Rails."

Hans Blix, appearing before the Security Council on March 3, made reference to intelligence authorities who "have claimed that weapons of mass destruction are moved around Iraq by trucks; in particular, that there are mobile production units for biological weapons." He acknowledged that food-testing mobile labs and mobile workshops "have been seen, as well as large containers with seed-processing equipment." Yet he and his inspectors found no evidence that Iraq had engaged in prohibited activities or used these labs as part of a program of making biological weapons.[92]

In May 2003, the United States reported the recovery of a suspected mobile biological weapons lab in northern Iraq. A senior administration official said that the truck resembled one of the mobile labs that Powell had described in his speech to the Security Council.[93] On May 28, the CIA and the DIA issued a joint report, stating that coalition forces "have uncovered the strongest evidence to date that Iraq was hiding a biological warfare program."[94] This shrill first sentence, similar to other intelligence studies, was not supported by the body of evidence presented. The report conceded that some of the features of the labs "are consistent with both bioproduction [of BW agents] and hydrogen production" for artillery weather balloons.[95] The screaming first sentence was followed by sections in the report that used such caveats as "probably," "possibly," "apparently," "suggesting," and "reportedly."

On May 30, from Poland, President Bush referred to the discovery of the trailers as proof of mobile biological weapons labs: "We found the weapons of mass destruction. We found biological laboratories." Promising to find more weapons "as time goes on," he criticized those "who say we haven't found the banned manufacturing devices or banned weapons, they're wrong. We found them."[96] The discovery gave Bush what seemed to be evidence to support the primary reason for going to war: weapons of mass destruction. However, the CIA/DIA report was far from definitive, and no trace of biological agents had yet been detected in the trailers.[97]

American and British intelligence analysts began to dispute the claim that the trailers were used for making deadly germs. Other purposes, more benign, seemed more likely. Iraqi scientists said that the trailers were used to produce hydrogen for weather balloons.[98] The State Department's intelligence division said it was premature to conclude that the trailers were evidence of an Iraqi biological weapons program. It was learned that the CIA and the DIA did not consult with other intelligence agencies before issuing the report, which was prepared for the White House.[99] Over time, engineering experts from the DIA came to believe that the most likely use for the trailers was to produce hydrogen for weather balloons and not biological weapons.[100]

Secretary Powell eventually conceded that the trailers were not mobile biological labs. On April 2, 2004, he blamed the CIA for his misconception and for relying on faulty sources.[101] In May, he spoke on national television about his regret in telling the Security Council that Iraq had mobile biological labs. He now felt that the CIA had been deliberately misled about the evidence. He suggested that the Iraqi engineer who provided the information had resorted to fabrication.[102] Powell sought answers from the CIA to explain how the various sources could be not only inaccurate and wrong but also deliberately misleading. The DIA had labeled one of the sources as a fabricator, but Powell was never warned about those concerns.[103]

In October 2004, U.S. inspector Charles Duelfer said that the trailers could not have been used for a biological weapons program and that the manufacturers of the trailers "almost certainly designed and built the equipment exclusively for the generation of hydrogen."[104] The Senate Intelligence Committee concluded that the statement in the NIE of October 2002 that Iraq "has mobile transportable facilities for producing bacterial and toxin biological weapons agents," overstated what the intelligence reporting suggested and "did not accurately convey to readers the uncertainties behind the source reporting."[105]

UNMANNED AERIAL VEHICLES

The NIE of October 2002 included a section on Iraq's unmanned aerial vehicle (UAV) program. It claimed that Iraq was "continuing to develop other platforms which most analysts believe probably are intended for delivering biological warfare agents." The NIE discussed Iraqi efforts after the Gulf War of 1991 to convert a MiG-21 into a UAV to carry spray tanks capable of dispensing chemical or biological agents. The report stated that Iraq had produced modified drop tanks able to disperse biological or chemical agents effectively. Before the Gulf War, Iraq had successfully experimented with aircraft-mounted spray tanks capable of releasing up to two thousand liters of an anthrax simulant over a target area.[106]

President Bush's Cincinnati speech warned that Iraq "has a growing fleet of manned and unmanned aerial vehicles that could be used to disperse chemical or biological weapons across broad areas." He expressed concern that Iraq was exploring ways of using these UAVs "for missions targeting the United States."[107] Two months later the State Department "Fact Sheet" drew attention to the UAVs. Although Iraq had denied any connection between its UAV program and chemical or biological dispersal, the department said that Iraq had admitted in 1995 that a MiG-21 remote-piloted vehicle was able to carry a biological weapon spray system. The department posed this question: "*Why do they deny what they have already admitted? Why has the Iraqi regime acquired the range and auto-flight capabilities to spray biological weapons?*"[108]

At his February 5, 2003, appearance before the UN Security Council, Secretary Powell claimed that Iraq had developed "ways to disperse lethal biological agents widely, indiscriminately, into the water supply, into the air." By modifying the aerial fuel tanks of Mirage jets, it could spray two thousand liters of simulated anthrax from the jet. According to Powell, an Iraqi military officer told UN inspectors in 1995 that Iraq intended to mount the spray tanks onto a MiG-21 converted into an unmanned aerial vehicle. This UAV would "constitute an ideal method for launching a terrorist attack using biological weapons."

Hans Blix and his inspectors were aware of the UAVs, or drones, but did not regard the vehicles as a likely method of distributing biological agents.[109] On March 12, 2003, about a week before the start of the war, the press had an opportunity to see one of the drones. Reporters thought it looked "more like something out of the Rube Goldberg museum of aeronautical design than anything that could threaten Iraq's foes." The plane's two engines, each about the size of a whiskey bottle, were attached to tiny wooden propellers, "looking about powerful enough to drive a Weed Whacker." Its wings and twinned tail fins were made of wood and stretched fabric. In early test flights, the vehicle ventured no further than two miles from the airfield. Iraqi officers said that the craft had been designed for reconnaissance, jamming, and aerial photography.[110]

In September 2004, the UN's chief weapons inspector concluded that there was no evidence that Iraq ever developed UAVs capable of dispersing chemical and biological agents. The UN report was consistent with earlier findings by U.S. Air Force intelligence analysts and the Pentagon's Missile Defense Agency that the drones were being developed for reconnaissance, not as part of a WMD program.[111] In its report of July 9, 2004, the Senate Intelligence Committee concluded that the assessment of the intelligence community in the key-judgments section of the NIE, that Iraq was developing a UAV "probably" intended to deliver biological warfare agents, "overstated both what was known about the mission of Iraq's small UAVs and what intelligence analysts judged about the likely mission of Iraq's small UAVs." It agreed with an air force footnote that regarded biological weapons delivery as a possible, but unlikely, mission. That assessment "more accurately reflected the body of intelligence reporting."[112] Other than the air force's dissenting footnote, the intelligence community "failed to discuss possible conventional missions" for Iraq's UAVs.[113] Further, the committee said that intelligence provided to it did not support the intelligence community's assessment that Iraq's procurement of U.S.-specific mapping software for the UAV "strongly suggests that Iraq is investigating the use of these UAVs for missions targeting the United States."[114]

RESTORING DEMOCRATIC CHECKS

The failure to find weapons of mass destruction in Iraq prompted many analysts to wonder how the Bush administration could have issued so many dire threats on the basis of so little evidence. Similar concerns were leveled at Congress. Why were members of Congress and their committees unable to see through the thinness of claims made by executive officials and demand persuasive evidence? Why was it thought necessary to vote on the Iraq resolution before the November 2002 elections instead of having inspectors enter the country and complete the search for WMDs?

Kenneth Pollack, who served as a military analyst with the CIA and the National Security Council, wrote a book one year before the war, arguing that military force would be needed to prevent Saddam Hussein from acquiring a functioning nuclear weapon.[115] When inspectors discovered no WMDs in Iraq, he published an article early in 2004 to address the evident intelligence failures. He recalls participating in a late spring 2002 meeting about the Iraqi threat. In attendance were nearly twenty former inspectors from the UN Special Commission (UNSCOM), which had been established in 1991 to oversee the elimination of WMDs from Iraq. A senior person put this question to the group: "Did anyone in the room doubt that Iraq was currently operating a secret centrifuge plant?" Pollack notes: "No one did."[116]

Obviously the individual asked a loaded question. It invited a false and misleading consensus because it required nothing in the way of evidence or even reasonable information. The question could have been put this way: "Did anyone in the room *know* that Iraq was operating a centrifuge plant?" Deliberating in the manner described by Pollack allows national security policy to be driven by assertions and claims, with the burden placed on skeptics to disprove something that no one ever had to prove. Solid or even reliable information is unnecessary. The opportunity for miscalculations and error is limitless, especially when assertions are presented in a climate of fear and apprehension.

The risk of acting on erroneous intelligence is especially grave now that the United States has made explicit what has always been implicit: the legitimacy of preemptive war. Making matters more grave is the decision by President Bush to take it to the next step: preventive war. He endorses the right to act not merely in response to an imminent threat but even to an *emerging* threat.[117] The record of going to war against Iraq underscores how national security can go wrong when intelligence is handled so irresponsibly. The heedless manner of justifying war most likely contributed to the failure to anticipate and plan for the widespread looting, violence, and insurgency that followed the quick military victory.

On June 18, 2003, Deputy Defense Secretary Paul Wolfowitz appeared before the House Armed Services Committee to hear Representative Gene Taylor (D-MS) ask whether the intelligence about the threat from Iraq's weapons was wrong. Taylor said he voted for the Iraq Resolution because of the administration's warning that Iraq had weapons of mass destruction. He told Wolfowitz: "A person is only as good as his word. This nation is only as good as its word. And if that's the reason why we did it—and I voted for it—then we need some clarification here." Wolfowitz replied: "If there's a problem with intelligence . . . it doesn't mean that anybody misled anybody. It means that intelligence is an art and not a science."[118]

That modest tone was wholly absent from the Bush administration when it justified war against Iraq. It consistently treated intelligence as a science, yielding certitude, not doubt or equivocation. The State Department issued a "Fact Sheet," not an assertion sheet. Powell told the UN Security Council on February 5, 2003, that he was presenting "not assertions" but "facts and conclusions based on solid intelligence." The position by the Bush administration was not merely that Iraq had weapons of mass destruction in the past and had used them against Iraqi citizens. Bush, Cheney, Rumsfeld, and other top administration officials insisted that Iraq *currently* had WMDs, particularly chemical and biological weapons, and had the capacity to deliver them. According to their analysis, the threat was imminent, not in the future.

In initiating a military action to oust Saddam Hussein, the United States would be creating a power vacuum. Without a government in place, civil disorder and violence were easily predictable. Yet even strong supporters of the administration concede that little thought had been given to securing the country and creating conditions that would allow for reconstruction, economic activity, and elections.[119]

In an effort to understand how military planners had so misjudged the war, a reporter asked Douglas Feith whether the administration could have done a better job of preparing for the occupation phase. Feith replied: "We don't exactly deal in 'expectations.' Expectations are too close to 'predictions.' We're not comfortable with predictions." Rumsfeld, he said, was especially sensitive to the limits of future knowledge. He called Rumsfeld "death to predictions" because his "big strategic theme is uncertainty."[120]

Uncertainty is part of the human condition, but no one in the corporate world, academic life, the scientific community, government, or any other sector would have a chance of success without having expectations and making predictions. Otherwise, people would simply stumble along and absorb whatever blows and mortifications came their way. Moreover, it is remarkable for Feith to state that the administration lacked expectations and was loath to make predictions. They said that Iraq had weapons of mass destruction. They thought, and repeatedly said, that Iraqis would treat U.S. troops not as occupiers but as liberators.

Multiple problems experienced during the occupation of Iraq led many in the media to do some soul-searching about the performance of reporters and editors. The *New York Times* admitted that it should "have been challenging reporters and pressing for more skepticism" instead of trying to rush scoops into the paper. The dependence on Iraqi defectors as sources of information was "not always weighed against their strong desire to have Saddam Hussein ousted." Articles supportive of the administration's claims garnered front-page attention, while follow-up articles questioning the original story were placed deep in the paper. Claims by Iraqi defectors were often taken at face value without attempting to verify their accounts.[121] Reporters who want their story on page one learn that the "sound of trumpets" can be more effective than a balanced, analytical piece.[122] The *Washington Post* found fault with its coverage of the case made for war, as did other publications.[123]

In the age of terrorism after 9/11, Congress and the public must have trust and confidence in the integrity and competence of executive officials. It is crucial for intelligence agencies to present information that is reliable and capable of producing sound policy. If trust is absent, so is popular control. Congress needs to discharge its institutional duties and supply needed checks and balances. The press needs to do a better job of scrutinizing governmental assertions. Given the record of the Iraq war, other countries will not take seriously the claim by the United States that it operates as a democratic republic and has both the capacity and the credibility to spread democracy abroad.

NOTES

1. *Weekly Compilation of Presidential Documents* 38:1716–17.
2. *Weekly Compilation of Presidential Documents* 38:1718.
3. 115 Stat. 224 (2001).
4. *Weekly Compilation of Presidential Documents* 38:1619.
5. *Weekly Compilation of Presidential Documents* 38:1625.
6. Karen De Young, "Unwanted Debate on Iraq–Al Qaeda Links Revived," *Washington Post*, September 27, 2002, A19.

7. Sebastian Rotella, "Allies Find No Links between Iraq, Al Qaeda," *Los Angeles Times*, November 4, 2002, A1.

8. Eric Schmitt, "Rumsfeld Says U.S. Has 'Bulletproof' Evidence of Iraq's Links to al Qaeda," *New York Times*, September 28, 2002, A8.

9. Karen De Young, "Bush Cites Urgent Iraqi Threat," *Washington Post*, October 8, 2002, A21.

10. James Risen, "Prague Discounts an Iraqi Meeting," *New York Times*, October 21, 2002, A1; James Risen, "How Politics and Rivalries Fed Suspicions of a Meeting," *New York Times*, October 21, 2002, A9; Peter S. Green, "Havel Denies Telephoning U.S. on Iraq Meeting," *New York Times*, October 23, 2002, A11.

11. James Risen, "No Evidence of Meeting with Iraqi," *New York Times*, June 17, 2004, A14.

12. Dan Eggen and Susan Schmidt, "Bin Laden Calls Iraqis to Arms," *Washington Post*, February 12, 2003, A1, A14; David Johnston, "Top U.S. Officials Press Case Linking Iraq to Al Qaeda," *New York Times*, February 12, 2003, A1, A16.

13. Walter Pincus, "U.S. Effort to Link Terrorists to Iraq Focuses on Jordanian," *Washington Post*, February 5, 2003, A17; Don Van Natta Jr. and David Johnston, "A Terror Lieutenant with a Deadly Past," *New York Times*, February 10, 2003, A1.

14. Dana Priest and Walter Pincus, "Bin Laden–Hussein Link Hazy," *Washington Post*, February 13, 2003, A20.

15. Walter Pincus, "Report Cast Doubt on Iraq–Al Qaeda Connection," *Washington Post*, June 22, 2003, A1.

16. Dana Priest and Glenn Kessler, "Iraq, 9/11 Still Linked by Cheney," *Washington Post*, September 29, 2003, A1, A15.

17. David E. Sanger, "Bush Reports No Evidence of Hussein Tie to 9/11," *New York Times*, September 18, 2003, A18; Dana Milbank, "Bush Disavows Hussein–Sept. 11 Link," *Washington Post*, September 18, 2003, A18; *Weekly Compilation of Presidential Documents* 38:1238.

18. "Hussein 9/11 Role Doubted," *Washington Post*, September 17, 2003, A28.

19. Stephen F. Hayes, "Case Closed: The U.S. Government's Secret Memo Detailing Cooperation between Saddam Hussein and Osama bin Laden," *Weekly Standard*, November 24, 2003, 20.

20. Walter Pincus, "CIA Seeks Probe of Iraq–Al Qaeda Memo Leak," *Washington Post*, November 18, 2003, A18; Walter Pincus, "Memo Exacerbates Defense-CIA Strains," *Washington Post*, November 20, 2003, A34; Douglas Jehl, "More Proof of Iraq-Qaeda Link or Not?" *New York Times*, November 20, 2003, A14.

21. Philip Shenon and Christopher Marquis, "Challenges Bush: A Chilling Chronology Rewrites the History of the Attacks," *New York Times*, June 17, 2004, A1, A15; Walter Pincus and Dana Milbank, "Al Qaeda–Hussein Link Is Dismissed," *Washington Post*, June 17, 2004, A1.

22. *The 9/11 Commission Report* (New York: W.W. Norton, 2004), 228–29.

23. Dan Eggen, "9/11 Panel Links Al Qaeda, Iran," *Washington Post*, June 26, 2004, A12.

24. *U.S. Intelligence Community's Prewar Intelligence Assessments on Iraq*, Report of the Senate Committee on Intelligence, S. Report 108-301, 108th Cong., 2d Sess. (2004), p. 322 (hereafter Senate Intelligence Report).

25. Senate Intelligence Report, 338.

26. Senate Intelligence Report, 346.

27. Thom Shanker, "Rumsfeld Sees Lack of Proof for Qaeda-Hussein Link," *New York Times*, October 5, 2004, A10.

28. Douglas Jehl, "A New C.I.A. Report Casts Doubt on a Key Terrorist's Tie to Iraq," *New York Times*, October 6, 2004, A12.

29. Walter Pincus, "Zarqawi Is Said to Swear Allegiance to Bin Laden," *Washington Post*, October 19, 2004, A16.

30. *New York Times*, October 3, 2004, 17.

31. "How White House Embraced Suspect Iraq Arms Intelligence," *New York Times*, October 3, 2004, 1.

32. Senate Intelligence Report, 95.

33. Michael R. Gordon, "Agency Challenges Evidence against Iraq Cited by Bush," *New York Times*, January 10, 2003, A10; Joby Warrick, "U.S. Claim on Iraqi Nuclear Program Is Called into Question," *Washington Post*, January 24, 2003, A1.

34. "Report on Nuclear Quest: 'Clarification' Is Needed," *New York Times*, January 10, 2003, A10.

35. "Nuclear Inspection Chief Reports Finding No New Weapons," *New York Times*, January 28, 2003, A11.

36. *Weekly Compilation of Presidential Documents* 39:115.

37. "Powell's Address, Presenting 'Deeply Troubling' Evidence on Iraq," *New York Times*, February 6, 2003, A15–16.

38. Senate Intelligence Report, 88–90.

39. Transcript of ElBaradei's remarks appear in the *New York Times*, March 8, 2003, A8.

40. Barton Gellman and Walter Pincus, "Depiction of Threat Outgrew Supporting Evidence," *Washington Post*, August 10, 2003, A1.

41. Senate Intelligence Report, 131.

42. Glenn Kessler, "Rice: Iraqi Nuclear Plans Unclear," *Washington Post*, October 4, 2004, A18. See also Jeff Gerth, "Rice Defends Going to War Despite Dispute about Iraqi Weapons," *New York Times*, October 4, 2004, A10.

43. For further analysis of the aluminum tubes question, see John Prados, *Hoodwinked: The Documents That Reveal How Bush Sold Us a War* (New York: New Press, 2004), 93–104.

44. Walter Pincus, "For Iraq Inspectors, 'Yellow Cake' and Other Quarries," *Washington Post*, October 10, 2002, A17.

45. U.S. Department of State, "Illustrative Examples of Omissions From the Iraqi Declaration to the United Nations Security Council," Fact Sheet, December 19, 2002 (emphasis in original).

46. Condoleezza Rice, "Why We Know Iraq Is Lying," *New York Times*, January 23, 2003, A27.

47. Dana Priest and Karen De Young, "CIA Questioned Documents Linking Iraq, Uranium Ore," *Washington Post*, March 22, 2003, A30.

48. *Weekly Compilation of Presidential Documents* 39:115.

49. David E. Sanger and James Risen, "C.I.A. Chief Takes Blame in Assertion on Iraqi Uranium," *New York Times*, July 12, 2003, A1, A5; Walter Pincus and Mike Allen, "CIA

Got Uranium Reference Cut in Oct.," July 13, 2003, A1. For details on the CIA's involvement with various drafts of the Cincinnati speech, see Senate Intelligence Report, 55–57.

50. Letter from Paul V. Kelly, assistant secretary of legislative affairs, U.S. Department of State, to Representative Henry A. Waxman, April 29, 2003, p. 1.

51. Transcript of ElBaradei's remarks appears in the *New York Times*, March 8, 2003, A8.

52. Joby Warrick, "Some Evidence on Iraq Called Fake," *New York Times*, March 8, 2003, A1, A18. Several anomalies undercut the authenticity of the documents. For example, a letter, allegedly signed by the foreign minister of Niger on October 10, 2000, bears the signature of Mr. Allele Elhadj Habibou, who was foreign minister in 1988–1989; letter of June 20, 2003, from Piet de Klerk, director, Office of External Relation and Policy Co-ordination, IAEA, to Rep. Henry A. Waxman.

53. Warrick, "Some Evidence on Iraq Called Fake," A18.

54. Walter Pincus, "CIA Says It Cabled Key Data to White House," *Washington Post*, June 13, 2003, A16.

55. Walter Pincus, "White House Backs off Claim on Iraqi Buy," July 8, 2003, A1; David E. Sanger, "Bush Claim on Iraq Had Flawed Origin, White House Says," *New York Times*, July 8, 2003, A1.

56. Walter Pincus, "CIA Asked Britain to Drop Iraq Claim," *Washington Post*, July 11, 2003, A1.

57. David E. Sanger and James Risen, "C.I.A. Chief Takes Blame in Assertion on Iraqi Uranium," *New York Times*, July 12, 2003, A1, A5.

58. Sanger and Risen, "C.I.A. Chief Takes Blame," A5.

59. Senate Intelligence Report, 64.

60. Walter Pincus and Dana Milbank, "Bush, Rice Blame CIA for Iraq Error," *Washington Post*, July 12, 2003, A12.

61. Sanger and Risen, "C.I.A. Chief Takes Blame," A5.

62. Richard W. Stevenson, "Bush Declares His Faith in Tenet and C.I.A.," *New York Times*, July 13, 2003, 1.

63. James Risen, "Bush Aides Now Say Claim on Uranium Was Accurate," *New York Times*, July 14, 2003, A7.

64. "Senior Administration Official Holds Background Briefing on Weapons of Mass Destruction in Iraq, as Released by the White House," July 18, 2003, 10, 12; www.fas.org/irp/news/2003/07/wh071803.html.

65. "Senior Administration Official Holds Background Briefing," 16. See www.fas.org/irp/cia/product/iraq-wmd.html.

66. Dana Milbank and Walter Pincus, "Bush Aides Disclose Warnings from CIA," *Washington Post*, July 23, 2003, A1.

67. Mike Allen and Dana Milbank, "Bush Takes Responsibility for Iraq Claim," *Washington Post*, July 31, 2003, A1.

68. Richard W. Stevenson, "President Denies He Oversold Case for War with Iraq," *New York Times*, July 31, 2003, A11.

69. Senate Intelligence Report, 72.

70. Senate Intelligence Report, 75.

71. Senate Intelligence Report, 77.

72. Senate Intelligence Report, 81. For background on the Niger story, see Prados, *Hoodwinked*, 163–74, 186–98.

73. Central Intelligence Agency, "Iraq's Weapons of Mass Destruction Programs," October 2002, 1.

74. CIA, "Iraq's Weapons of Mass Destruction Programs," 8, 10, 13.

75. Senate Intelligence Report, 300.

76. Senate Intelligence Report, 302.

77. Senate Intelligence Report, 286.

78. Senate Intelligence Report, 286.

79. Senate Intelligence Report, 295.

80. Senate Intelligence Report, 211.

81. Senate Intelligence Report, 188.

82. Senate Intelligence Report, 154–56.

83. Senate Intelligence Report, 160–61.

84. Transcript as printed in *New York Times*, February 6, 2003, A14.

85. "The Case against Iraq," *New York Times*, February 6, 2003, A34; William Safire, "'Irrefutable and Undeniable,'" *New York Times*, February 6, 2003, A35.

86. Keith B. Richburg, "Key Allies Not Won Over by Powell," *Washington Post*, February 7, 2003, A1; Julia Preston, "U.N. Envoys Said to Differ Sharply in Reaction to Powell Speech," February 7, 2003, A10; "Powell's Performance Earns Mixed Reviews," *New York Times*, February 7, 2003, A10; Sydney J. Freedberg Jr. and Corine Hegland, "The World Reacts to Powell's Case," *National Journal*, February 8, 2003, 440.

87. Douglas Jehl and David E. Sanger, "Powell's Case, a Year Later: Gaps in Picture of Iraq Arms," *New York Times*, February 1, 2004, 1; Glenn Kessler and Walter Pincus, "A Flawed Argument in the Case for War," *Washington Post*, February 1, 2004, A1.

88. Senate Intelligence Report, 253.

89. Senate Intelligence Report, 254.

90. Senate Intelligence Report, 255.

91. Transcript printed in *New York Times*, February 6, 2003, A15.

92. Transcript printed in *New York Times*, March 8, 2003, A8.

93. Walter Pincus and Michael Dobbs, "Suspected Bioweapon Mobile Lab Recovered," *Washington Post*, May 7, 2003, A1; Sabrina Tavernise, "A Suspected Weapons Lab Is Found in Northern Iraq," *New York Times*, May 10, 2003, A9.

94. Central Intelligence Agency and Defense Intelligence Agency, "Iraqi Mobile Biological Warfare Agent Production Plants," May 28, 2003, 1.

95. CIA and DIA, "Iraqi Plants," 5.

96. *Weekly Compilation of Presidential Documents* 39:690; Mike Allen, "Bush: 'We Found' Banned Weapons," *Washington Post*, May 31, 2003, 1.

97. "The Bioweapons Enigma," *New York Times* editorial, June 1, 2003, WK12. See also Dana Milbank, "Bush Remarks Confirm Shift in Justification for War," *Washington Post*, June 1, 2003, A18.

98. Judith Miller and William J. Broad, "Some Analysts of Iraq Trailers Reject Germ Use," *New York Times*, June 7, 2003, A1.

99. Douglas Jehl, "Agency Disputes C.I.A. View on Trailers as Weapons Labs," *New York Times*, June 26, 2003, A1.

100. Douglas Jehl, "Iraqi Trailers Said to Make Hydrogen, Not Biological Arms," *New York Times*, August 9, 2003, A1.

101. Glenn Kessler, "Powell Expresses Doubts about Basis for Iraqi Weapons Claim,"

Washington Post, April 3, 2004, A19; Christopher Marquis, "Powell Blames C.I.A. for Error on Iraq Mobile Labs," *New York Times*, April 3, 2004, A5.

102. David E. Sanger, "Powell Says C.I.A. Was Misled about Weapons," *New York Times*, May 17, 2004, A8.

103. Douglas Jehl, "Powell Presses C.I.A. on Faulty Intelligence on Iraq Arms," *New York Times*, June 2, 2004, A12.

104. Douglas Jehl, "U.S. Report Finds Iraqis Eliminated Illicit Arms in 90s," *New York Times*, October 7, 2004, p. A22.

105. Senate Intelligence Report, 188. For further background and the CIA/DIA report of May 28, 2003, see Prados, *Hoodwinked*, 270–92.

106. Central Intelligence Agency, "Iraq's Weapons of Mass Destruction Programs," October 2002, 22.

107. *Weekly Compilation of Presidential Documents* 38:1717.

108. State Department Fact Sheet, December 19, 2002.

109. Steven R. Weisman, "U.S. Says Blix Played Down Details of Banned Weapons," *New York Times*, March 11, 2003, A10; Walter Pincus, "Iraq Drone Scrapped after U.N. Inspection," *Washington Post*, March 11, 2003, A16.

110. John F. Burns, "Iraq Shows One of Its Drones, Recalling Wright Brothers," *New York Times*, March 13, 2003, A12; Rajiv Chandrasekaran, "Iraqi Officials Proudly Exhibit a Disputed, Dinged-Up Drone," *Washington Post*, March 13, 2003, A12.

111. Colum Lynch, "U.N.: Iraqi Drones Were No Threat," *Washington Post*, September 5, 2004, A28.

112. Senate Intelligence Report, 235.

113. Senate Intelligence Report, 236.

114. Senate Intelligence Report, 236.

115. Kenneth M. Pollack, *The Threatening Storm: The Case for Invading Iraq* (New York: Random House, 2002).

116. Kenneth M. Pollack, "Spies, Lies, and Weapons: What Went Wrong," *Atlantic Monthly*, January/February 2004, 80.

117. On June 1, 2002, at the U.S. Military Academy in West Point, President Bush stated: "If we wait for threats to fully materialize, we will have waited too long." *Weekly Compilation of Presidential Documents* 38:946. In his State of the Union address on January 28, 2003, he rejected the position of those who say "we must not act until the threat is imminent." *Weekly Compilation of Presidential Documents* 39:115.

118. Walter Pincus and Dana Priest, "Lawmakers Begin Iraq Intelligence Hearings," *Washington Post*, June 19, 2003, A16.

119. James Fallows, "Blind into Baghdad," *Atlantic Monthly*, January/February 2004, 58.

120. Fallows, "Blind into Baghdad," 53.

121. "The Times and Iraq," *New York Times*, May 26, 2004, A10.

122. Daniel Okrent, "Weapons of Mass Destruction? Or Mass Distraction?" *New York Times*, May 30, 2004, WK2.

123. Michael Getler, "Looking Back before the War," *Washington Post*, June 20, 2004, B6; "A Pause for Hindsight" editorial, *Washington Post*, July 16, 2004, A26; Howard Kurtz, "The Post on WMDs: An Inside Story: Prewar Articles Questioning Threat Often Didn't Make Front Page," *Washington Post*, August 12, 2004, A1; Howard Kurtz, "New Republic Editors 'Regret' Their Support of Iraq War," *Washington Post*, June 19, 2004, 1; *New Republic*, June 28, 2004.

AARP. *See* American Association of Retired Persons
abortions, 37–38, 208n18
Aerospace Industry Association, 251
Afghanistan: Bush, George W., and, 47, 49–53, 71–72, 78, 85, 104, 127, 268–69, 279; Taliban regime in, 49–50, 279, 290; war in, 50, 229
Africa, 295, 296
African Americans, 276
Agricultural Adjustment Act, 81n7
Agricultural and Consumer Protection Act of 1973, 172
agriculture, 218
AIDS research, 218
air-conditioning, 34–35, 55n11
Air Force One, 110
air pollution, 144
Alaska, 144, 175
Altman, Robert, 65–66
American Association of Retired Persons (AARP), 19–20
American Jobs Creation Act, 234. *See also* Foreign Sales Corporation/Extraterritorial Income Act
American Political Science Review (Neustadt), 187
America's Congress (Mayhew), 116
Americorps, 141, 175
Anderson, John, 89
Andrews Air Force Base, 226
Ansar al-Islam, 290
Appalachian Regional Development Act (1965), 174

Archer, William, 263n14
Arctic National Wildlife Refuge, 51
Arizona, 89
arms sales, 270
Arms Export Control Act, 270
Armey, Dick, 109
Arnold, Douglas, 262
Ashcroft, John, 49
Asia, 281
Atta, Mohamed, 291–92
"axis of evil," 50

baby boomers, 229
backdoor spending provisions, 136
Baker, Howard, 64
Baker, James A., III, 50, 64
Balanced Budget Act (1997), 96, 227
Balanced Budget and Emergency Deficit Control Act (1985), 225
"the barons," 132
Bartlett, Dan, 77
Baucus, Max, 239, 242–43
Belmon, Harry, 216
Bentsen, Lloyd, 65–66
Between the Branches (Collier), 111
Biden, Joseph, 42
bills, 172; agricultural, 172, 173; appropriation, 190, 224; civil rights, 34, 88, 158, 171; crime, 144, 176; divided government/major, 185; education, 197, 198, 200–201, 218; federal highway (1956), 171; highway reauthorization, 206; House spending, 71; job training, 173; landmark domestic, 174–75; message

politics/other, 196–97, *198*, 199–204, 200, 201; minimum wage, 175; omnibus, 128, 141, 175, 176; private, 129–30; and resolutions in Congress, 50, 128–30; tax, 251–52; veto of, 185. *See also* laws; legislation

Binder, Sarah, 39, 41

bin Laden, Osama, 50, 275, 291, 292–93

blacks, 34–35, 276

Blitzer, Wolf, 180n35

Blix, Hans, 51, 303, 305

Blunt, Roy, 241

Boeing, 235, 239, 240, 251

Bolling, Dick, 224

"Boll Weevils," 22m39

Bond, Jon R., 39

Bosnia, 281, 283

Boston Globe, 98

Bowles, Erskine, 67

Boxer, Barbara, 217

Bradley, Bill, 40

Brady, David, 42, 161

Brady Handgun Violence Act, 141, 175

Breaux, John, 46

Brock, William, 44

Brown, Hank, 40

Brumbaugh, David L., 263n6

budget(s): balanced, 3, 47, 227–28; bipartisan, 216–17; deficit politics and, 27, 217, 223–31; DOA (dead on arrival), 215; politics and, 27, 209; process, 3, 27; process in House, 214–23, *216*, *221*; process in Senate, 214–23, *216*, *221*; Reagan's, 225; summits, 225–27; surpluses, 47, 221–22. *See also* Bureau of the Budget; OMB

budget, federal: appropriations for, 222–24; balanced, 227–28; bipartisanship of, 230–31; deficits and, 223–31; early years of deficit, 224–25; executive branch's process for, 210–14; hearings/negotiations for, 215–18, *221*; on House/Senate floors, 219–20; leadership's role in, 231–32; legislative process for, 214–23, *216*, *221*; OMB's spending targets and, 211–13, *212*; par-

tisanship of, 230; pay-go rule with, 229; presidential appeals and, 213–14; process, 209–32; reconciliation for, 220–22, *221*; summits, 225–27; support for, 214

Budget and Accounting Act of 1921, 61, 211

Budget Act, 219, 220, 229, 248

Budget and Impoundment Control Act of 1974, 17, 145, 211, 223–24

Bunning, Jim, 253

Bureau of Intelligence and Research (INR), 293, 296

Bureau of the Budget, 17, 81n8, 187–88, 211. *See also* Office of Management and Budget

Burns, James MacGregor, 133, 158

Burr, Richard, 255

Bush, George H. W.: 1988 election of, 103; administration of, 64–65, 75, 115–16, 140, 145, 279; Congress and, 4–6, 5, 70, 101; electoral victories of, 155; legislative agendas of, 90, 91, 96, 98–100, 102, 155; vetoes of, 152, 162, 173; as vice president, 90

Bush, George W.: 2000 election of, 1–2, 24, 33–34, 37; 2004 election of, 1, 2, 24, 51–54, 85–88, 119–22; administration of, 19, 67–70, 113, 231, 257, 284; batting average of, 164–65, *165*, 180n41; Congress and, 3–7, 5, *15*, 15–19, 21–29, 33–34, 70–80, 85–88, 101–2, 104, 108–10, 151–77; Congressional polarization and, 47–52; conservative policy agenda of, 33–34, 47–48, 77; on education, 4, 91, 97; electoral victories of, 155, 156; first term of, 47–52; on FSC/ETI, 237, 257, 260, 261; legislative agendas of, 4, 77–80, 91, 96–97, 101, 108–10, 155, 177; public relations operations during, 77–78; response to 9/11 and Afghanistan, 47, 49–53, 71–72, 78, 85, 104, 127, 268–69, 279; second term of, 101, 183, *191*, 191–93, *193*; on Social Security privatization, 4, 48, 51, 70, 72, 91, 99, 102, 106; speeches of, 290–91, 294, 296,

297, 299, 302, 304, 313n116; tax cut
initiatives of, 48, 52, 70, 97, 102, 106,
238; vetoes of, 8, 9, 26–27, 173–74,
183, 205–6. *See also* Iraq War
Bush's Council of Economic Advisers, 243
business lobbyists, 273
Byrd, Robert, 66, 210, 222

California, 251
Calio, Nicholas, 111
Cameron, Charles, 184–86, 204, 207n4
campaign(s): finance reforms, 197, *198*,
202; governing and, 24; presidential,
24–25, 85–100
Campbell, James, 154
Camp David accords, 279
Cannon, Joseph G., 16
Cantwell, Maria, 247, 265n51
Capitol Hill, 22, 86, 233; presence, 108–9;
viewpoints from, 143–44; voting on,
139
Carter, Jimmy, 6, 24; administration of, 72,
73–74, 145–46, 279, 284; agenda of,
160–61, 174–75; electoral victories of,
89, 156; government-reform proposals
of, 95, 160–61; legislative successes of,
63, 81n11, 89–90, 94–95, 102, 152;
vetoes of, 160–61
Castle, Michael, 241
Caterpillar, 239, 240, 251
Central America, 270
Central Intelligence Agency (CIA), 277,
292–94, 299–302, 303–4
Chamberlain, Lawrence H., 132
Chao, Elaine, 244
Chemical Weapons Conference, 281
Cheney, Dick, 43, 50, 63, 68, 291, 307
China. *See* People's Republic of China
Christian Coalition, 274
CIA. *See* Central Intelligence Agency
civil rights, 62, 94, 171
Civil Rights Act of 1964, 34, 88, 158
Clean Air Act, 65, 175
Clean Waters Restoration Act of 1966, 175
Cleveland, Grover, 2
Clinton, Bill, 2; after 1992 elections, 3–4,

15, 141; after 1994 elections, 3, 13, 17–
19, 114, 127, 141–42, 163, 180n35;
after 1996 elections, 45, 91, 118–19,
121; administration of, 21, 65–67,
81n21, 112–13, 195, 202–3; batting
average of, 164–66, *165*; Congress and,
3–6, *5*, *15*, 15–18, 21–24, 34, 70, 104,
109, 117–19; Congressional Democrats
and, 2–4; Congressional polarization
and, 44–47; economic plan of, 210,
227, 231; first term of, 127; foreign policy of, 275, 283; impeachment of, 6, 10,
46, 271; legislative agendas of, 76–80,
90–91, 94–96, 102, 108, 116, 141–43,
152, 174–75; nominations of, 43; political career of, 6; second term of, *191*,
191–93, *193*; staff of, 21; on universal
health care, 45–46, 72, 75, 78–79,
82n37, 91, 95, 114; vetoes of, 8, 9, 152,
163, 173. *See also* Lewinsky, Monica;
New Democrat; Whitewater investigations
Clinton, Hillary Rodham, 82n37, 95
coal miners, 171
coastal zone management, 144
coattails: marginal, 156; negative, 16,
155–56; presidential electoral, 16, 154;
seat-gain, *155*, 155–57
Coca-Cola, 239
Cochran, Thad, 138
Cold War, 28, 140, 271–72, 279, 287
Collier, Ken, 111
Collins, Mac, 239, 240
Comprehensive Test Ban Treaty, 271, 284
concurrence, 164, 180n37
Congress, 2; 79th, 133; 80th, 133; 89th,
175; 90th, 175; 91st, 171, 172; 92nd,
172; 93rd, 172; 96th, 137, 145; 97th,
161; 103rd, 16, 41, 45; 104th, 12, 16,
41, 45, 142, 163, 173; 105th, 45–46,
173, *191*, 191–92, *193*, 195–97, *198*,
200, 200–204, *201*; 106th, 42, 45, 115,
173, 188, *191*, 191–92, *193*, 195–97,
198, *200*, 200–204, *201*; 107th, 27, 49,
71–72, *191*, 191–92, *193*, 237–38;
108th, 12, 27, 68, 71–72, 237–41, 261;

109th, 13, 205, 261–62; during 1965, 93; agenda of, 125; approval of, 141; bills/resolutions in, 50, 128–29; bipartisanship in, 6–7; Bush, George H. W., and, 4–6, 5, 70, 101; Bush, George W., and, 3–7, 5, 15, 15–19, 21–29, 70–80, 85–88, 101–2, 104, 108–10; Clinton, Bill and, 3–6, 5, 15, 15–18, 21–23, 72, 104, 109, 117–19; committees in, 129, 133–34; decentralization of, 13, 16–17, 21; delaying tactics within, 34, 45; Democratic control of, 14–19, 15, 35–38, 158–59, 161–63; democratization of, 13; "do-nothing," 43; election returns for, 16–19; foreign policy roles of, 267–87; internal configuration of, 157; majority-minority districts of, 35; members of, 211, 223, 269; during nineteenth century, 60–61; organizational reforms in, 153; output/workload of, 128–32, 131; as policy-making branch, 126–28, 157; political prerogatives of, 194; powers of, 8–11; presidents and, 3–7, 5, 21–29, 70–80, 85–88; presidents during nineteenth century and, 60–61; presidents during twentieth century and, 60n6, 61–62, 61nn7–8; presidents during twenty-first century and, 101–22; procedural prerogatives of, 194; public mood in, 172; redistricting of, 36–37, 55n14; Republican control of, 14–19, 15, 21, 35–38, 96–97; split control of White House/, 14–19, 15, 146, 152–53; structural reforms in, 159–60; textbook, 134, 157; U. S. Constitution and, 7–12, 9, 23–24, 59–60; voting in, 34, 129; White House and, 105. *See also* Democrats; government; House of Representatives; presidents; Republicans; Senate; veto bargaining
Congressional Budget Act (1974), 93
Congressional Budget Committee, 215, 216, 228, 275
Congressional Government (Wilson), 61
congressional polarization: Bush, George W., and, 47–52; causes of, 34–38,

55n11, 55n14, 55n18, 55n20; Clinton, Bill and, 44–47; decline of civility and, 41–44; gridlock and, 41; partisan, 38–44; presidents and, 44–52; roots of, 22–23, 33; waning center and, 39–41
Congressional Quarterly, 6, 13, 14, 51
Congressional Quarterly Weekly Report, 197, 198
Congressional Research Service, 275
conservative government eras: bipartisan, 26, 130, 131, 132–34, 157–59, 166, 168–69, 170
conservative party, 26, 130, 131, 140–43
Constitutional Convention, 60
Consumer Product Safety Act, 144
Contract with America, 3, 29n2; campaign, 13, 45, 77, 92, 142; provisions of, 17–19, 173; support of, 163
Coolidge, Calvin, 101
Cooper, Joseph, 161
corporations, U.S., 235; domestic, 240; foreign subsidies of, 235–36; multinational, 236, 239–41; taxation of, 235–36, 238–41, 257
Corwin, Edwin, 269
Crane, Philip, 238–40
Crane-Rangel bill, 239–40
crime, 144, 176, 197
Cuba, 273
Culture War? (Fiorina), 37
Czechoslovakia, 291, 292

Darman, Richard, 111, 189
Daschle, Tom, 42–43, 92, 97, 151, 245–46, 254–55
Davidson, Roger, 157
On Deaf Ears (Edwards), 113
Deaver, Michael, 75, 99
defense, 104; issues, 197, 198; spending, 161, 195, 218
Defense Intelligence Agency (DIA), 293, 303–4
Delaware, 88
DeLay, Tom, 44, 55n14, 99, 250, 252, 255
Democratic Caucus, 35
Democratic Leadership Council (DLC), 4

Democratic Party: Congressional, 21; discipline in, 4; unity votes by, 13, *14*
Democratic Study Group (DSG), 135
Democrats: in 1964, 89; in 1976, 89; during Clinton Presidency, congressional, 2–4; conservative, 39–40; control of Congress, 14–19, *15*, 35–38, 158–59, 161–63; control of House, 93–94, 97; control of White House, 14–19, *15*; "Dixiecrat," 34–35; House, 43–44, 94; on Iraq War, 51; liberal, 159–61; "Old," 4; priorities of, 194, 197–99, *198*, 208n18; Progressive, 161; recession-driven, 146; Senate, 3, 43–44, 97, 151; southern, 22, 34–35, 154, 158–59. *See also* New Democrat
Desert Storm, 6, 18. *See also* Persian Gulf War
DeWine, Michael, 253
DIA. *See* Defense Intelligence Agency
Dirksen, Everett, 175
DLC. *See* Democratic Leadership Council
Dole, Robert, 45, 91, 112, 118
Donovan, Robert J., 133
Dreier, David, 252
drugs, war on, 18
DSG. *See* Democratic Study Group
Duberstein, Ken, 64
Duelfer, Charles A., 301, 304
Dunn, Jennifer, 241
Durbin, Richard, 253

economy, 47
education: bills, 197, *198*, 200–201, 218; Bush, George W., on, 4, 91, 97; cuts, 8; "Ed-flex," 173; elementary/secondary, 91; goals, 175. *See also* No Child Left Behind Act
Edwards, George C., III, 72–73, 81n11, 103, 113
Edwards, John, 255
Eisenhower, Dwight D., *15*, 268; batting average of, 164, *165*, 166; electoral victories of, 154, *155*; legislative agendas of, 61–62, 107, 133, 145, 159; vetoes of, 171

ElBaradei, Mohamed, 293–94, 296–97
elections: 1996, 3, 45, 91, 118–19, 121; 2002, 3. *See also* presidential elections
elections, 1994: Clinton, Bill after, 3, 13, 17–19, 114, 127, 141–42; House after, 13, 17–19, 42, 114, 141–42, 162–63
elections, 2004: House of Representatives after, 1–2, 52–54, 87–88, 119–20; Senate after, 1–2, 52–54, 87–88, 119–20
Electoral College, 85
Elementary and Secondary Education Act (1965), 174, 200
Employment Act of 1946, 133
endangered species protections, 144
energy: consumption, 91; crisis, 72; tax subsidies, 245–48, 262
environment, 194, 273; concerns about, 18, 138; programs for, 8
Equal Employment Opportunity Act of 1972, 172
Equal Rights Amendment, 145
ethnic groups, 273, 276
ETI. *See* Extraterritorial Income Act
Europe, 235–37, 241, 263n13, 281, 290
European Union (EU), 235; complaints to WTO, 235–37, 263n13; tariffs, 241
Evans, Diana, 262
executive branch, 10–11; agencies, 23; internal politics of, 187–93, *191*, *193*; legislative relations, 18–19, 101–22, 144–45; policy directors in, 23; policy-making duties of, 126–28. *See also* presidents; White House; *specific presidents*
Executive Office of the President, 61, 188
export subsidies, 235–36. *See also* Foreign Sales Corporation/Extraterritorial Income Act
Extraterritorial Income Act (ETI), 236. *See also* Foreign Sales Corporation/Extraterritorial Income Act
Exxon-Mobil, 239

Fair Deal, 133. *See also* Truman, Harry S
Family and Medical Leave Act, 108, 141, 175
FDA. *See* Food and Drug Administration

320   *Index*

Federal Deposit Insurance Corporation Act, 81n7
Federal Election Campaign Act, 144
federalism, 2, 10
Federalist 73 (Hamilton), 59
Feith, Douglas, J., 291, 307
Fenno, Richard F., Jr., 129, 134
filibusters, 22; avoidance of, 230; breaking, 114; as delaying tactic, 34; minority party and, 40–41; use of, 40–41, 166, 221, 243
Fiorina, Morris, 37–38, 42, 53
Flake, Jeff, 250
Fleisher, Richard, 39
Florida, 1–2, 86, 251, 292
focus groups, 23
Foley, Thomas S., 5, 16, 111, 227
Food and Drug Administration (FDA), 253–55, 256–57, 260
Ford, Bill, 224
Ford, Gerald: administration of, 73–74, 136, 145; legislative successes of, 62, 144, 160; vetoes of, 160, 175
foreign policy, 28; actors, 272–75; changes since 1960s, 269–71; Clinton's, 275, 283; Congress's roles in, 267–87; historical trends in, 268–69; internationalist, 52, 271–72; laws, 167; Nixon's, 270, 279, 283; objectives of presidents', 79–80; powers of presidents', 61, 80n6; presidents' roles in, 267–87; Reagan's, 270–71, 279, 283
Foreign Sales Corporation/Extraterritorial Income Act (FSC/ETI), 27, 234; Bush, George W., on, 238, 257, 260, 261; coalition building on, 234–63; House on, 238, 249–52, 258–59, 265n57, 265n60; H.R. 4520 and, 249–52, 258–59, 265n57, 265n60; H.R. 1769 and, 238; repeal of, 236, 238–40; S. 1637 and, 241–48, 249, 253–60; Senate on, 241–48, 249, 253–60; stalemate over, 242–43
foreign sales corporation (FSC), 235–36
Fox News Sunday, 298
France, 290, 301

Frank, Barney, 217, 261
Franks, Tommy, 50
Freedom of Information Act, 172
Frist, Bill, 43, 92, 241, 245–47, 254, 262
FSC. *See* foreign sales corporation
FSC/ETI. *See* Foreign Sales Corporation/ Extraterritorial Income Act
FSC Repeal and Extraterritorial Exclusion Act (2000), 236
fundraising, 42

Gallatin, Albert, 61
Gallup polls, 49
GATT. *See* General Agreement on Tariffs and Trade
gender gap, 37–38
General Accounting Office, 275
General Agreement on Tariffs and Trade (GATT), 4, 6
General Electric, 235, 251
George Mason University, 92
Gephardt, Richard, 42, 111
Gergen, David, 66
Germany, 290
gerrymandering, 37–38, 55n18. *See also* redistricting
Giamo, Bob, 224
Gigot, Paul A., 98
Gingrich, Newt, 3, 96; as minority whip, 21, 35; as Speaker, 18–19, 41–42, 44–45, 91–92, 118, 142–43, 226. *See also* Contract with America
Goals 2000, 175
Goldwater, Barry, 89, 155
Gore, Al: 2000 presidential campaign of, 1–2, 37, 52; as vice president, 65, 141; voters for, 53–54
government: branches of, 7–12, 9; conditional party, 161; constitutional design of, 7–12, 9, 59–60; federal, 7; integrity in, 89; party, 158–59; party control of, 14–19, 15, 145–46; -reform proposals, 95; revenues, 138; shutdown of, 19, 45; system of, 11; unified party control of, 3–4, 14–19, 15, 22, 87–88, 114–15, 153, 164

government, divided, 176–77; divided
party control of Congress as, 14–19, *15*,
105–6, 139, 152–53, 164–76, *168–69,
170*; major bills and, 185; results of, 22;
split control of Congress/White House
as, 14–19, *15*, 146, 152–53; varieties of,
14–19, *15*
government eras, 130–32, 176–77; bipartisan conservative, 26, 130, *131*, 132–34,
157–59, 166, *168–69, 170*; conservative party, 26, 130, *131*, 140–43; liberal
activist party, 26, 130, *131*, 134–37,
144–45, 159–61, *168–69, 170*,
171–73; postreform/party-unity, 26,
130, *131*, 137–40, 161–64, *168–69,
170*; presidential leverage and, 153–64
Gramm-Rudman-Hollings Act, 225
Grand Old Party (GOP). *See* Republican
Party
Grassley, Charles, 233, 241–45, 256–59
Grassley-Baucus bill, 242–43
Great Britain, 296
Great Society: agenda, 88, 136, 154, 159,
172, 174; legislation, 44, 62, 94. *See also*
Johnson, Lyndon B.
Grenada, 281
Groseclose, Tim, 185–86, 204
Groseclose-McCarty model, 185–86

Habibou, Allele Elhadj, 311n52
Hadley, Stephen, 299
Haiti, 281
Halleck, Charlie, 175
Hamilton, Alexander, 59–60
Harkin, Tom, 243–46, 259–60
Harlow, Bryce, 107
Harry and Louise ads, 82n37
Hastert, J. Dennis, 42, 69, 92, 99, 143, 234,
240–41, 255, 260
Hatch, Orrin, 239
Havel, Vaclav, 291
Head Start, 214, 218
health care: managed, 197, *198*; universal,
45–46, 72, 75, 78–79, 82n37, 91, 95,
114
health insurance companies, 19–20
Higher Education Act of 1972, 172

highway, 171, 206
Hobbs, David, 109
homosexuality, 38
House Appropriations Committee, 18,
222, 224
House Armed Services Committee, 68–
69, 134, 307
House Budget Committee, 27, 209, 215,
216, 217
House Commerce Committee, 18
House International Relations Committee,
275
House Judiciary Committee, 10, 69, 142
House of Representatives: 104th, 12, 18;
108th, 12; during 1965, 93; after 1976
elections, 89; after 1992 elections, 3–4,
15, 141; after 1994 elections, 13, 17–
19, 42, 114, 141–42, 162–63; after
2000 elections, 2, 16; after 2002 elections, 3; after 2004 elections, 1–2, 24,
52–54, 87–88, 119–20; budget process,
214–23, *216, 221*; centralization of
power in, 3, 16–17; chairmen, 217–18,
224; committees, 18–19, 129, 133–34,
214–18, *216*; decorum, 42–43; Democratic Caucus, 35; Democrats' control
of, 93–94, 97; Democrats in, 43–44, 94;
elections, 11; floor, 219–20; freshmen,
18–19; on FSC/ETI, 238, 249–52, 258–
59, 265n57, 265n60; H.R. 8, 189; H.R.
4520, 249–52, 258–59, 265n57,
265n60; H.R. 1769, 238; incumbencies,
37, 55n18, 55n20; leaderships in, 4,
214; measures, 128–29; members of,
211, 223; office terms for, 11–12, 126;
one-minute speeches in, 197; operations of, 125; party-line voting in, 40,
46, 56nn37–38; Republicans in, 94,
119–20, 163; safe seats in, 23, 36–37;
scandals, 141; seat-gain coattails in,
155, 155–57; Speaker of, 18–19, 114,
214; spending bills, 71; subcommittee
chairs, 4; votes, 129. *See also* Congress;
specific committees
House Republican Conference, 3
House Rules Committee, 18, 35, 93, 115,
133–35, 188, 219, 251

House Select Committee on Intelligence,
    128
House Steering and Policy Committee, 35,
    136
House Use of Force Resolution, 71
House Ways and Means Committee, 18,
    35, 134, 136–37, 139, 220, 233, 251–52
Housing and Community Development
    Act of 1974, 172
Hughes, Karen, 77
Human Rights Watch, 274
Hunter, Duncan, 69
Hussein, Saddam, 50–51, 279, 307; al
    Qaeda and, 52, 290–93; WMDs and, 5,
    289, 295–302. *See also* Iraq; Iraq War
hyperpluralism, 20

IAEA. *See* International Atomic Energy
    Agency
IBM. *See* International Business Machines
impeachment, 6, 10, 46, 271
Imperial Presidency, 19
incumbency(ies): advantages of, 37,
    55n18, 55n20; House, 37, 55n18,
    55n20
independents, 37
India, 243
INR. *See* Bureau of Intelligence and
    Research
insourcing, 264n37
insurance companies, 71
intelligence agencies, 99
interest groups, 19–20, 42
Internal Revenue Service (IRS), 202
International Atomic Energy Agency
    (IAEA), 293–95
International Business Machines (IBM),
    239
International Monetary Fund, 271, 274
Iowa, 1
Iran, 50, 281, 292
Iraq, 71, 229, 306–8; aluminum tubes in,
    293–99, 311n52; biological/chemical
    weapons of, 299–302; Cheney on, 291;
    invasion of, 2, 44; mobile labs of,
    302–4; al Qaeda link, 290–93; threats

from, 29; unmanned aerial vehicles of,
    304–6; WMDs of, 5, 289, 295–302. *See
    also* Desert Storm
"Iraq's Continuing Programs for Weapons
    of Mass Destruction," 298
Iraq War, 33: Bush, George W., and, 47,
    49–52, 57n66, 279; Democrats on, 51;
    justification of, 289–308, 311n52,
    313n116
IRS. *See* Internal Revenue Service
Islamic extremists, 28, 287

Jackson, Andrew, 60–61, 127
Jacobson, Gary, 36, 53–54, 138
Jefferson, Thomas, 60–61
Jeffords, James, 3, 48–49, 67, 97, 114, 151,
    255
JOBS (Jumpstart Our Business Strength),
    242, 248
Johnson, Andrew, 10
Johnson, Lyndon B., 17; administration of,
    72, 187–88, 268, 278, 283; batting aver-
    age of, 164, 165; electoral victories of,
    89, 146, 154, 156, 159, 174; legislative
    successes of, 62, 81n11, 88–89, 93–94,
    102, 145, 174–75, 176; as majority
    leader, 134, 135. *See also* Great Society
Johnson, Nancy, 241
Jones, 104
Jones, Charles O., 160
Jordan, Hamilton, 63, 81n12
judicial branch, 10–11. *See also* Supreme
    Court

Kabul, 50
Kandahar, 50
Kasich, John, 219
Kay, David, 301
Kemp, Jack, 88–89
Kemp-Roth, 88. *See also* Reagan, Ronald
Kennedy, Edward, 233, 253
Kennedy, John F., 2, 62, 268; electoral vic-
    tories of, 155–57; legislative agendas of,
    89, 95, 158–59, 174–75. *See also* New
    Frontier
Kernell, Samuel, 72, 75

Kerry, John F., 1, 52, 85, 86, 248, 257, 259, 265n51
Korean War, 133
Kosovo, 281, 283
Kumar, Martha, 81n14
Kurds, 290

labor, organized, 4
Landrieu, Mary, 259–60
Latinos, 276
law(s): foreign policy, 167; making, 128–32, *131*, 136, 170–71, 234–35; price-control, 172; public, 130; "significant," 153, 164–76, *165*, *168–69*, *170*, 180n37, 188. *See also* bills; legislation
Leach, Jim, 36–37
League of Nations, 61, 268
Leahy, Patrick, 43
Leath, Marvin, 218
Legislating Together (Peterson), 103
legislation, 188; backdoor spending, 136; coalitions for, 25; global economic, 235–41; Great Society, 44; major, 16, 132, 197–99, *198*, 203; omnibus, 45; pork, 234; SAP/major, *200*, *201. See also* bills; laws; *specific legislation*
legislative activity, 126
legislative branch, 10–11; bicameral effects of, 115–16; -executive relations, 18–19, 101–22, 144–45; party control of, 14–19, *15*, 145–46; as policymaking branch, 126–28, 157. *See also* Congress; House of Representatives; Senate
legislative presidency, 125; in political time, 151–77; of Roosevelt, Franklin Delano, 125, 130, 132–33
legislative strategy: message politics and, 193–99, *198*; veto bargaining and, 193–99, *198*
legislative vehicles, 128
legislative workloads, 125–26, 129–30, 133, 136, 145–46
Lewinsky, Monica, 46, 82n37, 96
Lewis, Ron, 250
liberal activist party, 26, 130, *131*, 134–37, 144–45, 159–61, *168–69*, *170*, 171–73

liberals, 138, 145
Light, Paul C., 92
Lincoln, Abraham, 2, 61
Livingston, Robert, 143
logrolling, 157
Loomis, Burdett, 166
Lott, Trent, 42–43, 110, 118, 208n18, 239
Lugar, Richard, 237

Madison, James, 11, 61
Malbin, Michael J., 145
Mann, Thomas, 13
Mann, Thomas E., 145
Mansfield, Mike, 135
Manzullo, Donald, 240, 241
Massachusetts, 251
Mayhew, David R., 16, 114, 116, 136, 146, 152, 167, 204
McCain, John, 44, 202, 233, 246, 248
McCain-Feingold campaign finance reform, 202
McCarty, Nolan, 185–86, 204
McConnell, Mitch, 202, 244–45, 247, 253, 257, 259
McCrery, Jim, 241
McDermott, Jim, 46, 233
McGovern, Jim, 258, 265n60
McGovern-Fraser reforms, 160
McLarty, Mac, 65
media, 274
Medicaid: cuts, 8, 45; spending, 19, 229
Medicare, 88, 194; cuts, 8, 45; prescription drug bill (2003), 19–20, 44, 51, 108; proposals, 158; reforms, 20, 68, 70, 91, 175; spending, 19, 229
Meet the Press, 291, 296, 297, 298
message politics: other bills and, 196–97, *198*, 199–204, *200*, *201*; legislative strategy and, 193–99, *198*; majority message priorities in, 195–96, *198*, 199–204, *200*, *201*; minority message priorities in, 196, *198*, 199–204, *200*, *201*; policies/proposals and, 194–99, *198*; shared message priorities in, 195, *198*, *200*, *201*, 299–304. *See also* veto bargaining

Michel, Robert, 112
Michigan, 1
Microsoft, 235, 239, 240, 251
Middle East, 281, 291
Mikva, Abner J., 136
Mills, Wilbur, 134, 137
Minnesota, 1
minority party: filibusters and, 40–41; senators, 196
Missile Defense Agency, 305
Mitchell, George, 92, 111
Mogadishu, 274
Moore, Frank, 63
Morris, Dick, 149n43
Motor Voter Act, 141, 175
Muskie, Ed, 216, 224

NAFTA. *See* North American Free Trade Agreement
National Association of Manufacturers, 20
national debt, 225
National Defense Education Act (1958), 171
National Endowment for the Arts and Humanities, 45
National Environmental Policy Act of 1969, 144
National Guard, 259
National Industrial Recovery Act, 81n7
National Intelligence Estimate (NIE), 293, 298, 300–301
National Journal, 24, 39–40
National Labor Relations Act, 81n7
National Scenic Trails system bill, 175
national security, 104
National Security Agency, 292
National Security Council (NSC), 190, 278, 298
NATO. *See* North Atlantic Treaty Organization
Neustadt, Richard E., 72, 187, 188
New Deal, 81n7, 88, 132m, 144, 187. *See also* Roosevelt, Franklin Delano
New Democrat, 4, 44, 47, 91. *See also* Clinton, Bill
New Freedoms program, 61

New Frontier, 89, 95, 136. *See also* Kennedy, John F.
New Mexico, 1
New York, 88, 92
New York Times, 214, 308
New York University, 92
NGOs. *See* nongovernmental organizations
Nicaragua, 271, 283
Nickles, Don, 248
NIE. *See* National Intelligence Estimate
Niger, 296, 297–98, 300, 311n52
9/11 Commission, 28, 68–69, 292
9/11 Recommendations Implementation Act, 205
9/11 terrorist attacks, 2, 28–29, 49; legislation after, 67–68, 97, 143; post, 143, 272; response to Afghanistan, 47, 49–53, 71–72, 78, 85, 104, 127, 268–69, 279
Nixon, Richard M., 2, 10; administration of, 73, 107, 145, 187–88, 224; batting average of, 152, 164, *165*, 166–67; electoral victories of, 89–90, 97, 154; foreign policies of, 270, 279, 283; legislative successes of, 62, 72, 96, 144, 171–72; resignation of, 89, 152; vetoes of, 171–72
No Child Left Behind Act, 4, 51, 91, 108
nongovernmental organizations (NGOs), 274
North American Free Trade Agreement (NAFTA), 273; passage of, 4, 6, 47, 75, 141; votes for, 82n37
North Atlantic Treaty Organization (NATO), 279, 281
North Carolina, 255, 261
Northern Alliance, 50
North Korea, 50, 284
NSC. *See* National Security Council
Nunn, Sam, 40

Occupational Safety and Health Act of 1970, 144
Office of Management and Budget (OMB), 17, 23; central legislative clearance and, 187–93, *191*, *193*; "pass back" by,

212; recommendations, 209–10; reserve fund, 213; responsibilities of, 62, 63; spending targets of, 211–13, *212. See also* statements of administration policy

Oglesby, M. B., 111

Ohio, 1, 86

"the old bulls," 132

OLS. *See* ordinary least squares regression

OMB. *See* Office of Management and Budget

Omnibus Budget Reconciliation Act of 1993, 141

Omnibus Crime Act, 176

Omnibus Deficit Reduction Act of 1993, 175

O'Neill, Thomas P., Jr., 81n12, 94, 233, 240

ordinary least squares regression (OLS), 180n41

Ornstein, Norman J., 145

outsourcing, 243, 264n37, 273

Oval Office, 144

Panama, 63, 75, 270, 279, 281, 284

Panama Canal Treaty, 63, 270, 279, 284

Panetta, Leon, 21, 66–67, 82n23

parliamentary arms race, 41

party: "name brand," 194; systems, 127

party control: Congressional/presidential relations and, 151–77; divided Congressional, 14–19, *15*, 105–6, 139, 152–53, 164–67, *168–69*, *170*; of government, 14–19, *15*, 145–46; of government, unified, 3–4, 14–19, *15*, 22, 87–88, 114–15, 153, 164; of legislative branch, 14–19, *15*, 145–46; net effects of, 165; regression analysis during, 165–67, 180n39

Paster, Robert, 65–66

Patients' Bill of Rights, 196

Pearl Harbor, 275

Pell Grants, 172

Pelosi, Nancy, 240, 241

Pennsylvania, 1

Pentagon, 99, 305

People's Republic of China: humanitarian interests in, 281; outsourcing to, 243; trade with, 4, 6, 47, 273

Perkins, Carl, 224

Perot, Ross, 75, 90

Persian Gulf War, 65, 75, 115–16, 140, 271. *See also* Desert Storm

Peterson, 103

pharmaceutical companies, 19–20

pluralism, 19–20

Podesta, John, 67

Poland, 303

polarization, congressional. *See* congressional polarization

political capital, 69–70

political change, 34

political parties: during 1960s, 13, *14*; during 1970s, 13, *14*; control of government, 14–19, *15*; heydey of, 127; leadership of, 25–26; power of, 16; state-based, 12–13, *14*; systems within, 127; unity votes by, 13, *14. See also* congressional polarization; Democratic Party; Republican Party

political time, 126–28; legislative presidency in, 151–77; presidential leverage and, 153–64. *See also* government eras

politics: domestic, 268–69; "four-party," 158. *See also* message politics

Pollack, Kenneth, 306

polling, 23

postal reorganization, 144

postreform/party-unity government eras, 26, 130, *131*, 137–40, 161–64, *168–69*, *170*

poverty programs, 94

Powell, Colin, 50, 291, 294, 301–3, 305, 307

Prais-Winsten (AR 1) technique, 180n39

Presidency Research Group's Transition Project, 81n14

president(s): access to, 111–12; activist, 125, 132–33, 135; batting averages of, 164–67, *165*; bully pulpit of, 92, 113; campaigns' impact on, 24–25, 85–100; commissions/task force of, 70; Congress and, 3–7, *5*, 21–29, 70–80, 85–88;

Congress during nineteenth century
and, 60–61; Congress during twentieth
century and, 61–62, 80n6, 81nn7–8;
Congress during twenty-first century
and, 101–22; Congress/leadership of,
59–80, 80n4; contemporary, 64–70;
"crisis" components and, 71–73; Democratic, 158; electoral "coattails" of, 16,
154; electoral resources of, 154–57,
155; first-year's congressional dealings
of, 92–98; foreign policy objectives of,
79–80; foreign policy powers of, 61,
80n6; foreign policy roles of, 267–87;
hidden-hand, 159; legislative agendas
of, 61–64, 81n11, 88–92; legislative
roles of, 23–24; modern, 18; national
goals of, 70; office terms for, 11–12,
126; permanent campaign for, 74–75,
78–80, 82n37; policy contexts of,
115–16; positions/priorities of, 69–70;
postwar, 154–57, 155; powers of, 17–
18, 86; public approval/opinion and,
23–24, 72–73; public relations and, 23–
24, 73–74; as rational actors, 154; significant legislation and, 153, 164–76,
165, 168–69, 170, 180n37; State of the
Union addresses of, 169–70, 214; strategic coordinations/goals of, 116–20;
two-term, 2–3, 85; U.S. Constitution
and, 7–12, 9, 23–24, 59–60; wartime,
268, 278. *See also* Congress; legislative
presidency; veto bargaining; vetoes; *specific presidents*
presidential election, 2000: Bush, George
W., during, 1, 2, 24, 33–34, 37; outcome of, 1–2, 16; popular vote during,
2; Supreme Court and, 2. *See also* Electoral College
presidential elections: 1988, 103; 1992,
2–3; 2004, 1, 2, 24, 51–54, 85–88,
119–22; battleground states in, 11;
Clinton, Bill and, 3–4, 15, 141; minority winners of, 2; unified party control
after, 3–4, 16; voters in, 53
presidential vetoes. *See* vetoes
press, 23

Price, David E., 35
public affairs, 116
public policy, 152

al Qaeda, 29, 49; Hussein and, 52; Iraq
link, 290–93

Rangel, Charles, 236–40, 252
Rayburn, Sam, 135
Reagan, Ronald, 110; administration of,
137, 145; batting average of, 165,
165–67; budgets of, 225; communications' strategy of, 74–75, 77; electoral
victories of, 89, 97, 154; foreign policies
of, 270–71, 279, 283; legislative
agendas of, 88–89, 93–94, 109, 154,
161–62; on tax cuts, 88–89, 94, 137;
vetoes of, 173
recessions, 137, 146
Reconciliation Task Force, 224
redistricting, of Congress, 36–37, 55n14.
See also gerrymandering
Regan, Donald, 64
Reid, Harry, 245, 247
Republican(s): in 1980, 89; on balanced
budgets, 3, 47; control of Congress, 14–
19, 15, 21, 35–38, 96–97, 146; control
of White House, 14–19, 15, 146; federal government and, 3; gains in Sunbelt, 162; House, 94, 119–20, 163; liberal, 39–40; majorities, 1–3; priorities,
194, 197–99, 198, 208n18; Senate, 94,
119–20; Southern, 34–35. *See also*
Contract with America
Republican Conference, 18
Republican National Committee, 44, 75
Republican Party: ascendancy of, 127;
dominance/resurgence of, 127, 142–43;
unity votes by, 13, 14; voters' attraction
to, 34–35
Rhodes, John, 224
Rice, Condoleezza, 293, 295, 296, 297–98
Roberts, Pat, 261, 298
"Rockefeller Republicans," 22, 39
Roe v. Wade, 37
Roosevelt, Franklin Delano, 61, 101:

administration of, 146, 188, 268, 278; elections of, 127; legislative agendas of, 81nn7–8, 88, 102, 144, 158; legislative presidency of, 125, 130, 132–33. *See also* New Deal

Roosevelt, Theodore, 61, 268

Rostenkowski, Dan, 139, 220, 224

Roth, William, 88–89

Rousellot, John, 219

Rove, Karl, 77

Rubin, Robert, 65

Rumsfeld, Donald, 50, 63, 290, 291, 292, 298, 307

Russell, Richard, 134

Sandlin, Max, 250

SAP. *See* statements of administration policy

Sarris, Patti B., 136

Saudi Arabia, 270, 284

savings and loan crisis, 18

Schick, Allen, 139

Schlesinger, Arthur M., Jr., 7

school vouchers, 48

Senate: during 1965, 93; after 1976 elections, 89; after 1992 elections, 3–4, 15, 141; after 2000 elections, 1–2; after 2002 elections, 3; after 2004 elections, 1–2, 52–54, 87–88, 119–20; on appointees/nominees, 41, 43, 96; budget process, 214–23, 216, 221; centrists/moderates, 39–40; committees, 151; Democrats in, 3, 43–44, 97, 151; elections, 11; floor, 219–20; on FSC/ETI, 241–48, 249, 253–60; leadership of, 25–26, 114; measures, 128–29; members of, 211, 223; mid-twentieth-century, 134; nongermane amendments in, 166; office terms for, 11–12, 126; operations of, 125; parliamentary freedoms in, 242–43; partisanship in, 166–67; party-line voting in, 40, 46, 56nn37–38; powersharing in, 2; powers of, 10–11; Republicans in, 94, 119–20; Rule XXII, 114; S. 1637, 241–48, 249, 253–60; votes, 129. *See also* Congress; filibusters

Senate Appropriations Committee, 189, 210, 222, 224

Senate Finance Committee, 239, 241

Senate Intelligence Committee, 295, 298, 300, 304

Senate Select Committee, 292

September 11. *See* 9/11 terrorist attacks

Shogan, Colleen, 92

Sierra Leone, 275

Simpson, Alan, 40

Sinclair, Barbara, 163

Skinner, Sam, 65

Skowronek, Stephen, 127

Smith, Hedrick, 134

Smith, Howard W., 134

Snow, John, 251, 257

Social Security, 194; benefits, 91, 225, 229–30; Bush, George W., on, 4, 48, 51, 70, 72, 91, 99, 102, 106; privatization of, 4, 48, 51, 70, 72, 91, 99; reform, 19–20, 70, 91

Social Security Act, 81n7

Soil Conservation and Domestic Allotments Act, 81n7

Somalia, 274, 281, 283

South: air-conditioning, 34–35, 55n11; Deep, 89; Democrats in, 22, 34–35, 154, 158–59; solid, 34

South Africa, 270, 276, 281

Soviet Union, 140, 270, 279

Spain, 290

"stagflation," 137

Starr, Kenneth, 46

statements of administration policy (SAP), 205–6, 251; five phrases in, 189–93, 191; as formal mechanism, 188; major legislation with, 200, 201; messages/signals included in, 189–93, 191, 193; presidential veto threat in, 190–91, 191; process, 189–93, 191, 193; review of, 189; secretary's threat in, 190–91, 191; senior advisers threat in, 190–91, 191; signalling scale levels in, 191, 191–92, 203, 207n11; veto threats and, 189–93, 191, 193, 207n11

states, 10–11. *See also* federalism

Stenholm, Charlie, 217
Stephanopoulos, George, 65
Stockman, David, 225
stock markets, 47
Strahan, Randall, 139
Sumners, Joe, 154
Sununu, John, 64–65, 111, 246
Superfund, 20
Supplemental Security Income (1972), 172
Supreme Court: federalism and, 2; nominees, 96; rulings of, 61, 142; 2000 presidential election and, 2

Taliban regime, 49–50, 279, 290
tax(es), 8: bills, 251–52; credits, R&D, 251; cut, corporate, 233; cut initiatives by Bush, George W., 48, 52, 70, 97, 102, 106, 238; federal, 203; federal estate, 189; increases, 91, 108; Reagan on, 88–89, 94, 137; reductions, 194, 197, 198, 229; simplification, 91; structure, 70; subsidies, energy, 245–48, 262; U.S., 235–37; of U.S. corporations, 235–36, 238–41, 257; VAT, 235, 263n6
Tax Reform Act (1969), 172
Taylor, Gene, 307
Tenet, George, 291, 296–99
terrorism, 29, 49; insurance companies and, 71; war on, 29, 49–52, 205–6. *See also* 9/11 terrorist attacks
Texas, 36, 55n14, 251
Thomas, William, 233, 236, 238–41, 248–51, 255, 256–62, 263n14
Thune, John, 246
Thurow, Lester, 137
ticket splitting, 15–16
tobacco: buyout, 250–52, 253–56, 259, 265n57; issues, 187; regulation of, 253–55, 256–57, 260
Tower, John, 96
trade: with People's Republic of China, 4, 6, 47, 273; policies, 8; sanctions, 236
trade, transatlantic: conflict's origin, 235–41; war, 233–62. *See also* Foreign Sales Corporation/Extraterritorial Income Act

trans-Alaska pipeline, 144
Transportation Security Act, 71
triangulation, 91, 141, 149n43
Truman, Harry S, 2, 102; administration of, 146, 268, 278; legislative agendas of, 61–62, 133, 155, 158. *See also* Fair Deal
Truth in Security Act, 81n7

UAV. *See* unmanned aerial vehicles
UN Security Council, 50–51, 293–96, 301
UN Special Commission (UNSCOM), 306
United Nations, 274; funding for, 271; inspection teams, 51, 293, 301, 303–5; peacekeeping missions of, 275; Resolution 1441, 51; resolutions, 50–51
United States (U.S.): economy, 137; productivity, 137; revenues, 138; taxes, 235–37; troops, 281–82
United States v. Curtiss Wright Corporation, 80n6
Uniting and Strengthening America by Providing Appropriate Tools Required to Intercept and Obstruct Terrorism Act of 2001 (USA Patriot Act), 49, 71, 143, 173
unmanned aerial vehicles (UAV), 304–6
uranium, 293–99, 311n52
uranium oxide (yellowcake), 295–99, 311n52
urban mass transit, 144
U.S. Air Force, 305
USA Patriot Act. *See* Uniting and Strengthening America by Providing Appropriate Tools Required to Intercept and Obstruct Terrorism Act of 2001
USA Today, 214
U.S. Chamber of Commerce, 20
U.S. Constitution: Article I, 125; Article II, 125; compliance with, 241–42; Congress and, 7–12, 9, 23–24, 59–60; First Amendment, 20; presidents and, 7–12, 9, 23–24, 59–60; Twenty-Sixth Amendment to, 145
U.S. Department of Agriculture, 187, 277

U.S. Department of Defense, 71, 277
U.S. Department of Energy, 293
U.S. Department of Health and Human Services, 187, 277
U.S. Department of Homeland Security, 68, 71, 104, 151, 173–74, 237, 277
U.S. Department of Labor, 244
U.S. Department of Transportation, 277
U.S. State Department, 277, 293, 296, 302–3, 307
U.S. Treasury, 133, 136, 173, 237, 277

value-added tax (VAT), 235, 263n6
Versailles Treaty, 61
veto(es): of bills, 185; of Bush, George H. W., 152, 162, 173; of Bush, George W., 8, 9, 26–27, 173–74, 184, 205–6; Carter's, 160–61; chains, 185; of Clinton, Bill, 8, 9, 152, 163, 173; Eisenhower's, 171; Ford's, 160, 175; leverage, 154; line-item, 142; Nixon's, 171–72; pocket, 8, 30n13; politics, 167–76, 168–169, 170; power of, 59–60; Reagan's, 173; returned, 7–8; threats, 22–23, 26–27, 41, 173; threats/SAPs, 189–93, 191, 193, 207n11; usage of, 7–8, 9
veto bargaining: between branches, 199–204, 200, 201; as blame game, 185–86, 194–95, 204–5; central legislative clearance in, 187–93, 191, 193; as commitment game, 184–85; as coordinations game, 185–86; foundational theories of, 184–86; institutional context of, 183–206; legislative strategy/message politics in, 193–99, 198; role of, 184; as sequential game with complete information, 184. *See also* message politics
Veto Bargaining (Cameron), 184
Vietnam War, 17, 28, 269–70; end of, 89; opposition to, 41, 135, 268
Virginia, 251
vote(s): during 2000 Electoral College, 85; during 2004 Electoral College, 85; on Capitol Hill, 139; House of Representa-

tives, 129; for NAFTA, 82n37; party-line, 15, 15, 40, 46, 56nn37–38, 139; party unity, 13, 14, 162; political parties' unity, 13, 14; popular, 2; proxy, 18; recount in Florida, 2; roll-call, 25, 81n11, 109; Senate, 129; Twenty-Sixth Amendment and, 145
voters: black, 34; centrists, 38, 53; evenly divided, 37; for Gore, 53–54; in presidential elections, 53; Republican, 34–35; suburban/urban, 135
Voting Rights Act of 1965, 34, 88

wages, 175; minimum, 197, 198, 202; overtime, 244–48, 259
Wagner Act, 81n7
Wallace, George, 90
Wall Street Journal, 98
war: on drugs, 18; major, 268; powers, 10; on terror, 29, 49–52. *See also* Vietnam War
War on Poverty, 72, 174
War Powers Act, 281
War Powers Resolution of 1973, 17, 145, 270
Washington, George, 60, 125
Washington Post, 214, 233, 308
Watergate: post, 159; scandal, 10, 28, 41, 89, 146, 270
water pollution, 144
weapons of mass destruction (WMDs): Hussein and, 5, 289, 295–302; Iraq's, 5, 289, 295–302
Weekly Standard, 292
welfare: reform, 47, 142; social, 62; spending, 8, 19
Weller, Jerry, 241
West Virginia, 171, 210
White, William S., 134
White House: chiefs of staff, 23, 63–68, 81n14, 190; conferences, 70; Congress and, 105; coordination in, 64–70; Democratic control of, 14–19, 15; lobbying team, 109; policy staffs, 62–64, 81n10, 187; public relations operations of, 73–74; Republican's control of, 14–19,

15; split control of Congress and, 14–19, *15*, 146, 152–53; staff, 17, 112. *See also* executive branch; presidents; veto bargaining
White House Office of Domestic Policy, 190
whites, 34–35
Whitewater investigations, 119. *See also* Clinton, Bill
Whitten, James, 224
Wilson, Woodrow, 2, 61, 262, 268, 278
Wisconsin, 1
Wolfowitz, Paul, 307
women's rights, 276
Woodruff, Judy, 180n35
Woods, B. Dan, 103

World Bank, 274
World Trade Organization (WTO), 234, 274; compliant legislation, 237; disputes, 235–36; EU's complaints to, 235–37, 263n13; free trading laws of, 236; members, 235
World War I, 268
World War II, 137, 153, 268
Wright, Jim, 92
WTO. *See* World Trade Organization

yellowcake. *See* uranium oxide

Zarqawi, Abu Musab, 291, 292–93
"zero-sum society," 137

About the Contributors

Gary J. Andres is vice chairman for research and policy at Dutko Worldwide in Washington, D.C. He holds a Ph.D. from the University of Illinois at Chicago in public policy. Dr. Andres is the author of articles on politics, public opinion research, and Congress in a variety of publications including *Presidential Studies Quarterly*, *National Review Online* and *Roll Call*. He also writes a weekly column in the *Washington Times*.

Richard E. Cohen, congressional reporter for *National Journal*, joined the magazine's staff in 1973. Cohen has authored numerous books about Congress. Since 2001, he has been coauthor with Michael Barone of *The Almanac of American Politics*, the biennial "bible" of 535 Members of Congress. Other titles include a biography of Dan Rostenkowski, the former chairman of the House Ways and Means Committee; *Washington at Work: Back Rooms and Clean Air*; *Changing Course in Washington: Clinton and the New Congress*; and *Congressional Leadership: Seeking a New Role*. He is a graduate of Brown University and Georgetown University Law Center.

Richard S. Conley is associate professor of political science at the University of Florida at Gainesville. He is author of *The Presidency, Congress, and Divided Government* and editor of *Reassessing the Reagan Presidency* and *Transforming the American Polity: The Presidency of George W. Bush and the War on Terrorism*. His research interests include the presidency, presidential-congressional relations, and comparative executive politics.

Roger H. Davidson is professor emeritus of government and politics at the University of Maryland at College Park, and more recently a visiting professor of political science at the University of California at Santa Barbara. He is author of numerous books and articles concerning U.S. politics and policy making, especially Congress and legislative-executive relations. In 2002 he held the John Marshall chair at the University of Debrecen, awarded by the Hungarian Fulbright Commission.

C. Lawrence Evans is professor of government at the College of William and Mary and coeditor of the *Legislative Studies Quarterly*. He has published numerous books and articles about the U.S. Congress. During 1992–1993, he served as the staff associate for Chairman Lee H. Hamilton (D-IN), on the Joint Committee on the Organization of Congress.

Lee H. Hamilton is president of the Woodrow Wilson International Center for Scholars in Washington, D.C., and director of the Center on Congress at Indiana University. During his thirty-four years in the U.S. Congress from the 9th District of Indiana, he chaired the House Committee on Foreign Affairs (now International Relations). He recently served as ViceChairman of the National Commission on Terrorist Attacks upon the United States (the 9/11 Commission).

Louis Fisher is senior specialist in separation of powers with the Congressional Research Service at the Library of Congress, where he has worked since 1970. In 1987 he served as research director of the House Iran-Contra Committee and wrote major sections of the final report. His books include *Presidential War Power* (2nd ed. 2004), *American Constitutional Law* (6th ed. 2005), *Military Tribunals and Presidential Power* (2005), and *Constitutional Conflicts between Congress and the President* (4th ed. 1997).

Patrick Griffin is a longtime Democratic Party strategist. He has served as senior policy and political advisor to two Senate democratic leaders and as the chief lobbyist for President Clinton in his first term. He recently sold his ownership position in the successful bipartisan lobbying firm Griffin, Johnson, Madigan and Peck, which he cofounded with his former partner David Johnson eighteen years ago.

Stephen Ng is pursuing a J.D. at the University of Virginia School of Law. A member of Phi Beta Kappa, he graduated from the College of William and Mary in 2003 with a concentration in public policy. He is a winner of the Jack Kent Cooke Fellowship for academic excellence.

Mark J. Oleszek is a doctoral candidate in American politics at the University of California at Berkeley. His academic interests include congressional leadership and organizational theory. He is in the early stages of a research project examining Senate leadership, an interest born from work as a legislative aide to the U.S. Senate Democratic Policy Committee.

Walter J. Oleszek is senior specialist in the legislative process at the Congressional Research Service. He is a longtime adjunct faculty member at American University and the author of several books on the U.S. Congress.

Leon E. Panetta represented California's Central Coast in Congress from 1976 to 1992, during most of which time he also served as member and chair of the House Budget Committee. He was appointed director of the U.S. Office of Management and Budget in 1993 and served in that position until President Clinton appointed him chief of staff in 1995. Mr. Panetta, together with his wife Sylvia, directs the Panetta Institute for Public Policy.

James P. Pfiffner is University Professor in the School of Public Policy at George Mason University. His major areas of expertise are the presidency, American national government, and public management. He has written or edited ten books on the presidency and American national government, including *The Strategic Presidency: Hitting the Ground Running*, *The Modern Presidency*, and *The Character Factor: How We Judge America's Presidents*.

James A. Thurber is Distinguished Professor of Government and director of the Center for Congressional and Presidential Studies at American University. He is author or editor of twelve books and over seventy-five articles on campaigns and elections, Congress, congressional-presidential relations, interest groups, and lobbying. Recent publications include *Campaigns and Elections, American Style*, 2nd ed., edited with Candice Nelson (2004); *Congress and the Internet*, edited with Colton Campbell (2003); *Battle for Congress: Consultants, Candidates and Voters* (2001); *Campaign Warriors: Political Consultants in Elections*, edited with Candice Nelson (2000); and *Crowded Airwaves: Campaign Advertising in Elections*, edited with Candice Nelson and David Dulio (2000).

Stephen J. Wayne is a well known author and lecturer on American presidents and the presidency. Professor of Government at Georgetown University since 1988 and a Washington-based "insider" for over thirty-five years, Wayne has written or edited ten books, many in multiple editions, and authored over one hundred articles, chapters, and reviews that have appeared in professional journals, scholarly compilations, newspapers, and magazines. His best known work, *The Road To The White House*, is now in its 7th edition. Recently, he added a supplement to it on the 2004 presidential nomination process.